PAIN AND PROFIT
The Politics of Malpractice

Books by Sylvia Law

Pain and Profit: The Politics of Malpractice (co-author)

Blue Cross: What Went Wrong?

Rights of the Poor

Political and Civil Rights in the United States, Vol. II (co-editor)

PAIN
AND PROFIT
The Politics of Malpractice

SYLVIA LAW and STEVEN POLAN

1817

HARPER & ROW, PUBLISHERS
NEW YORK   HAGERSTOWN
SAN FRANCISCO
LONDON

To Our Parents
Edward and Alice Law
Isadore and Adele Polan

FIRST EDITION

Designed by Sidney Feinberg

Library of Congress Cataloging in Publication Data

Law, Sylvia A
  Pain and Profit.
  1. Physicians—Malpractice—United States.
2. Tort liability of hospitals—United States.
3. Insurance, Physicians' liability—United States.
I. Polan, Steven, joint author. II. Title.
KF2905.3.L38   346'.73'03   77–11535
ISBN 0–06–012546–2

---

78 79 80 81 82 10 9 8 7 6 5 4 3 2 1

Contents

Acknowledgments   *ix*

Preface   *xi*

1. An Introduction to Malpractice Law   1

   The historical development of the fault-based system of liability.
   Its economic and philosophic assumptions. The role of industry
   custom in determining the standard of care. Basic standards of
   malpractice liability.

   PART I. **THE MEDICAL SYSTEM**

2. The Maldistribution of Malpractice   11

   The maldistribution of medical services in the United States. The
   economics of the physician marketplace. The relationship between maldistribution of medical services and malpractice.

3. Bad Apples   28

   The nature, extent, and impact of chronic substandard practice.
   The effectiveness of state disciplinary procedures. Methods of
   professional self-regulation.

4. The Hospital: The Doctor's Workshop   51

   Malpractice in hospitals. The hospital's legal responsibilities for
   the quality of medical care. Hospital power to control physician

malpractice. Peer review. Economic incentives in hospital care. Hospital response to the malpractice crisis. Public and private controls in hospitals.

PART II. THE LEGAL SYSTEM

5. Lawyers: How Much Is Too Much?   81

The attorney's share of the malpractice dollar. The contingent fee. Deficiencies in legal representation. Do lawyers make too much money?

6. The Rules of the Malpractice Game   97

The degree to which legal changes have affected the number and size of malpractice awards. Myths of liability. Informed consent. Defensive medicine.

7. Techniques of Dispute-Resolution   120

The problem of delays. Obtaining expert testimony. Screening panels. Arbitration. Limitations on patient rights to compensation.

8. The No-Fault Alternative   149

The plans and their policy justifications. What is compensable? Deterring substandard medical practice.

PART III. THE INSURANCE SYSTEM

9. Malpractice Insurance: The Blood-Money Industry   161

The crisis in perspective. Group plans and monopolies. Surplus, reserves, and investments. Argonaut and industry opportunism. Rate-making and the failure of state regulation. The holding-company phenomenon. The possibility of federal intervention.

10. Insuring Insurance: When the Private Market Fails   195

The state response to the insurance crisis. Joint Underwriting Associations and the shifting of risk. Captives, self-insurance, and no insurance. The future.

11. Conclusions 206

Distorting the problem. Reform in the 1970's. Addressing root
causes.

Appendix—Excerpts from Gonzales v. Nork *215*
Notes on the Text *247*
Index *299*

Acknowledgments

Many people made substantial contributions to the creation of this book. In 1973, Judge B. Abbott Goldberg of the California Superior Court entered the largest verdict which had ever been given in a medical malpractice case up to that time. Judge Goldberg wrote an opinion, a portion of which is set forth in the Appendix, that brings to life the actual human problems involved in a medical malpractice case. This opinion has had some practical effect in encouraging measures to avoid injuries through malpractice. Judge Goldberg has given us encouragement throughout, and the benefit of concrete and cogent reactions to an earlier draft of the book. Stan Price, formerly Director of the National Health Law Project in Los Angeles, and Robert Harley shared with us valuable information and ideas. James Sheeran, New Jersey Commissioner of Insurance, and Phillip Stern, the Chief Actuary in that office, helped us to understand the problems of regulating the malpractice insurance industry.

Many students did important research, thinking and writing: Julia Spring, Jane Friedson, Randi Bloch, Rona Daniels, and Sandi Ingram. Many people provided access to important information and research materials; among those who were particularly helpful were Joe Diamond, Liz Hersch, and Deborah Bennington. Several people assisted in secretarial work and shared with us their reactions and insights: Susan McBean, John Plucinski, Alegra Sims, and Gretchen Yancey.

Ann Harris, our editor at Harper and Row, helped us to make the book intelligible and coherent. Barry Ensminger has given us enormous moral, intellectual, and practical support. Most important, all these people helped to make the process pleasant.

Preface

Medical malpractice is a problem that has come of age. In the past few years, it has demanded the urgent attention of the legislatures of every state, the state departments of health and insurance, the United States Congress, and many other private and public agencies. When these agencies and organizations were confronted with a sudden crisis arising from spiraling insurance premiums and insurance unavailability, they naturally looked to available sources of knowledge and information to see what might be done. Often the primary sources of information and ideas were the special-interest groups: the trial lawyers who make their living representing patients or doctors in malpractice cases; organized medicine; and insurance trade associations and companies.

Everyone recognizes that information provided by special-interest groups is bound to reflect and protect the interests of the group presenting it. But in this situation there are few alternative sources of information and ideas. Certainly, patients as a group do not have anyone to speak for them, either as people who are at risk of injury through medical treatment, or as the people who ultimately bear the costs of rising malpractice premiums. Often, conscientious and competent doctors are ill-advised and ill-served by the leaders of organized medicine who purport to represent them in the media and the legislatures. Lawyers, most of whom have little or no knowledge of the laws and procedures which bear on medical malpractice, are often represented only by those groups that have staked out a particular economic niche in the medical-liability market.

What results is an astounding amount of misinformation for popular and professional consumption. Well-motivated, highly intelligent physicians can hardly speak with their lawyer friends about this issue. Scarcely anyone trusts the insurance companies, though no one has much specific knowledge of how they operate. Professional polarization sets in. There is little worthwhile interchange.

This book is written for the many decent and conscientious lawmakers, regulators, and health administrators who must formulate policies in relation to medical malpractice and who need concise, accurate, and documented information and ideas in order to question, evaluate, and challenge the proposals which are inevitably pressed upon them by the special-interest groups. It is written for the many doctors who recognize that they are being unfairly penalized for their colleagues' derelictions and feel powerless to change this situation. Finally, it is written for the consumers of health services who wish to know what the malpractice "crisis" is really all about, and how it affects them.

One of the few disinterested sources of information and ideas about the medical malpractice problem is the 1973 *Report of the HEW Secretary's Commission on Medical Malpractice.* This is an excellent collection of data and ideas, but, unfortunately, it has not been disseminated and read as widely as it should be. Our book presents the major information and recommendations of the *HEW Report,* updates its data where that is possible, and sometimes takes issue with its approaches and conclusions. We hope that this book will make the important information gathered and presented in that 1973 *Report* more accessible. Much has happened in relation to medical malpractice since 1973, and we analyze those developments.

We do not represent any special interest or preconceived point of view. On the other hand, we believe that we do have some qualification to speak with authority on these issues. Although both of us are lawyers, neither of us has ever represented a patient or a physician in a medical malpractice case. The freedom to acquire specialized knowledge, without the bias and distortion which inevitably result when the acquisition of knowledge is financed to serve the interests of a particular group, is the special privilege and joy of working in an academic setting. New York University Law School has provided us with the intellectual, financial, logistical, and secretarial support which made this book possible. We both have long-standing interest and involvement in the developing area of the law which attempts to analyze and understand the legal structures that determine the shape of the medical-care delivery system in the United States. Sylvia Law teaches torts, or the law of personal injuries, of which medical malpractice is one branch, health law, and insurance. From 1970 to 1973, she worked with the Health Law Project of the University of Pennsylvania, a group funded by the government and private foundations to develop materials for teaching law students and lawyers the basic legal structures of medical-care delivery systems. Steven Polan became involved in problems of the organization of medical-care delivery while working for Congressman Bob Eckhardt and pursued these interests through his law-school career, both through academic work and as a staff assistant to the Health Committee of the City Council of New York. He now works as a lawyer and health specialist with Carol Bellamy, President of the N.Y. City Council.

We hope that this book is in the best tradition of responsible scholarship. Scholarly work demands an openness to the complexities of differing points of view, and documentation and evaluation of sources of knowledge. We have tried to provide them. But we do not believe that scholarly analysis must be confined to subjects which are esoteric, narrow, or banal. We hope that readers will find this book interesting, lively, and a useful resource in dealing with a major social issue of the day.

The theme of the book is that the causes of the malpractice crisis are multifaceted, hence solutions must be sought on many different fronts. The roots of the crisis run deep in the basic economic structure and moral assumptions of three major American institutions: medicine, the law, and the insurance industry. Therefore, solutions must of necessity address fundamental problems. Limited reforms are possible, and are suggested. But minor reforms, if they are to be effective even as stopgap measures, must be consonant with more fundamental solutions. As we will show, many of the recent attempted "reforms" are at best useless, and at worst will exacerbate existing problems. For these reasons, the malpractice crisis is not likely soon to disappear or be solved.

Although the focus of this book is medical malpractice insurance, much of the analysis is also applicable to other fields. After an introduction to general principles of liability, the first major section of the book discusses the ways in which the market for medical services and the organization and regulation of those services contribute to the rising costs of malpractice insurance. The second large section discusses the role of lawyers and the court system. The third and final section examines the insurance industry. In recent years, there have been large increases in the cost of all forms of liability insurance: product-liability insurance; the malpractice insurance of lawyers and other professionals; automobile-liability insurance. The information and analysis presented in the last two thirds of the book may be helpful in understanding the reasons for increases in the costs of liability insurance in areas other than medical malpractice.

The major work on this book was done in 1975 and 1976, and includes new developments through November 1977.

SYLVIA LAW
STEVEN POLAN

New York
December 1977

1

An Introduction to Malpractice Law

The Rise of the Fault System

Medical malpractice is one branch of the law of torts. In the most general terms, the tort law allocates the costs of losses resulting from human activity. The losses caused to people by other people are as diverse as human activity itself: damage to health, physical integrity, property, peace of mind, or reputation. Our discussion here focuses on physical injury to people. Tort suits are private legal actions in which one person seeks a remedy, usually money, for damages caused by another person.

The central question in each case is: "In what circumstances should the law require people to pay for injuries which they cause to other people?" Two prime purposes are served by singling out some people and making them pay for the injuries they cause to others: compensation of the victim; and deterrence of accidents or of behavior thought to be socially unreasonable.

One possible answer to the question, of course, is: Always. As a principle, it is simple and certain. Some cases will present difficult questions as to whether the person being asked to pay did indeed "cause" the injury. But any standard raises questions on the edges of the concept. If people were required to pay the victim whenever their actions caused physical injury to another, there would be strong incentives to be careful, and also to abstain from activities which are

1

dangerous to other people even when carefully done. Victims would be compensated whenever they could prove that their injuries were caused by the actions of another person, or at least, practically speaking, by a person with money or insurance.

This was in fact the operable principle of our own liability system until the last hundred years. The primitive Germanic concept, as applied in England after the Norman Conquest, was that "the doer of a deed was responsible whether he acted innocently or inadvertently, because he was the doer." From the 1500's to the middle of the nineteenth century, courts held to this basic view that people are responsible for their actions and must pay for the injuries they cause, but they began to recognize exceptions. The most important exception was the circumstance in which harm was caused indirectly rather than directly. In such cases, the victim was required to show either intentional wrongdoing or carelessness. When injuries were caused by the direct action of another person, courts began to recognize defenses of "inevitable necessity" or "unavoidable accident." Although in theory this assured that a person who was entirely blameless would not be required to pay, in practice literally no one ever succeeded in proving that an injury directly caused by human action was "inevitable."

In the last half of the nineteenth century, with the coming of the Industrial Revolution, the principle was stood on its head. The law abandoned the assumption that people should pay for the damage directly resulting from their voluntary actions. The exceptions swallowed the rule, and the rule became that the victim must prove "fault" in order to recover payment from the person who caused the injuries. Since the Industrial Revolution, the assumption has been that the victim should bear the economic costs of injuries caused by other people.

Adoption of proved "fault" as the basis for making one person pay for the costs of injuries caused to another was part of the larger social and economic revolution.

Perhaps one of the chief agencies in the growth of the idea of [liability based on fault] is industrial machinery. Early railway trains, in particular, were notable neither for speed nor for safety. They killed any object from a Minister of State to a wandering cow, and this naturally reacted on the law.

Adoption of fault-based liability was also part of a revolution in concepts and ideas: another manifestation of the individualism which underlies *laissez-faire* as a political philosophy. Perhaps the leading proponent of this philosophy in the law was Oliver Wendell Holmes. In his great work *The Common Law,* he searches for a single general principle upon which all liability in tort might be justly premised. "The general principle of our law," he states, "is that loss from accident must lie where it falls . . ." Holmes' principle is based on an assumption of fact, an empirical observation about the world.

A man need not, it is true, do this or that act—the term *act* implies a choice,—but he must act somehow. Furthermore, the public generally profits by individual activity. As action cannot be avoided, and tends to the public good, there is obviously no policy in throwing the hazard of what is at once desirable and inevitable upon the actor.

The supreme value placed on individual freedom of action, and the assumption that action is good in itself, are central to the concept of fault-based liability.

Obviously, this is not the only assumption that the law could make. For example, the law could take a neutral stance on the question of whether action or inaction is, in general, preferable. It could say that people are free to act, but that when action injures other people the actor should pay. Perhaps this is the notion embodied in the cliché that one person's freedom to swing a fist extends as far as the next person's nose. The common law prior to the Industrial Revolution took this sort of neutral stance on the question of whether action or inaction is, in its nature, preferable. Or, alternatively, the law could make a radically conservative assumption that, in general, inaction is to be preferred. This attitude is perhaps expressed in the canon of medical ethics which commands, "First, do no harm." Since we have never seen a tort-compensation system built on the assumption that in general it is better not to act than to act, it is difficult to imagine how such a system would work.

Today, liability based on "fault" is the major premise of the tort system. Malpractice, despite all hysteria to the contrary, is a fault-based system. Courts order doctors to pay patients for injuries inflicted in medical treatment only when the patient proves that the doctor was at fault. The most common way in which a victim proves fault is to show that the injurer acted negligently. Negligence has a common-sense and legal meaning which includes both *inadvertence,* or not paying proper attention in a situation in which a reasonable person would pay attention; and *recklessness,* deliberately taking a risk that a reasonable person would not take. The legal definition of negligence is that

The degree of care demanded of a . . . person is the resultant of three factors: the likelihood that his conduct will injure others, taken with the seriousness of the injury if it happens, and balanced against the interest that he must sacrifice to avoid the risk.

The formula's aura of precision is false. "Seriousness of injury," even if known, is not easily quantifiable. Often the likelihood of injury is calculable in only the foggiest sort of way. The interests which must be sacrificed to avoid the risk are numerous and various, and often impossible to value in an objective way. Striking a balance among these factors is rarely an easy task.

How are courts to make those judgments? Since the formula does not apply itself, the courts call on a venerable fiction of the tort law— the reasonable person—to apply the formula to particular facts. Would a reasonable person drive seventy miles an hour on a two-lane road on a rainy night? If the interest to be sacrificed to avoid the risk of a collision is the desire to get home ten minutes earlier, a reasonable person would not take the risk. But what if the driver was taking a sick child to the hospital? The interest to be sacrificed in avoiding the risk of an accident is now escalated, and perhaps a reasonable person would risk speeding. We all engage in this process every day, in governing our own conduct and in judging the actions of others.

With respect to the everyday activities of ordinary people, it has always been clear that the law's hypothetical "reasonable person" is an idealization. Almost everybody does foolish and careless things at one time or another. But the law's hypothetical "reasonable person" does not do foolish and careless things. The law requires a reasonable person on good behavior. As A. P. Herbert put it,

The Common Law of England has been laboriously built about a mythical figure—the figure of "the Reasonable Man." . . . He is an ideal, a standard, the embodiment of all those qualities which we demand of the good citizen.

The Reasonable Man is always thinking of others; prudence is his guide, and "Safety First," if I may borrow a contemporary catchword, is his rule of life. . . . He is one who invariably looks where he is going, and is careful to examine the immediate foreground before he executes a leap or bound; who neither star-gazes nor is lost in meditation when approaching trapdoors or the margin of a dock; . . . who never mounts a moving omnibus and does not alight from any car while the train is in motion; . . . who never drives his ball till those in front of him have definitely vacated the putting-green which is his own objective; . . . who never swears, gambles or loses his temper, who uses nothing except in moderation and even while he flogs his child is meditating only on the golden mean.

Although the reasonable-person standard has always been so idealized, judges and juries evaluating the conduct of ordinary people involved in everyday activities have been able to make judgments about what a reasonable person would do in a given situation.

But consider, for example, the question of whether a reasonable railroad runs broad-gauge cars on a narrow-gauge track. What does the jury, or even the judge, know about running a railroad? Not much. How can they evaluate the seriousness or likelihood of the risks created by this practice, or the interests which must be sacrificed to keep narrow-gauge cars on narrow-gauge tracks? Common experience does not help much. How can they acquire the knowledge needed to judge whether a reasonable railroad runs broad-gauge cars on a narrow-gauge track? One obvious way is to ask a person who runs a railroad. From the mid-nineteenth century until the 1930's, the "custom of the industry" largely determined what constituted negligence in a case that involved facts and judgment beyond the personal experience of ordinary people. Railroads charged with negligence for having injured a person by running a broad-gauge car on a narrow-gauge track could defend themselves by simply showing that this was customarily done in the railroading business. As one court said:

Even if the practice had been shown to be dangerous, that would not show it to be negligent. Some employments are essentially hazardous. . . . All the cases agree that the master is not bound to use the newest and best appliances. . . . "Reasonably safe" means safe according to the usages, habits, and ordinary risks of the business. . . . No man is held by law to a higher degree of skill than the fair average of his profession or trade. . . . Juries . . . cannot be allowed to set up a standard which shall, in effect, dictate the customs or control the business of the community.

In 1932, Judge Learned Hand was presented with a case in which two boats went down at sea while being towed by a tug that did not have a radio receiver. If the tug had had a radio, it could have received warnings of the impending storm and put into port. Even though radios had rapidly become popular most tugboats did not have them. Given that the cost of a radio was small relative to the risks involved in operating at sea without a current weather report, Hand held the tug company liable for the damage. He said:

[I]n most cases reasonable prudence is in fact common prudence; but strictly it is never its measure; a whole calling may have unduly lagged in the adoption of new and available devices. It never may set its own tests, however persuasive be its usages. Courts must in the end say what is required; there are precautions so imperative that even their universal disregard will not excuse their omission.

This has become the classic statement of the effect of industry custom in determining what conduct is negligent in almost every area of human activity. The practices of the industry are highly relevant. They show what is possible. For example, if some tugboats have radios and others do not, it is clearly possible to use them. Industry custom provides evidence of industry knowledge of the state of the art. Most important, custom shows how other knowledgeable people have struck the balance between the costs of accidents and the costs of avoiding them. Although industry custom is important and relevant, it is not finally determinative. Normally, courts must make an independent judgment as to whether the industry has acted reasonably in striking the balance between the risk of injury and the costs of avoiding the risks.

Medical Malpractice

Even during the period prior to the Industrial Revolution when ordinary people were held responsible for all injuries directly caused by their voluntary actions, the principles applied to physicians were more complex, and were designed to take into account the peculiar nature of medical practice. An early reported malpractice case, decided in 1767, involved a patient with a broken leg which had been bandaged and healed to the point that it could bear weight. The physician who was summoned to remove the bandage rebroke the leg and put on "a heavy steel thing that had teeth, and would stretch or lengthen the leg." The steel thing left the patient "ill and bad of it" months later. The patient's lawyer did not argue that the doctor should pay simply because injuries were the direct result of the doctor's treatment. Rather, the patient presented several doctors who stated that they would not rebreak the bone in these circumstances. The court held the doctor liable, saying:

It appears from the evidence of the surgeons that it was improper to disunite the callous without consent; this is the usage and law of surgeons: then it was ignorance and unskillfullness in that very particular, to do contrary to the rule of the profession, what no surgeon ought to have done;

It appears that even during the heyday of liability without fault, physicians were not to be held liable unless it was proved, on the basis of expert testimony, that the doctor's particular action demonstrated ignorance or lack of skill. The legal standard applied is the standard of the profession.

In the modern, industrial period, the assumption of the law is that the practice of medicine, like any other field of human endeavor, is basically good. Doctors are not required to pay simply because their actions produce injuries. Rather, malpractice liability is imposed only when the patient shows that this doctor did something that no reasonable doctor would have done in those circumstances. The patient must also show that this negligence caused the injuries which the patient suffered. The patient can recover only by showing that the doctor's conduct was unreasonable and that the unreasonable conduct caused specific injury.

Furthermore, the effect of custom is given greater weight in evaluating the conduct of professionals, including physicians, than in judging other forms of human activity. As we have seen, in most areas of the law, courts make an independent judgment as to whether customary practice is reasonable. In evaluating the conduct of professional people, the customary practices of the profession are presumed to be reasonable. In most areas of human activity, customary practice is simply important evidence of what is reasonable, while the customary practices of professionals are legally presumed to be reasonable.

Several reasons have been offered for this strict adherence to customary standards in medical cases. As Clarence Morris, probably the most influential writer in this area, puts it, "No other stand is practical. Our judges and juries are usually not competent to judge whether or not a doctor has acted reasonably." He recognizes that the law's uncritical acceptance of the customs of the medical profession "may be academically deficient in countenancing an excuse that may occasionally be based on the negligence of other doctors." But he argues, and courts basically agree, that this is necessary since there is no practical alternative.

One consequence of the strict adherence to customary practices in judging the conduct of professionals is that the law requires that expert witnesses explain what the customary standards are, and swear that customary standards were violated. As a practical matter, expert witnesses are important in many cases in which an injured person attempts to show that an industry practice was unreasonable. For example, as a practical matter, an expert would be needed to show the dangers of running broad-gauge railroad cars on narrow-gauge tracks. But when an injured person sues a professional, the requirement of an expert witness is not simply a practical necessity, but is demanded as a matter of law.

While there are extraordinary exceptions which will be discussed in Chapter 5, the standard rule in medical malpractice cases is that the patient must have an expert witness testify that the doctor's conduct fell below that of a reasonable physician. Furthermore, as a general rule, the doctor will not be found negligent if his or her conduct was acceptable to any reputable group of doctors. Courts will not attempt to determine whether another course of treatment might have been more appropriate so long as a treatment given was not inappropriate. Hence, in order to win a malpractice case, the patient must establish, by a preponderance of the evidence, supported by expert testimony, that the physician did something that no reasonable doctor would do, and that this produced injuries which the patient would not otherwise have suffered.

PART I

THE MEDICAL SYSTEM

2

The Maldistribution of Malpractice

Malpractice is not like lightning. Many doctors learning of large malpractice judgments have the sense that "It could happen to anyone," "There but for the grace of God go I," "Everybody makes mistakes sometimes." Remarks like this have little to do with malpractice. First, as we have seen, courts do not require doctors to pay unless the patient proves that the doctor did something no reasonable physician would have done.

Second, and more important, we can predict to a remarkable degree that some doctors are much more likely to have malpractice judgments rendered against them than others. For example, in 1972 the risk of a malpractice claim against a surgeon practicing in California was fourteen times as great as the risk of a claim against a general physician practicing in New Hampshire.

The *HEW Secretary's Malpractice Commission Report* found that most doctors and other health-care providers go through their entire professional lives without being sued. A relatively small number of physicians accounts for a disproportionately large number of the malpractice claims. For example, a study of physicians in Maryland showed that during the 1960's forty-six doctors in that state had more than one malpractice claim filed against them. If malpractice claims were distributed randomly over the population of Maryland doctors, the chance that this many physicians would have more than one claim against them would be about one in a million. By contrast, during the 1960's, 89 percent of the doctors in Maryland were never sued.

There is evidence that the number of doctors being sued for malpractice is on the increase. For example, a survey conducted by *Medical Opinion* magazine in 1975 showed that 26 percent of the doctors who responded to the survey had been sued at least once during their professional careers, while in 1971 only 17 percent of those responding to a similar survey had ever been sued. However, the general situation continues to be one in which most doctors are never sued and a relatively small, unevenly distributed group of physicians accounts for most malpractice claims.

Of course, it is not much comfort to an individual doctor to know that statistically the risk that he or she will be sued for malpractice is small. So long as any risk exists, most doctors will purchase insurance and the possibility of a suit will remain a source of anxiety. However, given the wide variation in the distribution of doctors and the similarly wide variations in malpractice rates, it seems useful to explore these distributional patterns to discover whether the maldistribution of services contributes to high rates for malpractice insurance. In this chapter we will discuss the maldistribution of medical services in the United States; the nature of the medical-care marketplace; and the relationship between the uneven distribution of medical services and malpractice.

Geographical Maldistribution

It is generally recognized that there is a serious problem in the geographic distribution of physicians in the United States. Certain parts of the country have an abundant supply of physicians, but many areas have none at all. Physicians are disproportionately located on the east and west coasts. For example, in 1972 there was one physician for every 504 people in New York and one physician for every 604 people in California, but only one doctor for every 1,340 people in Mississippi and one for every 1,400 people in South Dakota. These ratios reflect dramatic deviations from the national average of one physician for every 781 persons. In 1970, there were 132 counties in the United States that had no doctor.

There is also a serious disparity in the distribution of physicians between urban and nonurban areas. In 1972, metropolitan areas contained 73 percent of the population, 86 percent of all physicians, and 93 percent of all hospital-based physicians. The ratio of physicians per

1,000 population in metropolitan areas was 1.84, more than double the 0.82 ratio for nonmetropolitan areas. Furthermore within urban areas, distribution of physicians is affected by racial and economic factors. Doctors tend to concentrate in affluent, white neighborhoods. One study found:

> All the communities in Chicago and Suburbs which experienced rapid racial change and decreased socio-economic status since 1950 lost physicians. When maps showing an area with the greatest gains and losses of doctors are compared with maps depicting those areas with the highest socio-economic status and those whose population changed from white to black, two things become obvious. First, an influx of blacks resulted in an exodus of doctors. Second, the shift in the distribution of doctors was into the areas of highest socio-economic status.

In the ghetto areas of the Bronx, New York, the physician-patient ratio is one doctor for every 10,000 people.

This situation gets steadily worse. Between 1960 and 1970, the physician/population ratio increased by 34 percent in the five states which had the greatest proportion of physicians per population. (These states, in order of increase, are New York, Massachusetts, Connecticut, California, and Colorado.) By contrast, in the five states with the lowest physician/population ratios, the ratios increased by only 9 percent.

Maldistribution by Specialty

Even more serious is the maldistribution of physicians by specialty. The number of doctors has been increasing dramatically in recent years. First-year medical-school places grew from 8,759 in 1965 to 15,351 in 1976. But, despite these increases in the numbers of physicians, there has been a consistent and alarming decrease in the number of doctors in general practice. In 1949, 50 percent of all doctors were in general practice. By 1972, only 19 percent of all doctors involved in direct patient care were GP's. Between 1968 and 1972, while the absolute number of physicians was increasing rapidly, the number of GP's declined by 8 percent. By everybody's standards, there are simply not enough doctors providing the ordinary primary care.

The shortage of general practitioners has an immediate and devastating impact on people's ability to obtain needed health services. The corresponding surplus of surgeons and other specialists has an adverse impact which is more subtle but perhaps more destructive. In 1970, there were more surgeons than general practitioners working in the United States. If you think for one moment about the medical services that you, your family, and your friends need during the course of your lives, you will realize that it cannot possibly make sense to have more surgeons than GP's. There are more neurosurgeons in New York City than in the whole of the Soviet Union, and "you have 700 times as great a chance of having your head opened up here as you would in some other countries where the quality of care is also high." There are more neurosurgeons in Massachusetts for a population of 5 million than there are in England and Wales for a population of 50 million. Every major study of the subject agrees that there is an oversupply of surgeons in the United States. In 1976 a medical panel of the prestigious National Academy of Sciences found the problems of oversupply of specialists so severe that it called for an immediate federal freeze on increases in the numbers of medical specialists and surgeons being trained in the United States.

There are several stages in the training of a physician. Normally, a doctor receives a bachelor's degree, four years of medical education and an M.D. degree, and one year of training as an "intern." After the four years of medical school, the graduate is qualified to use the title of "doctor," but in most states may not yet practice medicine except under supervision in an internship program. During the internship, the doctor rotates through a variety of medical departments, normally in a hospital and under supervision. After the internship, he or she is eligible to become a fully licensed physician, legally free to practice all types of medicine. A person who stops training and begins medical practice at this point is a general practitioner. However, most doctors today continue their training as "residents" for an additional one or two years. "Residents" are licensed physicians working in an approved residency program, usually in a hospital. Residencies are offered in particular areas of specialization. After completion of a residency, a person may take an examination to be certified by the board in that specialty.

The choice of residency is critically important in separating specialists from doctors who provide general medical care. A person who wants to practice general medicine would usually take a residency in internal medicine, pediatrics, or family practice. (Family practice became a certified specialty in 1970.) Many physicians who choose residencies in these areas go on to become subspecialists within the larger specialty. For example, a resident in pediatrics or internal medicine may specialize in a particular organ, or even in a specific disease of a particular organ.

In 1975–76, the residency positions offered in the United States totaled 65,435. Of these, 3,832, or less than 6 percent, were in family practice. By contrast, 9,121, or about 14 percent, were in general surgery; in addition, 2,568 positions were offered in orthopedic surgery and 643 positions in neurological surgery. In 1974–75, the most recent year for which figures are available, only 80 percent of the residency positions offered in family practice were filled, while 94 percent of those offered in general and neurological surgery and 97 percent of those in orthopedic surgery were filled. Between 1950 and 1970, the number of surgical residencies offered in the United States increased more than 100 percent.

The American Medical Association claims that increasing numbers of young physicians are choosing careers in primary care. It is difficult to evaluate precisely the degree to which the number of primary-care physicians is increasing or decreasing in the mid-1970's. The AMA is the basic source of data on the kinds of work that physicians do, and there are serious limitations on the data it collects. For example, published AMA information on the distribution of physicians in the United States lumps together general practitioners and doctors certified in family practice. Furthermore, the work of many general practitioners includes a substantial surgery practice, but the AMA data do not inform us how many. Similarly, people trained in internal medicine or pediatrics may be either primary-care physicians or may specialize in particular diseases or organs, and the AMA data do not inform us of the breakdown. In addition, although the number of doctors certified as general surgeons is relatively small—8.2 percent in 1974—this figure does not include doctors who are certified in the surgical subspecialties. For example, in 1974, 2.9 percent of the doctors in the United States were certified in orthopedic surgery; 1.5 percent were certified in otolaryngology; 1.7 percent were certified in urology. The largest single category in the data published by the AMA on the distribution of physicians in the United States is "Other Specialties," which accounts for 27.5 percent of the doctors.

The Market for Medical Services

Dr. Charles C. Edwards, America's chief health official in 1974, said:

In the past, Federal policies toward specialty and geographic distribution of health professionals have relied too heavily on the notion that an increase in total supply would solve the distributional problems. If large enough numbers of health professionals are produced, it was reasoned, competitive pressure would force them to practice in non-metropolitan areas and in the medical specialties that offer lower income potentials, longer working hours, and/or relatively lower levels of prestige. Experience has shown this reasoning to be incorrect.

The laws of supply and demand do not work in the medical marketplace. The need for physicians does not induce doctors to enter a particular type of practice in an unserviced area. Probably the major reason for this is that, tragically and ironically, doctors can generally make more money for doing less work if they practice in specialties and areas where the human need is least. According to the AMA, the average net income for doctors working in surgical specialties is consistently higher, in both urban and rural areas, than the income of general practitioners or specialists in internal medicine. For example, in 1973, in communities of 50,000 to 100,000, doctors in general practice earned an average of $43,677 a year, specialists in internal medicine averaged $47,333, and surgeons averaged $62,320. Another recent study concludes that the median income for surgeons is 20 percent above that for all other physicians. *Medical Economics* reports the following median incomes for various specialties in 1975: general practitioners, $43,360; pediatricians, $48,330; family practitioners, $53,440; internists, $60,130; surgeons, $67,450; obstetricians, $72,380.

The reasons that surgeons make significantly higher salaries are found in the nature of insurance coverage for health services. First, a surgeon's services are much more likely to be covered by individual health insurance. In 1974, 75 percent of the civilian population had insurance coverage for surgical services, while only 59 percent had any coverage for outpatient doctor services. Second, health-insurance companies generally pay surgeons at higher rates. Blue Shield, which is controlled by the local medical society under most state laws, is the largest single private supplier of health-insurance coverage for physicians' services. Blue Shield generally pays physicians on the basis of "customary and prevailing" charges. In theory, this seems reasonable, if you assume that there is a free market which operates to assure that the customary and prevailing charges are in some way related to the supply of various kinds of physician and the demand for the services they provide. But there is no such market. In theory, the free-market dog should wag the "customary and prevailing charge" tail. But in this case, the tail wags the dog. This results because such a large portion of medical services is paid for by insurance rather than directly, and, more fundamentally, because health services in general, and surgeons' services in particular, are not subject to conventional market pressures.

The assumption of a free market for services is basic to our political and economic system. It is based on the concept that people cannot have everything they want, and the concept that no one knows what is best for individuals better than they do themselves. These principles, whatever validity they may have in the general economy, have little application to physicians' services. For the most part, medical services are, or are perceived as, undesired necessities rather than desired goods. Obviously, no one would "choose" an appendectomy over a hi-fi if she perceived a choice. Further, professional services are, in their nature, so complex and sophisticated that it is often impossible for an ordinary individual to make an informed judgment as to whether services are desirable or not. The inherent difficulty of informed consumer choice is made worse by professional restrictions on the dessemination of information about alternative medical care. The medical profession closely controls the supply of medical services. For all of these reasons, the laws of supply and demand do not assure that the supply of physicians will correspond to people's needs for medical care.

The publicly financed health-insurance programs have done nothing to correct this situation in which specialists who are in oversupply earn substantially more than primary-care doctors who are in acutely short supply. Indeed, the public health-insurance programs have made the problem worse. The largest publicly financed health-insurance programs are the Medicare program for the aged and the Medicaid program for the poor. Both of these programs, adopted in 1965, are based on a philosophy of extending health-insurance benefits similar to those purchased privately by the general population to these two particularly needy categories of people. Medicare has two parts: Part A, which is automatically provided to every person over sixty-five and which covers inpatient hospital services, and Part B, which may be purchased at individual option and covers a variety of outpatient services, not including routine physical examinations. This benefit structure obviously favors the provision and financing of in-hospital specialist services. The Medicaid program for the poor requires, in general terms, that states participating in the program make payment for "physicians' services" provided to eligible individuals. However, while the federal statute requires that the states pay full costs for inpatient hospital services, there is no floor on the amount which the state must pay for physician services. Following general insurance practices, most states pay more for specialist and inpatient services to Medicaid recipients.

There is yet another way in which the laws of supply and demand do not work with respect to medical services. The "need" for medical services is a decidedly pliable concept. There is substantial evidence, at least in relation to surgery, that supply determines demand, rather than demand determining supply. If there are more surgeons, there is more surgery. Dr. John Bunker, of Stanford, found that there were twice as many surgeons in the United States as in England and Wales, and that proportionately more operations were performed. His conclusion is that some of the surgery being performed in the United States is unnecessary. This conclusion is supported by a study conducted by Dr. Charles E. Lewis, of Cornell Medical Center. Dr. Lewis studied surgery in Kansas and found that there was a three- to fourfold variation in the regional rates for six common operations. The number of operations varied directly according to the number of available surgeons and hospital beds. "The results presented support a medical variation of Parkinson's Law: patient admissions for surgery expand to fill beds, operating suites, and surgeons' time."

Approximately fifteen million people in the United States undergo an operation under general anesthesia every year. These patients make up one half of all hospital admissions. Dr. Lawrence Williams, a board-certified surgeon, estimates that 20 percent of these operations are unnecessary, and that this estimate is probably conservative. Its accuracy is supported by the experience of one large union in New York City, which required that its members obtain a second consultation with a qualified and disinterested surgeon before undergoing an operation. They found that one operation in five was determined to be unnecessary when a second doctor was consulted. A 1977 study by New York Blue Cross/Blue Shield found that where people sought a second opinion on the need for elective surgery, the initial recommendations were not confirmed in 27 percent of the cases.

A House of Representatives Subcommittee on Oversight and Investigation has been studying the problem of unnecessary surgery for several years and has heard testimony from doctors across the nation who have published research on the question. The 1976 report of that committee reviews the recent evidence and criticisms which had been made of earlier studies, and concludes that 11,900 is a conservative estimate of the number of people who died from unnecessary surgery in 1975. While there is hot dispute over whether this figure is correct, the argument centers on whether the number is a couple of thousand less, as the AMA claims, or several thousand more. No one seriously disputes the fact that thousands of people die each year as a result of unnecessary surgery.

There is strong evidence that the devastation of unnecessary surgery falls most severely upon poor people who are eligible for Medicaid. The Investigations Subcommittee of the House Commerce Committee found that in 1975 the rate of surgery for individuals eligible for Medicaid was more than 100 percent greater than that for the American population as a whole. For elective surgery, the disparities were even greater.

Maldistribution of Health Services and Malpractice Rates

It is not necessarily malpractice when a surgeon performs an operation which another surgeon, before the fact, would have believed unnecessary. To hold a doctor liable for injuries growing out of an unnecessary operation, the patient must prove by expert testimony that no reasonable doctor would have believed an operation was necessary in the circumstances. But the number of physicians in a specialty or in a geographical area affects the number of malpractice claims in at least two ways, one benign and one problematic. The benign relationship between the distribution of doctors and the distribution of malpractice is that when there are more doctors and more people receiving medical care, there is more opportunity for a malpractice claim to arise. If there were no medicine, there would be no medical malpractice. This is not a particularly useful observation. It is, however, no different from the observation sometimes seriously made by physicians that if there were no malpractice lawyers, there would be no malpractice. A problematic relationship between the number of malpractice claims and the number of physicians may exist where there is a disproportionately large number of physicians in a given specialty or geographic area. In that case, the relationship between large numbers of physicians and the incidence of malpractice claims, as reflected by higher insurance rates, may reflect the unnecessary provision of higher-risk services which have inherent risks of causing injury to people.

Before looking at correlations between malpractice rates and distribution of excess physicians by area and specialty, it is important to note that these correlations must be viewed as suggestive rather than conclusive. Obviously, many factors influence the frequency of malpractice claims—among them, the availability of legal services, the quality of the doctor-patient relationship, and whether the people involved are litigious. (The poor present a glaring example of a lack of correlation between the provision of unnecessary surgical services and legal claims for medical malpractice. As we have noted, poor people are much more likely than the general population to be victims of injuries arising from unnecessary surgery. However, poor people on welfare rarely press legal claims for medical malpractice. The injured poor person has little incentive to press such a claim because welfare departments in all states require that, as a condition of receiving public aid, the poor person sign over to the welfare department any money that he or she receives from a personal-injury action. Further, as a practical matter, lawyers are not available to the poor because people on welfare suffer no economic loss when they are injured as a result of medical malpractice.) Other factors influencing the outcome of malpractice claims include regional differences in the legal rules and court systems. Further, malpractice insurance rates serve as our basis of comparison, and these rates depend not solely on the frequency and amount of malpractice claims made, but also on the relative profitability of the company providing the insurance, and on other factors. With these caveats in mind, some comparisons are useful.

According to the American Medical Association, in 1972 there were nineteen states in which the overall ratio of physicians to population was greater than 120 doctors per 100,000 people. If we look at the data on the costs of malpractice insurance in 1972, we find that twelve of the nineteen states in which coverage was most expensive for doctors are the states that had the largest supply of physicians.

A second gross comparison which is interesting to observe is that

of the insurance premiums for various types of physician and the over-
or undersupply of these physicians. Since the mid-1960's, most insurance companies and the Insurance Service Organization (ISO), an insurance rating bureau that collects data for rate-making purposes and is
owned and operated by its subscriber insurance companies, have classified doctors in five groups. Class I are physicians who do not do surgery.
Class II are physicians who do minor surgery or assist in major surgery
on their own patients. Radiologists are also included in this class. Class
III are physicians other than those in Classes IV or V who do perform
major surgery. Class IV physicians are specialists, including anesthesiologists, cardiac surgeons, general surgeons, gynecologists, otolaryngolo-
gists, plastic surgeons, thoracic surgeons, urologists, and vascular surgeons. Class V includes orthopedists and neurosurgeons. The rate of
malpractice insurance which doctors must pay goes up as the number
of their classification increases. The differing classifications and rates
are commonly thought to reflect the higher risks of the work performed
by the particular group. Doctors in Class V generally pay five times
as much as doctors in Class I. Doctors in Class IV pay four times as
much; those in Class III pay three times as much; and those in Class
II pay 1.75 times as much as doctors in Class I. These differential
rates have remained relatively stable since the mid-1960's. Because
we lack precise data on which specialties are most seriously oversupplied, it is difficult to determine the degree to which an oversupply
of specialists corresponds to increasing malpractice rates. Primary-care
physicians, who are most acutely undersupplied, pay the lowest rates.
Surgeons, who are generally in oversupply, pay generally high rates.
It is believed that neurosurgeons and orthopedic surgeons are among
the most acutely oversupplied physicians, and these doctors pay the
highest rates. Again, the usefulness of these correlations is limited because to an undetermined degree, they can be explained by the greater
risks inherent in the various classes of medical practice.

The most interesting and useful comparison is therefore that which
exists beween the degree to which surgeons are oversupplied and the
geographical differences in rates for these doctors. Because presumably
the risks inherent in surgical procedure remain relatively stable
throughout the country, this correlation should tell us something about
the degree to which malpractice arises from maldistribution.

If a list of the fifty states ranked according to the ratio of surgeons
to population is compared with a list of the fifty states ranked according

to the malpractice rates that surgeons pay, we find that surgeons in New York and California pay the highest malpractice rates, and New York, Massachusetts, and California are the three states with the highest ratio of practicing surgeons to population. If we expand the comparison to include the twenty-five states with the highest rates for surgical malpractice insurance, we find that eighteen of the states with the highest surgeon population ratios are also states in which malpractice insurance rates are high.

A 1976 study by the National Association of Insurance Commissioners, the first of its kind, confirms that the most serious problems of increasing malpractice claims exist in relation to the oversupplied specialty practices. The NAIC sought to examine a popular public view that poorly trained physicians are a prime source of malpractice claims. In several states, this assumption has led to proposals to strengthen educational requirements for physicians. The study found that "anesthesiologists, cardiac surgeons, neurosurgeons, obstetricians and gynecologists, orthopedists, plastic surgeons and thoracic surgeons generate a relatively high volume of claims." The NAIC's malpractice consultant, commenting on the data, said,

It has been commonly believed that poorly trained physicians were the major source of malpractice claims. This survey does not support that premise. What we are finding is a greater prevalence of claims among highly trained, certified specialists, particularly those practicing in a hospital setting.

Is it likely that the fault system and the corresponding malpractice insurance system can or will contribute to the solution of the problem of maldistribution of physicians by geography and specialty? Stories often appear in the press that a doctor is leaving a high-risk practice because of the cost of malpractice premiums. Almost invariably these stories regard the doctor as the victim of a system gone wrong. Considered in the context of existing maldistributions, if the risk of malpractice causes physicians to move to areas and specialties where their services are needed more, that may be a very good thing. In fact, however, it is doubtful that high malpractice rates have much direct impact on these physician decisions. In a 1975 survey, only 3 percent of all doctors studied said premiums motivated them to move to lower-risk population centers. A 1977 Rand study of California doctors, whose premiums have escalated faster than any others in the nation, showed that only five tenths of 1 percent had relocated because of high rates and only 2.1 percent said they were likely to do so.

Many factors influence a doctor's decision to practice in a particular area and choose a particular specialty. Malpractice rates play a relatively insignificant role in these decisions. If we are to correct the serious maldistribution of physicians, more direct action is needed. For many years, Congress has considered using federal funds to encourage doctors to serve in undersupplied specialties and areas of the country. A 1965 federal act established programs under which a portion of educational loans received would be canceled each year that the young physician practiced in an underserved area. The program was a failure. Less than 1 percent of those eligible took advantage of the loan-forgiveness program. In 1974, a more universal, and frankly coercive, program was approved by a Senate committee. It would have required that *all* new doctors practice for two years in an area of designated medical need. The requirement would have applied to all students who attended a medical school that received federal funds, whether or not an individual student had received any federal aid. Those who did not comply with the service requirement could not obtain a licence to practice medicine. Federal money would have assured that the young doctors practicing in underserved areas would continue to receive an income equivalent to the average for their specialty and experience.

This coercive solution to the problem of physician maldistribution was not adopted by the Congress. Instead, in 1976 Congress enacted a program providing a package of incentives to encourage medical schools and young doctors to meet the need for primary-care physicians. With respect to the schools, the law requires that a fixed proportion of the residency programs offered, 50 percent by 1980, be in "primary care." The law offers an attractive package of incentives to students to serve in underserved areas. Any physician who agrees to serve in an underserved area is guaranteed a salary equivalent to the national average earned in that specialty by a person with comparable experience. Additional grants of $25,000 are available to assist a doctor in establishing a practice in an underserved area. A student who agrees to work in an underserved area can receive federal subsidies covering full tuition, all educational expenses, and a stipend of $4,800 a year for living expenses for each year in medical school. This substantial student subsidy is repaid after graduation by the doctor's work in an underserved area: one year of work, at a salary guaranteed to equal the average which the physician could earn elsewhere, repays one year of student subsidization.

It is too soon to tell whether the new program will have the desired result. Whether the provisions requiring residencies in "primary care" are effective depends largely on how such positions are defined and whether there is effective monitoring of medical-school compliance. Internal medicine and pediatrics are traditional "primary care" residencies. But, as we have noted, there is an increasing tendency for residencies in these areas to become subspecialties which do not prepare a doctor for the actual practice of primary care. Is a residency focusing on pediatric hematology a position in "primary care"? Although residencies in family practice specifically prepare doctors to provide primary care, fewer than 6 percent of the residencies offered in 1975–76 were in family practice and many of these were not filled.

The package of incentives for individual physicians to settle in underserved areas sounds enormously attractive to people outside the medical profession. But many people within the medical schools are skeptical whether this new program will attract young physicians to serve in the areas in which they are most needed. There are many reasons for this skepticism. Prior loan-forgiveness programs have had almost no impact on the geographical maldistribution of physicians. Of the 300,000 medical- and dental-school graduates who had received federal health-professions loans as of 1973, only 86 physicians had obtained forgiveness for practicing in areas suffering health-care shortages. From 1973 to 1975, an additional 384 physicians had obtained forgiveness of either federal or private loans—a marked increase, but one which studies of the loan programs continue to characterize as "inconsequential."

The reasons which various federal studies offer for the failure of the loan-forgiveness programs include poor marketing of the program, student debts not substantial enough to make the forgiveness attractive, and the absence of a commitment to service on the part of students. Half of all medical students come from families with incomes in excess of $20,000 a year, as opposed to only 22 percent of the national population with income above that level. From a short-term financial point of view, young doctors do not feel strong pressure to take advantage of the loan-forgiveness program because most borrow at modest levels, are able to repay over extended periods of time, and are able to earn enough, even in the early years of practice, to meet their loan payments without significant hardship. From a long-term financial point of view, it is certainly to the young doctor's financial advantage to repay student loans and establish a practice in a geographical and specialty area where financial rewards are greater. Looking solely at finances, the new law does not provide affirmative incentive to young doctors to settle in underserved areas, but rather assures only that doctors will earn an "average" doctor's income, and relies in part on doctors' desire to serve in ways that are most useful.

Other factors are perhaps more significant than the financial incentives. After four years of medical school and two years of internship and residency in centers of high technology and sophisticated resources, many medical-school graduates are reluctant to take up a life of caring for people with relatively mundane ailments in a simpler and less stimulating setting. The standards of "quality care" which students acquire in settings where the newest technology and knowledgeable colleagues are available on a regular basis are not replicated in underserved areas. Young physicians in major urban settings do not want to leave the cultural opportunities which cities offer. So long as patterns of financing make it possible for physicians to choose to work in oversupplied specialties and geographic areas, and in fact provide them with long-range financial incentives to do so, it is difficult to believe that a loan-forgiveness program will provide sufficient incentive to correct the geographic and specialty maldistribution of doctors.

In all probability, the geographic and specialty maldistribution of physicians has an additional impact on the incidence of malpractice suits that goes well beyond the quantifiable correlations. The shortage of primary-care physicians means that growing numbers of Americans *never* have a personal relationship with a physician. Increasing specialization promotes the fragmentation and dehumanization of relationships between physicians and patients. Pursuing a malpractice claim is an arduous process for the patient. The patient must have a strong sense of outrage in order to sue. As we have seen, the root causes of the decline of primary-care physicians and the increase in hospital-based specialists lie in the economic incentives created by prevailing financing mechanisms and patterns of insurance coverage. The power of these financial incentives simply cannot be overstated.

The 1976 legislation attempts to provide a regulatory counterweight to the prevailing economic incentives. But it leaves untouched the *underlying* economic incentives. It provides a regulatory finger in the dike, but the surging power of fee-for-service medicine backed by insurance coverage for acute and specialty services remains. Regulatory Band-Aids which attempt to redress abuses without challenging underlying forces that produce the problems are destined to fail. When one such Band-Aid fails, we attempt another; and the regulatory bureaucracy becomes ever more complex, cumbersome, and truly oppressive.

The only way out of this dilemma is to address root causes. Theoretically, this could be done either by changing patterns of insurance coverage or by changing the fee-for-service method of paying for medical care. There are real limits to our ability to change patterns of insurance coverage to emphasize ordinary primary care, as opposed to acute catastrophic care. Acute catastrophic care is more expensive and more unpredictable. If forced to choose, both consumers and government programs will elect coverage for acute catastrophic service rather than ordinary primary care. If acute services are covered and ordinary ones are not, there is necessarily pressure to characterize more and more medical needs as acute or catastrophic in order to come within the scope of insurance coverage. Under these circumstances, of course, physicians continue to have incentive to work in those areas in which payment is assured.

The other alternative is to change the fee-for-service pattern of paying for medical care. A national health-care program, in consultation with physicians and others, could determine national needs for doctors and offer salaried positions for doctors in specialty and geographical areas to meet national medical-service needs. Young doctors would apply and compete for the positions available. Of course, some doctors would not obtain positions in the precise area of their choice, just as other workers in our society are forced to make choices among the jobs in which their skills are needed. Doctors, like most other workers, would be guaranteed a salary, and not forced to work on a piecework basis that turns what should be a healing relationship between patient and physician into a commodity relationship.

But a shift from fee-for-service medicine toward a system in which the need for physician services of various kinds, and the compensation for those services, is determined on a social basis is not politically "realistic." None of the proposals for national health insurance currently being considered by Congress adopts such an approach. Hence, the problems generated by fee-for-service medicine are likely to remain until the political framework that determines what is realistic changes radically.

Fault-based liability and the corresponding variations in malpractice insurance rates do not in fact play a major direct role in influencing physician choices about where they will practice and the kind of practice they will elect. However, these variations do play an important indirect role in alerting the public and the medical profession to the possibility that oversupply of physicians may lead to the provision of unnecessary services and corresponding increases in malpractice rates. However minor it may be, the direct effect of malpractice rates on the decisions of doctors to work where their services are needed is good.

3

Bad Apples

Doctors, being human, make mistakes. In this chapter, we first explore the issue of whether some doctors regularly practice substandard medicine. Second, we examine the effect which this group of doctors may have on rising malpractice premiums. Third, we consider the nature of professionalism and existing mechanisms to discover when a doctor's standard practice has fallen below professionally acceptable levels, to encourage improvement, or to limit the physician's authority. Finally, we consider the tension inherent in the need to control doctors who regularly injure patients and the need for fairness to the individual physician.

Chronic Substandard Practice

ITEM: On July 17, 1975, twin brothers named Marcus were found dead in their Manhattan apartment. One brother died of withdrawal symptons following severe long-term addiction to barbiturates. The other brother died of an overdose. Both were physicians on the staff and faculty of a prestigious New York hospital and medical school. Colleagues at the hospital reported that for some time prior to their death both men had behaved bizarrely. At first the hospital refused to comment on the deaths, and subsequently revealed that the brothers' hospital staff privileges had been withdrawn the day before the bodies were discovered.

ITEM: A 1976 editorial by two physicians in the influential *New England Journal of Medicine* comments, "Every physician knows some colleague who has to be watched carefully, an old friend or even teacher for whom he hesitates to bring down the curtain even though he knows that the man or woman has advanced beyond his or her competence." The editorial goes on to argue against federal legislation to encourage young doctors to provide primary care in underserved areas, and suggests that instead older doctors who are no longer competent in modern technology should be encouraged to provide ordinary primary care.

ITEM: In October 1974, in Sacramento, California, a $3.7-million-dollar malpractice judgment was entered against Dr. John Nork. The court found that Dr. Nork had performed dozens of operations that were "unnecessary, bungled, or both"; had coerced patients to undergo surgery with threats, intimidation, and false diagnoses; had written fraudulent progress notes; and had altered the recommendations of consultants. Dr. Nork's defense was that he was dependent on "uppers" and "downers" and hence not responsible for his actions. The court rejected this defense, saying that Dr. Nork seemed to have been motivated by a desire for money. A physician colleague said, "I don't believe the judge's conclusion that he did it out of greed, and I know damn well he wasn't on drugs. I suspect he was just really sick, and none of us saw it."

ITEM: Beginning in 1973, St. John's Hospital in Suffolk County, New York, began to receive reports that one of its neurosurgeons, Dr. Edward Altchek, was sexually molesting female patients in the hospital. After fourteen months, the hospital ordered that a female nurse accompany all male doctors examining female patients. Nothing was done to protect patients in Dr. Altchek's office or in the other hospitals at which he worked. A patient complained to the New York State Board of Regents. The board filed charges against the doctor in March 1976; in July 1976 hearings were held before the State Board of Professional Medical Conduct. By this time, Dr. Altchek could no longer attract patients in New York, and decided to apply for a Michigan license. In September 1976, the Suffolk County Medical Society and two colleagues at St. John's Hospital attested to the Michigan licensing authorities that Dr. Altchek's "ethical and professional character were beyond suspicion." In October 1976, the New York State Board of Regents wrote to Michigan that Dr. Altchek was a physician in good standing.

On October 11, 1976, he received his Michigan license; on November 11, 1976, his New York license was revoked. In April, 1977, the AMA Clearinghouse, which hospitals consult regularly to check on staff applicants, had no information regarding any disciplinary action taken against Dr. Altchek.

ITEM: A physician and professor of medicine writes an article analyzing the serious errors which he knows he has made in his professional practice. He concludes:

In each of these case histories more than one person was involved, so there isn't any safety in numbers. Error is also more likely to occur when you are tired, rushed or over-worked—so we must provide for adequate staffing at all times. Safety will have to come before cost effectiveness.

In addition to this kind of anecdotal information, there are a few systematic studies of the prevalence and nature of substandard medical practice and the characteristics of the doctors most likely to engage in such practice. One type of study focuses on medical error, looks at the care actually provided, and evaluates it against established professional norms. Of course, medical error is much broader than medical malpractice. Everyone—not only doctors—makes mistakes. Some mistakes are harmless. Legally, as we have noted, malpractice is a mistake which no reasonable physician would make, which causes an injury that the patient would otherwise not have suffered.

A 1973–75 study made by the American College of Surgeons and the American Surgical Association indicates that 796 of the 1,696 "untoward incidents" arising out of 1,493 surgical operations were avoidable. Another study of children being treated in a comprehensive-care project found that anemia was not recognized or treated in 45 percent of the children cared for in the program at any stage of their treatment; and one half of these children were still anemic at the end of the study. In other recent studies, only one quarter of the patients with severe gastrointestinal symptoms who presented themselves to the emergency rooms of either university or city hospitals were judged to have received minimally adequate care.

Another type of study of substandard medical practice focuses on the characteristics of individual physicians. There is no necessary connection between individual physicians' characteristics and legal malpractice. A doctor may be a convicted felon or an alcoholic or drug addict but still not injure people by practicing medicine below reasonable professional standards. Conversely, a physician who is a law-abiding teetotaler may injure a patient through substandard practice and be held liable for medical malpractice.

The major study of the characteristics of physicians who are subject to professional discipline has been done by Dr. Robert Derbyshire, who was for many years the head of the New Mexico State Board of Medical Examiners and the National Federation of State Medical Boards. He estimates that about 5 percent of the doctors actively practicing in the United States are "unscrupulous, unethical, delinquent or incompetent." Dr. Roger O. Egeberg, who was special assistant on health policy to the Secretary of Health, Education and Welfare, concurs in this estimate. Both of these authorities regard this figure as conservative. Although this is a relatively small proportion of all doctors, it amounts to 16,000 doctors. By this conservative estimate, it is likely that the life and health of more than twelve million patients are now at risk in the care of chronically incompetent doctors. In view of the responsibilities and authority of physicians, it represents a serious problem.

Basic legal responsibility for licensing physicians and certifying their continued competence to practice rests with the boards of medical examiners in the various states. The state medical board is a body created by state law and empowered to license and regulate physicians. It is separate from the medical society, which is a private professional association. Medical societies are usually organized in local as well as state units. Often societies will receive complaints about physician behavior, and may reprimand doctors or exclude them from society membership on the basis of misconduct. However, the medical society does not have legal authority to suspend or limit a doctor's right to practice medicine. That legal power is given to the state medical board.

Overall, the chance that an unfit doctor will have his license suspended or revoked is very slim. The National Federation of State Medical Boards reports that in 1973 only 20 medical licenses were revoked in the United States. In 1974, the figure was 47. In 1975, 67 licenses were revoked. During the four-year period 1969–73, there were more than sixteen states in which no doctor's license was revoked. (The figures are imprecise because some state boards deny the public access to any information about their actions.) In 1970, the medical boards in thirty-one states took no disciplinary actions whatsoever. In recent years, some states have strengthened their procedures for finding and disciplining incompetent doctors, but, nationally, very few licenses are revoked or limited.

Drug abuse is the most common ground for suspending or revoking a doctor's license to practice. Drug abuse accounts for almost half of the disciplinary actions taken by state boards. Although some doctors are disciplined for illegally prescribing narcotics for others, the most frequent ground for discipline is a doctor's own addiction. Narcotic abuse seems to be an occupational disease among doctors. A 1957 study estimated that while there was one addict in 3,000 people in the general population, the proportion among physicians was one in 100. A 1969 study estimated that there were 300 *new* physician addicts each year. In 1975, the *Journal* of the AMA stated that this figure was probably too conservative. Dr. Herbert C. Modlin of the Menninger Foundation estimates that 1.5 percent of U.S. physicians are addicted to drugs. Statistically, the chances of becoming a drug addict are higher for doctors than for ghetto youths.

Some of the reasons for drug addiction among physicians are understandable. Present patterns of medical education make work demands that are greater than those in most other jobs. The young doctor, exhausted by these demands, must deal with complex technology as well as with people at their most vulnerable. The pressures are intense. The drugs that provide stimulation or sedation are readily accessible. But, however well we may understand the causes of drug addiction among doctors, the facts are disturbing.

The second most common reason for which physicians are disciplined is mental incompetence. In most states, mental incompetence is not a ground for revoking or limiting a physician's license to practice except in the extraordinary situation in which he or she is formally declared incompetent or committed to an institution. Other grounds for disciplinary action include fraud and deceit in practice, conviction of a felony, alcoholism, unprofessional conduct, moral turpitude, fee splitting, and gross immorality.

Although criminal conviction is a ground for disciplinary action in most states, recent evidence indicates that physicians who have defrauded public medical-care financing programs are generally not prosecuted, and when they are prosecuted and convicted, there is seldom any follow-up action by the state licensing board. A 1976 Congressional study showed that fraudulent payments of $300 million are made each year to physicians under Medicare. The Justice Department is reluctant to prosecute physicians even when evidence of fraudulent practices is available. Frequently, financial settlements are made in order to avoid prosecution, so that the physician's corrupt practices never become known to the public or to state licensing boards. When physicians are prosecuted and convicted for Medicare fraud, the most common disposition of the case is simply to require the repayment of the money stolen. Of the 150 doctors convicted of Medicare fraud during the period 1970–75, only 14 served any time in jail and only 2 had their licenses revoked. In California, a doctor convicted of intentionally defrauding the Medicaid program by submitting bills for operations on fictitious patients contested board action suspending his license on the ground that the crime did not involve "moral turpitude." The courts rejected the doctor's argument and upheld the suspension. Though it may be inappropriate to bar a convicted physician from practice permanently when the board is convinced that he is repentant and will not repeat the fraudulent practices, the evidence is that in most cases Medicare fraud, practiced on patients as well as the federal treasury, does not result even in a reprimand from the professional disciplinary authority.

A study of the seventy-four disciplinary actions taken by the state board in New York during the period 1973–76 showed that the largest single reason for physician discipline—43 percent of the cases—was drug-related offenses. Another 21 percent of the physicians were disciplined as a result of criminal charges against them. The other repeated offenses were: sexual abuse, five cases; aiding and abetting unlicensed persons to practice medicine, four cases; mental disability, three cases; other miscellaneous matters, five cases. The New York state legislative committee's study comments on these findings, saying:

What this means is that the State agencies involved have only been able to deal effectively with a limited number of physician behavioral problems. The more complicated subjects of concern which are most directly related to patient care, such as medical incompetence, negligence, overutilization of medical service, unnecessary surgery or hospitalization, abandonment and fragmentation of medical care, are just not being dealt with under the current law, procedures and practices. Our survey of other states indicates that New York is not unique in this failure.

Malpractice, even gross malpractice, whether resulting from failing skill and intelligence, habitual failure to pay attention, overwork, or any other cause, is not a common reason for disciplining physicians. In the six years from 1970 through 1975, only eight physicians in the United States were disciplined for incompetence.

Malpractice Premiums and Substandard Physicians

The limited evidence available indicates that the habitually incompetent physician may have an important impact on the malpractice premiums paid by all doctors. Some facts are clear from the available evidence. First, the most rapid increases in malpractice judgments have been in relationship to very large claims. From 1967 to 1975, payments below $5,000 per claim increased from 5 to 8 percent a year. Payments below $25,000 increased from 10 to 12 percent; and payments in excess of $25,000 increased at a rate of more than 20 percent a year. The first malpractice judgment in excess of $1 million occurred in 1968. Between 1968 and 1975, there were at least twenty-five settlements or awards in excess of $1 million, most of these in the last two years. Eighteen were in California and thirteen of them occurred after March 1975.

Second, it is clear that a small proportion of malpractice suits accounts for a very large proportion of the total amounts paid by malpractice insurance companies. The NAIC report found that in 1975 claims of over $50,000 against individual physicians constituted only 3 percent of the claims made, but consumed 63 percent of the premium dollars paid out. These enormous awards, though they represent a small proportion of the total malpractice cases, consume a large part of the malpractice premium dollar. For example, when Dr. John Nork was held liable to Albert Gonzales for $3.7 million, that single judgment represented 12 percent of the total Northern California losses incurred by the American Mutual Liability Company in 1974. Of course, many factors affect the size of the judgment or settlement the patient receives: the severity of the injury; whether the patient is rich or poor; whether the patient is young or old. It costs more to compensate a wealthy young person with very serious injuries than to compensate a person who is poor, older, or less seriously injured. But in the case of Dr. Nork the largest part of the judgment, $2.7 million, was entered because the evidence showed that he had acted maliciously and incompetently in a large number of cases. Available data do not allow us to know what portion of these very large judgments is being entered against physicians who have demonstrated a pattern of malicious action.

Generally, malpractice insurers do not vary rates in accordance with any factors other than specialty, whether the doctor performs surgery, and geographical location. Hence, a doctor who has been held liable in one or more malpractice suits will pay the same premium as another physician in the same specialty and location who has never been sued. A doctor who has a serious problem with drugs or alcohol will pay the same rate as one who does not. The malpractice insurance companies take the position that it is not possible for them to predict more precisely than they now do which doctors are most likely to be sued for malpractice, or to make corresponding adjustments in premium rates. Further, predicting losses and determining appropriate insurance premiums depend upon insuring a large pool of people. The relatively small size of the doctor pool makes rate-making a difficult job which would be still more difficult if finer distinctions were drawn.

Despite these real problems, there are some ways in which insurance companies could use malpractice premium rates to assist in detecting and dealing with the incompetent physician. They could offer lower rates to doctors willing to undergo periodic physical examination to detect drug addiction, alcoholism, or serious physical or mental disabilities that interfere with the ability to practice. But, beyond this gross sort of screening, the insurance companies are skeptical, and probably rightly so, of their ability to identify those characteristics of physicians or physician practice that make it more or less likely that a doctor will be held liable for malpractice. Although it may be administratively feasible to offer lower rates to doctors who participate in programs of continuing medical education, there is no evidence that participation in such programs leads to better-quality medical practice, or decreases the likelihood that a doctor will be held liable for malpractice. Thus, competent and conscientious doctors, who are in the majority, must pay malpractice premiums which reflect not only their own risks but also the risks of the minority of physicians who are addicted, incompetent, or dishonest. All the evidence indicates that a small proportion of the medical profession is responsible for a very large portion of the rapidly increasing malpractice premium.

Professional Self-Regulation

Medicine is the prototype of a profession. Two main factors define a professional. First, a professional works in areas that require mastery of a large, complex body of knowledge. Second, the professional provides personal services which touch upon the core values of a society. Other defining characteristics of a profession flow from these two central factors. Professional training is a long and arduous process that builds the required technical competence that characterizes a professional's work and inculcates a commitment to the values of the profession. Because of the nature of professional work, the most common forms of social control of work in an industrial society, bureaucratic supervision and consumer judgment, are of limited applicability in controlling the work of a professional. Yet the need for social control of professional work is especially urgent because of values and interests at stake.

In theory, this dilemma is resolved by a strong emphasis on individual self-control, grounded in the long socialization process of professional education and the formal and informal control of the community of colleagues. Society as a whole accepts the professional's pledge of self-regulation through peer control, and grants in return privileges and advantages, such as high income, prestige, and professional autonomy against lay control and interference. As we have seen, when doctors are charged with negligence, as professionals they enjoy a unique position in the law in that the conduct of a physician is judged only by professional medical standards. The critical importance of the work that doctors do, the significance of the consequences when that work is not done well, and the absence of other means of social control over the quality of physician work all make effective peer review of professional conduct absolutely essential.

States have primary responsibility for the licensing and regulation of physicians. These functions have been assigned to the boards of medical examiners of the various states. Traditionally, these boards have been composed exclusively of local physicians. The license to practice medicine is granted on the basis of educational credentials and knowledge demonstrated at the beginning of the doctor's professional career. Once the license is obtained, the physician is authorized to practice in any field of medicine, and until recently there have been no further requirements to demonstrate continued competence.

The state medical boards are the only bodies with the legal authority to revoke or limit the doctor's general freedom to practice medicine. There are two other, more limited formal mechanisms for monitoring and controlling a doctor's practice. First, physicians in hospitals determine which doctors will have the "privilege" of admitting and caring for patients. Hospital-based peer review will be discussed in the next chapter. Second, in 1972, Congress enacted a law requiring that local and state Professional Standards Review Organizations (PSRO's) be established to review services financed with federal funds to assure that services are medically necessary, are provided at the most economic level consistent with the medical needs of the patient, and meet professionally recognized standards of quality established at the local level.

PSRO's are still in an early stage of development. Even when they are in full operation, it is uncertain whether PSRO's will have much direct impact on either the process of finding and disciplining problem physicians or on malpractice premiums. Like the present hospital-utilization review committees, the PSRO's may focus primarily on assuring that hospital services paid for by Medicaid and Medicare are necessary services. Review of the quality of medical care may be a distinctly secondary function. Although the PSRO has authority to investigate doctors and hospitals when it discovers problems in the course of its own review, it has no mechanism for receiving complaints from patients, hospitals, or physicians. The PSRO is intended to develop profiles on Medicare and Medicaid patients, hospitals, and doctors. Where the profiles reveal a pattern of unnecessary or substandard care, the PSRO may, after notice and hearing, exclude a doctor or hospital from participation in Medicare or Medicaid. The primary penalty which the PSRO will impose is denial of reimbursement for a particular service found to be medically unnecessary.

The profiles developed by the PSRO's on individual physicians, and PSRO sanctions imposed on physicians, could be a very useful source of information for state medical boards. Unfortunately, federal law now impedes access to PSRO data. The federal statute provides that the HEW Secretary shall promulgate regulations which provide for the public disclosure of PSRO data and information ". . . in such cases and under such circumstances as the Secretary shall by regulation provide to assure adequate protection of the rights and interests of patients. . . ." The most recent federal regulations, published in December 1976, provide that the PSRO may release only general statistical information which does not identify any particular doctor or hospital, and information which has already been published *and* is obtained from a source that does not label it as confidential. People working with PSRO's face criminal sanctions for the unauthorized disclosure of information gathered in their work. The Secretary of HEW should promulgate regulations making PSRO information about individual doctors and hospitals available to state medical boards, and the boards should be allowed to use the data in disciplining problem physicians. But even if federal regulations were to allow the disclosure of PSRO data to state boards, there is now no assurance that the boards in most states would actually receive the information. Other than Vermont and Florida, no state requires that PSRO's convey information and findings on substandard medical practice to the state licensing boards.

The PSRO statute provides immunity from civil claims based on the actions taken in connection with PSRO review. It also provides immunity to hospitals and physicians who act in compliance with or reliance upon PSRO standards and norms, so long as they exercise "due care." These are not likely to have much impact on malpractice liability, since, even without the immunity provision, it is difficult to imagine a situation in which a person could be held liable in a civil action for functions performed in connection with PSRO responsibilities, and even more difficult to imagine a situation in which a doctor or hospital could be held liable for malpractice when they had complied with the prevailing, published standards of treatment and had exercised due care.

Hence, state medical boards have the key responsibility for licensing physicians and for imposing limits on that license. It is widely acknowledged, even in professional medical circles, that state medical boards have done a wholly inadequate job of finding and disciplining chronically incompetent physicians. Furthermore, some of the inadequacies of state medical boards are correctable through rather simple legislative changes and modest expenditures of money. All that is required is that conscientious physicians and legislators make a judgment that it is important to develop a more effective means of dealing with incompetent doctors. There are a number of reasons why state medical boards have been ineffective. First, the laws of most states are inadequate both in defining the grounds upon which the board may act, and in providing a range of sanctions, limitations, or corrective measures which it may require. Second, the law in most states does not do enough to ensure that the boards will be provided with the information they need in order to act. Third, the boards are often not capable of carrying out the serious responsibility assigned to them because of inadequate staff and board leadership.

Legal Powers of State Medical Boards

A very serious omission in the legal standards defining the powers of state medical boards is that, in many states, professional incompetence, however gross, is not a ground for disciplining a physician. In 1973, professional incompetence was not a ground for discipline in thirty-five states. In 1975–76, eleven states enacted laws adding "malpractice" or "professional incompetence" or "gross or repeated malpractice" as a cause for medical discipline. Nonetheless, even following a period in which the problem of medical malpractice was before every state legislature in the country, the medical boards of many states still do not have explicit authority to discipline a physician for gross or repeated malpractice. This omission is shocking.

In the past, some conscientious state medical boards have been able to surmount the deficiency in their legal mandate. For example, in 1968, the physicians of the Kansas State Board of Healing Arts had before them evidence that during one year a doctor practicing surgery at a Kansas hospital had performed eleven operations which were unnecessary or seriously mishandled or both. Three of the patients had died. The Kansas statute empowered the board to discipline doctors for "unprofessional conduct," and enumerated fifteen grounds for such a finding, not including gross malpractice or incompetence. The board determined that the statutory language "unprofessional conduct" should be read to include extreme incompetence and, after giving the physician a full hearing and an opportunity to explain the evidence against him, revoked his license. The doctor challenged the board's action in court. A lower court held that, under the law, the board had no power to discipline a physician for extreme incompetence and restored his right to continue practicing medicine. The physicians of the state board appealed, and ultimately the Kansas Supreme Court upheld their action.

The court said:

The whole purpose and tenor of the healing arts act is the protection of the public against unprofessional, improper, unauthorized and unqualified practice of the healing arts. The goal is to secure to the people the services of competent, trustworthy practitioners. . . .

. . . No conduct or practice could be more devastating to the health and welfare of a patient or the public than incompetence; integral to the whole policy the legislature had in mind must be the power of the board to protect against it.

So, while it is possible for a state medical board to interpret its general powers as including the power to discipline incompetent physicians, this power needs to be made explicit. When a state board is forced to operate under such vague standards as "professional conduct," legal challenges to its actions are predictable. Further, the legal standard should inform physicians more precisely what is expected of them. The scope of judicial review of medical-board actions is broader when the board operates under words like "unprofessional" or "immoral" which have meaning in the general language as well as in the medical context. While a standard such as "incompetence" or "gross malpractice" is also general, these terms focus on characteristics which are particularly relevant to the physician's ability to practice medicine. For all these reasons, the state legislatures should make perfectly plain that the state medical boards have the power and responsibility to find and discipline physicians who are chronically and seriously incompetent.

A second serious omission in the statutory mandate of many state medical boards is the absence of a range of investigative tools and sanctions to deal with the variety of problems that afflict physicians. If the only sanction available to the state board is license revocation, the board will obviously be reluctant to apply it except in the most serious cases. However, there are many cases in which more limited sanctions may be more appropriate and, being more appropriate, may be more readily applied. Thus, probation conditioned upon treatment may be more appropriate for the doctor who is addicted to drugs or alcohol or has serious psychological problems. In the mid-1970's, several states enacted laws providing state medical boards with a broader range of powers including: limitations or restrictions on the right to practice medicine; public or private reprimand; requiring submission to medical examination, counseling, or treatment; requiring participation in a program of continuing education; or fines. The American Medical Association has endorsed legislation which would provide state boards with a broader range of investigative authority and sanctions. Recent improvements have been made in the laws of some states, but, in most states, legislative action is still needed to provide the state boards with the range of sanctions they need to act effectively.

Obtaining Information About Physicians

State medical boards do not have access to the information they need to do an effective job. Useful sources of information include patients, medical societies, hospital review committees, PSRO's, malpractice insurers, courts, and, most important, other physicians. In most states, none of these sources are tapped effectively. Furthermore, there is generally no agency which accumulates information about a particular physician on either a state or a national level. A doctor may have privileges suspended at one hospital and move on to another. A doctor may have several malpractice actions pending or decided adversely, yet no responsible authority has comprehensive information about such legal proceedings. Even in those rare instances where a state board acts to suspend or revoke a license, a physician can move on to another state, and there is no national reporting system which allows a state board or a hospital to obtain comprehensive information about the disciplinary proceedings or malpractice suits in which a physician has been involved.

At a minimum, the law should require that the state medical board be notified when some other responsible body has made a judgment that raises questions about the competence of a physician. For example, the law should require that the state board be notified when a hospital acts to suspend or limit a doctor's admitting privileges, when a court enters a judgment against a doctor, or when a medical society or PSRO imposes sanction on a doctor. Most states do not require reporting to the state medical board even after one of these agencies has made a judgment against a physician. State laws should also require that some charges against physicians be reported to the state board at the time the charge is made. For example, when criminal charges are filed accusing a physician of serious offense, the law should require that the state board be informed. Proof which is not sufficient to meet the high standards applicable in criminal cases might nonetheless be sufficient to justify some limitation on a physician's license to practice.

Unless all of these agencies are required to report to the state board, there will be no single place in which all relevant information about problem physicians is collected. Most states have done nothing to ensure that the findings of these various agencies will be collected in one place.

In the mid-1970's, a good deal of legislation dealing with these issues has been passed. Florida and Vermont have enacted the most comprehensive laws. They require that all medical disciplinary committees report to the state medical board when they take action against a physician. These include medical societies, hospital peer-review committees, and PSRO's. Other states have imposed more limited reporting requirements. Eleven have required that when a malpractice claim is filed, the insurance company must report to either the state medical board or the state insurance department. Thirteen additional states require only that a report be filed after a malpractice claim is settled or a judgment is entered. Four states have required that courts report to the state medical board when they adjudicate a physician mentally incompetent. Six states require that hospital disciplinary actions be reported to the state board. Five states require that the disciplinary actions of the state and local medical societies be reported.

Given that every state in the country enacted some form of legislation during the mid-1970's in response to the malpractice crisis, it is surprising to find that so many states still do not require these agencies to report to the state medical boards. Even if all these institutional sources of information were required to report to the state board, there would still be many cases in which the board had no knowledge of a physician who was addicted or who chronically practiced substandard medical care. All too frequently, hospital peer-review mechanisms do not function at all, or, if they do function, they allow the problem physician to resign and no formal action is taken. Malpractice actions do not arise until substandard practice produces a patient sufficiently angry to seek legal redress, and injured so seriously that a lawyer is willing to take the case.

Potentially, the people best able to identify doctors with problems and to provide reliable information to the state medical boards are other doctors. Today, doctors rarely report on the questionable practices or problems of their colleagues. In the Gonzales case, over a dozen physicians observed the fraudulent and incompetent practices of Dr. Nork, but no one filed a report with the state medical board, although one did advise a patient to file a malpractice action. When the Marcus twins died in New York, several physicians told newspaper reporters that the brothers' recent behavior in the hospital and operating room had been highly questionable. But none of these physicians had reported their observations to the state board.

There are many reasons why physicians do not report a colleague when they observe physical, mental, or drug problems or repeated demonstrations of incompetence. Perhaps most fundamental is that we are all taught from an early age that it is not right to "tattle." Joseph Conrad once observed that no one is more despised than an informer. Except in situations in which a community code of honor demands that we inform authorities when we observe breaches of the community standards, there is a strong ethic against "telling." Also doctors, like the rest of us, empathize with the problems of colleagues. We all know that there are times when we do not perform at top capacity. When we understand why another person may be unable to perform as well as possible, we are reluctant to condemn. Doctors probably also sense that providing information to a state medical board may be a waste of time; the medical community is well aware of the boards' general ineffectiveness. A doctor who reports on a colleague may have to spend time substantiating his or her observations, testifying before the board, and being available for cross-examination, which itself is a painful and difficult ordeal.

Though all these reasons are perfectly understandable, the situation which results is simply not tolerable. The "conspiracy of silence" among physicians is unacceptable to the general public, and it should be unacceptable to physicians. If ever there was a situation in which ethics and the law should require that the people who are best able to observe and report serious breaches in professional standards be required to do so, substandard medical performance is it. Both the nature of professionalism and the law of malpractice assume that self-policing will be the primary source of control of physicians' professional behavior.

The law does not and should not impose a general requirement that citizens must report violations of the law. But physicians enjoy a unique social position of privilege and responsibility. Nearly every state has long required by law that doctors report cases of drug addiction, child abuse, and gunshot wounds. The overwhelming evidence is that professional ethics do not motivate physicians to take their peer-review responsibilities seriously. The law must be changed to make it absolutely clear to physicians that they have a responsibility to provide state medical boards with information about colleagues who cannot or do not practice within minimally acceptable professional standards.

At the present time, only nine states impose such an obligation on physicians: Alabama, Arizona, Idaho, Illinois, Ohio, New York, Oregon, Utah, and Vermont. Three states—Alaska, Maine, and Virginia—require that doctors report when they have treated another physician for drug addiction, alcoholism, or mental illness. The Arizona law, enacted in 1971, compels doctors to report any information "which appears to show that a doctor of medicine is or may be mentally or physically unable to safely engage in the practice of medicine." It seems to have had a significant impact. Prior to its enactment, physicians rarely reported to the board about other doctors. Since its passage, about half of the complaints filed with the Arizona board have come from physicians, and about 75 percent of them have resulted in disciplinary action.

A more common legislative response to the problem of encouraging physicians to inform state boards about their peers has been to enact laws providing immunity from civil suit for persons providing information to disciplinary bodies. Such laws have been enacted in twenty-nine states. They are entirely unnecessary, because a person providing a state medical board with information already has immunity under the common law as long as the information is provided in good faith, even if it turns out that the information was false. As in the case of the Good Samaritan laws discussed in Chapter 5, it appears that the state legislatures are willing to provide explicit legal immunity against a nonexistent threat of civil suit, in the hope that it will encourage physicians to report to the state boards. But the Good Samaritan immunity against suits arising out of doctors' efforts to help at roadside accidents has not encouraged doctors to stop and help in emergencies. There is little reason to believe that this new immunity against a nonexistent threat of litigation will be effective in encouraging physicians to report to the state medical boards.

A further potential source of information about disabled or incompetent physicians is patients and the general public. A 1976 survey conducted in the New York area asked people where they would file a complaint about a physician. Not one person mentioned the state medical board, presumably because most people do not know that the board exists. Ten percent said they would complain to the local medical society. However, contrary to even relatively sophisticated popular belief, the local medical society does not have legal authority to discipline physicians. It may receive complaints and may in some cases suspend a physician's right to membership in the society. But in New York about half the physicians have never joined the medical society. A medical society has no authority over doctors who do not belong to it.

Patients do not in fact often file complaints with either medical societies or state medical boards. The only patient complaints filed against New York's Marcus twins involved delay in processing insurance forms. During the nine years that Dr. Nork practiced in Sacramento, only six patients filed complaints with the local medical society: five of them related to disputes over fees and one was from a patient complaining because Dr. Nork had refused to perform surgery!

Furthermore, patients do not have legal authority to trigger an investigation by a state medical board. In 1964, a woman named Mrs. Katz suffered severe and permanent brain damage under general anesthetic during childbirth when she was deprived of oxygen for twelve to fifteen minutes. Her brother and father brought a malpractice action against her physician and won. They also filed a complaint with the state medical board, and offered to produce evidence and witnesses at a board hearing. The board refused to hold a hearing, and the brother and father asked the courts to compel one. The Massachusetts Supreme Court ruled that the decision whether or not to hold a hearing was within the discretion of the board, and a court could not order it to do so.

Certainly the law should encourage the public to file complaints against physician behavior which seems dangerous, incompetent, or unethical. State medical boards could do much more to inform the public of their existence and to invite complaints. Either the state medical board or the state legislature could require physicians to post information about where patients can file complaints. Probably the most effective thing that a state medical board could do to encourage the public to bring information to its attention would be to develop a reputation for handling complaints in a way that encouraged patients to believe such complaints were taken seriously. For example, it would be a simple matter to provide individuals who filed complaints with copies of the ensuing correspondence between the state board and the doctor against whom the complaint was lodged. Some of the complaints received might be frivolous, or even vindictive; but to the extent that this was so, they could be handled expeditiously. If state boards effectively sought and handled patient complaints, not only would they have an additional pool of potentially useful information about physicians, but, perhaps more important, they would also provide an outlet for the anger that might otherwise vent itself in a malpractice action.

Staffing and Leadership

In addition to the inadequacies in the legal standards under which the state medical boards operate and their inability to gather the information needed for effective action, there are serious structural and staffing problems which often ensure that the state medical boards will not be able to do their job well.

In most states, the medical board is appointed by the governor from a list submitted by the state medical society. This process tends to produce boards dominated by general practitioners; over 60 percent of the physician members of state medical boards are not certified in any specialty. State boards tend to have an anti-academic bias which may not be justified in light of the highly specialized nature of modern medicine. State boards also tend to be composed of people who are quite old. Dr. Derbyshire found that the average age of state-board members was 58.3 years. In five boards, the average age of the members was over 65.

Certainly, general practitioners and older doctors have a great deal to contribute to the work of state medical boards. But probably the boards would function more effectively if they included a broader range of the professional medical community. Younger physicians are apt to be more up to date in their training and knowledge of recent developments in medicine. It would be very simple for the legislature to require that the state medical board be composed of people designated by professional organizations other than the state medical association, including nurse associations; the medical schools of the state; the state chapter of the National Medical Association, which represents black physicians; the state organization of the Committee on Interns and Residents; and the state chapter of the American Public Health Association, which is the largest organization of health professionals in the world.

Lay people should also be added to state medical boards. The HEW Malpractice Commission found that in the area of physician discipline "the public has a vital interest and we believe its voice should be heard." The presence of concerned and articulate lay people would provide a counterbalance to doctors' natural empathy with their colleagues. California has recently added substantial numbers of articulate, patient-oriented lay people to its state medical board. Early evidence is that this change in board membership is having a positive effect in making the board more active and effective.

None of the suggestions made so far would cost a penny. But if the state medical boards are to function effectively, one other change is needed which will require an increase in expenditures. In general, state boards are grossly understaffed. Staff is needed to act on complaints received, to communicate with the doctor against whom charges are made, to investigate, to maintain records, to present cases for board consideration, to advise the members of the board on their legal authority, and, when necessary, to defend the board's actions in court. The evidence is that, at present, the boards in most states are severely understaffed and unable to deal even with the very limited information now presented to them. Dr. Derbyshire reports that boards generally do not have the regular service of legal counsel.

In many states the attorney for the board is assigned by the attorney general. Often he is a junior member of the staff and the board might have different counsel at each meeting. It is not unusual for a strange attorney to be summoned to a board meeting on short notice with no opportunity to familiarize himself with the law or policies of the board.

Staff shortages are not limited to lawyers. One study reports that in 1970 the New York state board had twenty-three investigators for the New York City area, and by 1974 the number of investigators was down to four. In 1976, the New York board's staff consisted of an executive secretary, a lawyer, and twelve investigators. A 1977 report of the State Consumer Protection Board recommended that "there should be a dramatic increase in efforts to inform the public of the mechanisms available to lodge a complaint against a professional," and that staff be increased to handle complaints adequately. In New Jersey, from 1965 to 1971, the state board of medical examiners took no disciplinary action against any physician. In 1972, the state hired a full-time executive and expanded the board's budget; in the next two years, the board revoked ten licenses and persuaded three other physicians to surrender theirs.

In 1976, California substantially increased the staff of its state medical board, and created a number of local offices throughout the state to receive and investigate complaints about physicians. These offices serve as a means of gathering information about physicians who should perhaps be disciplined and of resolving complaints which might otherwise result in a malpractice suit. Although it is too early to evaluate the effectiveness of California's program, there is reason to believe that active, well-staffed state medical boards will do much to reduce both real and perceived needs to resort to malpractice actions.

Generally, state medical boards are financed through fees imposed upon licensed physicians. (In addition, better organized and motivated boards occasionally receive special grants from state or federal agencies to undertake specific projects.) The annual licensing fee is set by the legislature. In 1977 the California board had the largest budget in the nation—about $6 million, which was raised by imposing a licensing fee of $125 every two years on California physicians. Prior to 1976 the California licensing fee was only $25 every two years. Boards in most states have similarly low fees. There is some evidence of possibly wasteful expenditures on the part of state boards. (For example, is it appropriate to pay physician board members $35 an hour for attendance at meetings? Is it appropriate to hire expensive private counsel on an hourly basis when a salaried staff attorney could probably do work which was both more economical and effective?) Although licensing fees seem like an appropriate mechanism for financing the work of state medical boards, it is plain that substantial increases in these fees are needed in most states to enable the boards to do an effective job. The likelihood is that this expenditure could ultimately produce a savings in reduced malpractice premiums for most doctors.

Protecting the Doctor

Another factor that is sometimes cited as a barrier to effective action by state medical boards is the possibility that board action will be reversed in the courts. A doctor's license to practice, though a publicly conferred privilege rather than a private right, is also a form of liberty and property which is protected by the law. A physician is entitled to fair and due process before his or her license is suspended or revoked.

Because the right to practice medicine is so valuable, most physicians will do everything possible to challenge limitations on it. It can be expected that they will obtain first-class legal talent to present their claims. But if a board provides the due process the law requires and is itself represented by competent counsel, there is no inconsistency between the need to protect the public from incompetent physicians and the need to ensure that the individual physician is afforded a full and fair hearing. Since 1970, the Supreme Court has required that welfare recipients be afforded due process prior to the termination of aid. State welfare agencies have learned what due process requires, and have set up procedures and mechanisms to provide it in a routine and expeditious way. State medical boards could do the same. All that is required to enable state boards to meet due-process standards of fairness is the willingness and the staff to provide it. The requirement that individuals be afforded due process prior to the termination of state-granted rights or privileges has not paralyzed the state and prevented it from taking action against ineligible welfare recipients. It should not preclude state action against incompetent doctors.

Sometimes physicians who have been suspended by state boards have been able to persuade state courts to delay the action of the state boards. The HEW Malpractice Commission reports a number of cases in which doctors continued to practice for years, and to injure people, while the courts allowed delays in the enforcement of board orders. The commission recommended that states enact laws limiting the duration of judicial stay orders to the minimum period necessary to hold an adversary hearing, and assuring such hearings priority on court dockets. Maryland, Virginia, and Iowa have enacted laws specifically prohibiting courts from staying the action of a state medical board, and providing for a full and prompt hearing to review the board's decision. Prior to 1974, the California board was not entitled even to receive notice when a court stayed the board's order suspending a doctor's license to practice. A 1974 amendment requires that the board be given notice when a suspended doctor applies for a stay, and prohibits courts from staying such orders during the time of a hearing unless it appears that the board is unlikely to prevail in suspending a doctor.

In other states, the effectiveness of the medical board is undermined by state laws that require a process far more complex and cumbersome than is necessary to meet constitutional due-process standards. In New

York, *nine* separate administrative reviews must be completed before a doctor's license can be revoked, and this administrative process may be only a prelude to two additional levels of court review. A recent study of the New York procedures states that "the system bends over backwards to provide professionals with an unprecedented degree of due process which would not be tolerated if extended to criminal defendants or business regulatees."

Conclusion

The recent medical malpractice crisis provides powerful economic incentives for physicians to identify doctors who regularly practice substandard care. Apart from the financial impact which incompetent physicians have on the malpractice premiums of all doctors, decent doctors have a strong interest in improving the public image of the medical profession. Most fundamentally, one would think that doctors would be motivated by human concern and professional pride to do what they can to ensure that the public is protected from incompetent practitioners.

Organized medicine has done much to promote the belief that the causes for increases in malpractice premiums lie outside the medical profession. But the overwhelming evidence is that some doctors regularly provide care which is below any reasonable standard, and that inadequate effort is made to discover and discipline these physicians. Conscientious doctors could have an important impact on reforms within the medical profession. Their ability to affect other aspects of the malpractice problem may be more limited. Ultimately, physicians must play a major role in reforms within their own profession.

4

The Hospital: The Doctor's Workshop

Physicians often dismiss the *Nork* case as an atypical example of outrageous malpractice, so obviously deviant that no intelligent person would draw policy inferences from it. Although Dr. Nork was himself aberrational, to dismiss his story as exceptional is to miss the main lesson of the *Nork* decision. Mercy General Hospital of Sacramento, where Dr. Nork worked, was a typically "good" American hospital. It conformed to all accreditation, licensing, and government standards for quality care. Its papers were in order; its medical review system was in effect so that the appropriate boxes on the appropriate accreditation forms could be checked in good faith. Despite this, the hospital was unable to detect and stop even a blatant case in which a staff physician butchered at least fourteen patients through incompetence and fraud over a period of eight years. For this failure, the hospital was held liable for $1.7 million.

Another neurosurgeon, Dr. Moses Ashkenazy, has been called the east-coast Nork. In 1965, Dr. Ashkenazy left Houston for New York State after his Houston hospital privileges were revoked for performing an excess of surgery. Southside Hospital in Suffolk County, New York, refused his request for staff privileges after the chief of its Executive Board made phone inquiries of various Houston doctors. However, Dr. Ashkenazy was granted staff privileges at two other local hospitals, Smithtown General and St. John's. These hospitals relied on the letters of reference presented by Dr. Ashkenazy and on a favorable report by the AMA Clearinghouse. The chief of St. John's Executive Committee was later to say that Ashkenazy had a New York license, and "if New York State doesn't investigate, why should we? The hospital doesn't have the power or the money to investigate effectively." By 1966, the chief of surgery at Smithtown recognized that the amount of Dr. Ashkenazy's surgery was alarming, particularly laminectomy procedures. Requesting information from the specialty board as to an appropriate number of operations for the local population, he received the response, "It's your baby, you rock it." The hospital instituted a second-consultation rule for laminectomies, but a consulting physician later described it as a "sham" because the second physician's dissenting opinion was regularly ignored. Another neurosurgeon moved to the area and started to receive the bulk of referrals for the specialty. Dr. Ashkenazy, his practice dwindling, left Smithtown in 1974 of his own free will. As of this writing, the New York State Medical Practice Task Force, a special investigatory commission of the State Assembly established in response to the malpractice crisis, has so far identified twenty-three individual complaints with $28 million in outstanding malpractice claims against Dr. Ashkenazy. One million dollars have already been paid out. The hospitals involved have not been held liable.

The crucial significance of the *Nork* case is that, for the first time, a hospital was held liable for failure to adopt procedures to monitor the quality of medical care provided by a physician in the hospital. The decision has severely shaken American hospitals and their accreditation agency, the Joint Commission on Accreditation of Hospitals (JCAH). It has led to some honest self-examination and constructive reform. It has also led the American Hospital Association to urge its members to unite with doctors in advocating tort reform, lest the malpractice crisis atmosphere lead legislators to deal with other issues such as "relicensure, excess beds, PSRO and utilization review," all of which are summarily characterized as a "cure . . . potentially worse than the disease."

In this chapter, we examine the relationship between the organizational structure of hospitals and medical malpractice. In addition, we explore the legal standards and constraints imposed on hospitals, and show how the law has both discouraged and, more recently, encouraged hospitals to take responsibility for the care provided to patients.

Hospitals Are Dangerous Places

The HEW Malpractice Commission found that 75 percent of all reported malpractice takes place in hospitals. A 1977 study by the National Association of Insurance Commissioners shows that 79 percent of all claims arise from hospital injuries, and 83 percent of payments made in settlement are for injuries occurring in hospitals.

Further, malpractice claims are only the tip of the iceberg. An HEW study of medical records in two community hospitals disclosed that 7.6 percent of hospital admissions resulted in medical injury. Sixty-two percent of these injuries were either "major-temporary" or "permanent." Twenty-nine percent of the hospital injuries reported in the study were due to negligence, yet only 6 percent of these negligently caused injuries resulted in a claim against either the hospital or a doctor. While the usefulness of extrapolating gross national statistics of hospital-based injury based on the HEW study may be limited, there is little question that hospitals are extremely dangerous places. In a national 1975 survey of 10,000 nurses, one third said that they would not want to receive care in the hospital where they worked.

Doctors are primarily responsible for the increasing number of malpractice suits against hospitals. A consultant to the American Hospital Association reported in 1976 that hospital personnel-controllable claims, such as burns, medication mistake, and blood-transfusion error, were remaining relatively stable, but physician-controllable claims were increasing rapidly. The HEW Malpractice Commission found that, between 1967 and 1970, co-defendant claims, in which the hospital was named together with a member of the medical staff, increased at a more rapid rate than sole-defendant claims, where the hospital was named alone. The NAIC claims reports indicate that 65 percent of hospital losses by amount were based at least in part on physician error.

More than half of all patients making malpractice claims are in the hospital for surgical treatment. Within the hospital, the surgery suite is the most frequent site of injury leading to claims (38.7 percent), followed by the patient's room (33.8 percent), the emergency room (11.8 percent), and intensive- and cardiac-care units (1.1 percent). Looking not at the place of injury but at the primary treatment the patient received, 57.2 percent of all malpractice claims originate in the course of surgical treatment.

Malpractice claims against hospitals, like those against physicians, are not distributed randomly. In the period from 1967 to 1970, as the average number of claims per hospital rose from 1.026 to 1.862 per year, most hospitals were never sued. A small minority of hospitals accounted for the great majority of claims; 6.2 percent of all hospitals had five or more claims. These figures might be seen as confirming the obvious, that some hospitals are safer than others. But, at the present time, there is no statistical basis on which to evaluate the distribution of malpractice incidence among types of hospital, whether classified by financial structure, size, services offered, or some other factor. The American Hospital Association is now conducting such a study.

The Legal Structure

Traditionally, the law has not held hospitals accountable for the quality of medical care provided within the institution. There are two sources of law defining the institutional responsibility a hospital owes to its patients. First is the common law, developed by courts in the course of deciding medical malpractice claims brought against hospitals by patients who were injured while receiving care. The second is the public statutory and regulatory law, defining standards which hospitals must meet to be licensed, and, more recently, standards which hospitals must meet in order to receive insurance payments for services provided to patients eligible for Medicare or Medicaid. A third and extremely important source of standards for hospitals is the Joint Commission on Accreditation of Hospitals (JCAH). This is a private trade association which establishes and applies standards for the organization of hospital care. Through the years, these three sources of standards and legal requirements have developed in relationship to one another.

Until the 1940's, all charitable hospitals were legally immune from any liability for care provided to their patients. Over the past thirty years, immunity from liability has been whittled away or abolished by courts and by legislatures. But, as total immunity was abandoned, liability was imposed for only a small class of injuries occurring within the hospital. Until quite recently, the law has viewed the hospital as a hotel for the sick and a workshop for the patient's private physician, who was responsible for the medical care provided to the patient. Even today, many hospital admission forms state that the "patient recognizes that all doctors of medicine furnishing services to the patient

. . . are independent contractors and are not employees or agents of the hospital." The traditional common-law view places great emphasis on the independent contract between physician and patient, and the absence of any hospital control over the physician. To this date, most courts regard the physician as an independent contractor, so long as the parties structure the employment relationship to comply with the necessary formalities expressed in the decisions.

This legal view of the doctor as an independent contractor often bears very little relationship to the patient's or the public's perception of reality. Often a patient is assigned to a physician only after coming to the hospital clinic or emergency room. Patients normally look to the hospital and its entire staff to organize and carry out the treatment process. The hospital, in its fund-raising and public-relations efforts, presents itself as a unified, integrated community facility. Doctors, particularly hospital-based specialists who do not engage in private practice, often derive their entire income from hospital-based practice.

Hospital liability for malpractice can be established by one of two means. The hospital is vicariously liable, by the legal doctrine of *respondeat superior,* for negligent acts performed within the scope of employment by salaried employees. In practical terms, this means that the hospital is institutionally responsible for injuries negligently caused by administrators, nurses, technicians, salaried doctors, and support staff, but the hospital is *not* institutionally responsible for injuries negligently caused by doctors, because most hospital physicians are not salaried employees. In some instances, the hospital is not responsible even for the actions of a salaried employee. This arises most frequently in the case of a nurse who negligently injures a patient while assisting a doctor or carrying out a doctor's direct orders. By the doctrine known as the "borrowed servant," the nurse's negligence is then attributed to the doctor, not to the hospital.

The second way in which a hospital may be held liable for injuries inflicted on patients is based on the principle of corporate negligence. The law holds that the hospital owes certain direct, nondelegable duties to its patients, including furnishing and maintaining equipment, and providing safe buildings and grounds. Traditionally, the hospital's duty of care has been defined as "the degree of care, skill, and diligence used by hospitals generally in the community."

It is apparent that the legal requirements of common-law liability provide little incentive to hospitals to exercise responsibility for the medical quality of the care provided to patients. Before examining recent common-law changes expanding the responsibility of hospitals, it is useful to look at other legal and private mechanisms for encouraging quality of hospital care. The Joint Commission on the Accreditation of Hospitals has assumed dominant responsibility for defining and enforcing standards of quality in American hospitals. Founded in 1952, the JCAH is governed by representatives of the American College of Surgeons, the American College of Physicians, the American Hospital Association, and the American Medical Association. The JCAH surveys hospitals upon their request, and the hospital pays for the privilege of being surveyed. Given this organizing and financing structure, it is not surprising that the JCAH is, in the words of its director, Dr. John Porterfield, "what you would call industry oriented . . . [we] do the best that we can in a marketable product."

In addition to JCAH and common-law standards for the organization of hospital care, every state has requirements for the licensing of hospitals. Most of these state laws were passed to comply with the requirements for receipt of federal funds under the Hill-Burton Hospital Survey and Construction Act of 1946. These state laws emphasize minimal physical and safety conditions; the standards for state licensing are almost uniformly lower than those set by the JCAH.

Until 1965, accreditation had little legal or practical effect on most hospitals. The AMA required that teaching hospitals obtain JCAH accreditation in order to maintain a program for the training of interns and residents. All other hospitals could elect whether or not to seek JCAH accreditation; the decision was voluntary. If accreditation was denied, there were no practical adverse consequences to the hospital. In 1965, Congress, in enacting the Medicare program, recognized that it was necessary to specify which hospitals would qualify for payments for services provided to the elderly and which would not, but it did not want to undertake direct federal oversight of hospitals because this might well produce hospital resistance to the entire Medicare program. At the urging of the JCAH and the American Hospital Association, Congress provided that all hospitals accredited by the JCAH would be deemed to meet federal requirements for receipt of Medicare funds. While the federal law allowed HEW to develop standards for judging hospitals not accredited by the JCAH, those standards could not be higher than those of the JCAH. Hence, since 1965, JCAH accreditation has become a matter of substantial practical importance to most hospitals. Further, JCAH standards have achieved significant legal status under federal law. (More recent developments in relationship to federal regulation of hospitals participating in Medicare are discussed after examination of recent changes in the common-law standards.)

The first case to recognize a relationship between JCAH accreditation standards and common-law standards for determining hospital liability to a patient who was injured in the course of medical treatment was *Darling v. Charleston Community Hospital*, decided by the Illinois Supreme Court in 1968. Darling was a high-school football player who broke his leg during a game. He was brought to the emergency room of the Charleston Hospital, a small hospital accredited by the JCAH. The physician on duty, who had no recent experience in this type of case, applied a cast that interfered with blood circulation, resulting in gangrene and subsequent amputation. Darling argued that the hospital was negligent because it did not require this doctor to seek consultation with a specialist when the leg began to swell and smell, and because it did not provide sufficient nurses to observe whether there was circulation in the leg. The hospital defended on grounds that it had met the standards of other hospitals in the community, and that the patient had not produced experts to testify that Charleston had fallen below those standards.

Prior to this time, the custom of the community defined the limits of the hospital's legal responsibility, just as it still defines the limits of physician responsibility. But in the *Darling* case the Illinois court said that, in light of the obvious risks, the hospital could also be held liable for failing to comply with JCAH or state licensing standards. JCAH standards, which had as a formal matter been adopted by the hospital, required that the hospital provide "an adequate number of professional nurses"; the medical staff bylaws provide for "consultation between medical staff members in complicated cases"; "the members of the staff do not fail in matters of calling consultants as needed. . . ."

The decision's psychological impact has been great, but its practical effect has been less than overwhelming. Only nine state supreme courts have voiced approval of its essential holding, that the hospital board has a nondelegable duty to establish policies and procedures to monitor the quality of medical care in the institutions. In only four of these court cases was the hospital actually held liable for failure to meet the standard. In two cases, the courts recognized the applicability of *Darling*, but held that the patients had not proved any breach of the hospital's duty. In the three other cases, the court made favorable references to *Darling* in the course of reaffirming the power of a hospital governing board to dismiss or discipline a physician for medical misconduct. To some degree, the absence of malpractice suits based on failure to comply with JCAH standards can be explained by the fact that malpractice lawyers are quite familiar with the procedures for suing the physician directly, but are often unfamiliar with the mystical world of hospital regulations and standards.

However, the greatest limitation upon hospital liability based on failure to comply with JCAH standards rests on the nature of those standards. The JCAH standards and accreditation process require that the hospital show that it provides a "setting" in which good medical care is possible. Neither the standards nor the JCAH accreditation process attempts to determine whether or not minimally decent care is actually being provided. So long as the mechanisms are provided for in the hospital's rules and regulations, the JCAH does not attempt to determine whether the mechanisms are in fact being used effectively. Further, JCAH standards have not required that hospitals establish mechanisms for finding and limiting the practice of incompetent or fraudulent physicians.

It was this deficiency in JCAH standards which was addressed by Judge Goldberg in the *Nork* decision. Mercy Hospital in Sacramento was in full compliance with JCAH standards. Over the years, many people at Mercy Hospital had noticed that Dr. Nork had on particular occasions made serious mistakes, removed tissues that should not have been removed, and falsified medical records. While the JCAH-mandated review committees noticed these problems, there was no mechanism for compiling information or acting upon it. Each mistake or act of wrongdoing was viewed as an isolated incident. At the trial, in defense of the hospital's conduct, it was suggested that every dog is entitled to one bite. Judge Goldberg said that "this is not and has never been the law for dogs. . . . If it is not a good rule for dogs, it is not a good rule for doctors."

The JCAH, recognizing the serious implications of the facts revealed in the *Nork* case, sent its deputy director, Dr. Reed Nesbit, to testify at the trial. Dr. Nesbit acknowledged that nothing in the JCAH standards required hospitals to establish mechanisms for finding and dealing with a person like Dr. Nork. He testified that this case "is a classic example of how things can fall down between the cracks and not be picked up. . . . [T]here are cracks in the system which we, our whole medical world, have recognized and are working feverishly correcting. . . ."

Judge Goldberg recognized that Mercy had complied with all of the standards of the hospital community, state licensing, and the JCAH. However, he found that compliance with those standards was not sufficient to demonstrate reasonable care on the part of the hospital to protect patients against the risks created by incompetent and fraudulent doctors. Judge Goldberg said, "This may amount to holding the whole health care industry negligent. And if it does, so be it. Precedent is not wanting for such a holding."

Mercy Hospital also defended its corporate self on grounds that only physicians can review the work of other doctors, and that the hospital governing board had delegated to the medical staff all responsibility for the selection and supervision of physicians. State statutory law also required that hospital boards of directors function through a "medical staff [that] shall be self-governing with respect to the professional work performed in the hospital." Judge Goldberg found that, while the hospital board must operate through its medical staff, ultimately the board must retain legal and actual responsibility to ensure that the medical staff adopts standards to assure patients of quality care, and that it actually apply the written standards.

The *Nork* decision is only the decision of one lower California court. In most cases, hospitals are still effectively able to insulate themselves from legal liability by showing that they have behaved like other hospitals in the community, and have delegated to the medical staff all responsibility for the granting of staff privileges and the actual supervision of medical care. However, the decision has had an impact beyond its immediate legal effect. It was not appealed. It has not been publicly challenged by either the JCAH or the American Hospital Association. Indeed, there seems to be growing recognition on the part of these professional associations that hospitals must assume greater institutional responsibility to determine whether their facilities are being used by doctors who are chronically incompetent or fraudulent.

Unfortunately, hospital governing boards often are ill-equipped to challenge the dominance of the medical staff. Hospital trustees, typically, are affluent businessmen, certainly more sensitive to issues of finance and image than to the technical aspects of patient care. In a 1975 nationwide survey, more than half of all hospital board members listed their occupations as in the fields of business, finance, or manufacturing. The survey found that hospital trustees were overwhelmingly affluent, and that lower- and middle-income groups were substantially underrepresented. Although there has been some effort to integrate physicians into the board structure as a result of the *Darling* and *Nork* cases, this does not guarantee the level of either expertise or diligence necessary to evaluate the difficult medical questions facing the board. As a rule, a physician board member is either a retired physician not in touch with current hospital practices, or a member of the hospital medical staff whose main activity is to lobby the board and administration to meet the requests of the medical staff.

A major control that hospital boards can exercise over physician practice is in the granting or denial of admitting privileges. Admitting privileges refer to the physician's right to use a hospital facility to treat private patients. With rare exception, it is essential for private physicians to maintain privileges in good standing at one or more local hospitals. An ongoing Stanford University study indicates that the care taken in awarding staff privileges is one of the most important factors explaining wide disparities in surgical outcome among the institutions studied. In accordance with JCAH standards, most governing boards rely heavily upon medical-staff recommendations in the granting of admitting privileges. The process varies greatly from hospital to hospital. A 1971 study showed that in lax hospitals nearly everyone who applies for privileges is accepted, specialty applicants are not required to document qualifications, qualifications are not demanded, and the board simply rubber-stamps the recommendations of the medical staff. In five of seven New York City hospitals surveyed by the JCAH in 1975, there was no examination of applicants' physical or mental capabilities prior to the granting of staff privileges. In hospitals with more rigorous appointment procedures, records and training are more thoroughly reviewed, and appointments must be approved by the chief of the department in which the physician seeks to practice.

While the 35,000 physicians who are salaried hospital employees usually have contracts delineating the scope of their clinical practice, there is a great deal less specificity in defining the privileges of the 200,000 office-based physicians who can admit and care for their patients in hospitals. General practitioners with admitting privileges are normally allowed to perform surgery. Even where the appointment stipulates the scope of surgical practice, exceptions are granted routinely. As a result of these rather loose arrangements, nearly a third of all operations performed in the United States are done by people not board-certified to practice surgery.

In hospitals that do look to specialty qualifications, it is common to admit a physician to practice on the basis of board "eligibility" rather than board "qualification." Eligible doctors have completed the requisite training to qualify them to take the examination given by one of the national specialty boards. For example, Dr. Nork was a board-eligible surgeon who repeatedly failed the examination which would have made him board-qualified. In many hospitals, doctors are granted privileges when they are board-eligible, and they never bother to complete the process to become board-qualified.

Within surgical specialties, limitations on staff privileges are even rarer. Although simple surgical procedures can probably be performed equally well by most general surgeons, the mortality rate in high-risk operations can vary by a factor of ten to one, depending on the surgeon's formal qualifications.

The JCAH once proposed that each member of a hospital's surgical staff be certified by the chief of the department as to the types of operation which the surgeon could perform. The recommendation was greeted with such opposition from surgeons across the country that it was dropped by the JCAH. Since 1973, the JCAH has required that there be some broad delineation of the scope of the privileges granted to staff physicians in accredited hospitals. While it is recommended that the hospitals follow the parameters established by the national specialty boards, this is not required. No delineation is required *within* surgical specialties. Finally, delineation is not the same as limitation, and hospitals can continue to allow physicians to practice outside their delineated areas without risking their accredited status.

The lax procedures in most American hospitals for determining which doctors may perform surgery have a direct impact on medical injury rates and, most probably, on malpractice claims. First, the failure to restrict most physicians' surgical practice results in too much surgery being performed. In the 1970's, the rate of surgery in the United States has increased enormously. In 1971, there were 7,805 operations per 100,000 population, about the same as six years earlier. By 1975, there were 9,583 procedures for the same population group. A House subcommittee examining surgical care has determined that an alarming proportion of this surgery is unnecessary. It reported that in 1974, of the 14 million elective operations performed in the United States, 2.38 million were unnecessary, and that these unnecessary operations led to 11,900 needless deaths. As we have seen, the precise number of unnecessary operations and deaths, and even the terminology by which to characterize the problem, have been vigorously contested by the AMA. In 1977, the House subcommittee reopened its hearings on surgical quality and necessity. Dr. Eugene McCarthy, whose study was relied on by the committee in the development of its earlier report, testified again with updated findings. Citing the inflammatory effects of the term "unnecessary," Dr. McCarthy now referred to the problem as "surplus" surgery. The findings were nonetheless the same.

In addition to the problem of "surplus" surgery, another way in which the failure of hospitals to control surgical practices may lead to malpractice claims is the fact that the surgeon of questionable competence is not restricted. The American College of Surgeons and the American Surgical Association have jointly undertaken a study of all post-operative complications in ninety-five hospitals over a period of two and one half years. The study found that about one third of the 245 surgical deaths and one half of the other 1,696 surgical complications were preventable, and that more than three quarters of these "critical incidents" might have been avoided by surgeon action. In other words, a study conducted by the surgical profession itself indicated that negative surgical outcome is often related to physician competence.

It has often been suggested that the federal or state governments, or the JCAH, or hospitals independently, should require that surgery be performed only by board-certified surgeons. The suggestion has some appeal: its adoption would almost certainly reduce the amount of surgery performed. But the proposal is also a rather crude way of dealing with the problem, both because there are some areas of the country where there are not enough certified surgeons, and because it seems that many routine operations can be performed competently by noncertified physicians. Individual hospitals may be in the best position to make an independent evaluation of which physicians should be allowed to perform surgery, and who should be doing particular types of operation. Factors such as the surgical needs of the local population, the supply of surgeons, and individual physician experience could be considered in such a process.

Unfortunately, just as economic incentives encourage physicians to perform surgery, the hospital's economic interests are to keep physicians working and to keep its beds full. The Congressional Budget Office has estimated that a doctor generates an annual expense of $350,000 at each of the hospitals he uses. As long as control of hospitals is dominated by people who perceive the hospital's interest primarily in economic terms, it is vain to expect hospitals to institute programs that would limit the pool of doctors who can admit patients for surgical treatment, or effectively control the amount of surgery by those physicians who do have admitting privileges.

A hospital's ability to use the granting of staff privileges as a means of promoting quality medical care is also limited by the lack of any unified system of information interchange among hospitals. A physician whose privileges have been limited, suspended, or revoked at one institution may be appointed at another, without any certainty that the second hospital will be aware of the earlier disciplinary action. As we have noted earlier, hospitals often allow a physician who is found seriously deficient simply to resign. The doctor applies for privileges at another hospital, and when the second hospital asks the first for references, it will be told that the doctor resigned in good standing.

But the overwhelming reality is that doctors' hospital privileges are rarely revoked, suspended, or even limited. One reason is that there probably is little systematic review of the work which physicians do in the hospital. Since 1970, the JCAH has required formal "peer review," which typically consists of a medical-care evaluation committee that reviews patient charts on a random basis and presents findings and recommendations at monthly meetings; a tissue-review committee, which reviews surgical procedures and results; and infection committees which review procedures for reducing infection rates.

Testimony at the Nork trial summarized the gross structural deficiencies in these peer-review mechanisms. The review process was predicated on the assumption that the doctor was reporting honestly and the records were truthful and accurate. Review was based solely on the standards of the reviewer. It was random, infrequent, casual, uncritical, and sandwiched in among the doctor's other work. It did not include a comparison of the doctor's records and the nurse's notes. And, finally, no record was made of the doctor's demonstrated deficiencies, so that there was no common fund of knowledge available to the hospital.

Other examinations of the peer-review process have elicited similar findings. Testimony before a House subcommittee examining unnecessary surgery indicated that if a patient's chart showed a diagnosis compatible with surgery, the review committee was satisfied. No questions were raised as to the range of available options in a particular case, whether no surgery or minor surgery would be preferable treatment, or whether the particular physician should have referred the case to someone of a more refined specialty.

In addition to these basic structural weaknesses, under internal hospital peer-review structures the reviewers and the doctors being reviewed change places on a periodic basis. Physicians reviewing one another's work are dependent upon continuing referrals from one another. Economic pressure and fear of reprisal are also real and relevant considerations that cannot be divorced from a system which, because of its subjective nature, has a built-in capability to function in line with self-serving ends. A sociologist who spent two years observing doctors in three private university-affiliated hospitals quotes the chief of medicine at one hospital as saying that most physicians' mistakes were not discussed at review meetings because "it's got to be a cordial affair." According to the doctor, "Eighty percent of the mistakes made around here are swept under the rug." She summarized her observations of medical review:

[A]lthough the avowed purpose of these meetings is to review mistakes and prevent their recurrence, in actuality the meetings are organized and conducted in ways that absolve doctors from responsibility and guilt and provide the self-assuring and somewhat false appearance that physicians are monitoring each other and their standards of work. In case after case, physician errors are systematically excused and justified, and their consequences made to look unimportant.

The JCAH survey-and-accreditation process has done little to cure these gross defects of the peer-review process. The commission has been concerned with the capacity to perform, as demonstrated by the existence of the required committees, rather than with actual evaluation of performance. It looks to organization, not accomplishment. The credibility of the commission's quality-control activities has been further diminished by the secrecy under which the organization operates. The commission will not disclose what constitutes "substantial compliance" necessary for accreditation, it refuses to make public its findings and recommendations resulting from inspection, and it does not make a public announcement when a hospital loses its accreditation.

JCAH Response to the Malpractice Crisis

In response to the *Nork* decision and the rising public concern with the quality of hospital care, the JCAH in 1974 adopted new accreditation requirements for medical-care evaluations. It has made a major financial investment in its Quality Review Center, which has designed a model evaluation system called PEP (Performance Evaluation Procedure for auditing and improving patient care). Hospitals are now required to conduct some form of medical audit, using either PEP or some locally developed system that conforms to the list of "Essential Characteristics of an Acceptable Patient Care Evaluation Procedure" prepared by the commission. For a fee, the Quality Review Center will teach hospitals to use PEP, and will provide standardized audit-report forms which, if properly completed, will satisfy commission surveyors.

The characteristics of the PEP system are a direct reply to the criticisms of the JCAH in the *Nork* opinion. Criteria that permit direct review of the quality of care must be established; variations from established criteria must be identified and justified. Specific immediate action and follow-up are required, and results are to be reported to the governing board and chief executive officer. Most important, the system must produce a profile reflecting the clinical performance of each staff member.

The JCAH's marketing of the system is designed to appeal to physicians. The promotional literature emphasizes that "professionalism, not fear of punishment, is the operable motivation." It describes a "case history" in which the PEP audit showed that a high mortality rate in a hospital's coronary-care unit was due to a lack of electronic monitoring equipment. Using the information disclosed in the PEP audit, hospital physicians were able to pressure the board to appropriate funds for new equipment.

However, the harsh reality remains that if a review system is effective, it will sometimes reveal physician delinquency as well as innocence. Further, there must be a willingness to take appropriate action on the basis of audit findings. Although the JCAH will not reveal audit findings and resulting actions taken, it does list sample findings in its monthly *Quality Review Bulletin.* There are some impressive results in detecting procedures that were not justified by the patient's medical chart. But the only remedial actions undertaken as a consequence of these findings are educational: the physician is told of his error and how to correct it. This appears to be the common approach. The audit system has been in effect in the New York City municipal hospital system for nearly two years. In that period, not a single physician has had privileges suspended, revoked, or limited on the basis of the finding of the audit review. The JCAH deemphasizes privilege limitation or revocation as a possible audit result. It argues correctly that a physician against whom such action is taken can simply schedule work at another hospital. Unfortunately, the JCAH has not imposed standards which address this failure of coordination and communication among hospitals.

The commission did inform us of one case in which a doctor's privileges were limited on the basis of an audit disclosing many unnecessary appendectomies. Interestingly, this review was aimed at the particular doctor, and it was used to confirm what everyone already knew. In other words, the audit method did have the structural capability to detect and disclose base-line incompetence or fraud; so it can be used successfully where a sufficiently powerful group of doctors wants it to work.

Still, the new PEP system is dependent on the same mechanisms and motivations that have always characterized peer review. It relies on internal review which encourages cooperation between the reviewer and the reviewed and seeks to justify the doctor's actions if possible. Without commitment to a change in this pattern by a significant number of hospital physicians, the new audit will be another exercise in futility.

Review of particular audits is a regular feature of the *Quality Review Bulletin.* The analysis is thoughtful and precise. Unfortunately, the JCAH does not have the capability to review audits in such detail for its regular hospital accreditation surveys. The audit system will almost certainly suffer to the extent that the JCAH continues to rely, as it traditionally has, on the hospital's production of paper to satisfy standards. For example, in 1975, the JCAH surveyed seven New York hospitals, all of which had conducted medical-care evaluation studies. Instead of making detailed analyses of the substance of the survey, the JCAH noted as faults only the facts that the governing boards of two hospitals were not advised of the recommendations resulting from review, and that the surgical review of two hospitals did not include procedures in which no tissue was removed. In essence, the review was undetailed, and sought primarily to determine whether the basic structure was in order. Past experience indicates the deficiencies of this approach.

Hospital Response to the Malpractice Crisis

Expanded concepts of hospital liability and rising insurance rates have led some hospitals to institute risk-control programs that go beyond those required for accreditation. The most common approach is to hire a risk manager, usually a nonphysician, whose sole responsibility is to reduce the hospital's liability potential. The Florida legislature has enacted a statute requiring risk managers in all hospitals with 300 or more beds.

Some limited evidence suggests that risk-control efforts are particularly prevalent among hospitals that self-insure—that is, those that have forsaken the traditional insurance market and decided to pay malpractice judgments directly from hospital assets or, more typically, from specially established reserve funds. Because hospitals' premium rates have usually been established on the basis of the experience of all similar hospitals within the particular area or state, one hospital's favorable claims record has not normally been rewarded with a lower rate. Self-insurance may provide a direct financial incentive to reduce claims. The *New York State Malpractice Report* states that "[h]ospitals with the incentive of self-insurance appear to be engaged more aggressively in the reporting of incidents, claims analysis, and progress targeted in injury producing clinical setting or problem staff." In Florida, when a university hospital began self-insuring, staff reports of untoward incidents increased by 300 percent.

The success of these new risk-control efforts is likely to depend on a hospital's ability to tackle problems caused by physicians. These programs must do more than substitute for the private insurers' safety inspections that emphasize factors such as the disposal of explosives, chemical storage, and sprinkler systems. A 1976 HEW study suggests that the new hospital risk-control programs have still not been able to overcome bureaucratic constraints and professional obstinacy. It concluded that "[m]ost loss control and patient injury prevention programs for hospitals which exist today or are currently being planned do not attempt to address physician-related incidents, even though the majority of malpractice claims filed stem from physician-related causes." It went on to say that medical-staff members are unwilling "to subject their practices to hospital review or to become considerably involved in hospital management." Hospital officials were "not willing to press medical staff members to participate."

Physician Response to Increasing Peer Review

The medical profession has responded to pressures for more effective peer review with demands for guarantees of confidentiality and protection against liability from participation in peer-review activities. As we have noted earlier, physician fears of liability for participation in peer review have little basis in reality. But the fears are understandable in the light of the medical profession's general distrust of lawyers and the legal system.

Physicians fear suits from other doctors who are denied medical staff privileges. This fear is expressed both by the physicians sitting on review committees and by hospital trustees. However, courts have uniformly held that so long as the hospital provides basic procedural standards for fairness and opportunity for review, it has wide latitude in deciding who should be granted staff privileges. The courts will not independently evaluate an applicant's medical competence.

A second expressed concern is that candid committee discussions about professional competence and character may result in lawsuits for defamation of character. This fear is also exaggerated; few such lawsuits are initiated, and those rarely, if ever, establish liability. The common law has always protected such communications as long as they are made with a legitimate interest in patient care, in good faith, and without malice. Nonetheless, physician anxieties have led forty-one states to enact statutes providing immunity for defamation liability. In addition, hospital bylaws often require that each staff member sign a release absolving other staff members from liability resulting from participation in review activities. Whether such protections are granted by statute or contract, they add little to the existing protection provided by common law. To the extent that they are perceived as reducing liability possibilities, however unrealistic the possibility is, they may be useful in encouraging review activities.

The third concern voiced by physicians is the use of committee reports in malpractice litigation. Under the rules of evidence, such reports will not be admissible at trial, but it is possible that in some cases patients' lawyers will be allowed to examine such records in preparation for trial. The clear trend is for courts to deny patients' requests to examine committee reports. The policy articulated in such decisions is the "overwhelming public interest in having these staff meetings held on a confidential basis so that the flow of ideas and advice can continue unimpeded." Such protection has also been guaranteed by statute in at least twenty-four states, and such laws have uniformly been upheld by the courts.

Despite the widespread judicial approval of protections against examination of review-committee records, this issue poses difficult policy questions. By supporting confidentiality, courts implicitly favor peer review, as opposed to malpractice actions, as a means of discovering and discouraging substandard medical care. But restricting access to committee records and reports makes it very difficult to establish a failure of institutional responsibility of the sort that existed at Mercy Hospital. Though the *Nork* decision has already had a phenomenal impact on the JCAH and the operations of many hospitals, it is still only the opinion of one California lower court. The concept of hospital responsibility to monitor medical care will not readily be established in other states without the presentation of very strong and convincing evidence. As we have seen, the mere existence of the required committee structure is no guarantee of adequacy. The actual substance of review must be examined. Restricting access to documents will make that task difficult, and is likely to discourage other malpractice actions that might attempt to extend the legal force of *Nork* beyond Sacramento County. Establishing a plain and enforceable legal requirement of medical-staff and hospital responsibility for monitoring doctors and medical care might ultimately provide a better incentive for meaningful medical review than the guarantee of review-committee secrecy.

All these fears of potential legal liability serve as a convenient shield to avoid the more difficult and more deeply engrained problems encountered in peer review. As we have noted, professionals are reluctant to criticize their colleagues' work for a number of social and economic reasons. An enforceable legal requirement that serious monitoring take place, one that would leave physicians no choice but to act responsibly or be subject to penalty, might also be an effective way to change the professional tendency to look the other way.

Federal Action on Hospital Responsibility

As we have seen, the initial Congressional approach toward setting standards for hospitals which receive federal payments under Medicare and Medicaid was to defer to the JCAH, with respect to both setting and enforcing standards for hospital care. From the beginning, Congress recognized that the JCAH standards were deficient in that they did not require any institutional mechanism for review of the services actually provided to patients. Hence, the 1965 legislation supplemented JCAH standards by requiring that participating hospitals establish internal "utilization review" programs.

The 1965 statute required that a committee of physicians be established within the hospital to review the admission, length of stay, and professional services provided to federally funded patients, and to determine the medical necessity of extended stays. Although the program was mainly intended to control costs by preventing unnecessary hospitalization, it was also intended to monitor the quality of care provided.

Utilization review was predictably ineffective. Within the hospital, social and financial incentives discouraged physicians from serious examination of one another's work. Effective implementation of statutory requirements was not sought by either the federal government or the private agencies such as Blue Cross which were given administrative responsibility for the federal medical-care programs. By 1970, the Senate Finance Committee reported:

. . . the utilization review requirements have, generally speaking, been of a token nature and ineffective as a curb to unnecessary use of institutional care and services. Utilization review in Medicare can be characterized as more form than substance.

In 1972, in response to legal actions and public criticism questioning the propriety of total federal deference to the JCAH, Congress amended the law to allow HEW to promulgate standards for hospitals in addition to those of the JCAH, and to conduct independent federal reviews of hospitals accredited by the JCAH. HEW has never exercised this authority to promulgate additional standards for participating hospitals. In 1974, HEW conducted the first, and only, random survey of hospitals accredited by the JCAH. It reviewed 105 accredited hospitals, and 69 were found seriously deficient in major areas such as fire safety, adequacy of drug and medical records, and dietary-department controls. When most hospitals are substandard even by the limited JCAH standards, it is difficult to take effective administrative action in the context of a program which seeks to provide quality services to limited, and vulnerable, groups of society. If standards for hospital participation in Medicare and Medicaid are made significantly more rigorous, there is a danger that hospital services will become even less accessible for the poor and the aged. Certainly, more rigorous standards and more effective application of standards are needed, but it is not politically practical to impose them in the context of programs which deal only with limited and vulnerable groups of patients.

Professional Standards Review Organizations (PSRO's) were mandated by Congress in 1972; physician-created and -administered, these organizations were intended to correct the problems of in-hospital utilization controls by providing review through a local unit external to the hospital. PSRO's are designed to control costs by certifying the need for elective admissions and reviewing lengths of stay. In addition, PSRO's are to undertake medical-care evaluation studies (MCE's) that utilize locally developed standards of treatment. This would allow development of a profile on each practicing physician and institution.

Initially, PSRO's offered an important potential for effective review by moving the review out of the context of a particular hospital. However, this potential is not being realized. Federal law requires that the PSRO utilize the service of and accept the findings of hospital committees which the PSRO feels are capable of conducting review effectively. Through this provision, most PSRO activities are being delegated to the individual hospitals. The Bureau of Quality Assurance, the HEW division which administers the PSRO program nationally, has made clear its preference for in-house delegated review. No funding is available for PSRO review of hospital care until the hospital has been given a chance to formulate its own review plan. If a hospital is dissatisfied with the PSRO's disallowance of hospital review, an appeal procedure is available "to avoid any non-professional prejudice or bias by the PSRO in the acceptance or rejection of in-house review." The B.Q.A. has stated that any hospital with the JCAH-PEP system should qualify for delegated review. By 1977, over 70 percent of hospitals under review had been approved for full delegation.

The process is complete. We have come full circle. To eradicate the deficiencies of internal review, we have substituted another system of internal review. The responsibility to carry out in-house review, standards of compliance, and sanctions for noncompliance are all defined in a "memorandum of understanding" between the PSRO and the individual hospital. These documents are confidential, so the public has no opportunity to evaluate the adequacy of the hospital review process. Another opportunity for public accountability might have been through the disclosure of the institution and physician profiles that the PSRO will develop. Certainly, many patients would like to know, before treatment, about a doctor's or a hospital's competence and experience in a particular area. Profiles would also be useful to state licensing boards and hospital trustees. Under present B.Q.A rules, no one has access to the profiles. They will be coded and sent to the B.Q.A; and no one knows quite what will happen to them thereafter.

The first detailed federal evaluation of the PSRO program was released in draft form in late 1977. The government advisory panel's executive summary concluded "that PSRO implementation alone is not apt to cause significant changes in either hospital utilization rates or associated government expenditures." The study found that the PSRO program was not cost-effective, in that more was being spent on review than was being saved by reducing utilization rates. The PSRO quality-of-care component was not sufficiently established to allow the panel to draw conclusions. It did find, however, that those PSRO's conducting medical-care evaluations were not regularly doing re-audits, so that there was no feedback on recommended actions. Additionally, only a very few PSRO's had produced provider profiles.

Possible Reforms

Hospitals as organized social institutions, and as the source of most instances of malpractice, have great potential to control malpractice. As we have seen, legal, social, and financial incentives discourage hospitals from exercising institutional responsibility for the practice of medicine in the hospital. Two sorts of reform are possible. First are those which leave established patterns of financing and professional control essentially unchanged, and attempt to insure minimal quality of hospital-based medical care within the context of prevailing power relationships. The second sort of reform seeks more fundamental change in the financial and professional forces that determine the nature of hospital-based medical services. These two kinds of reform are not mutually exclusive.

We have suggested several examples of useful reforms of the first type. The law should make plain that hospitals have institutional responsibility to monitor the quality of medical services provided in the institution. More specifically, hospitals must be required to establish review mechanisms that collect information about individual physicians; review physician work on a systematic basis; and have a capability to identify doctors who falsify records or who do unnecessary or incompetent work. This review process should not rely exclusively upon people associated with the hospital, who have a direct incentive to protect the public prestige and finances of the institution. The review process should routinely include physicians who have no other association with the hospital. Hospitals must also be required to review seriously the qualifications of doctors seeking staff privileges, both initially and on a periodic basis after approval. The scope of privileges should be aligned with the abilities of the individual doctor. Where an injured patient establishes that injuries were caused by a physician who habitually did fradulent, unnecessary, or incompetent work that could have been detected and controlled by functioning hospital review procedures, the hospital as well as the physician should be held legally responsible. Whether legal responsibility rests with the board of trustees or with the medical board, some structure within the hospital must be institutionally responsible.

Most of this is essentially what was required by the *Nork* decision, and what is now required by the JCAH. Unfortunately, the evidence is that the JCAH accreditation process does not provide sufficient incentives to hospitals to take these institutional responsibilities seriously. Legislative or common-law change is needed in almost every state to make plain that hospitals have and must act upon this institutional responsibility, and will be held liable when failure to exercise it causes injury to a patient. Obviously, there will still be many cases of hospital-based malpractice on the part of individual doctors that will not result in hospital liability. This is as it should be. There will still be many cases of physician malpractice which even rigorous institutional review could not detect or prevent. These will not result in hospital liability. But where the facts show that institutional review could have found and controlled physicians who have injured patients, the institution should be held liable. Since this change would represent an expansion of hospital liability in nearly every state, it might mean a consequent increase in the costs of hospital malpractice insurance, at least to the extent that hospitals fail to establish and implement the review mechanisms now required by the JCAH and these failures result in injuries to patients.

Some observers have suggested that hospitals should be made institutionally liable for all malpractice taking place within their walls, and that hospitals, rather than physicians, should pay the bulk of malpractice insurance costs. Physicians would remain legally and financially responsible only for the care they give outside the hospital. This approach, known as "channeling," was proposed by the Virginia Department of Insurance, but it has not been implemented. The proposal is similar to that which we have just suggested in that it attempts to provide financial incentives to hospitals for more effective institutional monitoring of physician performance. It is dissimilar in that the hospital would be liable even for those actions which would not have been uncovered by diligent medical audit.

The major problem with channeling all liability incurred within a hospital to the hospital is that it may further insulate individual physicians from direct and personal responsibility for their own actions. It is sometimes suggested that physicians should share in the hospital's increased insurance expenses, though usually this has been proposed only as a measure to help the hospital through its early years of increased premium exposure, and certainly never in a manner that might relate an individual physician's contribution to his particular specialty or the riskiness of his practice. It would seem to be very difficult to structure a channeling system in which the hospital takes on legal liability and the physician, through financial contribution, retains a sense of personal responsibility.

Effective institutional review of physicians can reduce both the incidence of malpractice and insurance costs, whether charged to hospitals, doctors, or both. But to the extent that effective institutional review is stymied by the continued dominance of physicians in hospital decision-making, and to the extent that malpractice still occurs, channeling may easily result in malpractice insurance costs becoming but another diffuse and uncontrollable element in rising, reimbursable hospital costs. Further, there is real concern that such a shift might further increase health-care costs by encouraging doctors to treat patients in the hospital where the doctor does not risk a malpractice judgment, rather than in a less expensive, noninstitutional setting.

Another area in which there is much room for improvement is

the national accreditation process. The record of the JCAH is very poor indeed, both with respect to the standards it sets and to the way it goes about applying those standards. Major improvement can hardly be expected from a private organization, controlled by the hospitals and the medical profession, which perceives itself as "selling" a private service to hospitals. The reality is that the JCAH performs a vital public function which is financed, through Medicare, Medicaid, and Blue Cross, at public expense. We need a national, publicly accountable agency to set and apply standards for hospitals. The deliberations of such an agency must be open to the public; standards must be set through public processes; information generated by such an agency must be accessible to the public. Although hospital and physician interests should be represented in the governance and control of such an agency, many other interests which are now excluded must also be given significant voice: nurses, hospital social workers, other hospital workers, and organized consumers of hospital services. (In recent years, senior-citizen groups, labor unions, women's groups, and poor people's organizations have attempted to influence the governance and policies of hospitals across the country.) Either the JCAH should be replaced by a national, publicly accountable accrediting agency, or the JCAH should be required, as a condition to its continued role in Medicare, Medicaid, Blue Cross, or national health insurance, to make changes in its character such as those suggested here.

Another reform which would be useful in controlling the incidence of hospital-based malpractice is to require that only board-certified specialists perform certain high-risk procedures. Such a requirement could be imposed either by state law, or by federal law as a condition for participation in Medicare, Medicaid, or national health insurance. Exceptions to such a requirement could be allowed in emergency situations or in cases in which certified specialists are not available. Although hospitals should have primary responsibility for matching the scope of staff privileges with individual physician capabilities, there are powerful financial incentives that discourage hospitals from limiting physician privileges, particularly when the result is that *none* of the doctors associated with the hospital is allowed to do particular high-risk operations. But it is precisely these incentives that necessitate national certification, at least for complex operations.

We turn now to reforms which could reduce hospital-based malpractice through more fundamental changes in the financial and power relationships that characterize the delivery of hospital care. It has been widely noted that medical services are organized on an extremely hierarchical basis. Again and again, when instances of grossly substandard hospital care are exposed, many of the people who had knowledge of the problem doctor say, "What could I do? I am only a nurse." Or "I am fifteen years his junior." Particularly in smaller hospitals which have no salaried staff physicians, it is often the nurses who are best able to observe overall patterns of treatment. The system of private, office-based practice permits—in fact, encourages—physicians to insulate themselves from knowing what other members of the medical staff are doing. Most physicians simply do not take review and audit committees seriously.

Specific, concrete reforms could be adopted to involve younger doctors and other groups of hospital workers in review processes. For example, hospital workers should have the opportunity to make confidential reports to JCAH survey teams, and should be included on hospital review committees. These reforms, while of some use, will be of limited effect so long as the basic organizational structures for medical-care delivery are so rigidly hierarchical. To address this basic problem requires fundamental change in the nature of medical and nursing education, and in the organization of hospitals, that will encourage teamwork, mutual criticism, and self-criticism. It also requires reduction in the disparities in social and economic status between physicians and other hospital workers.

A second, related reform which could reduce the incidence of hospital-based malpractice would be to change the nature of hospital control and governance. As we have seen, hospitals today are controlled by physicians and by boards of trustees who are primarily interested in the financial health of the institution. These patterns of control dictate policies which are often not in the best interests of patients. Hospitals could be in fact the community institutions which they are now in name only. A hospital board composed of people representative of, and accountable to, the community served would have some of the same interests as the current business-oriented trustees, but it would promote policies of a fundamentally different nature. It would certainly be within the power of state governments to impose hospital-board membership requirements for nonprofit hospitals operating in the state. Likewise, federal policies of reimbursement, which now blindly follow the customs of the medical profession and hospital industry, might be revised to encourage hospitals to alter the composition of their governing boards so that such boards will be broadly representative of all the people served by and interested in the hospital. Such a board might be interested in establishing programs to reduce surgery, and in upgrading preventive health-care services.

A medical-staff committee composed of a broad spectrum of those who work in the hospital would have some of the same interests as current medical-staff committees, but it would promote other policies as well. Interests of hospital workers and patients are not identical, and both should be represented in the governing structure. But democratization of both groups could change the nature of hospitals, reduce the incidence of hospital-based malpractice, provide patients with a sense of satisfaction with their community institution that would reduce the motivation to sue, and allow patients to express dissatisfaction in ways that are more constructive than malpractice suits.

PART II

THE LEGAL SYSTEM

5

Lawyers: How Much Is Too Much?

The malpractice crisis is often characterized as a fight between two major professions: physicians and attorneys. "Battle lines are being drawn between the law and medicine; public confidence in both professions is being eroded by brickbats being thrown by both sides." Some doctors believe that lawyers, particularly patients' lawyers, are the heart of the problem.

The contingent legal fee . . . has become the golden calf of the legal profession. Every device known to human ingenuity has been used to divert attention away from it as the real cause of the proliferation in medical malpractice suits in this country.

The role of lawyers in relation to medical malpractice raises three issues. The first involves the effect of the contingent fee. The contingent-fee system means that the patient's lawyer is paid a portion of the money the patient recovers. If the case is unsuccessful, the patient's lawyer gets nothing. The lawyer's fee is "contingent" upon success. Is the contingent-fee system an effective means of making legal services available for legitimate claims and deterring unjustified and harassing lawsuits? A second issue is whether the lawyers involved in malpractice suits make too much money. A third issue is the question of who actually bears the costs of paying lawyers involved in malpractice suits, and who *should* bear these costs.

The Contingent-Fee System

Many doctors—or at least those who speak for the medical profession—believe that the contingent-fee system encourages lawyers to bring unjustified lawsuits. There is little evidence to support this belief. One half to three quarters of the alleged malpractice cases presented to lawyers are refused. The more experienced the lawyer is with malpractice law, the more likely it is that the case will be rejected. Expert medical opinion is obtained before any case is accepted, and it is the most important factor in a lawyer's decision whether to take a malpractice case. Patients often seek a lawyer because a doctor suggests that they have been maltreated by another physician. Hence, it is doctors who often decide whether a malpractice action will be brought.

A major criticism of the contingent fee rests on the fear that patients' lawyers will attempt to maximize their income by bringing unjustified lawsuits. Both common sense and the facts available refute this logic. When a lawyer takes a malpractice case and loses, he or she gets nothing. Even unsuccessful cases require a substantial amount of work: one study showed that, on the average, a lawyer spent 440 hours working on a case in which the patient recovered nothing. This is a lot of work, and no one in his right mind will do it unless there is some prospect of success.

In about 45 percent of all malpractice claims made against doctors, the patient receives some payment. In one study, in which malpractice insurers were asked to study randomly selected claims, the insurance experts found that 46 percent of the cases were "legally meritorious in terms of liability." The HEW Malpractice Commission concluded:

the number of claims judged to be meritorious by malpractice insurers and the number in which payment was made to the claimant would seem to indicate that the vast majority of malpractice claims are not entirely baseless, as often alleged.

Most of the malpractice cases in which the patient receives nothing are settled at a very early stage. In 1970, 28.6 percent of the malpractice complaints resolved were settled before any formal claim was made, and in three out of four of these cases the patient got nothing. An additional 21 percent of the potential cases were settled after a formal claim was made but before an actual suit was filed, and two out of three of these patients got nothing. Hence, almost half of all malpractice complaints are settled before a lawsuit is ever filed, and most of these patients do not recover anything. The patient who files a suit is far more likely to receive some money. In 1970, 38 percent of the malpractice complaints were settled after suit was filed but before trial; almost two thirds of these patients recovered some money. Five percent of the cases were settled during the trial but before a verdict. Three quarters of these patients received compensation. Despite a common popular belief that juries favor malpractice claimants, the jury finds for the doctor in more than 75 percent of those cases that go to the jury.

Any system of settling claims for injuries which the patient believes are the result of bad medical treatment requires some mechanism for sorting the valid claims from the frivolous. This process necessarily involves complex questions of law, fact, and medicine. The contingent-fee system provides lawyers with incentive to take cases that have a reasonable prospect of success, and to refuse those in which it is unlikely that the patient will be able to prove that the doctor acted unreasonably. The lawyer also has a financial incentive to do a good job in representing the patient.

Another strength of the contingent-fee system is that it allows people of moderate income to seek redress for negligently caused injuries. If a lawyer works 440 hours on an unsuccessful malpractice case and charges $50 per hour, the patient is likely to have to pay $22,000 to retain a lawyer to handle a malpractice case. Obviously, most people, however grievous their injuries and legitimate their claims, could not afford access to the legal system if the contingent-fee system were abolished. There is a serious question whether it would be constitutional to abolish the contingent-fee system without providing some reasonable substitute, since the practical effect of such a move would be to reserve the courts for the rich.

Because it is often likely that an insurance company will settle a nonmeritorious claim rather than spend a larger sum to win the suit in litigation, it is frequently argued that such nonmeritorious "nuisance" claims brought by unscrupulous lawyers have a significant impact on the malpractice problem. While it is understandable that physicians are distraught when an insurance company settles a suit in a manner which implicitly acknowledges physician negligence, and it is undoubtedly true that such cases do arise, there are no studies which quantify the problem. This may be because one person's injury is another's nuisance. But whatever such a study might report, small claims do not significantly impact on rising malpractice premiums. As we shall see in Chapter 10, it is the relatively few large claims which account for most dollars awarded to patients. Further, the contingent-fee system provides little incentive for lawyers to take these cases. A small settlement is simply not worth the time a malpractice lawyer must spend to get it.

Contingent fees are unethical in Great Britain. Many people point to this fact, and to the relatively low incidence of malpractice cases in England, and conclude that abolition of the contingent-fee system in the United States would be an effective means of limiting malpractice cases and controlling malpractice insurance rates. On one level, this analysis is absolutely correct. The problem is that injured patients with legitimate claims are left to bear the financial as well as the physical and emotional costs of their injuries, and a legal mechanism for discovering and controlling the behavior of negligent doctors is lost. Analogies with the experience of Great Britain may not be helpful because its society and, particularly, its health system are so different. Certainly, the American contingent-fee system does provide greater assurance that the ordinary citizen has access to legal services.

A major weakness of the contingent-fee system is that many people injured as a result of physician negligence are not able to obtain legal representation or redress. The same economic incentives that discourage lawyers from taking cases in which there is little prospect of success also discourage them from taking cases in which the prospect of success is good but the economic damage to the patient is small. Most lawyers indicate that the amount of economic loss is an important factor in their decision to take on a case. One study shows that New York lawyers will not institute a malpractice action unless the recovery is likely to exceed $25,000. Another study shows that most New York lawyers will not take a malpractice case unless the likely recovery exceeds $40,000. Such policies make it very difficult for poor people to find lawyers because their earning capacity, and hence the economic loss they suffer as a result of injury, is relatively small. Often lawyers require that an injured patient pay cash, in advance, to cover the costs of investigating a proposed malpractice claim. These costs, which may amount to a few hundred dollars, also create impossible barriers for poor patients with legitimate claims.

If the patient's economic loss is negligible, why should we be concerned about whether legal redress is available? First, to say that the economic loss is small is not an entirely accurate description of the patient's injury. Indignity and pain are legitimate interests which the law has traditionally protected, particularly when accompanied by physical injury. Second, a "trivial" economic loss of $25,000 is substantial to a low-income person. Third, when small claims go unredressed, the law does not operate to discover or deter a negligent physician until she or he has inflicted an injury so serious that it commands the attention of a malpractice lawyer. The HEW Malpractice Commission reported that the most serious problem with the contingent-fee system was that the negligently injured patient whose potential for recovery was low was unable to obtain legal services. It recommended that "legal aid must be provided to injured patients whose cases, though small, appear to be meritorious."

Another commonly perceived drawback of the contingent-fee system is that it encourages lawyers to argue for excessive, unjustifiable recoveries. It is quite clear that lawyers do strive to recover as much money as possible. This raises two questions. First, should the lawyer do otherwise? Second, are successful claimants actually receiving excessive recoveries? To answer the first question, the attorney, as an advocate for his client, is professionally obligated to argue for as high a recovery as can be justified. The legal system provides other checks—opposing counsel, judges, and juries—to counterbalance the overzealous lawyer. No doubt the system is incapable of detecting every attorney abuse that might lead to an exaggerated recovery. But, on the whole, the available evidence indicates that malpractice claimants as a group are not receiving excessive recoveries. The American Insurance Association studied claims resolved in 1974, comparing claimants' financial recoveries with their actual reported out-of-pocket losses. The study found that "most award ranges show that the average case is undercompensated." While the study shows that people receiving more than $50,000 usually got more than their out-of-pocket costs, the total amount of undercompensation from successful claims exceeded the amount paid in overcompensation. Further, as will be discussed more fully in the next chapter, "overcompensation" is money paid for pain, suffering, or other loss which does not have a direct out-of-pocket cost.

In summary, the contingent-fee system provides powerful and efficient economic incentives to encourage lawyers to take cases which involve serious injury and have a reasonable prospect of success, and to refuse cases in which there is little evidence that the physician's conduct fell below that of a reasonable doctor. The major weakness of the contingent-fee system is that people who have suffered modest economic loss are left with no means of legal redress.

Despite these incentives, there are of course instances in which lawyers press baseless claims, or act maliciously or unscrupulously in suing a doctor. Sometimes the lawyer is motivated by personal ill-will, and in other cases the lawyer fails to exercise due care in determining whether there are facts to support the patient's claim. Professional self-policing of lawyers suffers from many of the same problems that characterize the medical profession.

The law provides some remedies to the doctor who is harassed by baseless and malicious litigation, and these are being used increasingly. The AMA has encouraged local groups to establish funds and programs to aid doctors in instituting countersuits against lawyers who have filed baseless malpractice claims, and, as of 1976, such programs had been established in ten states and were being considered in eight others. The mere fact that a malpractice suit is unsuccessful does not establish that it was malicious or the lawyer negligent, any more than the fact that medical treatment was unsuccessful establishes that the physician was negligent. In an adversary system, it is important that people have access to the courts for claims whose chance of success may be less than certain. While it is important that doctors have a legal remedy against lawyers who bring malicious or baseless claims, the evidence available indicates that in the vast majority of unsuccessful medical malpractice cases, the patient has had a probable claim which a lawyer could pursue in good faith without fear of sanction.

Do Malpractice Lawyers Earn Too Much Money?

Much of the criticism of the contingent-fee system is generated by a popular belief that patients' lawyers are getting very rich. With respect to earnings, the question of how much is too much is always difficult. The report on lawyers' fees for the HEW Malpractice Commission states that "we have no social and philosophical basis for determining the 'worth' of lawyer services." Let us look first at the simple question of how much malpractice lawyers in fact make, and then consider some criteria for judging whether this is too much.

The method of payment for malpractice lawyers depends on whether the lawyer is working for the patient or for the doctor. Patients' lawyers are almost always paid on the contingent-fee basis. Doctors' lawyers are normally paid on an hourly basis by the company that insures the doctor. Generally, lawyers tend to work for either patients or doctors, not for both. In 1970, the average hourly fee of doctors' lawyers was $50. This figure includes overhead costs (secretaries, office space, Xeroxing, etc.), so the lawyer's personal earnings are less than that.

Computing the fee of the patients' lawyers is more difficult. About half the lawyers who act for patients charge a fixed contingent fee. The most common rate is one third of the amount recovered, though many patients' lawyers take a larger percentage and a few take as little as 25 percent. Other patients' lawyers charge a sliding percentage, depending on the stage at which the claim is settled. The most common sliding-scale percentages are 33.3 percent if the case is settled before trial, and 40 percent if it is settled after trial begins. The HEW Malpractice Commission estimated that in 1970 the average effective fee of patients' lawyers operating under the contingent-fee system was $61 to $63 per hour, including overhead costs. This figure was based on reports from patients' lawyers on the number of cases won and lost. The commission study states that the effective hourly fee is probably an overestimate because the lawyers tended to forget the cases that they lost. In a survey of lawyers active in malpractice work, the patients' lawyers said that they had won 84 percent of their cases, and the doctors' lawyers in the same survey said that the patients won only 62 percent of the time. A national survey of a cross-section of lawyers in private practice confirmed this bias: patients' lawyers said that they won 80 percent of the time and doctors' lawyers said that the patients won only 46 percent of the time. In another study of claims closed in 1970, the Malpractice Commission found that the patients received some money in 45 percent of the claims filed. Therefore, considering the fact that the patient's lawyer gets nothing unless the patient wins, $61–$63 per hour is certainly an overstatement. How much of an overstatement is unclear.

Turning now to the question of whether malpractice lawyers earn "too much," four comparisons and corresponding criteria may be illuminating. First, what proportion of the malpractice insurance dollar goes to lawyers? Second, how do the earnings of doctors' lawyers and patients' lawyers compare? Third, how do the costs of lawyers' services in malpractice action compare with the costs of lawyers' services in other areas? And, fourth, how do the earnings of lawyers compare with the earnings of other workers?

There is an astonishing lack of concrete information on the portion of the malpractice insurance dollar that goes for attorneys' fees. However, all the evidence that is available indicates that lawyers (for both patients and doctors) receive a larger portion of the malpractice premium dollar than patients do. One estimate is that patients receive 28 cents of each premium dollar versus 24 cents for the doctors' defense, 18 cents for the patients' legal services, and 30 cents for insurance-company expenses. Another estimate is that patients receive 30 cents, as opposed to 15 cents for the patients' lawyers and 55 cents for the doctors' lawyers and insurance-company expenses. Still another estimate is that 38 cents goes to the patients, 35 cents to the patients' lawyers, and 27 cents to the doctors' lawyers and other insurance-company expenses.

Can it possibly make sense to spend more on the process than on the objective the process is supposed to achieve? Of course, the process of malpractice litigation serves more objectives than simply compensating negligently injured patients. It also discovers and controls negligent and dangerous medical practice, and protects physicians from unjustified claims. Certainly, "justice" costs money. Nonetheless, it seems clear that the large portion of the malpractice insurance dollar that goes for lawyers' fees is not producing a corresponding quantum of "justice" in terms of any of the goals of the process.

A second comparison which may be useful in considering whether malpractice lawyers make too much money is that between patients' and doctors' lawyers. The HEW Malpractice Commission assumes that approximate equality in the compensation of the two sets of lawyers in these cases is important. This goal seems sound. From the prospective of the individual worker, people are often most concerned that there be equality between themselves and others whom they encounter on a day-to-day basis who have similar qualifications and do similar work. Further, in an adversary system, particularly one which raises such large issues of public interest as medical malpractice, it seems important to have advocates of approximately equal skill on each side. While the relationship between quality representation and economic compensation may not be direct, economic inducements are both more powerful and easier to control than other factors that affect the quality of legal representation. Thus, public defenders argue on principle that their salaries should be on a parity with those of the public prosecutors.

In recent years, several states have limited the amount which can be paid to patients' lawyers in malpractice cases. The New Jersey Bar Association adopted one of the first controls on contingent fees. The "New Jersey sliding scale" limits patients' lawyers to 50 percent of the first $1,000; 40 percent of the next $2,000; one third of the next $47,000; 20 percent of amounts between $50,000 and $100,000; and 10 percent over $100,000. In Ohio, the state legislature directed the state Supreme Court to promulgate a schedule of "graduated maximum contingent fees" that an attorney representing a patient in a medical malpractice action may recover, and prohibited fees in excess of one third in cases which are not appealed. A 1975 California law limits malpractice attorneys' fees to 40 percent of the first $50,000 recovered, one third of the next $50,000, one fourth of the next $100,000, and 10 percent of any recovery in excess of $200,000. The New York courts have also adopted a sliding-scale limit to contingent fees. These sliding scales should encourage lawyers to take smaller claims, discourage them from pushing for very high recoveries, and place an outside limit on the overall compensation of patients' lawyers.

A second type of limitation on contingent fees is a flat limit on the proportion of a patient's recovery which may go to the lawyer. In Oregon and Tennessee, the amount which a patient's lawyer can take is limited to one third of the recovery. In Idaho, the limit is 40 percent of the recovery. Laws such as these place no effective limit on the amount which the lawyer may take when the recovery is large, and may have the effect of further discouraging lawyers from taking cases in which the recovery is likely to be small.

There are two problems with all these limits. First, all deal exclusively with patients' lawyers. The HEW Malpractice Commission indicates that doctors' and patients' lawyers are in the same compensation ballpark. To the extent that effective controls are placed on the fees of patients' lawyers, an undesirable inequality arises between the compensation of patients' lawyers and doctors' lawyers. The second, more fundamental problem is that these reforms do not have any real impact. The legal limitations are not very different from the prior arrangements which were actually made between patients and their lawyers.

A third useful comparison is that between the earnings of malpractice lawyers and those of other lawyers. In terms of earnings, malpractice lawyers and personal-injury lawyers appear to be about in the middle of the legal profession. Lawyers working in the following major areas commonly earn more than personal-injury lawyers: corporations, banking, insurance, labor, antitrust, and admiralty. Lawyers who commonly make less than personal-injury lawyers are those working in domestic relations, collections, tax, probate, and criminal law. Probably the single most important factor affecting the amount that lawyers earn is the wealth of their clients. By and large, it is only the relatively wealthy who need legal services with respect to banking, corporate, or antitrust problems. By contrast, it is the poor who generally need legal services in criminal or collection matters. Therefore, it is not surprising to find that personal-injury lawyers fall in the middle of the legal-earnings spectrum. Injuries arising out of medical malpractice are distributed over the population on a relatively democratic basis; but insurance and the economic status of doctors and hospitals provide greater resources for paying lawyers than exist with respect to other democratically distributed legal problems.

There is another, more direct way in which the client's wealth determines the lawyer's likely earnings. A relatively wealthy client pays more for the same legal service than a relatively poor client does. The correlation is clear with respect to patients' lawyers. Lawyers operating on a contingent-fee basis earn more as settlement amounts increase, and the same injury is worth more, in the eyes of the law, when it is inflicted on a rich person than on a poor person.

The Bureau of Labor Statistics of the United States Department of Labor gathers and analyzes data on the jobs and earnings of American workers. The BLS classifies lawyers into six groups on the basis of an estimate of the "difficulty of the legal work" and the "responsibility of the job." A primary criterion which the BLS uses to make these classifications is the monetary value of the legal work to a client. The BLS assumes that, by definition, legal work involving a matter worth $1 million is more "difficult" and "responsible" than legal work involved in a matter worth $100,000. Even though performing a particular legal service—closing a property sale, setting up a corporation, reaching a child-support agreement—may involve the same legal skills and actions irrespective of the amount at stake, the BLS classification reflects the reality of the legal marketplace.

Perhaps the fees of medical malpractice lawyers should be regulated more stringently than the present insignificant limitations on contingent fees. The unusual public interest at stake in malpractice litigation, the astronomical costs of malpractice insurance, and the fact that such a substantial portion of the malpractice dollar now goes to attorneys might justify more drastic limitations. To preserve fairness and equality within the context of an adversary system, it would seem necessary to impose restrictions on the fees paid to doctors' lawyers as well as patients' lawyers. It would certainly be possible to control the fees of doctors' lawyers through regulations of a state insurance department, state insurance legislation, stipulating that no more than a fixed amount per hour could be paid from insurance funds to lawyers representing physicians charged with malpractice and covered by an insurance policy issued in the state. Limits on contingent fees could then be adjusted downward to produce approximately equal restrictions on the amounts paid to patients' lawyers.

Of course, malpractice lawyers would object strongly to such measures. They would argue that it would be inequitable to restrict their fees while leaving other lawyers free to earn whatever the market will bear. Lawyers able to earn more by doing other types of work would be less interested in malpractice cases. The quality of representation in the malpractice cases might decline. The public interest in malpractice disputes, which supports limitations on the fees of lawyers working in this area, might suffer as it became more difficult to obtain lawyers to represent patients and doctors in malpractice cases and the quality of representation declines.

At this point, a central dilemma emerges. On the one hand, attorney fees consume the largest portion of the malpractice dollar. In a very real sense, doctors are correct in alleging that rising malpractice premiums primarily benefit lawyers rather than injured patients. If the costs of medical malpractice insurance are to be controlled effectively, it seems inescapably necessary to deal with the major component of those costs, which is the money paid to lawyers. Although there are ways to streamline the settlement process for malpractice dispute (as discussed in Chapter 7), the simple fact is that resolution of disputes as complex as those which arise in medical cases requires the service of skilled advocates.

On the other hand, the earnings of patients' lawyers are not out of line with those of doctors' lawyers. The earnings of malpractice lawyers are not out of line with those of lawyers generally. This central

dilemma forces us to question whether these are the appropriate comparisons, or whether the problems must be addressed in a context
larger than medical malpractice.

One way to do this is to consider whether the excesses in the cost
of legal services in medical malpractice are simply one aspect of a
larger problem of excesses in the cost of legal services in general.
Because lawyers, like doctors, provide a professional service, the tradition is that the market is not an appropriate mechanism to allocate
and control the cost of legal services. Although the Code of Professional
Responsibility says that a lawyer may not enter "into an agreement
for, charge, or collect an illegal or clearly excessive fee," the prohibition
has not been enforced. There is no reason to expect that lawyers'
fees will be reduced by professional self-regulation. Until 1975, bar
associations took action against lawyers who charged *too little*. In that
year, the U.S. Supreme Court held that minimum-fee schedules violated the antitrust laws and were illegal. Recent changes in the law,
including prohibition of bar-association minimum-fee schedules and
the lifting of historic bans on lawyer advertising, may promote greater
competition among lawyers. These changes should affect the accessibil-
ity and cost of routine legal services which the client pays for out-of-
pocket, such as divorces and wills. But we cannot expect that a somewhat greater degree of competition in the legal marketplace will result
in a significant decrease in the overall cost of legal services relative
to other services, or significant reductions in the cost of legal services
in malpractice cases.

If we assume that the problem of excessive legal costs in medical
malpractice is essentially a problem of excesses in the general cost
of legal services, one remedy would be to control the cost of all legal
services. One lawyer proposes that

There should be a limit on the amount lawyers can earn—say something ridiculous like $200,000. Other services with publicly granted monopoly power have
limits—the utilities, for example. Lawyers are given monopoly access to the
nation's prime method of private dispute resolution, the courts. The public
can expect something in return. An income ceiling may make the bar less
top heavy, more decentralized. It will tend to spread the work around. If
members of Congress can accept income limits from outside work, why can't
lawyers who also hold positions of public trust?

The suggestion has merit. The problem with it—as most lawyers would be quick to point out—is that other groups, such as corporation executives and successful business people, are free to earn "ridiculous" amounts of money. Many people who exercise "publicly granted monopoly power" earn as much as or more than lawyers—for example, public-utility executives and, most notably for our purposes, doctors. Indeed, doctors are the only major occupational group in this country that, on the average, earns more than lawyers.

Significant restrictions on the compensation of malpractice attorneys are necessary if a greater proportion of the malpractice insurance dollar is to reach injured patients. However, restrictions on the earnings of malpractice lawyers, or lawyers generally, are inequitable in terms of comparisons with the earnings of other professionals, particularly doctors. It is only when we compare the earnings of malpractice lawyers with the earnings of all workers that the lawyers' compensation seems excessive. And, in that context, the earnings of nearly all doctors and lawyers are excessive.

The distribution of income in America is wildly disproportional. The poorest fifth of the population earns about 5 percent of the total income, and the richest fifth earns over 40 percent of the income. With very few exceptions, both lawyers and doctors are firmly established in the top fifth. The situation of those at the bottom is desperate, both in absolute terms and in relation to the wealth of other members of the society. As we have seen, an effort to think equitably about the fact that the largest portion of malpractice premiums goes to pay lawyers forces us to think broadly about the general distribution of income.

The gross disparity in the distribution of income in the United States is certainly relevant to the immediate question of attorneys' fees in malpractice cases and may also be relevant in a more fundamental way to the crisis in medical malpractice insurance. To be poor is a disaster, in terms of both social approbation and day-to-day economic reality. To be middle-class is to be insecure. As the level of social insecurity becomes more acute, the need to insure individual security becomes more intense. As traditional societal sources of security—the extended family, the supportive community, the family physician—atrophy, the importance of financial security increases.

Injured patients often must attempt to obtain financial redress through malpractice suits because they find themselves faced with staggering medical bills, lack of rehabilitative services, and the horrendous prospect of being "poor." Patients are aware that doctors, whether or not they have insurance, are much better able to bear the financial costs of patients' injuries.

Probably the only way to address the problem of maldistribution of income and wealth, and the social insecurity generated by that maldistribution, is through reform of the federal tax structure. Most often, tax reform is considered in terms either of the impact of particular loopholes or of general equitable considerations. The case for tax reform is seldom presented as a practical measure for approaching and dealing with concrete social problems, among which are those that arise in relationship to medical malpractice insurance.

Who Should Bear the Legal Costs of Malpractice?

The general rule in American law is that each party bears the costs of his or her own attorney. The rule is different in other places. For example in Great Britain, the party who loses the litigation is often required to pay all legal fees.

In medical malpractice, the costs of physicians' lawyers are generally paid by the insurance company which has insured the physician, and the costs of the patients' lawyers are paid on a contingent-fee basis from whatever settlement the patient recovers. As a formal matter, the amount which the patient with a successful malpractice claim recovers does not include any recovery specifically allocated to the payment of attorney fees. Hence, these fees come out of the amount which the jury has determined the patient should be paid to compensate for the costs of medical bills, lost wages, disfigurement, and pain. As we have seen, a patient's lawyer working on a contingent-fee basis receives nothing when the patient loses. Lawyers set their fees to take account of this fact. Hence, as a practical matter, the patient who has a successful malpractice claim pays the costs of legal services provided for his claim and, in addition, helps to finance legal services provided to patients whose claims proved to be unsuccessful. Although the jury is not specifically informed that the patient's lawyer will take a portion of the recovery which it awards, jurors are usually aware of this fact, and may inflate awards to take account of it.

Why does the insurance company pay the cost of the doctor's lawyer, yet make the patient pay the lawyer's fee out of the recovery? One possible justification is that the doctor purchased the malpractice insurance, including insurance against the legal costs involved in defending the malpractice action. The doctor paid the premium. The theoretical argument is that if the patient wanted this sort of legal insurance, he should have purchased it himself. In practice, however, prepaid legal coverage of this sort is not available. Further, the problem with this justification is that even though it is the doctor who pays the premium, the costs of medical malpractice insurance are borne by the patients, either directly when they pay doctor and hospital bills, or indirectly when they buy medical insurance or pay taxes to finance publicly sponsored medical-insurance programs.

Another possible justification for imposing the costs of attorneys' fees on the injured patient is that it would not be possible to use the contingent-fee system if patients' lawyers were paid out of malpractice insurance funds. As we have seen, the contingent-fee system serves important functions assuring that patients without financial resources will have access to attorneys, and providing attorneys with the incentive to take claims which have a good prospect of success, while rejecting those which do not. However, it would be feasible to preserve the contingent-fee system and, at the same time, provide that the patient's lawyer should be paid out of malpractice insurance funds rather than out of the patient's pocket, particularly as there is increasing state regulation of the terms of the contingent-fee arrangement. It would be a relatively simple matter to provide that the attorney of the successful malpractice claimant should present his or her bill to the insurance company for payment, rather than to the injured patient. If the claim were unsuccessful, the patient's lawyer would still recover nothing. The patient's lawyer could be prohibited from seeking additional compensation from the patient.

It is difficult to conceive of any legitimate reason for the present arrangement. The insurance funds, which ultimately come from the patients, pay the fees of the doctors' lawyers while the fees of the injured patient's lawyers come from the amount the patients receive if the lawsuits are successful. To the degree that juries now increase the amounts of awards to help cover the costs of the injured patients' lawyers, presumably they would stop doing so if the law required that patients' lawyers be paid, on a contingent basis, out of malpractice insurance funds.

The real reasons for this disparity in the source of funds of patients' and doctors' lawyers are tradition, the powerlessness of patients as a class, and the fact that if a law were now adopted providing for the payment of patients' lawyers out of malpractice insurance funds, there would necessarily be an increase in medical malpractice premiums. Since the crisis of medical malpractice insurance is largely a crisis of rising premiums, there is understandably little interest in reforms that would increase those premiums still more. Nonetheless, there is no reason why a state could not require that the costs of patients' lawyers as well as doctors' lawyers be met out of malpractice insurance funds. The idea has much to recommend it in terms of equity and the real needs of patients who are injured as a result of negligent medical treatment.

6

The Rules of the Malpractice Game

The most popular legislative response to the malpractice crisis has been to change the legal standards defining malpractice. These changes are premised on an assumption that it has become significantly easier for patients to prove medical malpractice, and that these changes in legal standards have had a significant impact on malpractice premiums. The vice-president of the National Association of Independent Insurers lists "changes in the legal standards" as the primary cause of the malpractice crisis: "Erosion of legal defenses [and] changes by many state courts in legal concepts have made it easier for patients to obtain favorable judgments." A physician/lawyer member of the HEW Malpractice Commission says that judicial decisions modifying the standard of proof in malpractice cases are "all designed to induce in the mind of the average physician the concept that he is guilty until proved innocent." Congressman Waxman of California says that the standard used to judge the practice of medicine "almost approaches a standard of strict liability."

But the evidence is that these assumptions are false. Therefore, legislative action based on them is likely to be ineffective and, in some cases, destructive. Because the authors' view of the law differs so sharply from popular beliefs held in medical, insurance, and legislative circles, we will support our unorthodox views in some detail. But even more important and more interesting is an effort to understand why such erroneous impressions of legal standards are so widely and firmly held. Medical malpractice decisions are accessible to anyone who reads; grounds for recovery are a matter of public record. How could matters of public record become so seriously distorted in the minds of people who are both intelligent and concerned? This chapter focuses on the standards by which the law judges physician behavior.

As we have seen, medical malpractice is just one type of a larger class of cases in which an injured person attempts to recover compensation by proving that: there has been an injury to an interest which the law protects; the person sued failed to exercise the care or skill that a reasonable person would use in the circumstances; and there was a sufficiently close causal relationship between the injury and the failure to act with due care. Although medical malpractice is generally similar to other forms of negligence, establishing proof of medical malpractice has been considerably more difficult because of the law's requirements concerning expert testimony. The necessity for a medical expert, as we have seen, grows out of the fact that doctors are judged by existing standards of the medical profession. Not only is an expert required in almost every case, but until recently, because the law judged physicians solely by the standards of other physicians in the same local community, the expert has had to be one who was familiar with the practices of the particular community.

For example, in 1968, a Michigan lower court dismissed the claim of a family whose child was permanently retarded because the pediatricians who treated the child for several years had not tested for phenylketonuria (PKU). As the family was unable to find a Detroit doctor willing to testify, it presented two recognized outside medical experts, one from Chicago and another from Los Angeles. The experts testified that when a pediatrician was testing and treating a child unable to perform mentally and physically as normal children could, he ought to have administered a test for PKU. The court ruled that Chicago and Los Angeles were not communities similar to Detroit and the expert testimony was therefore inadmissible. The court's justification for the locality rule was that country doctors should not be held to the same standards as physicians who work in great urban medical centers where they have an opportunity to keep abreast of current developments in medical practice. In 1970, the Michigan Supreme Court reversed the lower court, holding that "geographical conditions or circumstances control neither the standard of a specialist's care nor the competence of an expert's testimony."

In another 1968 case, an anesthesiologist practicing in New Bedford, Massachusetts, argued that physicians from Boston should not be allowed to testify on behalf of a patient who was injured as a result of an allegedly excessive dose of anesthetic. New Bedford is a community of 100,000 people located fifty miles from Boston. The trial court upheld the doctor's defense that New Bedford doctors could not be held to Boston standards. The Massachusetts Supreme Court reversed, saying that "with the rapid methods of transportation and easy means of communication, the horizons have been widened, and the duty of a doctor is not fulfilled merely by utilizing the means at hand in the particular village where he is practicing." The court said that the appropriate standard is

whether the physician . . . has exercised the degree of care and skill of the average qualified practitioner, taking into account the advances in the profession. In applying this standard it is permissible to consider the medical resources available to the physician as one circumstance in determining the skill and care required. Under this standard some allowance is thus made for the type of community in which the physician carries on his practice.

Even today, Massachusetts goes further than most states in rejecting the locality rule; but, through the 1970's, an increasing number of courts have required that doctors who hold themselves out as specialists be judged by the national standards, and that general practitioners be held to the standard prevailing in similar communities, not simply the standards of the particular town in which the doctor practices.

This erosion of the locality rule has made it significantly easier for an injured patient to establish medical malpractice. This is not primarily because doctors are now being judged by higher standards. For decades, medical education has taken place entirely at nationally accredited medical schools. Physicians are certified in specialties by national certification boards. Medical journals and information on drugs are distributed on a national basis. The significance of the erosion of the locality rule is not that it changes substantive standards, but rather that, as a practical matter, it makes it easier for the patient to find an expert to testify.

Expert testimony is critical in a malpractice suit. One half of the lawyers studied by the HEW Malpractice Commission said that the availability of an expert was the single most important factor in deciding whether to take a case, and the rest listed it as a very important factor. The difficulty of finding medical experts to testify is well known. A Boston study found that 70 percent of the doctors polled would refuse to testify on behalf of a patient in a suit against a surgeon who had mistakenly removed the wrong kidney, despite the clear merit of the claim. When the patient has to find an expert from the same community as the doctor sued, the task is often impossible because doctors, most of whom will not testify for a patient in any event, are even more reluctant to testify against a physician from the same community. But now it is significantly easier for patients to pursue a malpractice claim simply because the pool from which expert testimony can be drawn has expanded.

The erosion of the locality rule has probably had a greater impact on the increase in malpractice claims in recent years than any other change in the law. But there has been little effort by physicians or insurance companies to legislate its return. This is curious. Given that state legislatures, at the urging of physicians and insurance companies, have placed a primary emphasis on changes in legal rules in response to the malpractice crisis, and given that the erosion of the locality rule has probably increased the number of malpractice cases, why has this means of limiting malpractice claims been ignored? It may be because it is simply so obvious that a national standard, particularly for judging specialty practice, is more appropriate. It may be that physicians are less disturbed by the notion of being judged by other professionals, even from outside of their local area, than they are by legal rules that allow physicians to be judged by community standards, even in the narrowest of circumstances. Certainly, most of the legislative changes in legal standards have focused on those narrow circumstances in which the law allows a physician to be judged by standards other than those of the medical profession.

While there has been no movement to reinstate the locality rule in states where it has been modified, since 1975 two state legislatures and one state supreme court have reaffirmed the locality rule. A 1975 Tennessee law provides that physicians must be judged by the standards of doctors in the same or similar communities. Patients must produce medical experts who have practiced for at least one year in the state of Tennessee, or a "contiguous bordering" [sic] state. In Louisiana, a 1975 statute requires that physicians be judged by the standards of the profession in the same community or locality. In 1976, the Arkansas Supreme Court held that the locality rule still applied in the case of a surgeon who was practicing in a small town in the state. It is likely that these responses are prompted, at least in part, by the knowledge of rising malpractice premiums and a sympathetic sense that doctors should be allowed to retain the benefit of the locality rule, however difficult it is to justify as a matter of policy.

We turn now to the question of when, if ever, physicians can or should be judged by standards other than the standards of the medical profession. As we have noted, in most areas of human endeavor, even though the customs and practices of the industry are most significant in determining the required standard of care, courts rather than the industry determine what constitutes due care. In areas other than medical malpractice, courts frequently deal with matters which are complex and highly technical. Expert testimony is often necessary to show what precautions are feasible and effective. When all the evidence is in, it is the court, or the jury under instruction from the court, that does the weighing to determine whether, in light of the probability and seriousness of the injury and the cost and feasibility of the alternative precautions, the action was reasonable.

In contrast, in a medical malpractice case, there is a fixed general rule that the person injured must produce expert medical testimony that the doctor did something no reasonable practitioner would have done. It is the medical profession itself, as represented by the expert witness, that does the weighing of risks, probabilities, and cost of alternative precautions. It is not enough for the injured patient to present the court with facts and evidence that would allow the court to weigh and determine whether the doctor's conduct fell below that which would be expected of a reasonably prudent person. This represents legal recognition that medicine is a holistic art rather than a rulebook, formula science.

But although this recognition may be generally appropriate, it also creates problems. In medicine, as in other areas of human activity, a "whole calling may have unduly lagged in the adoption of new [methods]." Also, as a practical matter, it is even more difficult to obtain an expert witness who will judge another physician as unreasonable than it is to obtain an expert witness who will testify as to the facts upon which such a judgment can be made. The two areas of the law which seem to disturb physicians most, and which have been the primary focus of legislative action to change common-law rules, are *res ipsa loquitur* and informed consent. These represent the two major exceptions to the general rule that physicians will be held negligent only on the basis of the sworn testimony of another physician.

Res Ipsa Loquitur

London, 1860. Whilst walking in the public street past Boadle's General Store one John Byrne was struck with a falling barrel of flour, knocked to the ground and seriously injured. There was one witness who said he saw the barrel fall from Boadle's window. The employees at Boadle's were quoted as saying, "I just work here," and "I didn't see nothing."

Byrne sued Boadle & Co. He told his story, and the people from Boadle & Co. said nothing. The trial judge dismissed the case, saying Byrne had failed to present affirmative evidence that Boadle & Co. was negligent. Why did the barrel roll onto Byrne's head? Is it possible that it was moved by lightning? Did an interloper sneak undetected into the Boadle premises and push it onto the hapless Byrne? Gnomes, perhaps? All these things are possible, but not likely. Common sense tells us that the probability—the overwhelmingly probable answer— is that someone in Boadle's shop was careless. Common sense tells us this because, first, Boadle had control over the premises and the flour barrel, and, second, flour barrels do not normally fall on the heads of passersby unless someone is careless. On appeal, the Court of Exchequer said that, given these two factors, Byrne had made a *prima facie* case of negligence, and if Boadle had an explanation or excuse which showed that the barrel fell for some reason other than the carelessness of his employees, he should have come in and given it.

Does this not seem rather obvious and simple? The person injured must still prove negligence, but there are situations in which something happens that does not happen unless someone is careless, and in which there is some individual who has control over the situation. The common-sense inference is that the person in control of the situation was careless. The situation speaks for itself—or, translated into Latin, *res ipsa loquitur*. Lord Shaw later commented, "If that phrase had not been in Latin, nobody would have called it a principle."

In most states, when the injured person has established that the injury occurred in a situation in which injuries do not happen unless someone has been negligent, and that the person being sued was in control of the situation, the effect is simply to permit the jury, if it chooses, to make the common-sense inference that the person in control was negligent. Simply that *res ipsa* is held to be applicable does not necessarily mean that the person injured will prevail. The burden of proof remains on the person injured. The person sued has an opportunity to offer other explanations for the injury, but, whether or not he does so, the jury must still find that the person injured has established that it is more likely than not that the injuries were caused by the negligence of the person sued.

In a medical malpractice case, the application of these principles means that the patient must establish that the injury is the sort of thing that does not happen unless someone is negligent, and that the person sued was in control of the situation in which the patient was injured. In most states, including New York, *res ipsa* may be used only in a narrow class of cases in which it is possible to infer from common knowledge that the injury is the sort of thing that doesn't happen unless someone is negligent. The classic examples are cases where a sponge or surgical instrument is left in the body after an operation, or where the wrong patient or the wrong organ is operated on. Since 1970, juries have been allowed to infer from common knowledge that the physician in control of the following situations was negligent: During kidney surgery, a patient was placed under a hypothermal blanket; subsequently, she developed gangrene in her legs and feet, and the feet were amputated. A patient, in intense pain and under shoulder-manipulation treatment in the hospital for six days, was not X-rayed to discover that the shoulder was dislocated. A patient suffered a severe injury to her elbow, necessitating a skin graft, and a physician administered a dose of medicine which greatly exceeded the manufacturer's instructions, and then failed to observe the precautionary measures recommended.

Courts in most states have been quite conservative in determining when negligence can be inferred from common knowledge. Thus, in 1972, a New York court held that negligence could not be inferred when a patient lost sensation in his hand after blood was drawn from the arm. Many cases have held that negligence cannot be inferred when a patient is paralyzed after spinal anesthetic.

The application of *res ipsa loquitur* in medical cases does not represent the application of any special or more stringent rule to doctors. What *is* special about the use of *res ipsa* in medical malpractice cases is that, in the situations in which it is allowed, it replaces the usual need for expert testimony. It is shocking to believe that a patient would have difficulty finding a medical expert to testify that a reasonably prudent doctor does not leave a sponge in the body—shocking but true. Although *res ipsa* was adopted to obviate the difficulty that patients have in obtaining expert medical testimony, in most states this special need for *res ipsa* in medical cases has not led to a more liberal use of the doctrine.

A few states do allow a more expansive use of *res ipsa loquitur.* There are three aspects to the slight liberalization of doctrine. First, in some states, a patient can rely on *res ipsa* even though common experience does not provide the knowledge to allow the jury's inference of negligence from the facts of the situation. In these cases, the plaintiff must provide expert testimony that the injury in question does not happen unless the doctor is negligent; but it is still *res ipsa,* because the physician's *specific* act of negligence is not demonstrated. For example, the Washington Supreme Court in 1972, relying on both common knowledge and the testimony of an expert that the injury could not occur without negligence, allowed the application of *res ipsa* when a patient was left paraplegic after radiation treatment for a malignant tumor. In 1973, a Washington intermediate appellate court allowed the jury to infer negligence in a case in which an expert witness testified that paralysis does not result from spinal anesthetic if proper care is exercised.

A second aspect of the more liberal application of *res ipsa,* allowed in a few states, typically relates to claims against hospitals rather than physicians. In a 1944 California case, a patient woke up from an appendectomy with sharp pains in his shoulder which eventually developed into paralysis and atrophy of the muscles of the shoulder and arm. The patient sued all the people who had been responsible for his care while he was unconscious. The court allowed the use of *res ipsa loquitur,* citing two factors. First, the injuries must be "unusual" or "rare" or the sort of thing that does not occur unless someone is negligent. Second, the patient must be under the control of a group of people at the time the injury occurs. The court said that

where a [patient] receives unusual injuries while unconscious and in the course of medical treatment, all those [people] who had any control over his body or the instrumentalities which might have caused the injuries may properly be called upon to meet the inference of negligence by giving an explanation of their conduct.

A third factor, that the injury was remote from the site of treatment, is also considered necessary by most courts which allow this application of the doctrine.

The criteria and justification for applying *res ipsa loquitur* against a hospital as opposed to a physician are slightly different. In an action against a physician, the justification is that since common knowledge tells us that some injuries, such as the wayward sponge, do not happen unless the person in control is negligent, a patient should not have to produce expert testimony to establish what we know through common knowledge. In an action against an institution, the standards for using the doctrine are similar, but the need for it arises from the unconscious patient's inability to fix fault on a particular individual. During the 1970's, California courts allowed the use of *res ipsa loquitur* in a case in which, on the day after a hysterectomy, a patient developed internal hemorrhaging and a deteriorating condition over a ten-hour period, during which doctors and nurses noted her condition and did nothing to treat her, and she died. In 1973, a Louisiana court allowed use of the doctrine in the case of a fourteen-year-old boy who emerged from surgery on his elbow with a severe lesion on his thigh and genitals sufficient to raise serious questions about his future potency. An Ohio court in 1974 allowed use of *res ipsa loquitur* in a case in which a patient who had been undergoing twice-weekly hemodialysis treatment went into shock and died during a treatment. There was evidence that the death was caused because some of the patient's blood, which was used to prime the machine, had become contaminated while it was being stored in the hospital for several days.

The third aspect of the liberalization of *res ipsa* is a variation on its application in suits against multiple defendants. It represents the most extreme extension of the doctrine, and it has been adopted in only one state. In 1975, the New Jersey Supreme Court allowed the application of *res ipsa* when the tip of a forceps broke off into the plaintiff's spinal canal during surgery, resulting in severe complications and additional surgery. The plaintiff sued the doctor and the hospital for their negligence, and the distributor and manufacturer of the instrument for breach of warranty. The court determined that at least one of the defendants was necessarily liable, that it was not possible for the plaintiff to prove which particular defendant or defendants was at fault, and, most significantly, that it was therefore permissible to shift the burden of proof to the defendants and force each to come forward with any evidence which might establish nonculpability.

Statistically, *res ipsa loquitur* has been an issue in only a very small portion of malpractice cases—about 5 percent of the cases appealed since 1900. In about half these cases, patients were not allowed to use the doctrine. A study of all malpractice claims resolved in 1974 showed that only 8 percent involved an allegation of *res ipsa,* and that in many of these cases the *res ipsa* allegation was not a serious aspect of the controversy. A study by the National Association of Insurance Commissioners of claims resolved over a seven-month period in 1975 and 1976 showed only one claim from a total of 3,461 in which *res ipsa* was an issue.

In New York, where the medical society urges abolition of the doctrine, the report of the Governor's Special Advisory Committee on Medical Malpractice concludes:

The abolition of the doctrine would not produce more outcomes favorable to the health care provider. It would only require additional expert testimony, in situations where they are not really needed, thus increasing trial costs.

In other states which allow the use of *res ipsa* by an unconscious patient injured while under the control of a group of people, the effect may be somewhat greater. But even in these more liberal states, "abolition" of *res ipsa loquitur* would effect only a minuscule number of cases. Further, most cases affected would be those in which a patient wakes up from an operation with an unusual injury to a part of the body other than that being treated. We question the justice of a "reform" which denies a patient in this situation any means of forcing those responsible to explain the injury.

Despite all this, proposals to "abolish *res ipsa loquitur*" are commonly made by medical societies and insurance companies. *Medical World News* reports, "The most popular legislative proposals likely to be introduced this year [1976] are reforms in the states' tort laws, such as elimination of *res ipsa loquitur.* . . ." Some states have already enacted such laws. The attempts to abolish *res ipsa loquitur* reveal common misconceptions about the meaning of the doctrine. Thus, a 1967 Alaska law, which is often referred to as the first law abolishing *res ipsa loquitur,* requires that juries be instructed that "injury alone does not raise a presumption of the physician's negligence." Actually, juries have never been allowed to infer negligence simply from the fact that the patient is injured. Similarly, a 1975 Washington law requires that the patient prove that the doctor "failed to exercise that degree of skill, care, and learning possessed by other persons in the profession and that as a proximate result the patient suffered damages." Courts have always required this, the new statute does not tell us how a patient is going to establish lack of due care, and the new law does not necessarily have any effect on *res ipsa loquitur.* Similarly, Tennessee is often cited in popular and scholarly articles as a state which has limited the use of *res ipsa.* The 1975 Tennessee law provides that "there shall be a rebuttable presumption that the defendant was negligent where it is shown by proof that the instrumentality causing the injury was in the doctor's or doctors' exclusive control and that the accident or injury was one which ordinarily doesn't occur in the absence of negligence." This is simply a restatement of the existing common law.

Finally, Nevada enacted a law in 1975 which is also referred to as a limitation on the use of *res ipsa.* It provides that a patient can prove physician negligence without expert testimony in cases of five kinds, including a foreign object unintentionally left in the body, a fire or explosion during treatment, an unintended burn to the body, an injury suffered to a part of the body not involved in the treatment, and a surgical procedure performed on the wrong patient or organ. This new statute actually makes it easier for a patient to prove malpractice. For example, in any case in which there is an injury to a part of the body not being treated, there is a presumption of negligence, whereas at common law the patient had to show that such an injury was the sort of thing that does not happen unless those in control are negligent.

In summary, efforts to "abolish" *res ipsa loquitur* seem either to have no effect at all or to make it easier for the patient to prove negligence. Given that *res ipsa loquitur* is really nothing more than a Latin tag for a common-sense inference, it is probably difficult to eliminate its use. An analogy can be made to the efforts of one state legislator, disturbed by the inconvenience to geometers caused by all the numbers following the decimal points in Pi, to pass a law making Pi equal to 3 inside the bounds of his state. Circles, of course, would be resistant to this change. Probably the common-sense inferences allowed under the name *res ipsa loquitur* will be similarly resistant to legislative efforts to abolish the familiar reasoning process.

Informed Consent

Prior to the 1960's, the law governing a patient's consent to treatment was very simple and not often invoked. The law required that the patient consent before treatment was instituted. The scope of the patient's consent defined the scope of the doctor's authority to treat. If the physician exceeded the scope of the patient's consent, he or she was liable. The issue was not whether the consent was informed—that is, whether the patient had sufficient information about the risks of treatment—but whether consent had been given. No expert testimony was required, simply testimony about what happened. Patients were allowed to recover for unauthorized medical treatment in three types of case: First, when the doctor operated on the wrong organ or the wrong patient. Second, when the doctor's actions amounted to a form of fraud, as, for example, where a doctor persuaded a woman that submitting to his sexual advances would cure her medical problems. A doctor's silence sometimes constituted fraud, in cases where a doctor failed to inform a patient of a significant result that was certain to follow treatment—for example, when a woman was not told that a hysterectomy would make her sterile. The third class of cases was those unusual instances in which a patient affirmatively limited the doctor's power to treat. For example, in 1914, a New York woman agreed to have a tumor examined under ether. She told the doctors, nurses, and anesthesiologist that she was not consenting to surgery, but only to "examination under ether." The doctors performed the operation nonetheless, gangrene set in, and her hand was amputated. She sued the hospital, and lost because the hospital was not responsible for the doctor's actions. In the course of dismissing her claim against the hospital, however, Benjamin Cardozo described the rights of a patient in relation to medical treatment.

Every human being of adult years and sound mind has a right to determine what shall be done with his own body; and a surgeon who performs an operation without his patient's consent commits an assault, for which he is liable in damages. [Citations omitted.] This is true, except in cases of emergency where it is necessary to operate before consent can be obtained.

In the 1960's, in response to the growing sophistication of medical technology, there was a rapid change in the legal standards used to determine whether a physician's actions had exceeded the patient's consent. Courts began to recognize some obligation on the part of physicians to disclose to the patient the known risks of the recommended treatment. Dean William Prosser describes this development, saying:

[I]t began to be recognized that this was really a matter of the standard of professional conduct, since there will be some patients to whom disclosure may be undesirable or even dangerous for the success of the treatment or the patient's own welfare; and that what should be done is a matter for professional judgment in the light of applicable medical standards. Accordingly, the prevailing view [in the 1960's was] that the action, regardless of its form, is in reality one for negligence in failing to conform to the proper standard, to be determined on the basis of expert testimony as to what disclosure should be made.

There are several problems in using expert medical opinion to define what information should be conveyed to a patient when a particular treatment is proposed. Through the 1960's, it became increasingly apparent that there was no ascertainable professional standard. Some doctors provided a good deal of information, and others very little. Given this diversity, it would obviously be difficult if not impossible for one doctor to swear that another doctor had provided less information that is "customarily" provided by physicians in the community. As one court put it,

the reality of any discernible custom reflecting a professional consensus in communication of option and risk information to patients is open to serious doubt. We sense the danger that what in fact is no custom at all may be taken as an affirmative custom to maintain silence.

A second problem with a legal standard which looks to local professional custom to determine how much information should be conveyed to a patient is that it incorporates the social and cultural biases of physicians. The best evidence of the impact of these biases is in those studies which report on physician communications with terminally ill cancer patients. While there is absolutely no legal obligation for a physician to disclose the likelihood of death when the possibility arises naturally and not as a risk of a treatment procedure, studies focusing on this situation do give some indication of physician attitudes which would be relevant in other disclosure situations. One study, probably the most comprehensive examination of the practice in a major U.S. teaching hospital, showed that in 73 percent of the cases in which death from cancer was anticipated, the physicians made a judgment not to tell the patients of that fact. All the patients who were informed that they had a terminal illness were white, male, private patients who needed the knowledge in order to "settle their affairs." Although patients who were poor, black, or female were not directly informed that they were dying, the overwhelming majority of them suspected it and were left to face death in a state of uncertainty.

A third problem with a legal standard which relies on professional custom to determine what information the doctor should convey is that there is a wide gap between many physicians' beliefs about the adverse effects of disclosure and the evidence available from systematic studies. For example, one study of what doctors tell their cancer patients, and why, revealed that only 14 percent of the doctors studied had firsthand knowledge of the results of any disclosure policy other than the one they followed. Research has revealed that physicians are much more afraid of death than patients, and that they are more disturbed by the prospect of death than are their dying patients. Yet studies have demonstrated that disclosure is the best preparation for successful therapy. The patient who can anticipate pain and discomfort is better able to cope with it when it occurs. A hospital which allows patients to see their own medical records has found that 93 percent of the patients report that this reduced their anxieties. Another study, in which patients about to undergo angiograms (X-rays of blood vessels) were given detailed information about the procedure, reports that while 35 percent of the patients found the information disturbing, 80 percent of them also said they were glad to receive it.

The most fundamental problem with a legal standard that looks to professional custom to determine how much information a doctor should convey in obtaining consent to treatment is that it fails to weigh the interest which competent adults have in determining what is to be done with their bodies. As we have seen, the basic negligence standard requires that the probability and seriousness of risks that may occur if certain precautions are not taken be weighed against the costs involved in taking such precautions. Conceptually, it is very difficult to apply these principles in the context of informing a patient about options for treatment. Is providing information about a patient's condition and choices a precaution? A precaution against what? What are the risks involved in giving a normal adult such information? Viewed in this light, the so-called "negligence" standard of the 1960's was less a negligence standard than a judicial judgment—that the question of how much information should be conveyed to a patient should be determined by the medical profession.

During the 1970's, a growing number of courts have required that doctors provide as much information as a "reasonable person" would need in order to decide whether to undergo treatment. The Circuit Court of Appeals for the District of Columbia was among the first to adopt an informed-consent standard oriented to the patient's need for information. The case involved a young man with a bad back. The doctor performed a laminectomy without informing the patient that the procedure involved a small risk of paralysis. The young man became paralyzed as a result of the operation; he sued the doctor for failing to warn him of this possibility. When the physician defended on the basis of a customary medical practice not to warn of this risk, the court rejected the notion that the "physician's obligation to disclose is either germinated or limited by medical practice." The court required disclosure of all material risks, regardless of professional custom. Two exceptions were noted in which a physician could treat a patient without providing full information: in circumstances where the physician was confronted with an emergency, and where the physician could show that specific medical harm might flow from the disclosure of information. But, with these two important exceptions, the basic standard required that the physician provide such information as a "reasonable patient" would need to make a treatment decision.

Courts in at least eight states have now adopted informed-consent standards based on the needs of a reasonable patient. These decisions represent a significant conceptual shift in the law. The key difference in the new standard is the absence of the requirement that the patient produce expert medical testimony that the doctor's behavior was below professional standards. The easing of this requirement is a profound shift from the traditional deference the tort law has given to professional prerogatives. As a practical matter, expert testimony may still be necessary to establish the risks involved in the treatment, and the consequences likely to have ensued if the treatment had not been given. But once this expert technical information is provided, the standard for judging whether the patient was sufficiently informed is a community standard. This is one of the rare instances in which the medical profession has said, "This is a question of medical expertise" and the society as a whole, through the law, has said, "No."

The reasonable-patient standard remains an objective one. The doctor will not be liable because a particular patient had an individual, idiosyncratic desire for more information than a reasonable patient would want. A reasonable patient does not need to be informed of risks which are obvious or of risks which are extremely uncommon. The patient needs to be told only those things that may influence the judgment of a reasonable person who is deciding whether to undergo treatment.

Further, the patient charging insufficient information must establish that any reasonable patient might have *refused* treatment if fully informed. It is not enough that this particular patient, with the benefit of hindsight and the disability of a bad outcome, says that he or she would have refused treatment if full information had been provided. Where the benefits of the treatment far outweight the risks, the patient's claim that he or she would have forgone treatment if fully informed will not be credible. The burden of proof remains on the patient, who must establish two things: that the doctor provided less information than a reasonable patient needs in order to make an informed decision, and that if such information had been provided, a reasonable patient might have refused to consent.

The standard is artfully imprecise. What are uncommon and obvious risks? How does one evaluate whether the predicted benefits of treatment outweigh the risks? These are certainly not easy questions, but neither are they beyond the jury's realm of capability. In practical effect, these determinations are probably made by jurors asking themselves what they would want to know, and what decision they would make about a particular treatment with the benefit of that knowledge. The result, as evidenced by the number of malpractice claims based on an informed-consent theory, is that patients have a very difficult burden to meet.

The shift of a few states to the "reasonable patient" informed-consent standard, despite its great conceptual importance, has had almost no practical effect on either the volume or the outcome of malpractice cases. The HEW Malpractice Commission reported that, as of 1971, there had been only ninety appellate decisions from all states in the history of the nation in which consent was a major issue. Since 1971, there have been a substantial number of appeals in which patients have attempted to persuade courts to adopt a consent standard based on a reasonable patient's need for information, but most of these appeals have failed. A National Association of Insurance Commissioners study of claims resolved over a twelve-month period in 1975–76 reports that lack of proper consent or inadequate disclosure of information was raised as an issue, be it substantial or inconsequential, in only 3 percent of all cases. Even in the landmark decision that first defined informed consent in terms of the patient's need for information, the patient ultimately lost. When the case was resubmitted to the jury after the appeal, the jury found that, while a reasonable patient would want to know about the risk of paralysis with the laminectomy, the patient had failed to prove that, thus informed, a reasonable person would reject the treatment.

Changes in informed-consent standards have been among the most popular legislative actions in response to the malpractice crisis. The nature of many of these changes reflects the confusion and misunderstanding of physicians and legislators concerning both the meaning of the new informed-consent standards and their actual impact on the number of malpractice claims. Malpractice lawyers, on the other hand, who understood the practical limitations on the use of informed consent no matter how the doctrine might be defined, were willing to compromise on this issue in the state legislative battles.

For example, in 1975 New York enacted a statute severely restricting patients' rights to be informed about proposed treatment. Courts in New York had previously adopted an informed-consent standard based on the informational needs of a reasonable patient. The new law returns to the medical profession the power to determine how much information must be provided to patients in obtaining their consent for treatment. New York courts are now required to dismiss actions not supported by expert medical testimony that the physician fell below the informational standards common in the local medical community. The New York legislature had before it information showing that actions for failure to obtain informed consent have no measurable effect on malpractice premiums. In the entire history of New York, there had been only one case in which money was paid solely on an informed-consent theory. In 1975, Idaho also adopted a law providing that physicians should be held to the informational standards of other doctors in the same community.

Iowa, Louisiana, Ohio, Utah, and Washington adopted laws which provide that written consent to treatment will be presumed valid if it meets certain requirements. These laws require that the consent form "set forth in general terms the nature and purpose of the procedure, together with the known risks, if any, of death, brain damage, quadriplegia, paraplegia, the loss of function of any organ or limb, or disfiguring scars associated with such procedures, with the probability of each such risk if reasonably determinable." The form must also acknowledge that "all questions asked about the procedure have been answered in a satisfactory manner." The Ohio law provides in addition, that the written consent will not be presumed valid if the person signing it was not able to communicate in English. The information required by these laws is as great as or greater than that required by the common law even in those states that have adopted informed-consent standards geared to the needs of a reasonable patient. Here again, as with *res ipsa,* some of the new laws intended to limit patients' rights seem either to have no effect or to make it easier for a patient to prove a claim.

Nevada and Georgia have adopted laws which seriously limit patients' rights to sue for lack of informed consent. The 1975 Nevada law provides that the physician is conclusively presumed to have obtained adequate consent if he has "explained to the patient in general terms without specific detail" the procedure to be taken, the alternative methods of treatment, if any, and the "general nature and extent of the risks involved, without enumerating such risks." Georgia has taken more extreme action. In 1971, the Georgia legislature passed a statute which required written consent to the "general terms" of treatment. In 1975, during the malpractice crisis, the Georgia Court of Appeals interpreted the statute for the first time. It determined that the physician's duty of disclosure does not include an obligation to reveal the risks of treatment. In effect, the doctrine of informed consent has been nullified in Georgia.

Before leaving the subject of informed consent, it is useful to explore briefly the relationship between the consent doctrine and the subject of defensive medicine. "Defensive medicine" generally refers to modifications of medical practice based not on professional judgment, but rather on the doctor's perceived fears of a malpractice action. It takes one of two forms. "Positive defensive medicine" is the overuse of diagnostic or treatment procedures which are medically unjustified or unnecessary. "Negative defensive medicine" refers to those procedures or activities which a physician refuses to undertake because of the fear of a later malpractice suit.

The concept of defensive medicine is a subjective one. One doctor's defensive medicine may be another's prudent medical practice. However, it does seem to be the case that many doctors (70 percent, according to an AMA poll) *believe* they are practicing defensive medicine. It also seems to be the case that when medical practice is studied in a controlled and systematic way, defensive medicine is not practiced as widely as physicians commonly believe. There is another factor. When a doctor prescribes X-rays, tests, consultations, or hospitalizations which are of marginal usefulness, it is difficult to gauge to what degree he or she is influenced by the fear of malpractice and to what degree by the fact that the patient has insurance which is paid on a fee-for-service basis.

Three important points are worth noting in relation to defensive medicine. First, it should be apparent by now that the tort law is intended to affect human behavior. It is supposed to encourage people to take precautions which a reasonable person would take to avoid risks of injury; and it is meant to have this effect on doctors just as it does on everyone else. Second, with the very limited exceptions which have been discussed here, the tort law as applied to doctors is based entirely on the professional judgment of other doctors. Finally, and perhaps most usefully, in most situations in which a doctor might feel that he or she should modify treatment behavior because of a fear of a potential malpractice action, the doctor could as well, or better, deal with the situation by providing the patient with full information and allowing the patient to decide what is to be done.

Take, for example, the situation of a child with a head injury. There is evidence that many physicians in this situation order X-rays that are of marginal medical usefulness. One study of 570 children admitted consecutively to a hospital emergency room for head trauma showed that although skull X-rays were taken in each case, in only one instance did the results of these X-rays alter the course of treatment. The physician confronted with this situation has two choices: He or she can order the X-rays, as a defense against a subsequent malpractice claim. Or the physician can say to the parent, "I could order X-rays. I do not really think they are needed for the following reasons. . . . And of course exposure to X-rays has the following risks. . . . You could observe your child at home and bring him back in the following circumstances. . . . Or you could have the X-rays. Which do you want me to do?" This procedure could be adopted in any situation in which responsible professionals might disagree on the need for the test, or its usefulness. The parent who declined the X-rays in these circumstances would not be able to win a malpractice claim subsequently, even if it did prove later that the X-rays would have provided useful information. In addition, the patient (or, in this case, the guardian) who has thus been given responsibility for the decision is probably less likely to be sufficiently outraged to go through the difficult process of attempting to institute a malpractice claim. This example can be multiplied manyfold. Similarly, a doctor who is contemplating an innovative treatment, but who feels restrained by fear of a malpractice action, can provide himself with legal protection by communicating fully to the patient the risks and possible advantages of the treatment contemplated. It is likely, of course, that many patients, being understandably conservative about their own bodies, would reject the innovative or experimental procedure, particularly where more conservative, established treatment was available.

We now turn to the question of why so many physicians, and the medical societies that represent them, believe that a physician is legally "guilty until proven innocent." Certainly, simple lack of information is part of the answer. Medical students, interns, and residents report that the subject of malpractice liability is one of the most common topics of shop talk among them. But not a single medical school in the nation requires a course in which physicians in training are introduced to the basic law affecting their practice, and 40 percent of the medical schools do not even offer such a course. Lawyers and law students find that it is difficult to see a doctor without becoming engaged in a discussion of malpractice liability, and that the level of misinformation in such discussions is so high that communication is impossible. Yet we know of no medical society which offers a course on the basic law affecting physicians. Professional medical publications frequently offer statements about legal standards which are casual, offhanded, misleading, or just plain wrong; and they seldom attempt to provide any systematic, documented, or balanced view of the law as it affects physician behavior.

But simple ignorance compounded by fear is only part of the problem. An excellent example of the ability of the medical profession to avoid information and cultivate misinformation about the law is found in the history of the Good Samaritan statutes. These statutes provide legal immunity to physicians who stop to render aid in an emergency. This means that if a doctor helps in an emergency and does something that even in the circumstances of an emergency situation no reasonable physician would do, he cannot be held liable for his actions. The statutes have been passed in at least forty-three states, and exist because many doctors believed there was a danger that they would be sued if they stopped to render emergency aid. State legislatures wanted to do all that they could to encourage doctors to offer help when emergency aid was needed.

Despite the widespread belief to the contrary among the medical profession, *there is not one single reported case,* in any state, in the entire history of the country, in which a doctor has been held liable because the treatment he provided at a roadside accident or on the street was below professional standards. Even more disturbing, the AMA reports that even after enactment of these laws, only half of the doctors studied said they would stop to help at a roadside accident. The proportion was not affected by whether or not the state had a Good Samaritan law providing the doctors with immunity. Nonetheless, in 1975, as part of their response to the malpractice crisis, the legislatures of sixteen states extended their Good Samaritan laws to include new groups of people such as nurses, lifeguards, policemen, practical nurses, physicians' assistants, and ski-patrol personnel; and to new situations, as, for example, in an ambulance and, in Wyoming, in a hospital.

A major focus of physician fear and misinformation about the law grows out of the possibility that a doctor's conduct will be judged by other than professional medical standards. This fear is understandable, since the complexity of the human body and of medical knowledge and technology does make it difficult for lay people to judge the quality of medical care in many instances. It is also understandable because doctors must be acutely aware of the enormous gap between the godlike image of the doctor projected by the medical profession and the general culture, and the uncertainty and imprecision which, of necessity, must characterize much of a doctor's daily work. Lay people and the law recognize all of this. Although such fears are understandable, they are not reasonable.

As we have seen, in medicine the custom of the profession is the final determinant of the legal standard of reasonable care. We have also seen that the exceptions, in the areas of *res ipsa loquitur* and informed consent, are very narrow indeed. Only one court, in Washington in 1974, has ever held a physician liable when the doctor has followed the standards of his profession. The case involved an ophthalmologist who saw a thirty-two-year-old patient regularly for a period of a year and a half. Although the doctor observed that the patient had visual-field problems, he delayed administering a test for glaucoma, relying on the standards of the ophthalmology profession which do not require giving routine tests of internal eye pressure to patients under forty years of age. The patient suffered permanent injury because of the delay in treatment. The court said, "We find this to be a unique case." The factors which made the case unique were that: the doctor relied upon a fixed professional rule of thumb rather than a complex, individualized medical judgment; the disease was controllable if detected; and the test was "simple," not dangerous, and "relatively inexpensive." This case has not been used as a precedent in other states or applied to other situations within the state of Washington. Its uniqueness is indicated by the fact that it has produced as much legal commentary as any malpractice decision in recent years. The critical point is that it involves a situation in which the physician was operating on the basis of a rule of thumb that was, in turn, based on statistical data as accessible to the court as to the ophthalmologists who set the standard. It was not a case in which the physician was exercising his best individual judgment in light of a complex of facts and information available to him. With the exception of this case and the *res ipsa* and informed-consent cases discussed earlier, the law remains that physicians can be found negligent only when the patient proves that the physician's conduct fell below professionally determined standards.

Even more puzzling than the question of why doctors remain so misinformed about the nature of the legal standards governing malpractice is why state legislatures have made modifications of the legal standards so important a part of their efforts to deal with the malpractice crisis. The problem of rising malpractice premiums needs more effective solutions. Modifications in the law of *res ipsa loquitur* or informed consent may be temporarily effective as placebos to the medical profession, but they are not designed to deal with the real causes of increases in malpractice premiums. Many of the members of state legislatures are themselves lawyers. Although they might legitimately be expected to have a better understanding of existing legal standards and their effect on malpractice premiums, lawyers in fact often have little understanding of the law outside their own areas of practice and interest.

Probably two factors account for the popularity of changes in the legal standards as a response to the malpractice situation. First, the doctors and the insurance companies wanted these changes. The patients' lawyers, who had the most accurate understanding of the practical effects, knew that such changes would not make any significant difference. The second and perhaps more important factor is that reforms which can be accomplished by changing the words of a law, or the legal standard, are always easier to effect than reforms which require the expenditure of public funds or the creation of an agency to administer them. Dealing with the maldistribution of physicians is probably beyond the power of any single state legislature. Setting up a mechanism to identify and control physicians who chronically practice substandard medical care is enormously difficult. Regulating the rate structure and reserves of an insurance company, whether private or public, is an overwhelming job. But revising a legal rule is easy. In this case, it is not likely to help.

7

Techniques of Dispute-Resolution

The process of resolving malpractice disputes is expensive, time-consuming, difficult, and unpleasant for everyone involved. The costs of dispute-resolution consume a substantial portion of the malpractice insurance dollar. Delays of several years between the filing of a malpractice claim and its settlement are not uncommon. During this time, injured patients often lack the resources they need to mitigate the effects of their injuries, to obtain rehabilitative services, and sometimes simply to live. Long delays between injury and settlement produce a situation of uncertainty which, in turn, requires that insurance companies retain large sums of money for claims which they may have to pay in future years. The process of finding out what happened, preparing evidence, obtaining expert witnesses, and settling disputes is arduous. Much of the time, the process fails to give either patients or physicians a sense that justice has been done.

Many of the recent responses to the medical malpractice crisis have been directed toward reform of the dispute-resolution process. Among these responses are limitations on the time period within which malpractice actions may be filed; changes which will make evidence more available and encourage the early settlement of disputes; proposals to remove malpractice cases from the judicial system and settle malpractice claims through arbitration; and limitations on the amount of damages which may be recovered in a malpractice action. This chapter

120

considers these proposals. Proposals for imposing liability on a no-fault basis are discussed in Chapter 8.

There are two types of delay in settling malpractice claims: first, patients may delay in informing the doctor that there is a reason for complaint; second, there may be delay in the final settlement of the dispute after the patient has informed the doctor that a claim exists. These two kinds of delay present two different problems in insuring malpractice. In the first situation, in which claims have not been reported but may be asserted at a later date, the insurance company must guard against risks about which it has absolutely no information. In the insurance business, these claims are known as "incurred but not reported," or IBNR's. In the second situation, in which the claim has been reported but not settled, the insurance company has much more information with which to work. Normally, when a claim is first reported, the insurance company will evaluate the likelihood that the doctor may eventually be forced to pay, and the amount that the patient may receive. Both evaluations involve considerable uncertainty. The money for these reported (though still unsettled and uncertain) losses is set aside in "reserve" in insurance-company accounts. We first consider reforms to encourage the prompt filing of claims, and, second, reforms designed to encourage early settlement.

Time Limits

In every state, statutes of limitations require that legal claims be initiated within a fixed period of time. The primary purposes of these laws is to prevent the prosecution of stale claims, and to avoid the need to decide disputes after memories have failed and information is lost. The specified time limitations vary according to the nature of the legal claim; thus, a six-year period is common for contract claims and a three-year period is common for personal-injury claims.

The clock for bringing a personal-injury action normally begins to run at the time the injury is inflicted. With respect to injuries inflicted during medical treatment, this general rule is sometimes unfair. An instrument left in a patient may not be discovered until after the time for bringing suit has passed. Because of the obvious injustice of applying the statute of limitations strictly in such cases, most states have allowed a number of exceptions.

The most important exception is the discovery rule, which provides that the time clock for bringing suit does not begin to run until the patient discovers the injury, or could have discovered it with reasonable diligence. The discovery rule was originally adopted in cases involving foreign objects left in the patient. In some states, it has been extended to cover other situations in which the patient does not have opportunity to know that injury exists. A second exception applies where the physician has knowledge of the malpractice and fraudulently conceals this information from the patient. Under this exception, the statute of limitations does not begin to run until the fraud is exposed. A third exception is the continuous-treatment rule, which provides that the time period for bringing suit does not begin until the treatment is completed. This exception recognizes that a patient's reliance upon a doctor may prevent acknowledgment that an injury has been caused by the malpractice of a doctor in whom the patient has implicit trust. Finally, most state laws provide that the time period for bringing suit does not begin until the patient is legally able to sue. In the case of children, this means that the time limit does not commence until the child reaches maturity, although the parents may sue on the child's behalf at any time before then.

In 1975 and 1976, legislatures in at least thirty-one states acted to tighten restrictions on the time limits within which medical malpractice actions must be filed. The laws took three basic forms. In some states, the general time period in which a malpractice lawsuit may be filed was shortened. For example, New York reduced the general time for filing a malpractice suit from 3 years to 2.5 years. Some states eliminated the exceptions that had been created by the courts. Thus, Texas requires that a malpractice suit be filed within two years and allows no exceptions even in cases in which the patient could not have discovered the injury within that time, or in which the doctor fraudulently conceals the injury from the patient. Some states limited the exceptions which would justify delay in filing suit. For example, the North Dakota law excuses delay only in cases where the physician fraudulently conceals the negligence. Iowa allows delay only when a foreign object is left in the patient and could not be discovered.

This legislative action is based on a perception that there are unjustifiable delays in the filing of malpractice claims, and that these delays contribute to the need of malpractice insurance companies to maintain large amounts of money in "reserve" against future liability; and on the assumption that the time which elapses between an incident of alleged malpractice and the reporting and settlement of malpractice claims might be shortened by restricting the time within which suits must be filed. The evidence in support of these propositions is far from clear.

The National Association of Insurance Commissioners' study of claims paid from July 1975 through June 1976 shows that after two years the overwhelming majority of malpractice claims have been reported and finally settled. Within two years, 84.2 percent of all incidents were reported and 82.5 percent of the claims were closed. Among children, 80.4 percent of the incidents were reported within two years and 76.6 percent of the claims were closed. Less than 2 percent of all incidents of malpractice remain unreported after five years. The data collected by the HEW Malpractice Commission showed a slightly longer delay in the reporting and settlement of malpractice claims. Some New York data show notably longer delays, and the reasons for the differences between the New York data and the national statistics are not clear; but it is most probable that in this area of experience, as in many others, New York is simply different from the rest of the country.

The weight of the evidence is that restrictions on the time for filing malpractice suits are not likely to have a significant impact on malpractice premiums. When the law simply shortens the general time period for filing suit, attorneys file sooner than they otherwise would. This is not necessarily bad—it simply is not significant.

The major problem with laws which limit exceptions to the general time limits or, as in Texas, completely eliminate the exceptions is that, in a small number of cases, a patient with a valid claim will be barred from asserting it before he ever has a chance to learn that there is any reason to believe that the doctor acted negligently. Patients in Texas or North Dakota may find surgical instruments inside themselves and have no opportunity for legal redress. Although these statutes provide insurance companies with somewhat greater certainty in knowing the point at which claims are barred, they do so at the expense of an occasional innocent individual who is denied any opportunity to assert a valid claim.

Some states have also shortened the time for the bringing of actions by or on behalf of injured children. Children are not legally capable of suing on their own, and the traditional rule was that the statutory time for filing suit did not begin to run until the child reached majority. The new time limits assume that the injured child can rely on his parents to bring suit where there are grounds for it. The assumption seems entirely reasonable; but because most parents would be diligent in pursuing the legal claims of their injured child, a law forcing them to do so is not likely to reduce the number of malpractice cases. This conclusion is supported by the fact that 88.3 percent of all incidents involving minors are reported within three years of occurrence. Furthermore, only 15 percent of the malpractice insurance payments made in 1975–76 involved a minor.

Encouraging Settlement

Patients and their lawyers need information to determine whether a malpractice claim exists. Information is often difficult to obtain. Several studies show that health-care providers often refuse to release patient records to either the patient or the patient's lawyer until after suit has been filed or formally threatened. This forces the patient to threaten suit simply to obtain information. It also contributes to delay by forcing preparation of cases which might be recognized as lacking merit if the records were available at an early stage. Further, the evidence is that full disclosure of information promotes patient satisfaction and reduces the suspicion and distrust that sometimes motivate patients to institute malpractice actions. Despite all this, so far as we can determine, not a single state has passed a malpractice reform law that gives patients the right to obtain their own medical records.

Doctors also have problems obtaining information about malpractice claims. Patients' attorneys may foreclose opportunities for negotiation and settlement by not informing the physician when the patient has a complaint. The formal legal complaint is sometimes the first notice provided to the physician or the insurance company. In 1975, California dealt with this problem by providing that an attorney may be guilty of unprofessional conduct unless ninety days' notice is given before filing suit for medical malpractice. A new Utah law requires that the patient's lawyer give the doctor notice of the claim ninety days before filing suit.

When a patient has obtained basic information from his medical records and the physician has been informed about the existence of a complaint, expert evaluation is needed to determine whether there is basis for a malpractice claim. Several major studies have noted the difficulty which patients and, indeed, doctors sometimes have in obtaining experts to evaluate the merits of a claim and to testify. One approach to this problem is to establish a screening panel which can evaluate medical malpractice claims and offer the parties an opinion on the merits of the claim. A screening panel serves two functions. It provides a means of discouraging the prosecution of baseless claims, and it gives the parties access to expert evaluation and guidance. For several years, medical societies in a few areas have offered the services of screening panels to parties in malpractice cases, on a voluntary basis. The utility of these voluntary panels has been limited, primarily because often the lawyers for doctors and insurance companies would not allow their clients to submit to a process in which the patient is more likely to obtain helpful information than is the physician.

Prior to 1975, only New Hampshire required by statute that malpractice cases be submitted to an expert screening panel before the case could be heard in court, and New Jersey required the use of panels by court rule. In 1975 and 1976, the legislatures in twenty-five states enacted laws establishing expert screening panels for medical malpractice cases.

Most of the new screening-panel laws require that malpractice disputes be submitted to the panel before they can be *heard* in court. The panels vary in both size and composition. All panels contain physician members, and some also include lawyers, judges, and lay people. Some require a physician member in the same specialty as the doctor charged with malpractice. The panels also follow differing procedures. Some provide for hearings and others act on the basis of written documents. Some allow arguments and cross-examination and others do not. In general, the proceedings of the screening panels are more informal and less adversary than normal court procedures. Some panels make findings as to the probable existence of negligence, proximate cause, and the need for expert testimony. Others also make a finding as to the amount of damages. A critical issue in the operation of malpractice screening panels, and a point of variance among the new laws, is whether the findings of the panel should be admitted in a subsequent judicial trial.

It has been argued that if the findings of screening panels are not admissible, the panels may be unfair to physicians and ineffective in limiting the volume of malpractice litigation. The patient is provided with an expeditious and inexpensive means of obtaining information and expert opinion. Even if the panel's finding is in favor of the physician, the patient can still try to persuade a jury that the doctor was at fault, and he suffers no penalty from the findings of the screening panel. This criticism may be unduly pessimistic. As we have noted, there are strong economic incentives to discourage patients' lawyers from spending further time and effort on baseless claims. Also, the composition of screening panels is biased, to some degree, in favor of physicians. Therefore, some claims which the screening panel rejects can nonetheless reveal a situation in which a patient does, and should, have a reasonable prospect of success in a judicial proceeding that is less biased toward the medical profession.

Others argue that the admission of the finding of the screening panel would undermine the patient's constitutional rights. Even if a panel's finding is not binding, it is assumed that it will be so persuasive that its admission will effectively destroy the patient's right to a trial by jury. Since the composition of the panels is weighted toward medical professionals the profession is, in effect, given the power to make judgments on issues which the state and federal constitutions guarantee parties a determination by a jury of their peers. An American Bar Association study suggests that allowing admission of panel findings may be counterproductive since the panel finding then acquires so much weight that the "procedure is likely to become increasingly formal and take on all the trappings of court room litigation."

Courts have divided over the constitutionality of admitting the finding of the screening panel in a subsequent judicial proceeding. The Supreme Court in Illinois and lower courts in Tennessee and Ohio have held that it would violate the constitutional right to jury trial to allow screening-panel findings to be admitted. The Florida Supreme Court reluctantly upheld a provision allowing the introduction of panel findings into evidence at trial, saying that the provision ". . . reaches the outer limits of constitutional tolerance." The Appellate Division of the New York Supreme Court upheld the admission of unanimous panel findings, noting that the judge could instruct the jurors that the panel's conclusion was not binding upon them, and that parties are given the right to question panel members to attempt to "neutralize" the finding of the panel. A lower court in Nebraska held that panel findings could be admitted as expert evidence which should be available to the jury.

At least two states, Massachusetts and Arizona, impose further penalties on parties who go to court after a screening panel has found against them. Both states require that patients who seek to go to court after a screening panel has found that there is no basis for liability must post a bond of $2,000, to be paid to the doctor to defray legal costs if the doctor ultimately prevails in court. In Massachusetts a judge may increase the amount of the bond required. In both states the amount of bond required may be reduced if the patient is indigent, but it can never be totally waived. In Arizona a doctor who chooses to contest liability in court after a screening panel has found evidence of malpractice must also pay a $2,000 bond to help defray the patient's costs if the patient ultimately prevails. In Massachusetts the bond requirement is entirely one-sided; doctors are never required to post bond even if the screening panel has determined that the doctor should be held liable.

Both of these provisions represent a sharp departure from the normal American rule that each party to the litigation bears the cost of his or her own attorney's fees irrespective of who wins the litigation. The Massachusetts law imposing a bond requirement on patients but not doctors who seek judicial review after an adverse screening-panel finding seems blatantly inequitable.

Apart from the inequity inherent in conditioning access to the courts upon the ability to put a substantial sum of money up front, this sort of penalty may ultimately reduce the utility of screening panels. An American Bar Association study concludes: "Penalizing the loser, whether through cost bonds or some other device, will have the effect of making the panel procedure more formal and the atmosphere less amicable. Any success penalties might have in deterring litigation is outweighed by the damage penalties would do to the entire panel process."

Is there any evidence that screening panels are effective in accomplishing their intended purposes? Although conclusive data are not yet available, it seems that screening panels are helpful in reducing the costs—in time, money, and unnecessary hassle—of the process for resolving malpractice disputes. Studies of the voluntary screening panels established by medical societies and bar associations in the 1960's show that in nonurban areas the panels had a significant effect in encouraging settlement. In urban areas, screening programs were less successful in this respect. The speculation is that the panels have greater effect where there is closer cooperation between the legal and medical professions. Even when the panels do not succeed in encouraging settlement, they have focused and clarified the issues to be settled at trial.

Arbitration

Many people see arbitration as a solution to the problems in the judicial resolution of malpractice disputes. Arbitration is a private procedure for the resolution of disputes. The agreement between the parties determines the precise form of arbitration. Generally, the primary differences between the court system and the arbitration system are: in court, decisions are made by a judge or jury, whereas in arbitration, decisions are made by arbitrators selected by the parties; courts require formal written papers and formal pretrial procedures, and in arbitration there is only a simple statement of the nature of the dispute and no pre-"trial" proceedings; courts decide cases in accordance with pre-existing law, but arbitrators decide what is "just" in each individual case; in court, parties may appeal rulings on questions of law, but arbitration decisions are final. The proponents of arbitration claim that it is cheaper, faster, and less traumatic than court proceedings. Arbitration has proved to be an effective means of resolving disputes in many areas that involve complex technical issues such as commercial-contract, labor-management, and securities disputes.

For many years, most states have had general laws authorizing agreements to submit disputes to arbitration and specifying some of the provisions which such agreements must contain. From 1975 to 1977, in response to the medical malpractice crisis, eleven states passed laws specifically authorizing voluntary binding arbitration for medical malpractice claims. Eight of these laws give the parties the power to agree to arbitrate future claims; three apply solely to existing disputes.

Despite this legislative activity and the fact that parties have been free to agree to arbitrate medical malpractice disputes in most states for many years, the number of medical malpractice disputes submitted to arbitration has not been large. Data of the American Arbitration Association (AAA) show that arbitration was completed in 55 medical malpractice cases during the period 1972–77. Twenty-six of the closed cases were submitted to arbitration after the dispute arose; all the other 29 cases arose in California. The AAA estimates that, as of 1975–

76, total arbitrations represent about .01 percent of all malpractice claims closed.

Because of constitutional provisions guaranteeing people the right to submit legal disputes to a court and a jury, arbitration can be used as an alternative means of settling disputes only when both parties agree to it. Agreements to arbitrate can take several forms. After a dispute arises, the parties may agree that it should be resolved through arbitration. Another type of agreement to arbitrate is that contained in a contract offered by a group health service, such as the Kaiser Foundation Health Plan in California. A third type of agreement to arbitrate, and the one that is of primary interest in the context of the medical malpractice crisis, is an agreement between a patient and a doctor or hospital, entered into at the time treatment begins, in which the parties agree that any dispute which may arise in the future will be settled by arbitration. These agreements are now being offered to patients in New York and California.

Only the Southern California Arbitration Project has been in existence long enough to generate significant information about how arbitration actually works in medical malpractice cases. The project, which is sponsored by the California Hospital Association and the California Medical Association, began in 1969. In this project, in one group of hospitals the patients and the hospitals agreed that disputes arising out of a particular hospitalization would be settled through arbitration. Their experience is compared with a comparable group of hospitals and patients which had not made such agreements. In November 1975, a major study of this project, funded by HEW, was published. This study is a primary source of information about how arbitration of medical malpractice disputes actually works.

Two basic dilemmas arise when arbitration is used to solve the problems of the present dispute-resolution process. The first dilemma is that those characteristics which make the judicial process cumbersome and inefficient generally assure fairness to each side. To the extent that arbitration procedures are substantially different from judicial proceedings, there is likely to be some cost in terms of fair process. To the degree that arbitration provides processes and procedures similar to the present judicial system, it may be plagued by similar burdens and complexities.

The second dilemma revolves around the fact that both state and federal constitutions contain constraints against laws which would *require* arbitration as the exclusive means for resolving disputes between doctors and patients. Because the constitutions prevent the state from forcing arbitration on an unwilling party, a court must in fact first determine that the parties' agreement to arbitrate is knowing and voluntary.

With respect to the first dilemma, consider the basic question of who should decide malpractice disputes. Undoubtedly, the fact that judges and juries lack medical expertise exacts a cost in terms of time, money, and unnecessary bad feelings. Arbitration uses some decision-makers who have expertise in the area of dispute and do not need to be educated in each case. This makes the process more expeditious. In commercial or labor disputes, this expertise works to everyone's benefit. Experimental projects in malpractice arbitration have used arbitrators who have knowledge of medicine and the law applicable to malpractice disputes. For example, in the Southern California Arbitration Project, the arbitrators include one representative of the doctors and hospitals, one attorney, and one "consumer." The consumer member is always "a business industry leader who was extremely sensitive to the 'value of the dollar.' " An arbitration program sponsored by the medical society and the hospital association in New York uses a similar panel. Each party has an opportunity to select arbitrators from a list prescreened by the medical society and hospital association. The new arbitration laws follow a similar pattern.

A panel composed of a doctor, a lawyer, and a business leader has more expertise to decide a dispute expeditiously than do a lay jury and judge. But such a panel may also decide disputes differently. Efficiency may be purchased at the price of fairness to the injured patient, who might have received a more sympathetic hearing from a lay jury and judge. In a judicial proceeding, both sides have an opportunity to question prospective jurors and learn about their backgrounds and predispositions. In the Southern California Arbitration Project, neither side has much information about the proposed arbitrators, or any opportunity to talk with or question them. Representatives of both doctors and patients report that the fairness of the process is undermined by the lack of opportunity to know more about the arbitrators prior to selection.

Similar conflicts exist with respect to the rules for the conduct of hearings. Judicial rules of evidence are sometimes cumbersome and inconvenient. But these rules are designed to protect parties—in malpractice cases, both doctors and patients—from biased or unreliable testimony. Similarly, the judicial procedures for discovery of information held by an opposing party may cause delays and increase legal costs. But unless arbitration provides similar procedures, parties may be prejudiced by an inability to obtain information or plagued by unnecessary or abusive searches for information. Much can be done to improve rules of evidence and procedures for discovering information. But such reforms are not necessarily achieved, in a fair and balanced manner, by simply opting out of the judicial system and adopting arbitration.

The right to appeal raises similar conflicts. Normally, arbitration decisions are final and may not be appealed. The right to appeal questions of law makes judicial dispute-resolution more time-consuming and can delay final determination; but the right to appeal also protects parties from the possibility that the initial decision-maker (the judge or the jury) was biased or misunderstood the law. Lawyers representing both patients and doctors in the Southern California arbitration process were disturbed most by the lack of opportunity for appeal. Both sides were sometimes reluctant to allow large claims to go to arbitration, and preferred to use the court process even though the parties had previously agreed to arbitrate. Lack of appeal may discourage the use of arbitration. Parties are reluctant to put all their eggs in one basket. Still, there may be another aspect to this issue, because the California study indicates that the lack of appeal may also encourage parties to settle claims.

Proponents of arbitration claim that its major advantages over judicial dispute-resolution are greater speed and lower cost. Again the Southern California project provides the major source of information. The evidence is that claims arising in the arbitration group were settled or closed somewhat more rapidly: 22.5 months from the time the incident occurred, on the average, for the arbitration group as compared to 25.1 months for the control group.

Evaluation of the costs of dispute-resolution is more complex. Three major cost elements in dispute-resolution are the patient's expenses, the doctor's expenses, and the system's costs. Looking first at the costs of maintaining the system, a fundamental difference between resolving malpractice disputes in the courts and in arbitration is that the costs of maintaining the courts is a public expense, whereas the costs of arbitration are paid by the parties. Brochures encouraging patients to agree to arbitration generally point to the fact that the patient will not need to pay more than a fixed amount for the costs of arbitration—for example, $500. A patient who prosecutes a malpractice claim through the judicial process does not need to pay anything for the cost of maintaining the court system, beyond nominal filing fees. There are no data on the relative "systems" costs of resolving malpractice disputes through arbitration rather than in court, but, obviously, one effect of adopting arbitration is to shift these costs from the tax-paying public to the parties to the dispute.

There are data on the costs of defending malpractice claims in arbitration. In the Southern California project, from 1970 through June 1975, the average costs of defending a malpractice claim were $508 for the arbitration group and $601 for the comparative group. This is a considerable difference in the costs of the doctors' insurance companies. No data have been collected on the costs of the attorneys who represent patients in arbitration, or the arrangements for payment of their fees.

The most significant cost element at stake in a malpractice dispute is the amount paid to the patient for injuries suffered. The question of whether payments to patients are likely to differ under arbitration is obviously of critical importance to both patients and doctors. The limited data available from the Southern California project indicate that the total amounts paid in settlement to patients who agreed to arbitration were less than the total amounts paid to patients who did not agree to arbitrate. Between 1970 and 1975, the total amount paid in settlement of malpractice claims by the arbitration-group hospitals was $931,678, and the total amount paid by the comparative group was $1,324,881. There was also a difference in the average amount paid per malpractice claim closed: the arbitration-group hospitals paid an average of $3,882 per claim closed and the comparative group paid an average of $5,941. Within the arbitration group, a slightly higher proportion of the claim-settlement money went to patients with claims under $1,000, and a significantly lower proportion of the money went to patients with claims over $40,000.

We turn now to the second problem inherent in using arbitration to settle disputes between doctors and patients—i.e., assuring that parties knowingly and voluntarily consent to arbitration. In the early common law, agreements to arbitrate were regarded as against public policy and unenforceable. The common-law bias against arbitration was

based on the belief that allowing unlimited delegation of judicial powers to lay persons to decide unknown future disputes was inherently
objectionable. Perhaps judges were simply trying to protect their own
turf.

In the twentieth century, public and judicial attitudes toward arbitration have changed substantially, and in many situations arbitration
is now favored as a matter of public policy. State and federal laws
allow parties to make enforceable agreements to arbitrate in a variety
of circumstances. But a valid agreement to arbitrate must be based
on the knowing and voluntary consent of the parties. Legislative proposals have been introduced in some states to force parties to arbitrate
medical malpractice disputes. No state has adopted such a law, though
a 1976 Puerto Rican law requires mandatory binding arbitration of
malpractice claims. In addition, a recent Michigan law requires hospitals purchasing malpractice insurance in the commercial market to
offer patients an arbitration option, and South Dakota requires that
health-maintenance organizations offer arbitration. Laws which force
parties to arbitrate a medical malpractice dispute raise serious constitutional questions under the federal constitutional guarantee of due process of law, and under the guarantee of trial by jury, which is protected
by the constitutions of forty-eight states.

The arbitration plans currently being promoted by medical and
hospital associations in California and New York involve agreements
prepared by the medical and hospital associations, with advice from
the American Arbitration Association. These form agreements, in
which parties agree to arbitrate disputes arising in the future, are presented to individual doctors and hospitals, who are encouraged to join
the program and offer the arbitration option to their patients. Doctors
and hospitals that decide to offer the arbitration option present the
agreement to the patient when he or she first seeks treatment.

Ensuring that the parties have consented to arbitration on an informed and voluntary basis is enormously difficult. The question arises
with respect to both patients and doctors, though practical difficulties
of ensuring informed and voluntary consent are much greater in relation to patients. Doctors and hospitals normally have thorough advice
of counsel and extensive debate within their professional associations
before they decide to propose arbitration to their patients. The recent
laws endorsing the concept of voluntary agreements to arbitrate medical malpractice disputes specify the form which such agreements must

take to be valid. But even in states which have such laws, courts will continue to scrutinize such agreements to determine that they have been made knowingly and voluntarily. It is unlikely that the legislature could deprive the courts of this power without running afoul of the constitutional protection of the right to trial by jury.

Looking first at the requirement that consent to arbitrate must be knowing, how much does a patient need to know? It would seem probable that, at the least, he or she would want to know the information about arbitration presented in the previous pages of this book. One major problem is that partisans of arbitration are interested in getting as many patients as possible to agree to arbitrate, and are not willing to present even this limited information about the relative advantages and disadvantages of arbitration and litigation. The Bar Association of the City of New York has criticized literature distributed by the American Arbitration Association and by the medical and hospital societies as "selling documents" that do not provide a balanced picture of the choice for arbitration. In response, the proponents of the New York arbitration plan frankly acknowledge this view of their literature. They contend that arbitration offers a possible solution to the medical malpractice crisis which can work only if a substantial number of people agree to it.

Even if full and unbiased information is presented, many patients will simply not understand it. One solution might be to require, as has the state of Texas, that agreements to arbitrate are valid only if "concluded upon the advice of counsel to both parties." Such a requirement would present no problem for doctors or hospitals, who normally will not enter into an agreement to arbitrate without the advice of counsel, whatever the requirement of the law. But there would be formidable practical problems to providing counsel to advise patients whether to sign such agreements. Furthermore, it is possible that some lawyers would advise patients to refuse to sign, not on the basis of the client's best interests but on the basis of the lawyer's self-interest. In addition, apart from perceived self-interest, many lawyers sincerely favor the judicial system, with which they are more familiar.

As difficult as it is to obtain knowing consent, there are even greater problems to assuring that the patient's consent to arbitrate is voluntary. Is a patient's consent voluntary when the doctor or hospital offers the arbitration option on a take it or leave it basis? May a doctor or hospital say to a patient, "If you want my services, you must agree to arbitrate"? The proponents of both the California and New York arbitration plans have stated that they do not believe that a plan offered on such a basis could be considered voluntary. Revised consent forms in New York specifically state that medical care will not be refused or altered because the patient has rejected arbitration. However, under both the New York and California plans, the patient must inform the doctor or hospital whether he or she accepts the arbitration option. A committee of the Association of the Bar of the City of New York proposed that the arbitration agreement which the patient had accepted or rejected be submitted only to the American Arbitration Association, which administers the program. The bar group found that

if the physician or the hospital is to receive a copy of the agreement and the patient knows this, the execution of the agreement by the patient may not be voluntary because he or she will feel some compulsion to comply with the express or implied desire of the hospital or physician that the agreement be executed.

Representatives of physicians and hospitals take extreme offense at the suggestion that some patients might believe that a doctor would treat them differently if the patient refused to sign a paper which the doctor wanted the patient to sign. If the agreements accepting or rejecting arbitration were submitted to a neutral party, such as the AAA, the physician or hospital would not learn whether or not the patient had signed until the time a dispute arose. Why does a doctor or hospital need to know whether or not a patient has signed an arbitration agreement before a dispute arises? The question has been put to the promotors of the New York arbitration plan repeatedly. Either no aswer has been forthcoming, or those speaking for the doctors explain that the physician-patient relationship is a "total relationship" and whether or not the patient has agreed to arbitrate is indeed relevant in the treatment situation.

Another issue critical to the question of voluntariness is whether the patient has an opportunity to revoke the agreement once it has been signed. In considering this issue, it is useful to distinguish between agreements with hospitals and agreements with doctors. In the Southern California project, the agreements to arbitrate covered only incidents arising out of the particular hospitalization for which the agreement was signed. The patient was free to revoke the agreement to arbitrate within thirty days after discharge from the hospital. Obviously, in some cases the patient will know by the time of discharge whether there is likely to be a malpractice dispute arising out of the hospitalization. The New York plan for hospitals adopts this procedure: arbitration agreements extend only to the specific hospitalization for which they are signed, and may be revoked by the patient within thirty days after discharge.

In contrast, the New York arbitration plan for physicians provides that the agreement to arbitrate may be revoked only within thirty days after it is signed; if not, it lasts in perpetuity. In a typical case, a patient would see a physician for a routine visit and sign an arbitration agreement, and the thirty days would pass without incident. Then, perhaps many years later, a malpractice claim would arise. The patient is bound to arbitrate by an agreement signed years before the conduct giving rise to the claim even occurred. The New York Medical Society recognizes that it is a bit far-fetched to characterize this as a knowing and voluntary agreement, so doctors are encouraged to get the patient to renew the arbitration agreement every few years. But whether or not the doctor obtains such renewals, the medical society maintains that the patient would be perpetually bound by the agreement once signed. It seems unlikely that these agreements will be upheld by the courts.

One possible resolution to these problems is to require that agreements to arbitrate medical malpractice disputes be revocable at any time prior to participation in the arbitration process. The disadvantage of this is that fewer claims would be arbitrated. The advantage is that after a dispute arises, a more informed judgment can be made as to whether arbitration is an acceptable means of resolving it. If arbitration really offers benefits to both parties in some cases, then there is no reason to believe that the parties would not choose it when it is preferable. Agreements to arbitrate controversies already under way have historically received more favorable treatment from the courts.

It is clear that, at least initially, agreements to arbitrate will be scrutinized by courts. Whether courts will uphold them depends on a finding that agreement to arbitrate is knowing and voluntary. It does not serve anyone's interest to organize a program for the signing of arbitration agreements which will subsequently be held invalid by the courts. At least part of the reason that physicians and hospitals are interested in arbitration is the belief that it will result in smaller amounts being paid to patients. Would an informed person voluntarily agree to a settlement procedure that was likely to result in a smaller recovery for injury suffered? Of course not, unless there were some significant countervailing benefit. Perhaps the greater speed and informality of arbitration offer such a benefit. The findings of the California project that patients with relatively small claims are likely to do better under arbitration, would make arbitration more attractive to patients if it were offered only with respect to small claims. It is also in these cases that the costs of judicial dispute-resolution are highest relative to the amounts at stake in the substantive dispute. But if arbitration is so beneficial to patients that an informed patient might choose it voluntarily, it may be correspondingly less attractive to doctors, and less effective in reducing the costs of malpractice premiums.

Agreements to arbitrate future medical malpractice disputes have been scrutinized by courts in New York and California. There were two major California cases in 1976. In the first, the California Supreme Court upheld an agreement to arbitrate entered into between the Board of the State Employees Retirement System and the Kaiser Foundation Health Plan. A state employee was injured in a Kaiser Foundation hospital and sought to avoid arbitration. The court found that the board, in negotiating contracts on behalf of state employees, was in a position analogous to a labor union. The law provides unions with broad authority to agree to arbitration of disputes which its members may have with third parties. The court found that the negotiation of the agreement to arbitrate was "between parties possessing parity of bargaining strength." The court also noted that the patient was not forced to accept the Kaiser plan, with its arbitration provision, but rather "enjoyed the opportunity to select from among several medical plans negotiated and offered by the Board. . . ." Finally, the court stated that arbitration offers benefits, in terms of speed and economy, to both patients and providers, and that public policy favors such agreements. Each of these factors—bargaining parties of equal strength, an opportunity for the patient to choose medical care without being forced to arbitrate, and a finding that arbitration offers real benefits to patients as well as providers—seems crucial to the court's decision upholding the agreement to arbitrate.

In the second case, a California Court of Appeals invalidated an agreement to arbitrate, with one judge dissenting. It was signed by a Mr. Wheeler when he was hospitalized for routine tests, which left him totally paralyzed and unable to speak or otherwise communicate except with his eyes. The agreement to arbitrate was contained in the general consent form presented at the time of admission. The form said that the patient could reject arbitration by simply placing his initials next to the arbitration provision, or by notifying the hospital within thirty days of discharge. Just above the signature line, the form stated that the patient had read the form and received a copy of it. Mrs. Wheeler testified that her husband had not in fact read the form, and had not received a copy.

The court found that because of the disparity in power between the hospital and the patient, the contract was one of adhesion. Normally, contracts of adhesion are ones that the stronger party offers to the weaker party on a take-it-or-leave-it basis. In this case, even though Mr. Wheeler had the choice of rejecting the arbitration option, the court found that

absent notification and at least some explanation the patient cannot be said to have exercised a "real choice" in selecting arbitration over litigation. We conclude that in order to be binding an arbitration clause incorporated into a hospital's "CONDITIONS OF ADMISSION" form should be called to the patient's attention and he should be given a reasonable explanation of its meaning and effect, including an explanation of any options available to the patient.

Contracts of adhesion are not *per se* invalid. Obviously, many form contracts are offered to consumers on a take-it-or-leave-it basis. But where the contract is one of adhesion, its provisions must be normal and reasonable. If unusual provisions are included, they must be stated in clear terms and brought to the attention of the weaker party. The court criticized the agreement offered to Mr. Wheeler because it was included in the general consent form, his attention was not directed to it, and it referred to "any legal claim or civil action in connection with this hospitalization," without specifically using the word "malpractice."

A New York court refused to enforce an agreement to arbitrate signed by a Czechoslovakian woman in her doctor's office. The woman alleged that the doctor handed her a piece of paper saying, "This is for the operation." She did not have an opportunity to read the agreement before signing; she was not given a copy of it. The court said that for a patient "to waive her rights under the Seventh Amendment to a trial by jury, a very clear understanding must be had by her of the nature of the agreement which was signed."

Neither the New York nor the California courts prohibit voluntary agreements to arbitrate future medical disputes. Indeed, both California cases recognized that arbitration is a favored means of resolving disputes. But the cases do suggest that if such agreements are to be upheld, they must be offered in such a way that patients have an opportunity for a knowing and voluntary choice. Providing patients with such an opportunity for choice is a very difficult process.

Limits on the Amount of Recovery

The simplest approach to the problem of high malpractice recoveries, and correspondingly high premiums, is to limit the amount of recovery for injuries suffered because of the malpractice of physicians or hospitals. Limits on patients' recoveries have been adopted recently in many states. One form of limitation simply provides that patients cannot recover more than a fixed amount in a malpractice action. These flat limitations, or "caps," will be discussed first. Other laws limit the kinds of damages which patients may be paid and will be discussed later. Still other laws, limiting the liability of a physician or an insurance company without restricting the patient's right to recovery, are discussed in Chapter 9 with other changes in state insurance laws.

Since 1975, eight states have enacted laws placing an absolute limit on the amount of compensation a patient can receive for a single injury. The Idaho law provides that a patient may receive no more than $150,000 for injuries resulting from a single course of treatment or occurrence. In North Dakota, Indiana, Louisiana, Illinois, Nebraska, and New Mexico, the limit is $500,000; in Virginia, the limit is $750,000. These limits affect only patients who have suffered harms so grievous that the proven loss is greater than the statutory limit.

As a matter of principle, laws restricting the amounts recoverable by seriously injured patients are outrageous. The actions of many people contribute to the malpractice crisis: doctors, hospitals, lawyers, insurance companies, and perhaps patients who press frivolous claims. No one suggests that the crisis is caused by patients who suffer very serious injuries. The crisis will not be solved by forcing the most seriously injured into dependency on friends, families, or welfare. Although we all ultimately pay for soaring malpractice premiums through rising health-care costs, it seems grossly unjust to impose a disproportionate share of these costs on people who are unfortunate enough to be seriously injured as a result of negligent medical treatment.

Do the state and federal constitutions place any limit on the power of a state legislature to make the most seriously injured patients bear a portion of the economic costs of the injuries negligently inflicted on them? Before addressing this issue, it is important to note that the question has never arisen before, because state legislatures have never before done anything quite like this. State legislatures have abolished common-law rights in situations in which changing social conditions have destroyed the basis for the rights. For example, the common law gave a man the right to sue anyone who "alienated" his wife's affection for him. This right was based on a concept of a husband's ownership of his wife, and as that concept has eroded, courts have found that the legislature is free to abolish the corresponding right. States have a good deal of latitude in changing the rules of conduct required in particular situations, even though this necessarily means that people no longer have a "right" to expect others to behave in ways that the law had previously required.

A somewhat different situation has arisen where rules of conduct are left unchanged and state legislatures abolish common-law remedies as part of a program to provide compensation for injuries through alternative means. Common examples of such legislative intervention are workers' compensation and automobile no-fault programs. Under both these programs, the injured individual loses some common-law remedies, but in exchange is given an alternative remedy which provides certain payment regardless of fault.

Laws denying full compensation to people who suffer the most serious injuries as a result of medical malpractice are quite different from either of these earlier kinds of legislative action. Presumably, physicians still owe it to their patients to act with reasonable care. The rule of conduct is not being changed. The seriously injured person must still prove malpractice. Nothing is given to the seriously injured in exchange for the abolition of the right to receive compensation for proved losses above a fixed amount. Never before in American legal history has a legislature abolished the right of the most seriously injured to receive full compensation for personal injuries caused by the unreasonable action of another, without providing any substitute remedy.

Hence the question of whether there are constitutional limits on the power of the legislature to abolish seriously injured patients' right to full compensation is new and courts must decide it in accordance with general constitutional principles. Three constitutional limits have been suggested. The first relies on concepts of due process and essentially says that when the legislature abolishes a common-law remedy, it must provide some reasonable substitute or *quid pro quo.* Although many judicial statements have declared that a reasonable substitute is essential, the question has not been clearly and finally settled.

A second argument rests on state constitutional clauses prohibiting "special" legislation. The general purpose of these provisions is to prevent legislation that bestows favors on preferred groups or localities. The Illinois Supreme Court has held that the law denying recovery for damages above $500,000 in malpractice cases was arbitrary and violated the state constitutional prohibition against special legislation. However, as a principle of general utility, the standards for determining what constitutes special legislation are unclear. In some states, the courts have held that the standards for determining whether legislation violates the constitutional prohibition on "special" laws should be the same as those used for determining whether legislation violates constitutional guarantees of equal protection.

A third possible constitutional restraint on legislative power to limit malpractice recoveries is the requirement of equal protection. Essentially, the doctrine of equal protection requires that state-created classifications of people must bear some reasonable relation to the legislative purpose sought to be achieved. The state laws restricting recovery for injuries suffered by patients create two classes of citizen. Those who are injured by the negligence of anyone other than a physician or hospital may recover in full for the injuries they suffer, but those in the second, disfavored class—people who are injured by medical negligence—are limited in the amount they may recover. In fact, the second classification contains two subclasses, because patients who are less seriously injured are legally entitled to full recovery, while the seriously injured constitute a disfavored class who can recover only a portion of their damages. The constitutional issue is whether these classifications bear a reasonable relationship to the legislative purpose intended to be served.

In recent years, courts have applied three standards in examining the relationship which must exist between a legislative classification and the purpose the law is seeking to serve. The most rigorous standard applies to situations in which the classification is made on the basis of a "suspect" criterion such as race or lineage, or where the right at stake is a fundamental one—usually a right enjoying independent constitutional status, such as the right to vote. Where the classification is suspect or the right is fundamental, courts normally require that there be a very close relationship between the classification and the purpose served by the classification. Further, the purpose served by the classification must be an important interest of the state. Those defending the classification have the burden of showing that it serves a "compelling" state interest which could not be achieved in any other way. There is little reason to believe that the classification that separates people injured as patients and people injured in other ways is "suspect," or that the right to recover money for personal injuries is a "fundamental" one. However, two Ohio lower courts have held that recent legislative limits on malpractice recoveries violate equal protection because the restriction does not promote a "compelling" state interest.

A second standard used to judge the relationship between a legislative classification and the goal it serves is a very relaxed one which asks simply whether any possible justification can be imagined to support the legislative classification. This standard applies where the classifying characteristic is not suspect and the rights at stake are not of fundamental importance. It gives the legislature a large amount of latitude. This relaxed standard traditionally applies in judging state tax classifications and economic regulations. More recently, the relaxed standard has been applied in judging classifications which allocate social-service benefits. In instances in which courts decide that this very relaxed standard of equal protection is appropriate, legislative classifications are almost invariably upheld. Some constitutional scholars have argued that this is the appropriate standard to be used in judging limits on malpractice recoveries, and that, under this standard, the state is free to deny recovery to the most seriously injured victims of medical malpractice.

A third standard sometimes used to judge the relationship between a legislative classification and its purpose lies somewhere in the middle. Some legal scholars and U.S. Supreme Court Justices believe that this single middle-level standard is the one which should be used in all cases. It demands simply that the classification must be

reasonable, not arbitrary, and must rest upon some ground of difference having a fair and substantial relation to the object of the legislation, so that all persons similarly circumstanced shall be treated alike.

On the one hand, it does not demand "compelling" justification or a precise correspondence between the classification and the goal. On the other hand, it is not sufficient for an imaginative lawyer to be able to offer some hypothetical justification.

This standard was recently adopted by the Idaho Supreme Court, which was asked to examine the validity of that state's law placing a limit of $150,000 on the compensation available to seriously injured victims of malpractice. The stated purpose of the Idaho law was to assure that malpractice insurance was available to physicians and hospitals at a reasonable price, and thus to assure "the availability of such hospitals and physicians for the provision of care to persons of the state." The court found that there was no factual basis in the record for judging whether the limitation on malpractice recoveries would actually contribute to the stated goal. The court said:

it is argued that by limiting the amount of recovery it was intended to create a more stable basis for prediction of malpractice losses and thereby encourage the entry into Idaho of new insurance carriers at lower, more reasonable and more competitive rates. We are unable to judge the accuracy or completeness of these assertions on the record presented here.

It is argued that the Act is a necessary response to a "crisis" in medical malpractice insurance in Idaho, but the record does not demonstrate any such "crisis." Further, there is no evidentiary basis presented here to either support or refute the relationship between the limitations created by the Act and the abatement of the alleged crisis. Although two insurance carriers are withdrawing from the malpractice field in Idaho, seven remain, one of whom is offering to insure physicians left uninsured by the recent withdrawals.

The court examined the literature identifying the causes of the malpractice crisis on a national level, and noted that increases in malpractice premiums seemed to result, nationally, from four factors: an increase in injuries caused by medical practice; an increase in the number of suits filed; an increase in the amounts recovered; and, finally, difficulties in determining reasonable premium rates. The court also noted that there was no evidence relating Idaho problems to those on the national level, and that Idaho had only .5 percent of the general practitioners, .2 percent of the surgeons, and .8 percent of the hospital beds of the nation. The court said:

The record here presents no factual basis for understanding the nature and scope of the alleged medical malpractice crisis nationally or in Idaho. It is thus impossible for this Court to assess the necessity for this legislation and whether or not the limitations on medical malpractice recovery set forth in the Act bear a fair and substantial relationship to the asserted purpose of the Act.

For these reasons, the Idaho Supreme Court sent the case back to the trial court to give the parties an opportunity to demonstrate a relationship between the limitation on compensation of the seriously injured and the purpose of the act.

The data of the National Association of Insurance Commissioners indicate that the new ceilings on compensation for the seriously injured are not likely to affect malpractice premiums greatly. NAIC statistics show that, in the eight states which have enacted such ceilings, there were only thirty-six cases in which more than $50,000 was paid to an injured patient in 1975–76. In Idaho, where the statutory limit is $150,000, there was no case in which a patient was paid more than $50,000. In the other states, the statutory limit is $500,000 or more, and during the period studied there was only one case, involving an Indiana patient who received $1 million, which would have been affected by the statutory limit. While the statutory limits are not likely to have a significant impact on medical malpractice premiums, they do have a devastating effect on the occasional individual who is seriously injured by negligent medical treatment and can prove large economic loss either because the injury occurred early in life or because the patient's substantial earning power was destroyed.

The attitude of the Idaho court has been sharply criticized by some legal scholars.

Whether the reforms will have the desired effect, is almost impossible to predict. . . . Social legislation developed by representative legislative bodies is seriously frustrated by judicial inquiry into matters of hopeless speculation. It is precisely in situations where no one can truly predict with any degree of certainty that social legislation will or will not accomplish its goal that the legislature must be given deference by the courts in its attempts to achieve social change.

One result of the approach taken by the Idaho court is that it is "likely to embroil this legislation in years of litigation in each of the various states."

This objection certainly has force. The Idaho court recognized the importance of the concept of judicial restraint as it cautions against substituting judicial opinion of expedience for the will of the legislature. Nevertheless, blind adherence and over-indulgence results in abdication of judicial responsibility.

Further, many factors support the kind of scrutiny demanded by the Idaho court. While the right to recover compensation for medical injuries is not "fundamental" in the traditional sense, it is obviously a right of very great importance to the seriously injured. Similarly, although the classification distinguishing between medical injuries and other sorts of injuries is not "suspect" in any traditional sense, it bears some of the characteristics of suspect classifications. In medical malpractice, one very powerful class of people creates and imposes risks on another, relatively powerless class. In many other types of personal-injury case, risks are created and borne by all those participating in the activity on a relatively equal basis, as, for example, the risks involved in use of the highways. As a practical matter, severely injured patients are not an identifiable or organized interest group that can assert its claims in the legislature. Finally, it is fairly clear that if legislative limits on the recovery for serious injuries are constitutional, they will be constitutional whether the limit is $500,000, $150,000 as in Idaho, or less. Since the line demarcating the limit on liability is in its nature arbitrary, legislatures have broad latitude in fixing this limit at one point or another. If the caps are accepted as constitutional and malpractice premiums continue to rise, there will be pressure for lower limits on the amount of recovery.

It is difficult to predict whether courts will find that caps are constitutionally acceptable. As we have indicated, there is much uncertainty in prevailing equal-protection doctrine. Further, state malpractice laws have been challenged in state courts under both state and federal constitutions, and the courts have rested their decisions on both state and federal grounds. It seems likely that this pattern will continue and that each state supreme court will judge the validity of the caps without the national guidance of a decision by the United States Supreme Court.

Some states have considered other forms of limitation on the damages recoverable in medical malpractice actions. One type of proposal would eliminate recovery for "pain and suffering." This type of recovery is particularly infuriating to doctors because the damages are inescapably subjective and not easily quantifiable. The term "pain and suffering" is misleading. This is the rubric under which all noneconomic loss is recoverable. For example, if a person with a sedentary job loses a leg as a result of proven medical negligence, his earning capacity may not be affected by the loss of the leg. But most people would agree that living life without a leg represents a significant loss, even if it is not reflected in earning capacity. This sort of loss is compensated under the heading of "pain and suffering." California has placed a ceiling of $250,000 on the amount recoverable for "non-economic loss" caused by a health-care provider. Ohio has placed a ceiling of $500,000 on the amount a patient may be paid for noneconomic loss.

A third form of limitation on damages in malpractice cases would abolish payment for punitive damages. Punitive damages, as the name implies, are a device for penalizing the wrongdoer. Negligence alone, however gross, does not justify imposing punitive damages. In order to recover punitive damages, the injured person must show that the person causing injury acted intentionally, fraudulently, with malice, or with such a conscious and deliberate disregard of the interests of others that his conduct may be called willful or wanton. The money penalty imposed on the person causing injury is paid to the person injured. North Dakota and Idaho enacted laws prohibiting the payment of punitive damages in medical malpractice cases, though court order has prevented the Idaho law from going into effect.

A final type of limitation on damages deals with the treatment of resources received by the patient from "collateral sources." The traditional common-law rule is that payments from collateral sources cannot be taken into account to reduce the liability of the person sued. For example, if an injured person has health insurance which pays a portion of his or her medical costs, the person causing the injury will nonetheless be required to pay the full costs of damages, including any medical costs already paid by the health insurance. Several reasons support this general principle. If the person who negligently caused injury is allowed to benefit from the fact that the person injured had a collateral source of benefits, the deterrent effect of the law will be reduced. Further, the person injured has often paid for the collateral benefits through premium payments or in other ways. Why should people who have the foresight to insure themselves against injury be penalized relative to those who choose not to buy personal insurance? Opponents charge that the collateral source can produce a "windfall" for the person injured. The person injured recovers twice for the same damage:

once from his or her own personal medical or income-replacement insurance and a second time from the liability insurance of the person who caused the injury.

There is growing sentiment that the individual should not be allowed to recover more than once for the same damage. But even if that principle is accepted, a question arises as to which insurance should be primary and which should be secondary. If the injured individual's private Blue Cross insurance is considered primary, for example, then the damages that the negligent doctor is required to pay will be reduced by the amount paid by Blue Cross. If, on the other hand, the doctor's liability insurance is considered primary, then when negligence is proved, the doctor's insurance company would reimburse Blue Cross for its payment of the patient's medical costs.

Theoretically, there are several criteria which could be used to determine which sources of payment should be primary and which should be secondary. If our purpose is to make the fault system of liability as effective as possible in deterring unnecessary injuries, then doctor's liability insurance should be the primary source of payment for injuries resulting from the fault of another person. Coordination of benefits can be accomplished by requiring that health-insurance and income-replacement policies contain a clause giving these insurers the right to recover for payments they have made if and when liability is established. If, on the other hand, our objective is to spread the costs of medical injuries as widely as possible, then health-insurance benefits, and particularly those financed by the government, should be the primary source of payment, and the doctor's insurance company should be required to pay only those costs not covered by some other form of insurance. Factors of administrative convenience may dictate that one or another form of insurance be primary in some situations.

Theoretical considerations aside, it is soaring malpractice premiums that have commanded immediate political concern in most states. Although premiums for health insurance, both public and private, often rise at rates comparable to rising medical malpractice premiums, the people who bear these costs do not have the political clout of the doctors and hospitals who bear the immediate costs of rising malpractice premiums. Hence, many states have adopted laws making medical malpractice insurance secondary to other collateral sources of compensation for injuries caused by the fault of medical practitioners. Seventeen states have adopted laws which require that damages assessed against a party at fault in a medical malpractice action be reduced by the amounts which the injured person has received from other sources. These laws apply exclusively to medical malpractice actions, and do not extend to other types of personal injury. It is not at all clear why, as a matter of policy, there should be a different rule for medical cases than for other kinds of personal injury cases.

One Ohio lower court has held that the changes in Ohio law relating to collateral sources in medical cases violate equal protection because there is no reason to treat medical cases differently from other types of personal injury. The court said:

There is no satisfactory reason for this separate and unequal treatment. . . . [I]t is not the business of government to manipulate the law so as to provide succor to one class, the medical, by depriving another, the malpracticed patients, of the general protection mandated by the constitution.

It may be doubted that this decision will be followed by other courts, since the injured person is still fully compensated despite changes in treatment of collateral sources. It is the Medicaid and Medicare programs and Blue Cross, Blue Shield, and other private health insurers who are injured by collateral-source rules of the type being adopted. Since their injury is merely financial and somewhat indirect, it is unlikely that they will ultimately succeed in challenging legislative judgment in this area.

According to an American Bar Association study of recently enacted laws, the only change in tort law which is likely to have a measurable impact on premium costs is the repeal of the collateral-source rule. They estimate that in a "typical" state which broadly repealed the collateral-source rule, the reduction in malpractice dollars awarded would be about 20 percent. However, a number of factors limit the potential reductions in malpractice premiums. First, it is uncertain whether courts will uphold the laws modifying the collateral-source rule in medical cases. Second, if juries know about the changes in the collateral-source rule for medical cases, they may adjust their verdicts upward. And, finally, for these and other reasons, insurance companies will not reduce premiums on the basis of changes in the law, but rather will wait until the legal changes are actually translated into reductions in insurance dollars paid.

8

The No-Fault Alternative

Many people, contemplating the intractable causes of the malpractice crisis, advocate a move to a "no-fault" system of compensating patients for injuries arising out of medical treatment. Under no-fault, injured people can recover a specified sum simply by showing that they were injured in a particular way—e.g., by an automobile, at work, during medical treatment. In exchange, common-law rights to sue in court for negligence are limited or abolished. The two facts most often cited in support of no-fault proposals are that, first, most patients who suffer injuries as a result of medical treatment never receive any compensation; and, second, a large portion of the malpractice premium dollar does not reach injured patients. In addition, some no-fault proponents question whether fault-based liability has any positive effect in encouraging more prudent behavior on the part of doctors and hospitals. Others suggest that the fear of liability leads to defensive, unnecessarily costly, and risky medical practice. Some favor no-fault as a means of allowing a more humane and healing relationship between patient and physician by removing the possibility that they will someday be in an adversary relationship. Many no-fault proponents point to the alleged success of no-fault in relation to workplace injuries and automobile accidents.

The no-fault alternative is generally advocated as a concept rather than as detailed legislation or specific insurance policies and contracts to be adopted by patient and physician. Issues which any no-fault system must address include: a definition of what constitutes an event giving rise to a right to compensation; the standards for determining the amounts to be paid to injured patients; the source of funds to pay patients; a mechanism for collecting and retaining the funds for compensating patients; and, finally, a mechanism for resolving disputes over whether a patient is entitled to compensation.

Defining what constitutes a compensable event is enormously difficult. It is fairly easy to determine whether an injury results from use of an automobile. It is somewhat more difficult, but nonetheless manageable, to determine whether an injury or illness arises out of employment. In contrast, it is extremely difficult to decide whether a particular injury results from medical treatment, from the condition that brought the patient to the physician in the first place, or from some other factor. Two methods to determine when a patient is entitled to compensation have been advocated. The first and more general approach would provide no-fault payments whenever the injury "is more probably associated in whole or in part with medical intervention rather than with the condition for which such intervention occurred, and is not consistent with or reasonably to be expected as a consequence of such intervention." In short, patients will be entitled to payment when medical treatment has unexpected results. This standard is enormously difficult to apply. What is "expected" varies not only with diagnosis but also with the condition of a particular patient—whether the patient is old or young, in generally good health or in poor health. It is likely that there would be as much room for dispute under a no-fault program promising payment on the basis of such an uncertain standard as there is under the present fault-based system. The nature of the disputes would be different, and perhaps less acrimonious. However, the range of potential disputes in a system promising payment whenever an "unexpected" injury results from medical intervention would be much larger than under the present system, in which the patient must make a plausible claim that the doctor was at fault.

Because of this serious problem, other no-fault proponents advocate a more limited program that would provide compensation only for a narrowly specified list of adverse consequences resulting from particular medical treatments. These proposals attempt to identify outcomes which are both readily recognizable and usually avoidable if good medical care is provided. No-fault benefits would be provided for these specific adverse outcomes. The fault-based system of liability, and hence the need for medical malpractice insurance, would be preserved for adverse outcomes not included on the lists. For example, a proposed list of events which would give rise to a right to no-fault benefits following general surgery includes: foreign bodies left in the patient; burns acquired during the operation; injury resulting from severance of an indwelling plastic catheter; neurological deficit resulting from intramuscular injection; injury resulting from mistaken identity: injury resulting from inadvertent intravascular injection of local anesthetic; post-operative wound dehiscence in a noncancerous patient under forty-five; tetanus infection after wound treatment; severe reaction to tetanus antitoxin. Payment would be provided when death or central-nervous-system injury followed a very simple surgical procedure such as an abortion or a tonsillectomy. This approach avoids the major administrative problems inherent in vague general standards for determining whether an injury was "caused" by medical treatment or by some other factor.

The difficulty with this more specific approach to no-fault liability is that it does not apply to many of the cases which now produce malpractice litigation. It does not include compensation in situations where the injury is sometimes but not always unavoidable. For example, the proposal would not include compensation for death or irreversible injury to the central nervous system occurring during an appendectomy or obstetrical procedure. It would not include compensation for the paralysis suffered by patients from laminectomies performed by Dr. Nork. Physicians would still be liable for negligently inflicted injuries not included on the list, so doctors and patients would have to continue to pay for fault-based liability insurance as well as for the new no-fault benefits. Disputes as to the nature and extent of injuries caused by medical practice would remain. Further, there would inevitably be disputes as to whether a particular injury fell within the specified scope of the no-fault liability agreement. As in the present workers'-compensation system, there would be some cases in which the injured person attempted to obtain no-fault benefits by showing that a particular injury was within the scope of the coverage, and other cases in which the injured individual would attempt to show that the injury was not covered so that the potentially larger damages available at common law could be sought.

In short, there is little reason to believe that either of the major models of no-fault compensation would reduce the number of cases subject to dispute. Indeed, the number of such cases might actually increase, since the universe of cases in which a possible claim to benefits might be made would increase. The issues subject to dispute—the extent of injury and whether an injury was caused by medical treatment—are difficult simply because physiological processes are inherently complex. It seems likely that the parties would want to be represented by attorneys, particularly in contested cases. The experience in workers' compensation cases confirms this. In 1974, injured claimants in New York State secured legal representation in more than 18,000 cases. Yet there were fewer than 13,000 cases where the insurance carrier contested its own liability. In other words, nearly every claimant with a contested claim had a lawyer, and many with uncontested claims also chose to have an attorney.

The overwhelming likelihood is that no-fault medical insurance would be astronomically more expensive than malpractice liability insurance. The primary reason for this is that a larger number of people would be entitled to compensation. Proponents of no-fault medical insurance, like the proponents of no-fault auto insurance, argue that even though a larger number of people would be entitled to compensation, costs could be kept manageable because no-fault offers opportunities for savings in administrative costs, and elimination of duplicate payments and damages for noneconomic loss. As we shall show, these potential savings are ephemeral.

There are two ways in which it is claimed administrative costs might be saved by a move to no-fault insurance. First, there might be less need for costs associated with dispute-resolution. But, as we have seen, the likelihood is that a comprehensive medical no-fault plan would produce at least as many cases subject to dispute, and that the disputes would be as complex as those which now arise under fault-based liability. A narrowly specific no-fault plan avoids these problems, but fault-based liability insurance would then continue to be necessary. Second, there might be potential for savings in the way in which insurance premiums are set and collected, reserves established, and insurance companies administered. However, experience with workers'-compensation and automobile no-fault does not support a belief that a move to no-fault insurance reduces administrative expenses, reserves, or profits. Additionally, our analysis of the malpractice insurance industry will show that the industry tends to increase reserves when the potential liability for insured risks is uncertain. The uncertainty factor in moving to a no-fault system would be very high at least for many years, and industry reserves would most likely show a corresponding increase.

It is possible to reduce costs to some degree by eliminating duplicate payments for injuries resulting from medical services and requiring that malpractice judgments or medical no-fault payments be secondary to other sources of compensation such as Social Security or Blue Cross. But, as we have shown, state legislatures are already moving to eliminate duplicate payments by requiring coordination of insurance benefits. It is not necessary to adopt no-fault in order to eliminate duplicate payments. The limited savings which may be realized in this way are already being taken in many states.

Similarly, the amounts paid to people suffering injury as a result of medical treatment could be reduced by eliminating damages for all non-economic loss—pain, suffering, disfigurement, disability. But, as we have noted, damages for these non-economic losses often serve a very important function, and whether it is sound policy to eliminate them is questionable. Even if it is determined that such damages should be limited or eliminated, it is not necessary to adopt a no-fault program in order to do so. Some states have already imposed limits on the amount of non-economic damages which may be recovered by people injured through negligent medical treatment.

Another way in which a no-fault program might realize savings is to reduce the compensation for economic losses. Existing no-fault programs provide less than full replacement for lost salaries. For example, the National Commission on State Workmen's Compensation Laws found that, in 1972, the maximum workers' compensation payment for a family of four was less than 60 percent of the average wage in thirty-two states. In half the states, the maximum weekly benefit did not equal the federal poverty line. Fourteen states limit total *lifetime* benefits to $35,000 or less. Automobile no-fault programs also place limits on the amount of economic loss recoverable, though the limits are generally higher than those in the workers' compensation programs.

In sum, it is likely that a no-fault program for the compensation of injuries resulting from medical treatment would be much more costly than present fault-based liability insurance. The only way in which a no-fault program might produce significant cost savings is by prohibiting injured patients from bringing common-law actions for negligence and providing a no-fault "benefit" which does not compensate most people for their actual economic loss.

Even assuming that a no-fault system of payment for injuries resulting from medical treatment would be much more expensive than the present malpractice liability insurance, there may be sound reasons to adopt such a system. For example, some people support no-fault simply because most people who are injured as a result of medical care receive no compensation in a fault-based system. Although this is undoubtably true, it is difficult to know why people injured in the course of medical treatment should have any greater right to compensation than people injured by the actions of people other than doctors or, for that matter, by natural disasters, disabling diseases, or malnutrition. All these people suffer grievous disability through no fault of their own. All could be helped by a program guaranteeing income and necessary medical and rehabilitative services. But it seems more sensible to address these problems through national health-insurance and income-maintenance programs than to create a separate benefit program for people injured in the course of medical treatment. Much of the current concern about reform in relation to national health insurance and welfare is directed to the need to place financing for these programs on a more progressive basis. A no-fault program for people injured in medical treatment would probably be administered through private insurance companies, and hence would almost necessarily be financed through premiums raised on a regressive basis. (A tax system can be progressive because the government can force people who have more money to pay more. An insurance company cannot, as a practical matter, charge higher rates to richer people and lower rates to those who cannot afford to pay.) However sympathetic we may be to the plight of people injured in the course of medical treatment, it is difficult to imagine any reason of principle or practicality that would justify setting up a special income-maintenance or health-insurance program for this particular category of needy people.

Another justification sometimes offered in support of a more costly no-fault program is the desire to conform to the classic economic model and have the prices of particular activities accurately reflect the costs which the activity generates. For example, the rallying cry in support of workers' compensation was that the cost of the product should bear the blood of the worker. Similarly, in relationship to automobiles, if motoring produces a certain amount of human injury, then perhaps everyone who owns a car should share in the costs of those injuries and be forced to consider those costs in deciding whether to buy a car. Economists call this goal the "internalization" of costs to the activity which generates them.

Does the objective of internalizing costs make sense in relationship to medical treatment? The argument would be that if medical treatment produces a certain amount of human injury, the medical-care prices should include the cost of those injuries which treatment generates. Then when people decide whether or not to obtain medical care, the price of the medical service would reflect the costs of treatment, including the injuries which treatment causes. This sort of thinking is absolute nonsense in relationship to medical services. As we have seen, the market for medical services shares few of the characteristics of the classic economic model. Further, the problem of distinguishing between those adverse outcomes which are the result of treatment and those which are the result of other factors is relevant here, since the costs to be internalized are only those generated by the activity—treatment—and not the total costs arising from human illness and injury.

One final issue must be addressed in evaluating no-fault proposals for medical injuries, and that is the question of deterrence. A primary purpose of the fault-based system of liability is to encourage doctors to take due care, and to penalize those who cause injury to patients through negligent practice. As we have seen, the fault-based system of liability has played an important role in exposing the failure of hospitals and professional review mechanisms to identify and deal with habitually incompetent or fraudulent physicians. Fault-based liability discourages some doctors from practicing beyond their capabilities. Liability-insurance costs have had some limited effect in encouraging doctors to practice in less risky specialties and less overdoctored areas of the country. On the negative side, fault-based liability produces some unnecessary and costly testing and hospitalization, though this could be avoided if doctors were willing to tell patients when tests are of marginal utility.

For all the very real problems in fault-based liability for medical negligence, this is often the only practical means available to patients for exposing, punishing, and deterring substandard medical practice. For this reason, it may well be dangerous to patients, and to the conscientious majority of the medical profession, to abandon fault-based liability. Proponents of medical no-fault have two answers to these fears. First, they suggest that voluntary expansion of professional peer review might offset the need for fault-based liability. Given the abysmal history of professional self-policing, which has generally improved only in response to pressures generated by increases in fault-based liability or by an aroused public outside the profession, this hope is naïve. Second, they rely on the general theory of internalization which suggests that if an enterprise is forced to bear all the costs of the injuries it generates, people who engage in that activity will be motivated to exercise appropriate levels of care. Given the peculiarities of the market for medical care, the decentralized nature of the "enterprise," and the difficulty in determining what injuries are generated by the activity of physicians, it is very difficult to apply this theoretical answer in the real world.

Certainly a major argument in support of automobile no-fault proposals was the observation that the fear of fault-based liability had had little effect in encouraging people to drive more carefully. If people were not motivated to drive carefully by their own instinct for self-preservation, it was difficult to imagine that the fear of liability would encourage better driving. Driving is, in this regard, very different from medical treatment. The doctor who practices substandard medicine creates enormous risks to the patient, but no particular risks to himself apart from the fear of liability. When people are in a situation in which all those who participate in an activity reciprocally generate *and* run risks of injury, it may be more appropriate to distribute costs on a no-fault basis or to let risks lie where they fall. But when one class of people—in this case, doctors—generates risks and another class bears them, there is a much greater need for mechanisms to encourage greater caution, and to shift the economic costs of loss when due care has not been exercised.

In relationship to workplace accidents, the workers' compensation system largely eliminated the role of the courts in defining the care which an employer must exercise to protect the workers' health and safety. The overwhelming evidence is that the no-fault workers' compensation system has not provided appropriate incentives to employers to exercise reasonable care in protecting workers' health and safety. In 1970, in response to this situation, Congress enacted the Occupational Safety and Health Act, which establishes federal standards and enforcement mechanisms for workplace safety.

In sum, there is little reason to support a no-fault system for compensating injuries arising from medical treatment. Such a system is likely to be far more expensive than the present malpractice liability insurance. Although more people might be compensated, it is difficult to imagine any reason of practicality or principle for assuring compensation for people who are injured in the course of medical treatment, as opposed to those who are injured in other ways. A no-fault system would eliminate even the limited role which the law now plays in encouraging the exercise of reasonable care in the provision of medical treatment, and would deprive patients of the only mechanism now available to them to trigger scrutiny of substandard medical practice.

PART III

THE INSURANCE SYSTEM

9

Malpractice Insurance:
The Blood-Money Industry

In December 1976, a committee of the National Association of Insurance Commissioners met to consider data its staff had compiled showing the profitability of each line of insurance in each state. The report disclosed the explosive information that malpractice insurance, in the year of the industry's "crisis," was, on the whole, a *profitable* line for the industry. While the operating profit (which measures income from premiums and investments against losses, expenses, and taxes) for all lines of insurance had been 1 percent in 1975, for malpractice insurance it had been 9 percent. The data disclosed that in only five states—California, New Hampshire, North Dakota, Oklahoma, and South Carolina—did the industry suffer losses.

Most of the state commissioners who make up the association had previously accepted the industry's position that malpractice was a losing proposition and had, accordingly, approved substantial rate increases for both 1975 and 1976. Hence, disclosure of this information could prove a source of great embarrassment. It was argued by many of the state regulators that the profitability data were misleading because they did not consider the impact of increases in industry reserves for unreported claims, or the money set aside in expectation of claims being filed.

The committee voted not to release the report, though many state departments were then considering 1977 premium requests. In June 1977, the NAIC again considered the profitability data, and decided to release the data accompanied by a caveat concerning possible inaccuracies. Though the caveats have been released, the long-suppressed data have yet to be officially disclosed.

The NAIC has disclosed profitability data for the 1976 policy year. Malpractice insurance profits, without considering reserves for unreported claims, had risen to 20.1 percent, as contrasted to industry-wide profits on all lines of 4.3 percent. For the first time, the NAIC also prepared a profitability analysis taking into account the industry-established reserves. As we shall explore in some detail later in this chapter, reserving practices, particularly for unreported claims, are highly speculative and easily susceptible to manipulation. By this report, malpractice profits in 1976 were 1.1 percent, as compared to an industry-wide figure of 2.4 percent.

While NAIC was attempting to suppress the 1975 profitability data, *Medical Economics* reported that the American Medical Association had misled the public about the increasing burden of physicians' malpractice premiums. The AMA had estimated that the average doctor's premium in 1975 had risen to $7,887 and had publicized this figure. It arrived at the sum by taking a 1973 survey figure and projecting it to 1975 on the basis of the highest recent premium hikes of six insurers. *Medical Economics* surveyed 6,600 physicians in private practice and found that half had paid no more than $3,000. Despite the publicity about malpractice premiums of $25,000 and up, only one doctor in seventy had paid that much for 1976 coverage. The *Medical Economics* report concluded that

although the median cost of malpractice insurance has gone up 58% in a single year, for most private practitioners it still represents no more than 3% of gross receipts and 9% of total professional income. For a majority of M.D.'s, then, malpractice premium boosts alone can't be used to justify the 13% average rise in fees in 1974 and the further hike of 12% [in 1975].

Still, it can be legitimately argued that physicians may be paying excessive amounts for malpractice insurance. The NAIC study of all claims resolved over a twelve-month period in 1975–76 reports that the average loss per physician on a national basis was $668. The averages range from a low of $36 in Maine to $1,503 in Arizona. Obviously, insurance companies have significant expenses aside from these loss payments; further, insurance premiums are normally established to cover losses from incidents *occurring* within the year which the policy is written rather than for losses paid in that year. Nevertheless, these national averages are surprisingly low, and they will certainly be useful in evaluating the industry's premium demands.

The essence of these reports is that the malpractice insurance industry, even before it pushed through many huge rate increases, was doing quite well for itself without unduly burdening the economic health of the great majority of American physicians. If this were so, one must ask why an insurance "crisis" happened, a crisis which was used to force further substantial rate increases and to justify restrictions on patients' rights to recover for medical injuries. This question, which has never been satisfactorily resolved, is the major focus of this chapter. A second and related question is whether state insurance departments, which are primarily responsible for the regulation of insurance, are capable of evaluating the insurance-industry position properly, and of coping with the pressure generated by the industry's requests for rate hikes under the threat of withdrawal. In Chapter 10, we will examine recent insurance reforms meant to alleviate the problem of unavailability of malpractice insurance.

Answering the first question, why the malpractice crisis happened, has been difficult mainly because data on the actual industry experience have been so sparse. To evaluate the industry's position, one must begin, at the minimum, with some reliable data on premiums, losses, and investment income. Some information that would be useful is in fact unknowable. Malpractice insurance is peculiar and difficult because claims for any recent policy year are not yet fully reported and settled. This factor, coupled with changing claims trends that make past experience an unreliable gauge for predicting the future, means that neither the industry nor the investigator has an accurate measure of a most essential figure—the actual losses for recent policy years.

Still, much that *is* knowable is not being reported to the regulators or the public. Unfortunately, in the area of data collection, most state regulators have pursued a policy of benign neglect, and the industry has not voluntarily pooled data in any intelligible manner. As a result, there is an almost total lack of hard, deep, and reliable data in the two critical areas of concern for policy-makers: the actual claims experience of the companies, and the profits and losses sustained in this line of insurance. The resulting uncertainty in defining the scope of the malpractice problem was itself a problem of crisis proportions for those who were called upon to respond to the pressures generated from the industry and physicians in 1975.

Malpractice data have been collected from insurance carriers in two ways. Companies must report premiums, losses, surpluses, reserves, and investment income to state regulators in a form prescribed by the National Association of Insurance Commissioners. But because malpractice is a relatively minor line of coverage, the data have traditionally been lumped together with other lines of liability insurance. With no separation, an outsider cannot judge the industry's actual loss experience and profitability in this individual line. Only in 1975 did the NAIC begin to require that malpractice premiums and losses be stated separately.

The only central agency for the collection of specific claims data is the Insurance Services Office, a rating bureau and advisory organization owned and operated by the insurance companies. Participation in ISO is voluntary; the HEW Malpractice Commission found that many major malpractice insurers did not report, or reported only partial data, to the ISO. This problem is further compounded by the fact that the accuracy of the data ISO collects and disseminates is almost universally discredited. Inaccuracies in ISO data were first noted in the HEW report, and they have continued to the present time. A 1975 malpractice rate-making decision of the New York Insurance Department said, "ISO's loss and premium statistics contain gross errors, are incomplete and therefore lack credibility."

In many instances in which the industry has been asked to supplement the information contained in the state and industry reports, it has been less than cooperative. For example, the HEW Secretary's Committee reported that some companies had refused its requests for data. Later, in 1975, the Argonaut Company pulled out of the New York and New Jersey markets rather than submit to the scrutiny of those states' insurance departments.

Since late 1975, the National Association of Insurance Commissioners and the industry have participated in a survey of closed malpractice claims which is providing valuable information hitherto unavailable. In addition, much new information unavailable to state regulators at the time of the crisis has been pried loose from the industry in subsequent applications for premium increases.

To understand the crisis of malpractice insurance availability, we begin with a picture of the industry as it approached the mid-1970's. There had been a steady decline in the number of companies writing a substantial amount of malpractice insurance, dropping from fifty in 1965 to twelve in 1975. The companies and physicians were increasingly interested in doing business only through group plans, usually sponsored by a state or local medical society. In 1973, the HEW Commission reported that "in contrast to the individual market, where many carriers have left the market or are passively seeking new business, a number of carriers indicated that they are actively seeking group business."

The pattern in Connecticut was typical. Prior to 1971, eight companies competed for the state's medical market. Then when the state medical society established a group plan with Aetna Life and Casualty, the remaining carriers were effectively driven from the state. Aetna was in turn shut out of other markets. Thus, it pulled out of New Jersey when the Federal Insurance Company signed a group contract with that state's medical society.

The decline of the individual market and the growth of the group market made perfect economic sense from the industry's perspective, and also appealed to most physicians. This common self-interest caused individual companies to carve out states and parts of states, and to write policies on a virtual monopoly basis in a particular territory. For the companies, the group plans meant the guarantee of a high premium volume which would justify the considerable investment in establishing the particular expertise necessary to underwrite malpractice successfully in a state or local area. In addition, the HEW Commission suggested that the relationship established through the group plans could be quite advantageous for the companies in selling substantial amounts of other forms of insurance to group members. For the physician, the group plans were heralded as an end to the problem of escalating premiums and insurance availability.

The individual market, on the other hand, was not attractive to insurers. Because the bulk of the market was covered through the group plans, selective underwriting of the limited individual market was not worth the company's time or investment. The HEW Commission reported that the companies did little to encourage this type of business. Insurer participation was further diminished by inflexible underwriting policies. Although group plans would sometimes quote a higher than normal rate for the high-risk practitioner—that is, one who had a history of nondefensible claims—the individual market would provide coverage only at a standard rate and only for good risks. Physicians who were denied coverage through the individual and group markets would normally turn to the unregulated "surplus" lines, or to Lloyd's of London.

The emergence of group plans as the dominant form of malpractice insurance coverage for both individual practitioners and institutions has several significant ramifications. First, it gives the group which sponsors the plan an important advantage in terms of recruiting of members and exercising influence over its members. A physician would hesitate to contravene society policies when it might result in his being forced to obtain insurance in the undependable individual market. New Jersey, recognizing this problem, now requires the state medical society's plan to cover any physician desiring coverage, regardless of membership.

Second, the monopoly position enjoyed by a particular insurance company put physicians at the mercy of the insurer. At the end of 1974, one of eleven insurance companies (Employers Insurance of Wausau, Travelers, St. Paul, Hartford, Aetna Casualty and Surety, Argonaut, Medical Protective, Chubb, CNA, INA, and Shelby Mutual) held a virtual monopoly position in forty-seven states. In each of these states, the insurer was in a strong position to demand and get a rate increase of virtually any size. In effect, the territorial monopolies, created through the joint efforts of the industry and medical societies, set the stage for the crisis which was to come. With the general property-liability insurance industry reeling from the combined weight of severe underwriting losses and the stock-market downturn of 1973–74, the point was reached at which each company knew that no other company would undercut it, no matter what its demands. The constraining influence of potential competition was no longer present.

Two company actions early in 1974 gave a fair indication of the impending "crisis." The St. Paul Fire and Marine Insurance Company demanded an 82 percent increase in premium rates for North Carolina physicians. The Insurance Commissioner found that the premium hike was clearly excessive and that 5 percent was appropriate; but he was forced to allow the higher amount because St. Paul threatened not to renew its policies unless the increase was granted. No other company offered to take St. Paul's business. In the middle of the same year, Employers of Wausau withdrew its twenty-five-year-old coverage of the New York State Medical Society plan. After some initial difficulty in finding a replacement carrier, the society had no choice but to accept the Argonaut Insurance Company's offer to replace Employers at a 93.5 percent increase in rates.

The vulnerability of the group plans to the industry's demands was now evident. Later in the year, Argonaut, for reasons that will be explored, decided on a policy of selective market withdrawals and premium hikes. With no other company or companies ready to fill the market voids left by Argonaut's hasty actions, an insurance availability crisis began. In other states, the individual companies servicing the group-plan monopolies perceived a combination of both the opportunity and the need to increase premiums, and acted to do so. These are the rough outlines of the progress of the crisis.

Malpractice insurance is but a minute part of the general property-liability insurance industry, as distinct from life and health insurance. The fortunes of the property-liability business as a whole dropped precipitously in the period 1972–75. These general industry conditions go far toward explaining why the threat of competition for the group-plan market vanished, leaving the insured physicians and hospitals so vulnerable. The industry's underwriting profits, which represent the difference between premiums paid in and claimed losses, were over $1 billion in 1972. They became zero in 1973, dropped to a $2.6 billion loss in 1974, and bottomed at a record deficit of $4.4 billion in 1975. Underwriting losses in lesser amounts have not been uncommon or unexpected over the past twenty years; losses and gains have tended to come and go in a cyclical pattern. In periods of adverse underwriting results, the industry has normally been able to accept and absorb losses because they have been more than offset by investment gains. Two former insurance commissioners, Richard Stewart from New York and Richard Roddis from California, who were the first to explain the malpractice crisis as an outgrowth of this broad industry picture, explained the logic behind this pattern as follows:

The technique of insurance rate-making (with its emphasis on past experience as the chief basis for predicting costs), coupled with competitive euphoria and regulatory lag, causes inflation to have deadly results on underwriting results. But in the past that same inflation tended to be accompanied by increases in the value of equity securities in which property-casualty insurers invested larger and larger proportions of their portfolios.

Insurance-company executives recognized the threat to this predictable pattern by the emerging economic developments of the early and mid-1970's. The inflation which was mainly responsible for the adverse underwriting results did not increase the value of the insurance companies' stock holdings, which normally account for about one third of their total investments. Instead, the value of the stock holdings declined, and every company suffered losses in the listed market value of its stocks. Companies which sold securities when the market was depressed took substantial actual losses.

The California Auditor General examined the investment experience of that state's malpractice insurers and confirmed the extent of the losses. In 1974, unrealized losses from investments in common and preferred stocks reduced the surplus, which represents the money held by the company to make up for any underwriting loss, by approximately $109 million, or 43 percent of total surplus. For the companies which dominated the malpractice market nationally in 1974, the Best Co. reports that every one except Medical Protective suffered a significant loss in the book value of its investments.

Unrealized losses are anxiety-provoking, yet a company could still hope that the stock market would recover. When the depressed stock is actually sold and the loss is realized, it is panic-inducing. The two companies which were mainly responsible for triggering the malpractice availability crisis not only sustained unrealized losses during 1974, but chose to bail out of the market and sustain actual losses. Argonaut unloaded all the common stock it held in non-affiliated companies, losing $21.4 million. St. Paul lost $28.5 million on the sale of its investments.

Roddis and Stewart write that "the effect of these events on the psychology of insurer managements cannot be overestimated." That psychology is molded by one of the basic laws of business. The level of risk that the company can assume, as expressed by its premium volume, bears a direct correlation with the company's surplus. In the language of the industry, this is called the premium-to-surplus ratio. The relationship is critical because when premiums are insufficient to cover all losses arising from claims, the claims must be paid out of surplus. In a bullish market, it makes good sense to expand underwriting commitments of even a riskier variety, sustain some surplus drain from the underwriting loss, and watch the surplus actually swell from the increase in the value of investment income. When surplus drain from underwriting loss is accompanied by a falling market, it gives insurers cause for particular concern. They must take a long and hard look at those underwriting lines which pose uncertain underwriting risks. The *Wall Street Journal* noted this development in October 1974 when it reported that availability problems were beginning to occur in malpractice, as well as products-liability and auto insurance for minority groups.

The malpractice line was subject to special scrutiny for a number of related reasons. First, insurers went into this line for its investment potential, and not with any expectation of significant underwriting profits. The particular characteristics of the malpractice-claim settlement process—specifically, the extended length of time a company could hold and invest premium income—encouraged companies to underwrite malpractice on the assumption that investment income would far outdistance any possible underwriting deficit. As an industry executive told a Senate subcommittee in 1975, "If it were not for investment income, many companies would have discontinued writing malpractice years ago." In 1974, the investment opportunities for use of this premium income looked far less attractive.

When investment gains no longer justified writing malpractice insurance, the actual claims experience took on greater importance. Both the frequency and amount of claims were increasing, though the marvels of the industry's record-keeping give us no precise measure of these increases. Added to these already recognizable problems was the HEW report of a year earlier, which indicated that only a small fraction of potential malpractice incidents were resulting in claims. Malpractice policies are written on an "occurrence" basis, which means that the insured is covered for all claims arising from incidents in the policy year, no matter when the claims are reported. The companies feared that premium rates set to cover the expected occurrences of a past year would be inadequate in light of these more recently recognized claim trends and claim possibilities.

Most companies, reflecting on these rather discouraging events, set premium rates for existing business to cover the worst possible loss contingencies and did not seek new business. For other companies, more drastic actions were needed. The risk of insolvency for the smaller companies was real: in 1975, the California Commissioner declared two malpractice insurers insolvent. The Auditor General was later to report that the lure of investment income, which had never materialized, had caused these companies to compete at rates which could not sustain future claims.

The implication of this analysis thus far is that the timing and abrupt-ness of the malpractice crisis were generated more out of the economic insecurity of the industry as a whole rather than by factors strictly related to malpractice. The original economic rationale for going into this line of business had disappeared: relying on investment gain to offset investment loss was no longer an operable assumption. The com-panies perceived a threat to their life-blood, the steady accumulation of unrestricted capital. To the extent that they could act to alleviate any threat of further capital erosion by cutting back less important lines which posed uncertain risks, they did.

It is also important to note at this point whom the companies chose to bear the burden of their investment losses. Company stockholders, who normally derive the greatest benefit when investment results are favorable, might have been called upon to shoulder some of the risk of underwriting loss. This could be done either by cutting back on dividends or by raising more capital through the sale of more shares. Argonaut, St. Paul, Hartford, Medical Protective, and Chubb all suf-fered underwriting losses in 1974 on their total business. All five compa-nies also saw the market value of their investments take a severe drop. Yet all managed to pay dividends to their stockholders. For Argonaut, it was the first dividend declared since 1968. The payment of dividends produced a further direct drain on surplus. The decline in surplus was used to justify policies whose main effect was to burden doctors and, ultimately, their patients, even though they, unlike the stockhold-ers, would not normally share in the benefits of any investment gains. These dividend payments also reflect the important fact that, despite the market downturn and the underwriting losses, these companies were making money. Although the value of the companies' stock port-folios declined, their investments were still providing sufficient income to offset the underwriting loss of the majority of the dominant companies.

This account of the reasons for the malpractice crisis based on the industry's rational response to a deteriorating investment market ex-plains much, but not enough. It is unsatisfactory in a number of re-spects. It does not mesh well with the state-by-state profitability picture presented by the NAIC report. It does not explain why most companies did not take any drastic action until after Argonaut had begun to an-nounce huge premium increases and market withdrawals. It does not consider why companies sought premium increases of 100 percent rather than 50 percent, or 400 percent. It does not explain why observers in many states perceived the carriers' drastic actions as totally unrelated to the malpractice experience of that particular state. In short, the analysis does not explain how what might have started as a rational and logical response became an industry-wide panic.

In analyzing the surveys of the malpractice crisis in individual states, one is struck by a common factor. With the possible exceptions of New York and California, insurance companies were making decisions and forcing state political responses on the basis of events and perceptions which seem to have had little to do with the reality of the local malpractice situation. The chairman of the Health Committee of the Wisconsin House of Representatives, commenting on the rate hikes of St. Paul, Shelby Mutual, and Continental Insurance Co. for his state, said:

In none of these cases was there any indication that the insurance company decision was based on Wisconsin information or experience. As a matter of fact, the responses indicated that these changes reflected national policy. Again, it appeared that Wisconsin was being affected by a national crisis which was totally unrelated to its own malpractice experience.

In Idaho, the Argonaut-affiliated company, Argonaut Northwest, informed the state's Director of Insurance that the company would drop its malpractice policies because it had been suffering adverse experience in that line in the larger states, though not in Idaho. The director of the Massachusetts Special Malpractice Commission put it quite bluntly: "We were the victim of someone else's experience."

On the basis of what experience, if not that of the actual profitability of the policies of the individual state markets, did the industry manage to scare itself into a national panic? The evidence points to the actions of a single company, Argonaut, which responded decisively to what it claimed was adverse loss experience in several of its state markets. Other carriers were quick to follow Argonaut's lead, either withdrawing, or utilizing rate-making mechanisms that could be easily manipulated to satisfy the company's particular level of panic.

Argonaut began operations in 1957 as a workers' compensation insurer, and expanded into the hospital-liability field for those hospitals which purchased its compensation insurance. In 1969 Teledyne, Inc., a rapidly expanding conglomerate oriented to defense technology, acquired Argonaut. It was the parent company's first acquisition in the insurance field. After the corporate shift, Argonaut greatly expanded its participation in the medical professional-liability market. Between 1971 and 1974, Argonaut took over the plans sponsored by medical societies in eight states, including the major markets of New York, Massachusetts, Flordia, Pennsylvania, and Northern California. In a market generally devoid of competition, Argonaut competed where it had to. In California, Florida, and Nevada, the company offered lower premium rates than were charged by the previous insurers. Argonaut also extended its hospital coverage to encompass twenty-nine state-hospital-association plans. By 1974, the company held an unusually high 36 percent of its business in the "liability other than auto" category.

The Argonaut-Teledyne management adopted the traditional wisdom that investment gain would be sufficient to overcome underwriting losses that its predecessor insurance companies claimed to be sustaining. Judging by Argonaut's rapid and unprecedented expansion, one might assume that the company thought it had a winner. Bruce Woolery, Argonaut's former president, was later to testify that management relied upon the tax benefits flowing from the conglomerate structure to make the malpractice expansion a lucrative venture. According to Woolery, "The plan was that we may have an underwriting loss from time to time, but a modest loss that would be permissible in the long run because we were consolidated with Teledyne insofar as our tax credits were concerned." This consolidated tax return meant that the profit-making parent, Teledyne, could take tax credits for Argonaut's underwriting losses, credits that would be unavailable to the insurance company if it were filing a separate return. The income generated by the tax credits would be returned to Argonaut to be invested on a long-term basis to overcome the contemplated underwriting deficit.

In a 1975 suit between the Florida Medical Association and Argonaut, Woolery testified that the company had estimated that its first-year loss, in 1973, would be 10 percent more than its earned premium. Referring to the corporate income-tax rate of 48 percent, Woolery said that "we should in effect get 48% of the 10% back in tax credits from Teledyne." Argonaut would "invest the money in tax exempt bonds having a dividend yield of 7.5% or higher." Because the payout of loss dollars was figured to stretch out over at least twelve years, "if we had a 10% loss over a period of a dozen years, [we] would end up with an after tax profit of 30%. And that was the basis under which we went into the medical malpractice field."

By 1974, Argonaut's claimed underwriting losses were significant. After a net profit of $18.3 million in 1973, the company experienced an underwriting loss of $104 million in 1974, which the company attributed mainly to its malpractice line. Because the reporting of malpractice data was submerged in the catch-all "liability other than auto" subline, there is literally no way of telling exactly how much of this projected loss actually came from malpractice. Investment income of $12 million was insufficient to make up for the underwriting disaster.

Projections of these dismal figures were reported to the Teledyne corporate hierarchy well before the year's end. The conglomerate's income for 1974 would be less than half of 1973 earnings, down to $31.1 million from $65.4 million. Teledyne's management placed the blame squarely on Argonaut. Its first move, in September 1974, was to withdraw the tax credits upon which Argonaut had relied to make its business profitable. Woolery testified that that tax credit would have added at least $21 million to Argonaut's surplus. That cut, according to Argonaut's former president, "curtailed our ability to write business. And had we known that was going to happen, the management of Argonaut would not have gone into malpractice to the extent we did."

When the Argonaut managers expressed their displeasure with Teledyne's actions, they were fired. Nine of the insurer's principal officers left the company in the last three months of 1974. At year's end, Teledyne reached again to drain its subsidiary's surplus: Argonaut declared a $10.5 million dividend, payable to its sole stockholder, Teledyne. The California Insurance Department's subsequent financial examination of Argonaut also showed that by investing in low-yield, tax-exempt Treasury notes in 1974 and 1975, Argonaut had sacrificed its own income to produce tax benefits for Teledyne.

Teledyne's bleeding of Argonaut stands in sharp contrast to the policies adopted at the same time by other insurance holding companies toward their corporate underlings selling malpractice insurance. In late 1974, the *Wall Street Journal* reported that the St. Paul Co. had transferred "cash and other assets" to the St. Paul Fire and Marine Insurance Company in support of its eroding surplus and capital. In January 1975, it reported that Aetna Life and Casualty had pumped $50 million into Aetna Casualty and Surety. Apparently, these companies were willing to weather the short-term difficulties in the expectation that the market would improve. Teledyne was not willing to take this chance; it chose to take what it could get from Argonaut.

Similarly, the new Argonaut corporate officers initially attempted to take what they could from the physicians and hospitals they were insuring. In December 1974, Argonaut announced a 197 percent increase for policy-holders in the New York State Medical Society plan. This rate hike was on top of the 93.5 percent increase made only six months earlier, when its old management first entered the New York market. It announced to 4,000 Northern California physicians, that it was canceling its group coverage, but would write individual coverage at premium rates that increased the former rates by as much as 380 percent. Significantly, these first-announced Argonaut major price increases were in two states that do not require approval of rates by the state insurance department before they go into effect. Argonaut knew that the industry's general condition made it most unlikely that anyone else would offer a lower rate than it was demanding. The company had mapped its tactical strategy. The crisis had begun.

Argonaut's New York plan fell through almost immediately when the state's insurance superintendent invoked a never-before-utilized provision of the State Insurance Code which allowed him to suspend the increase. He called a public hearing for January 9, 1975, at which time Argonaut could justify the premium hike. When confronted with the possibility that its actuarial projections would be subject to the scrutiny of one of the country's more capable departments, the company opted to leave the state instead. It would continue coverage at current rates for the duration of its remaining six-month contractual commitment, then depart.

Argonaut also attempted to force rate increases in other states under the threat of withdrawal. In Pennsylvania, the Insurance Commissioner granted a 206 percent rate increase with the proviso that the company stay in the state for four more years. In Florida, where the medical association was still debating whether to accept the old Argonaut management's demand for a 75 percent increase, the new management upped it to 96 percent. Challenged in a lawsuit by the Florida Medical Association, Argonaut was forced to stay until year's end, collecting the lower rate. By midwinter, convinced that it could not get the rates it demanded in every state, Argonaut announced that it would pull out of the professional-liability market entirely. The company would stay in the hospital-liability market, although it would cut back its commitments by 75 percent. Notices of cancelation and/or nonrenewal were issued for all hospitals in fourteen states; in fourteen others, it requested rate increases ranging from 300 to 545 percent.

Before discussing the ways in which other companies reacted to the market dislocations created by Argonaut, we take one final look at the Argonaut balance sheets. All of Argonaut's actions were premised on the claim of a severe underwriting loss for 1974. The New Jersey Insurance Department's analysis of Argonaut's year-end financial statement reveals that this year in which the company claimed to be losing so much money actually ended with an increase in Argonaut's cash balance. Its surplus declined by $99 million, attributable mainly to the claimed underwriting loss and the dividend payment to Teledyne. The underwriting loss, however, is not a measure of the dollars actually paid out. It is only a guess of future liabilities, based on known and expected claims. By predicting such a loss, the company could justify the transfer of surplus funds to bolster its reserves (the money set aside to pay off expected claims) by $135.2 million. In effect, the surplus funds suddenly became a reserve liability, with no actual loss in capital. From the judge's order in the Florida case, we learn that "Argonaut's actuary was told to recalculate the reserves required to cover Florida malpractice claims and to propose an even larger increase to the FMA." In other words, the company was shifting surplus funds to reserves, a move that would justify higher premiums. While reserves are technically listed as a liability on the company's books, the company still has the money, and the extent to which it will ever lose any or all of it is open to question. As we shall see, the standards for determining appropriate reserves are very vague and subjective and allow a great deal of room for maneuvers such as Teledyne's.

Argonaut's drastic actions cannot be understood solely in terms of its actual experience in the malpractice market. It is not disputed that malpractice was an increasingly bad risk, particularly in the large states in which Argonaut was writing insurance. Further, the company made particularly bad investments in the stock market. It was one of only two major malpractice insurers whose income on investments was insufficient to overcome their claimed underwriting losses for 1974. One company official was quoted in the *Wall Street Journal* as saying that the company's investments in the stock market took a beating "and the Teledyne people panicked." But a prime reason for Argonaut's drastic actions was that Teledyne realized that there was simply no reason why Argonaut should not play out its hand with the attempted rate increases and then quit. The conglomerate's managers were not insurers by profession; they had no commitment to this line of business. Henry Singleton, board chairman and driving force behind Teledyne, explained in an interview with *Forbes:* "We could have taken a pencil and written off not just the loss, but the entire company. It wouldn't have hurt us."

Under Teledyne's guidance, Argonaut announced its commitment to insure only lines of manageable risk. This meant primary concentration on its workers' compensation line. It also meant overseas expansion. Since the Teledyne takeover, Argonaut had begun to go foreign, establishing new markets in Great Britain, Canada, and Israel. For Argonaut, and for the insurance industry in general, the newly discovered foreign market means higher profitability. A company's underwriting portfolio can more easily be pitched to the most profitable lines. The cream of the insurance market can be skimmed off, with little regulatory pressure to cover less attractive lines. As one industry official explained to the *Wall Street Journal,* "Abroad, we try to run a Cadillac. Here we wouldn't dare tell Denenberg [former Insurance Commissioner of Pennsylvania] that auto [insurance] stinks and we're getting out."

Argonaut's actions were watched with great interest by the rest of the malpractice insurance industry. In some respects, other malpractice companies could readily perceive ways in which they differed from Argonaut. Argonaut was a small company which had gone into some of the worst malpractice states with little experience in this specialized form of coverage. Now directly under Teledyne's control, Argonaut could hardly be expected to behave like an old-line insurance company. Still, the other companies recognized that their loss experience on this line was uneven at best, and certainly not very predictable. There was no unified, consistent response to the growing problem. Contrary to the popular assumption, most of the major companies writing malpractice insurance did not withdraw from the market, and they have not withdrawn to this point. The AMA's October 1976 market-survey report indicates that Hartford, Aetna, INA, CNA, Travelers, Medical Protective, and St. Paul were all continuing to write coverage on a large-scale basis. Even Arogonaut was continuing coverage in California, Hawaii, and Pennsylvania.

Evaluating the actual scope of the 1975 crisis, we see that there were extreme availability problems for at least a short period in the states Argonaut left, in those where, as we shall see, St. Paul pulled out because it was refused permission for its new "claims made" policy, and in Southern California, where the Chubb-owned Pacific Indemnity Corporation canceled individual coverage for 2,500 physicians. Physicians not covered under group plans, particularly those in high-risk specialties, were also subject to cancellations or nonrenewal in many areas throughout the country.

The major companies remaining in the market, all experiencing the surplus decline discussed earlier, and recognizing the extreme volatility of the malpractice situation, were unwilling to plug the market gaps automatically. They were, however, quite willing to use the crisis atmosphere in other states as an unsubtle pressure on their existing policy-holders. So long as insurance was kept available, the companies knew that physicians and state regulators would be likely to go along with the price tag. Travelers increased Arizona's premiums by 107 percent for 1975, and demanded hikes of 350 percent and 485 percent in Northern and Southern California in 1976; Aetna increased Delaware's premium by 75 percent and Utah's by 70 percent; Hartford increased New Hampshire's rates by 100 to 200 percent. Premiums for hospitals everywhere increased by even greater percentages. In New York, average annual premiums per hospital bed jumped from $348 in 1974–75 to $1,447 in 1975–76, a 316 percent increase in one year. Still, for most physicians (with the notable exception of many in California) the major issue was availability, with the increased premiums clearly taking a position of secondary importance. The premium cost, after all, could be passed on to the patients.

Rate increases were no doubt called for by the recent surge in claims and losses. The question is how much was appropriate. At this point, one begins to see how the lack of a credible body of claims statistics gave the industry both problems and opportunities. State regulators, who in some cases were being pressured by the medical society to approve any rate so long as the company would stay, were simply incapable of challenging the industry's figures effectively. The rate hikes could sail through. As former Pennsylvania Commissioner Denenberg wrote, "The carriers win almost by default. There's no one whose job it is to contest the companies' figures and projections. The insurance companies are always there, their actuaries and lawyers swarm through state insurance departments like cockroaches."

Setting malpractice rates is a particularly troublesome task for a number of reasons, most significantly because the recent instability in claim trends makes the past a not altogether reliable basis for predicting the future. The resulting uncertainty makes the process extremely subjective: a company's vision of the future will affect the way it chooses and uses data. To the degree that a particular company is scared of a particular risk, data can be legitimately interpreted to justify a higher rate. To the extent that an entire industry panics with respect to an entire class of risks, the line between interpretation and manipulation becomes thinner, and the rates rise excessively.

As Denenberg notes, there is normally no one to challenge the industry's rate-making data. Since the time of the crisis, some of the country's more aggressive regulatory departments have begun to scrutinize malpractice rate requests, and medical societies have hired their own analysts to do the same. As a result, for the first time, we have a few small glimpses inside the industry's rate-making methods. The available evidence suggests that at least some segments of the industry have not hesitated to cross the line from interpretation to manipulation.

There are three basic steps in setting a premium rate. First, the actuary chooses a credible body of physician or hospital exposures and claim experience; he uses the malpractice loss experience of the insured group, or a group sharing similar characteristics, for a recent year or years. Second, since many losses for the chosen period have not yet been settled or even reported, a development factor must be introduced to reflect these considerations; it predicts ultimate losses for the base period on the basis of known losses. Finally, once ultimate losses have been reasonably determined, projections known as trend factors are calculated to determine at what rate and by what dollar amount claims will increase or decrease in the future.

Each of these steps provides opportunity for legitimate disagreement. The choice of an experience base presents particularly difficult problems. The universe of malpractice exposure is both small and fragmented. As compared to fire and health insurance, where the data base includes millions of policy-holders, malpractice insurers must rely on the experience of 300,000 physicians and 7,000 hospitals nationally. Within these groups, different specialties and geographic locations have markedly different risks. The credibility or reliability of the data is further diminished by the dearth of reliable reporting mechanisms to pool the loss experience of a fractionalized market. These factors lead to a situation in which the value of past data in predicting future losses is mathematically ill-defined and unclear.

For the insurance companies, the choice of rate base has a pronounced impact on the final determination of rates. For example, Argonaut's 1975 demand for the Northern California rate increase was based on the previous carrier's loss experience in a wider geographic area. The California Insurance Commissioner did not challenge the rate increase when it was requested. Yet former Argonaut president Woolery subsequently testified that the area used by his company was unfair because it included Sacramento County and the multimillion-dollar Nork award, a loss which accounted for 12 percent of the estimated California losses of the carrier, American Mutual Liability.

The entire industry appears to use the same device on a wider scale by relying on national data for rate-making in individual states. The actuary can assert legitimately that the loss experience of any individual state, with the exceptions of New York and California, is insufficient in terms of sample size to predict future losses. A wider data base must be utilized. Insurance companies use a combination of local experience and national data, generated either by the Insurance Services Office or independently by the company. But, as we have shown, the incidence of malpractice is wildly uneven from state to state. Use of a formula which assumes that claims are evenly distributed severely distorts rate-making determinations. Insurance companies tend to use national data in all states except New York and California, and to incorporate California and New York experience in arriving at its figures for all the other states. This means that doctors in all these states are paying higher rates because of the high-risk experience of doctors in those two states and in several other high-risk states. But when the companies set rates for New York and California, they do not use national data. In short, the insurance companies pick the data base that will produce the highest premium rate. There is no consistent principle for determining whether rates should be set on a state, regional, or national basis.

The distorting effect of including the New York and California experience is illustrated by the NAIC's report on average indemnity paid per physician on a national and state basis. Nationally, the average loss per physician over the twelve-month report period ending in June 1976 was $668. In California it was $1,381, and in New York, $749. Eliminating the data from both these states, the national average is reduced to $532, or by 20 percent. The geographic distribution of the very large claims was particularly uneven. There were 726 reported settlements of over $50,000; these represent only 3 percent of total claims, but 60 percent of all indemnity paid. California had 196 large claims and New York 108, or, together, 42 percent of the national total. Six states had no claims over $50,000; twenty-four states had no more than three large settlements during the reporting period. Yet the premiums for covering these large settlements were calculated in most states as if they occurred on a random basis.

Another distortion results from incomplete ISO data. Companies report to the ISO on a voluntary and irregular basis. If companies with good experience do not report to the ISO, its rates will be unjustifiably high. Thus, the 1976 rate request in Masachusetts was inflated, in part, because the Medical Protective Company, which insured about 15 percent of Massachusetts doctors, did not report to the ISO. Since this company writes only on a selective basis for better risks, inclusion of its experience would ultimately reduce the rates.

Companies' reserving practices and settlement policies provide additional opportunities for manipulation of premium rates. Loss development, as previously mentioned, requires the projection of ultimate losses from known losses. The famed "long tail" of malpractice—the period of time it takes for all claims to be reported and settled—and the changing economic and legal conditions affecting claims and settlements along the length of the tail make this process particularly troublesome. The insurance industry claims that the long tail is the primary reason for imprecision. Reserves must be established for the reported claims and for those that the insurer suspects have been incurred but have not yet reported (usually abbreviated IBNR). Reserves are also established for the expenses that the company expects to incur in handling the claims. Development is the actuary's periodic analysis of the company's actual losses and reserves to determine changes over time.

Reserve levels have a significant impact on premium rates. If a company's reserves are lowered for reasons other than an actual predicted decline in losses, then the premiums will be too low. If a company increases its reserves unjustifiably, then the rate will be inflated. There are many reasons why a company's reserves may be an inaccurate statement of its actual and potential liability. A company nearing insolvency may understate its reserves in order to stabilize its surplus and appear more secure. A company which wishes to hold capital for investment purposes, or to hide profits from taxation, may channel the funds into its reserves. A company which is simply scared of future claim potentialities may bolster its reserves to justify higher premiums.

Whatever a carrier's particular motivation and practice may be, there has been little public accountability in insurance companies' reserving practices. Companies are free to shift reserves from line to line, or state to state. The state insurance departments do not have the capacity to examine any company's total reserve structure. On the federal level, the IRS theoretically has the power to check reserves to make certain that they are not overstated, but it has normally relied on the judgment of state regulators, who have simply not been very demanding. Companies have not been required to submit information on reserves established for individual claims, information which could later be checked against the amount actually paid. The New York City Bar Association's Malpractice Report states:

We believe the Department has failed to monitor adequately the activities of insurance companies with respect to medical malpractice insurance and does not routinely test insurance company reserves or otherwise review with care the data and actuarial principles employed in rate setting.

Because the individual companies' reserving practices have never been subjected to real scrutiny, there are few data in this area. The HEW Commission reported that company reserves were understated between 1960 and 1970. In recent years, with the recognition of the worsening malpractice-claims experience, industry reserving policies appear to have changed. If a company increased its reserves to an adequate level, development of losses indicated by those reserves would result in a corresponding premium increase to a level attuned more realistically to eventual losses. If a company began to overstate its need for reserves, excessive premium increases could be justified in the short term.

We have already seen that the Florida federal court found that Argonaut began pumping huge amounts into its reserves just prior to demanding rate hikes. It is unclear whether Argonaut and other companies merely recalculated their reserves to realistic levels or took advantage of an opportunity to over-reserve. There is some evidence indicating that in recent years the malpractice insurance industry has overstated the reserves set aside for reported claims. For example, in 1974, when St. Paul requested an 82 percent rate increase for North Carolina, a task force from the state insurance department made an on-site review of the company's claims files at its home and local offices. Its examination concluded that claims reserves for claims actually paid were overstated by 33 percent, and that 19 percent of all reserves were held for claims which were settled without payment. In another example, the New Jersey Hospital Association commissioned a study of Argonaut's reserving practices on claims reserved and settled between 1971 and 1974. The study showed that reserves were 268 percent greater than were necessary as indicated by the actual settlement amount. Finally, the Health Policy Analysis Program at the University of Washington reports that Argonaut reserved $382,000 for a group of Washington claims which were subsequently closed with total payments to claimants of $7,000.

Insurance-company discretion with respect to reserves for reported claims is large. The discretion with respect to reserves for unreported claims is unlimited. To the extent that the long tail keeps claims hidden for long periods, projections of losses which may not exist can be legitimately asserted, reserves can be maintained, and investment income made. Until the recent release of the NAIC claims survey, there really was little quantitative measurement of the severity of the long tail. The NAIC report tends to confirm the industry's contention that claims take a long time to settle, though probably not so long as previously suspected. NAIC data tend to contradict the industry's claim that a large number of claims is still unreported several years after the policy year has elapsed. The significance of the second finding is that the carriers' policy of setting aside huge reserves in contemplation of claims yet to be reported is unjustified, and that development factors based on any recent flow of dollars into those reserves are inaccurate.

The NAIC reports that in cases where some payment is eventually made, on the average thirteen months elapse from the time the malpractice incident occurs until it is reported to the insurance company; on the average, the claim is finally settled thirty months after the incident occurred. These averages do not tell the entire story, for the larger claims tend to be the ones that take the longest to settle. However, in terms of the industry's actual knowledge of its potential liabilities based on reported claims, the NAIC reports that 62.2 percent of all incidents, representing 47.2 percent of ultimate indemnity payments, are reported within one year. Within two years, 84.2 percent of all incidents are reported, representing 76.2 percent of all payments. By the end of the third year, the industry has knowledge of 93.7 percent of all claims, representing 89.3 percent of all dollar losses. The tail may be long, but it is so very thin that its impact on the uncertainty quotient has surely been exaggerated.

Another way in which development can be distorted is by a claims-settlement speed-up process in the period preceding the year in which the new policies are to be rated. In 1976, New York's Joint Underwriting Authority (JUA), the state-mandated pool of private insurance carriers forced to write malpractice coverage after Argonaut's withdrawal, utilized the loss experience of Employers of Wausau to justify a proposed 90 percent increase in premium rates. This attempted increase was stopped when Employers disclosed in a letter to the State Insurance Department that during 1972 the company had begun a general effort "to close out severe cases as fast as possible [because] cases with a large potential severity have a tendency as they remain open to be significantly influenced by the inflationary pressures." On the basis of the discovery of the distortion in settlement experience, which would result in a higher loss-development factor, the Superintendent refused to allow any increase.

We have no way of knowing whether Employers' policy of closing large claims in the years just preceding the crisis was also pursued by other companies. If it was, rate-making in any state using such data would have been severely distorted. In compiling rate-making data used by many companies, the ISO does not take such distortions into account. It "theorizes that one company's possible reserve strengthening or accelerated payout rate is offset by another company's reserve slippage or payout slowdown." It is questionable whether this assumption is valid at a time when every company is cognizant of those inflationary pressures to which Employers responded.

Finally, the development factor can be unjustifiably increased by the use of national data in individual state markets. For example, a $20,000 claim in one state might eventually develop into a $10,000 loss. In another state, the prospect of a high jury award might lead another company to settle the same claim for $15,000. It would depend upon the company involved, its perception of a particular state's judicial climate, and its willingness to settle quickly at a higher figure to avoid heavier loss-adjustment expenses.

Once ultimate losses are computed by multiplying reported losses by a development factor, the losses are adjusted to reflect recent trends. Specifically, losses are multiplied by a claim-frequency trend factor to reflect changes in the average number of claims filed against physicians, and by an average-cost trend factor to reflect any trend of increase or decrease in the average cost per claim. Assuming, as the ISO does, that "rising damage awards are primarily responsible for the recent increases in premiums," the use of a nationwide average-claim-cost trend factor reflecting the severe losses of New York and California might severely distort premiums. Again, the industry fails to collect data and then capitalizes on uncertainty. The ISO suggested a national average-claim-cost trend factor of 10.2 percent for the Massachusetts JUA's 1976 filing. Because this figure represents the average national increase in the size of awards, it includes the numerous large settlements in New York and California. We know that these states have a disproportionately greater number of large awards than their physician population might indicate (California has 3.3 times as many physicians as Massachusetts, but 24 times as many awards over $50,000). Unfortunately, the available data do not tell us if awards in these states are growing faster, both as to number and amount, as compared to other states. The likelihood is that they are, which, when translated into a national-trend multiplier, means rate distortion.

The rate established from the process just described may be subject to downward adjustment to take into consideration investment income. As we have already seen, the great potential for investment income, based on the long period during which the malpractice company holds collected premiums, is one of the major reasons why insurers get into this business. The NAIC report verifies that the companies do hold a healthy proportion of the premium dollar for extended periods. Two years after the injuries have taken place within the policy year, the companies have paid out less than 20 percent of ultimate indemnity dollars. After three years, the payout is still only 41 percent, and after five years it has reached 78 percent. There is considerable disagreement as to the magnitude of investment income and wide variation in state regulatory treatment of this income.

The industry sometimes argues that investment income is insignificant, and that inadequate premiums are eaten up almost immediately by claim settlements. The evidence does not support this claim. Even in California, where the Auditor General projects a large ultimate underwriting loss for the carriers, it was reported that malpractice companies had collected $450 million in premiums over the fifteen-year period 1960–74 and, up to that point, had paid out claims worth only $200 million. Investment income was estimated to be $100 million. The Insurance Commissioner of North Carolina reported that the one company writing almost all the malpractice coverage in that state had actually paid out in dollars for claims and loss-adjustment expenses less than 20 percent of the premium dollars collected over the past seventeen years.

The actual investment income the industry has earned is a subject of some mystery, mostly because traditionally it has not been included as a factor in rate determinations. The industry, of course, seeks to minimize estimates of investment income. An industry spokesman told the Senate Health Subcommittee that the rate of return for malpractice premium investments was only 2.9 percent before taxes in the years 1971–73. At the same hearing, J. Robert Hunter, the Federal Insurance Administrator, testified that the industry realizes 7 percent annually, and 35 percent over the entire period that the malpractice premium dollar is held.

The length of time that a company can hold the premium dollar is subject to similar distortion. The industry has always sought to maximize the length of the claim-reporting and settlement process for rate determinations. Now that regulators are beginning to look at investment income, there is an opposite incentive to minimize this period. One might assume the companies realize that they cannot have it both ways, but they try. The Massachusetts JUA's filing assumed that it would receive interest on funds for 96 months. In the same filing, however, its development factor was computed over a 123-month period, which assumes that not all claims would be paid until the expiration of this longer period. While most states require insurance-department approval for premium increases, the McGill Commission in New York reported that only a handful of jurisdictions even mandate the inclusion of investment income as a component in the justification for new premium filings.

Recently, there has been some movement toward "open rating" and "file and use" statutes. Under these systems, which are now operating in seventeen states, companies need not get prior approval for price increases. It is assumed that a company will take into account all of its costs and potential gains, including investment income, to set the lowest possible competitive rate. This assumption is of dubious

validity in the malpractice insurance market, where territorial monopolies have all but eliminated competitive pricing.

With the recent recognition that competitive forces are not operating in the malpractice insurance market, prior approval has been re-
adopted for malpractice insurance in most states. In New York, for
example, the Superintendent invoked powers under the competitive-
pricing law and Unfair Insurance Trade Practices Act to suspend and
call for review of Argonaut's proposed increase for 1975. Later, the
legislature granted the Superintendent explicit authority to review
and approve malpractice rate increases. The New York Insurance Department is now requiring that investment income be considered. As
a result, the New York JUA's rate request in 1975 included an invest-
ment-income component of 18 percent. The department's own review
showed that the company's investment figures could not be supported,
and calculated the return at 30 percent.

Many other states are now requiring that investment income be
taken into account. Unfortunately, these efforts are still haphazard
and uneven. Massachusetts has gone the furthest in this area. By statute,
the Commissioner as he sets the rates must consider "investment and
potential income." The words suggest that the company's potential
investment income should be considered, rather than the company's
claim of a particularly disastrous investment experience. At the minimum, the Commissioner can hold the companies to the investment
income that can be anticipated from low-risk Treasury securities. This
requirement would have been particularly relevant to the Argonaut
experience, investing in a low-yield note to Teledyne's benefit and
against its own.

As most companies utilized the crisis atmosphere to push through
rate increases for existing business, the St. Paul Co. opted for a different
tactic. This company indicated its willingness to insure in any state
in which the insurance department would approve the use of its new
claims-made policy form. This type of coverage, common in other professional-liability fields, is for claims brought within the policy year,
regardless of when the incident giving rise to the claim actually occurred. The great advantage for the insurer is that premiums can be
calculated for one year based on the claims experience of the past
year. Because there is no need to predict losses years ahead, most of
the pricing problems coming from the "long tail" are alleviated.
Claims-made means that the company is risking less; its pricing mecha-

nism is more responsive to changing conditions.

For St. Paul, this also meant that it could initially charge lower rates than those required by companies writing traditional policies, because many of the claims coming in during the first years of the policy would be already covered by the doctor's old policy. While St. Paul readily acknowledged that claims-made would ultimately cost physicians as much as the present system, the promise of availability at a lower rate at this particular time helped it to gain approval for its new policy form in thirty-five states for physicians, and in thirty-eight states for hospitals.

Physicians initially opposed St. Paul's new policy form, because they knew that upon retirement they would have to purchase a "reporting endorsement" to cover claims made in the years following the termination of their practice. They were understandably reluctant to place themselves in a position where St. Paul could demand any price for this continuation of coverage or deny it altogether. After St. Paul made a contractual commitment to its policy-holders that coverage for these "tail" claims would be available and demonstrated how premiums would be calculated, opposition lessened. Now, even many of the physician-owned companies are using the claims-made approach.

The claims-made policy form may provide yet another problem for the insured physician. The policy application or renewal form often asks the doctor if he knows of any treatment incident likely to result in a claim. If such an incident or incidents do exist, and the doctor reasonably suspects he will be sued, he may be inviting the company's refusal to insure if he answers truthfully. On the other hand, if he does not answer truthfully, the company could disclaim liability for the incidents. There is no reasonable alternative for the physician.

Unfortunately, a still greater danger of the claims-made system is posed to patients. There is simply no guarantee that a physician will buy coverage for a sufficient number of years to cover claims after he has left practice, or that his estate will purchase insurance for claims made in the years following his death. These problems are not so serious for hospital insurance, because the institution is likely to remain insured. One might argue that even under an occurrence system there is no guarantee that a physician will have coverage. However, with an occurrence policy, both the patient and other physicians working with the doctor in question can determine by the present existence or nonexistence of a policy whether the particular doctor will be able to respond in damages for claims arising from current incidents. If there is no coverage, one can choose whether or not to be treated by or work with the doctor. With claims-made, there can be no guarantee that coverage will continue. This is a serious problem and it has not been considered by state insurance departments in the rush to assure availability. The problem becomes more important when one contemplates the difficulties in switching back to an occurrence system from a claims-made.

There is no doubt that many of the more capable state departments are now beginning to uncover some of the many ways in which the industry has exploited the vagaries of rate-making. This has been particularly true of malpractice insurance for several reasons. First, the obviously difficult problem of projecting losses in this line makes the subjectivity more apparent and the manipulations more straightforward. Second, the crisis proportions of the problem, coupled with the seemingly excessive premium requests, focused public attention on the department's responsibilities. Finally, the consumers of this specialized line of insurance could afford to organize and contest the industry's figures and projections.

In addition to the specific regulatory problems of malpractice rate-making, there are broader policy questions involving the capability of state insurance departments to regulate adequately the more complex and at least equally cost-significant machinations of this national industry which is becoming increasingly international. Specifically, there are serious questions about the ability of an individual state to cope with the recent restructuring of the industry into the holding-company system. The insurance industry is now organized so that individual companies are merely components of grand financial complexes, either insurance holding systems or multi-enterprise industrial conglomerates. In the case of malpractice insurers, we have seen that Argonaut is a subsidiary of the conglomerate Teledyne, which owns a total of sixteen insurance companies. St. Paul Fire and Marine is a part of the St. Paul Co.; Phoenix is a part of the Travelers Corporation; and Aetna Casualty and Surety is owned by Aetna Life and Casualty. The list could go on. The major impetus behind the holding-company development, which began in the mid-1960's, was the recognition that insurance companies have large holdings of liquid assets, the use of which is subject to some state-imposed restrictions for the benefit of policy-holder security. By diverting money upstream to the parent holding company, the assets can be utilized with greater flexibility.

The shifting of assets and liabilities between the various corporate entities scattered across the country tends to destroy the state regulator's attempt to ascertain the true financial posture of an individual company. For malpractice insurance specifically, there is real cause to question the ability of the regulatory process to monitor and control asset transfers which allow a company to appear to be no longer able to insure a particular risk, or to justify rate revisions.

Today, federal law establishes many basic ground rules for most major commercial enterprises in the United States. That so complex a national business as insurance continues to be within the regulatory province of the states, and exempt from the federal antitrust laws, is unique. In 1869, the U.S. Supreme Court held that insurance was not interstate commerce, and hence not subject to federal control. When the court reversed itself in 1944, Congress immediately enacted the McCarran-Ferguson Act, which mandated continued federal deference to state authority. It is a testimony to the political strength of the industry that it has managed to keep things this way.

Why does the industry prefer state regulation? First, it knows its way around the state legislatures and can greatly influence insurance legislation. In Illinois, a group of legislators from both houses were asked to examine state regulation of the insurance industry. Their 1973 report, evincing a degree of candor quite unusual for such self-analysis, stated:

The obvious question is why good [insurance] legislation cannot of its own weight pass through both houses and be enacted by the governor. The answer is simple. Each and every year we are more in awe of the insurance industry. Some of [its] lobbyists have a veto power second not even to the governor.

The composition of the legislature certainly tells part of the story. Twenty-one of 58 members of the Illinois Senate and 40 of 174 members of the House were licensed insurance brokers. Two dozen more legislators had direct ties to the industry, as officers or directors of companies, or as their attorneys. The insurance committees' chairmen were drawn from among this group; they, after all, possessed the technical expertise.

Such a pattern of industry domination is not limited to Illinois, though the degree of its pervasiveness obviously varies from state to state. In its report on the Illinois study, the *Wall Street Journal* suggested why industry lobbyists have such leverage at the state level. Since state legislators typically lack staff of their own, they are more heavily dependent than their Washington counterparts on the technical expertise of lobbyists. The industry's representatives benefit not only from this ease of access, but also from the relative lack of scrutiny by the press corps at the state level.

The resulting collective body of state insurance codes has been described by a leading authority, Spenser Kimball of the University of Wisconsin Law School, as "a rubbish heap without parallel in the law-making of modern man." The primary focus of insurance regulation in this country has been to prevent insolvency. Prior approval of rates, for example, is not intended to keep premiums low, but rather to assure that companies will be able to meet all future policy obligations. While there is no question that financial solvency is a valid state concern, it is also clear that procedures designed many years ago to guarantee solvency do not meet the new regulatory challenges of an industry which has moved toward conglomerate organization and has begun to withdraw selectively from coverage of certain types of risk.

The state financial examination of insurance companies, conducted by personnel of the insurer's corporate home state, is the cornerstone of the existing regulatory process. It is the only method by which public examiners regularly scrutinize a company's internal record-keeping and evaluate its financial position, both independently and in relation to its corporate cousins in the holding-company chain. These examinations, once completed, are sent to all states in which the insurer does business. While the paramount priority of the examination is to ensure solvency, this is also the time when the regulators could verify the accuracy of figures presented for rate-making purposes.

In addition to the special problems presented by the holding-company phenomenon, the adequacy and utility of these examinations are initially suspect on simpler grounds. The New York Superintendent, in commenting on the system of financial examinations, said that "vast amounts of time and energy are devoted to the production of information that is only marginally useful in determining the current condition of the insurer." Examiners were criticized as being content to file updated versions of their earlier reports and making little effort to uncover new matters. The standards of evaluation were called a "confusing jumble of statutes and rules." Perhaps the usefulness of these reports is best demonstrated by the fact that neither the New York nor the Massachusetts department, in response to our requests, was able to locate a copy of the most recent examination of Argonaut conducted by the California department in 1974.

The general weaknesses of the examination system are magnified when the complexities generated by the holding-company phenomenon are taken into account. By the late 1960's, insurance regulators readily perceived the opportunities for funneling assets from insurance into unrelated business activities. In 1969, *Best's Review* found that the diversion of surplus funds had already significantly restricted subsidiary insurers' underwriting capacity. The response of the NAIC and most states was to require regulatory-department approval for upstream dividends, which amount to direct payments to the parent holding company, exceeding 10 percent of policy-holder surplus or exceeding net investment income for nonlife insurers. New York gave its Superintendent authority to examine any company in the holding-company chain; and, as of October 1976, the NAIC was considering such a change in its model laws.

In the opinion of most insurance regulators, the statutory and administrative changes enacted thus far have not been adequate. It is indeed difficult to require that two parties to a transaction act as if there were an arm's-length relationship between them when in fact one is dominated by the other. In response to a survey conducted by McKinsey and Co., in a report for NAIC, 94 percent of the state commissioners and chief examiners expressed concern about their ability to detect and control "milking" of the insurer by the parent through dividends or exchange of assets, use of the insurer's funds or credit for questionable purposes, and short-term transfer of assets to conceal financial difficulties.

The NAIC Subcommittee on Insurance Holding Companies recognizes that the requirement of approval for extraordinary dividends does not cover all potential abuses arising from intercorporate transfers. Its October 1976 report stated that "there is presently no means of including [in the dividend calculation] any unpaid tax refunds due and owing the subsidiary arising out of a consolidated tax return." This, it will be recalled, was one of Teledyne's many tricks. The report also suggested that other unpaid obligations to the subsidiary could escape inclusion in the dividend calculation.

From specific rate applications to the financial juggling between the individual companies of a multicorporate whole, the insurance industry has mastered the rules of the state system. In instances where a particular state attempts to do more in the way of regulation, the insurers do not hesitate to incorporate elsewhere and be examined there. In New York, strict regulatory legislation has already led to the migration of a substantial number of insurance companies from the state.

There is now growing support for federal intervention in the business of regulating insurance. In 1976, a Presidential Task Force on Antitrust Immunities recommended that the industry's antitrust exemption be lifted. Still the states would be permitted to retain responsibility for financial reliability. In light of the industry's ability for financial maneuvering when each state is limited to looking at only a particular piece of the corporate puzzle, the proposed retention of state responsibility for financial examinations may be ill-advised. Federal assumption of some responsibilities in this area at least offers the potential for regulatory review of corporate finances at the same national level on which the industry operates.

Since the insurance industry has succeeded in keeping the federal government out of insurance regulation, it is not surprising that reforms in malpractice insurance have come only at the state level. These state solutions, which will be explored in Chapter 10, can be generally characterized as stopgap actions meant to guarantee the availability of insurance in the private market. Several malpractice-insurance solutions were proposed in Congress during the height of the 1975 crisis. Though their passage was never a serious possibility, they do point the way to some fundamental policy issues that should be included in thinking about malpractice insurance in the long term. These issues may be especially relevant if Congress, in the course of its eventual consideration of general insurance-regulatory problems, begins to formulate special remedies for those troubled lines of insurance which the industry would rather ignore.

The most basic issue is the wisdom of public policies designed to encourage participation of private companies in the malpractice market. Senator Nelson and Congressman Hastings have proposed that the federal government provide reinsurance for all malpractice claims exceeding either $25,000 or $200,000, depending upon the proposal. It is assumed that the threat of cripplingly large awards is keeping companies out of the market and reducing the possibility of price competition. The reinsurance mechanism would diminish the scope of any one carrier's liability for large settlements. Still, in the absence of a public subsidy to the fund, there would be no reduction in the total sum of losses that an extremely limited number of insurers would be sharing. The legislation as proposed, did not provide for such a subsidy. J. Robert Hunter, the former administrator of the Federal Insurance Administration, which administers other federal insurance programs, predicts that, without public financial support, reinsurance availability would have only minor impact on the market.

Should the public furnish such support to maintain participation of private companies in the market? The answer might vary depending on the characteristics of the line of insurance. A malpractice-insurance subsidy would be going to health-care providers, by way of insurance companies, and be reflected in reduced premiums. Physicians as a class are one of the most affluent groups in the society, so such a subsidy is not likely to be looked upon by most as a very fair solution. Additionally, to the extent that high premiums are causing providers to be more risk-conscious, a premium reduction could diminish that incentive. For a line of insurance in which the subsidy benefits would be distributed more equitably, the answer might be different.

The value in maintaining a private-sector role in malpractice insurance, and the relative benefits which might be achieved by establishing an alternative public system, are also important considerations. The traditional wisdom is that the profit motive in the private sector, coupled with effective public regulation, can best serve to distribute premiums and losses equitably and efficiently. The recent market dislocations and industry manipulations, induced at least partly by factors unrelated to malpractice, belie such optimism.

Further, it is questionable whether the private sector, in light of the partnership it enjoys with the medical societies, would ever be able to implement loss-reduction programs effectively. When Senator Kennedy proposed legislation to establish a publicly administered program of malpractice insurance, he specifically intended that the physician's need for insurance be used to mandate quality controls that would ultimately reduce malpractice itself. Federal malpractice insurance, under the Kennedy bill, would be available only to doctors accepting expanded PSRO review of their services. Compliance with federal regulations concerning professional and institutional licensing were mandated. Further, physicians would be required to participate in a program of second surgical consultations. Proposals for federal controls were vigorously opposed by both organized medicine and the insurance industry.

Other reforms not easily accomplished through state regulation of private industry could easily be included in publicly controlled federal insurance mechanisms. At the minimum, there can be no confidence that premium rates are being determined fairly until a reliable and complete national data base is established, with realistic geographic and specialty distinctions. If accurate loss data were available, it might be possible to determine that there are more meaningful exposure bases than individual specialty classifications for physicians and occupied hospital beds for institutions. With this knowledge, the safer practices of some physicians and institutions could be reflected in lower rates. Premiums, for example, might be tied to the kind and number of patients treated, the amount and types of surgery performed, the use of anesthetics, the physician's use of drugs or alcohol, and a range of other relevant variables. Although some hospital-association plans and companies writing individual physician policies have adopted some of these factors for rate-making, there has been no reported movement in these directions by private carriers writing coverage through plans sponsored by medical societies. For the most part, the private companies would still rather insure a doctor at a standard rate or not at all. State regulators have never seen it as their function to encourage more responsive rating mechanisms, and there is serious doubt as to whether they are capable of performing these functions on a state-by-state basis.

For the state to use its regulatory authority over the insurance industry as a means to influence physician behavior is itself a recognition of the absence of direct controls over professional practice. When the government seeks to impose safety standards on the automotive industry, it makes this effort directly, not by requiring that auto-insurance companies insure no cars without seat belts. It is admittedly a roundabout way of getting at a problem, but this is now one of the ways which are realistically available. So long as malpractice claims continue to escalate, malpractice insurance will remain a problem for providers, and a potential source of public leverage. In the next chapter, we will explore how the problem of malpractice insurance availability is now being handled, and the implications of the continuing failure to structure an insurance system which more directly confronts many of the deficiencies that characterize the private market.

10

Insuring Insurance:
When the Private Market Fails

State legislatures across the country convened their 1975 sessions recognizing that malpractice insurance might soon be unavailable in the private market. Some commercial insurers were hastily retreating from the field, others were demanding substantial rate increases. Doctors were threatening to curtail nonessential medical services. That threat became real when, in May 1975, thousands of Northern California physicians began a work slowdown. A crisis atmosphere prevailed nationwide, both in states that faced real availability problems and those that did not. The financial stakes were high, the political pressures intense. The immediate solution in thirty-four states was to authorize the establishment of a Joint Underwriting Association, a consortium of private insurance companies that could, if necessary, be forced to write medical malpractice insurance without risk of loss or opportunity for profit. The JUA was a realistic solution to the availability crisis because it could be authorized and established almost instantly, and because it was acceptable to the interested parties involved in the legislative struggle. In short, it emerged as the common denominator of practical political expedience.

In a few states, other insurance mechanisms were established, to complement or provide an alternative to the JUA. These include patient-compensation funds, stabilization reserve funds, and reinsurance facilities. Like the JUA, these measures are designed to guarantee the continued availability of malpractice insurance, by transferring the

195

risk of unpredictable loss from the insurance industry to health-care providers or to the public. All these devices are essentially stopgap measures meant to provide time for legislatures to develop means to reduce malpractice claims, and to allow opportunity for other insurance alternatives to develop. Provider groups have used this reprieve to capitalize and establish physician- and hospital-owned insurance companies—mutual and captive insurance companies. This chapter describes the legal mechanisms that allow creation of the JUA's and ensure continued availability of malpractice insurance, and the new forms of insurance organization that are developing in the late 1970's. While it is too early to know the actual experience of these new insurance companies, it is possible to examine their structural characteristics, and to consider the problems that are likely to arise.

While the JUA's differ from state to state, they have the same underlying structure. Liability insurers operating in the state are forced to provide malpractice coverage jointly, and to share temporarily any resulting underwriting losses. In return for their cooperation and participation, the insurance companies are assured that underwriting losses can be recouped, and they are permitted to continue selling their more lucrative and stable lines of insurance. The legislation normally authorizes the state's insurance commissioner to establish a JUA upon determining that malpractice insurance is no longer available in the voluntary market on a competitive basis. Typically, separate determinations must be made for the physician and hospital markets. By the end of 1976, these determinations, for at least one of the markets, had been made in seventeen of the states which had enacted JUA legislation. Most states have limited the JUA's operations to two years, though others provide longer periods or no limitation.

When the JUA begins operating, it writes policies in the name of the association. Some states allow companies remaining in the market to assign their existing malpractice policies to the JUA. A few states make the JUA the exclusive source of malpractice insurance, to prevent companies from skimming the best risks for themselves and leaving the rest to the association.

JUA's are run by a publicly appointed board of directors chosen from the ranks of the insurance industry, usually complemented by representatives of providers and the public. The board formulates a plan of operation, which is reviewed and approved by the insurance commissioner. In some states, the JUA has hired a staff to administer the company and service policies, but in most states actual day-to-day work is contracted to one or more private carriers. The St. Paul Co. has been especially active in contracting for this servicing function; it now operates the JUA's in Massachusetts, Maine, Virginia, South Carolina, Texas, and Arkansas.

The member companies of a JUA have little or no contact with its operations. Their participation will be required only if premiums and other income sources are insufficient to cover losses. If this were to happen—and it has not yet occurred anywhere—assessments would be made against the member companies in proportion to the premium amounts they collect in the state from all insurance which forms the basis of their association membership. The types of insurance which a company might write to force its participation in a JUA, and its contribution to an assessment pool, varies from state to state. If a company is ever assessed for excess losses, it will then recoup that money through the various methods provided by state law.

In most JUA's, the policy-holders will ultimately pay for all malpractice-insurance awards, whether or not the initial premium charges were sufficient. The most common approach is to use a retrospective rating plan whereby excess losses are recouped through surcharges against policy-holders. In fifteen states, stabilization reserve funds are collected in advance from JUA policy-holders as a contingent reserve to pay excess losses. In these states, policy-holders are required to contribute an amount usually equal to one third of their annual premium until the stabilization reserve fund reaches a predetermined capital level. These funds were established primarily at the insistence of the insurance industry, to provide an easy and certain method of recouping assessed losses.

Patient-compensation funds, established in six states, are also funded by surcharges imposed on policy-holders. Unlike the stabilization funds, which will be drawn on only if the premiums are inadequate, the patient-compensation fund pays all settlements over $100,000. The doctor or hospital needs only to purchase liability insurance for the base limit of $100,000. Any recovery in excess of the base figure will be paid from the patient-compensation fund. The rationale behind these funds is that the private sector will be willing to insure against malpractice risks so long as it is insulated from the large losses.

Reinsurance plans are an alternative device and have been established in three states. The purpose of these plans is to keep the private market operating on a competitive basis by requiring private companies to write policies in their own name, but allowing them to assign to the state reinsurance facility any policies which they have determined to be bad risks. New Jersey requires that any company doing business in the state and writing malpractice insurance anywhere must also write malpractice insurance in New Jersey. Losses sustained on risks assigned to the reinsurance facility are pooled and, like a JUA, are made up by payments from a stabilization reserve fund.

Hence all of these devices—JUA's, stabilization reserve funds, patient-compensation funds, and reinsurance facilities—have essential similarities. All rely on the private liability-insurance companies. All require or encourage private companies to write malpractice insurance by assuring that if premiums are insufficient, there will be a fund for the recoupment of deficits. Funds for recoupment are raised from surcharges on physicians and hospitals. Let us now examine some state-created insurance mechanisms which do not share these common characteristics.

North Carolina was the only state to implement a plan which required insurance companies to participate in the insurance of malpractice risks without also providing assurance that the participating companies would be able to recoup the losses which they might suffer. The state Supreme Court found that the state's attempt to create a mandatory reinsurance exchange was unconstitutional because it forced insurers having no experience in malpractice to write coverage without providing them with any protection against risks which they did not seek to bear.

Other states allow JUA's to take the significant, often unnoticed step of transferring some of the risk of insuring medical malpractice to policy-holders in other lines of insurance or to the general public. Ten states permit insurers participating in the JUA to recoup losses by adding a surcharge to the premiums of policy-holders purchasing other forms of liability protection. In this way, drivers, home-owners, and businessmen might all be required to subsidize physicians' and hospitals' malpractice premiums. Twelve states permit the insurance companies to deduct the excess-loss assessments from premium taxes owed to the state, in effect providing a public subsidy to health-care providers. Neither of these provisions has yet been subjected to judicial scrutiny.

JUA's were widely adopted because they provided the solution most politically palatable to the self-interested parties involved in the legislative struggle. For physicians and hospitals, the JUA's guarantee that insurance will be available, though without any promise of price stability. The medical societies were quick to accept this solution when the possibilities of state insurance was posed as an alternative. New York State Senator Lombardi reported that the medical profession was vehemently opposed to the use of a state fund and viewed it as another step toward "socialized medicine" and further governmental intervention in the practice of medicine.

Similarly, important segments of the insurance industry, after initial opposition, were able to accept the JUA because the alternatives were seen as worse. State-administered insurance was rejected because, as Senator Lombardi said, the "insurance companies feared that the government's entry into the malpractice field would be a forerunner of more governmental activity in insurance." Reinsurance plans were held in disfavor because they would require individual companies to evaluate policy-holder risks, establish a rate, write a policy, and decide whether or not to reinsure. When the American Insurance Association, which represents most of the malpractice insurers, announced its support of the JUA concept and began to circulate a model bill, battle lines were drawn within the industry over who would be required to share in the pool. The American Life Insurance Association was especially active, and usually successful, in convincing state legislators that the life and health insurers should not be included in the JUA. The National Association of Independent Insurers, representing mostly auto and property insurers, lobbied generally against the JUA and, specifically, against including the association's constituent companies. In most states, all liability insurers were included in the JUA, though a few states excluded auto and workers'-compensation insurers.

The industry was at best a reluctant partner; it could not wholeheartedly support the JUA. While the JUA does not expose insurance companies to financial risk, as a matter of principle the industry hesitated to approve any publicly coerced participation in the market as a condition of doing business in a state. Specifically, the industry was concerned that this solution might be adopted to address the growing problems of products-liability insurance, which could soon dwarf those of malpractice. Nevertheless, the industry, after realistically assessing its options, recognized the inevitability of some form of pooling device in many states, and decided that its best course was to make certain that its interests were fully taken into account in the legislative debate.

The JUA's were a hurried political compromise, and not designed to provide a lasting approach to the insurance problem. The Illinois commission that studied malpractice noted that "the JUA is only a short term emergency remedy. The Commission observes that the JUA does not reach the cost problem although it does make coverage available. The JUA does nothing to address the underlying causes of the malpractice problem."

The ability of the JUA's to perform even their limited mission is open to doubt. The adequacy of their performance is not likely to rise above the level of the industry's commitment. The underwriting manager for New York's JUA, the Medical Malpractice Insurance Association (MMIA), stated the industry's position quite clearly: "Our association members would prefer that the MMIA disappear." A staff paper prepared for the New York study commission reported on the State Insurance Department's early efforts to get the companies to implement the new JUA law:

It [the JUA] has no operating personnel of its own, and for months physicians and hospitals have had great difficulty establishing communications with it. Only with a great push from the department have the reluctant insurance companies moved to create the MMIA and establish a corporate framework. The Superintendent's comments to the panel expressed such dissatisfaction that he proposes to secure authority to discipline the principals.

Once the JUA began operating, its reviews were no more favorable. The New York Superintendent's February 1976 evaluation of the MMIA noted, "The Association's operating personnel are drawn from the participating insurers and reflect their principals' views, and it would appear as a consequence that there has been a noticeable reluctance to make the association serve the public need in the manner contemplated by the Legislature." The executive director of one hospital insured by the JUA observed that "the carriers assigned to the individual hospitals were shanghaied into this job and are doing as little as possible for as high a fee as possible. As a result not only are the carriers dissatisfied with their role, but the hospitals are dissatisfied with the services being rendered."

The primary concern of the insurance companies participating in the JUA's is to make certain that premiums are set high enough to preclude any possibility of later assessment. To do so, the JUA will engage in rate-making machinations similar to those of the private individual companies. The Massachusetts Rating Bureau, a state agency which reviews regulated industries' rate applications, reported that its "analysis of the JUA filing [was] made difficult because in several exhibits there appear what we call 'mysterious' figures. They are mysterious because nowhere in the filing or exhibits is there any explanation of what factors were used in arriving at the numbers." That the companies have no opportunity to profit from the JUA means, according to the St. Paul Co. executive who coordinates the company's servicing obligations, that "the incentive for holding down claims is not there." The New York Superintendent's report indicated the predictable result of this perspective: the state's JUA had not engaged in any loss-prevention or loss-control programs. Since most JUA's, as nonexclusive insurers, will be a dumping ground for the bad risks that can't get coverage elsewhere, the consequences of this attitude could be very serious.

Providers' dissatisfaction with the performance of the private sector, in both its voluntary and its coerced forms, is leading to the establishment of many physician- and hospital-owned insurance companies. Physician-owned mutual companies are operating in thirteen states, and they capture most of the market wherever they are established. Hospital captives have been established in at least fifteen states. Unlike the pooling arrangements, the captives are heralded as a permanent solution to the providers' insurance problems. As competitors of the JUA's, the captives will obviously succeed—the insurance industry is likely to do everything possible to make the JUA an unappealing, noncompetitive source of coverage.

In some respects, the captive is a viable alternative to the commercial insurance sector. It will be able to correct many of the suspected abuses of the rate-making process. As the president of the Pennsylvania Medical Society remarked, in supporting formation of a captive company, "One of the greatest problems now is the suspicion that we do not have all of the facts. In a captive we know where all of the money is all of the time." The captive will be able to gather data on its own and design risk-control programs based on local needs. Its promoters also promise that costs and premiums can be held down by sophisticated evaluation of claims, speedy settlement of meritorious cases, lower overhead, and a conservative investment policy. One policy of the captives may, however, be counterproductive. One of physicians' greatest complaints against the private companies has been their willingness to settle arguably nonmeritorious cases to avoid legal expenses; the captives promise to fight these claims through the legal process. Though this may have a soothing effect on physicians, who understandably do not like to have claims settled against them, it may also have a devastating effect on premiums.

While the captives are likely to correct many of the abuses of the rate-making process that have characterized the commercial market, it is not clear that they will give any more serious attention to programs for reducing medical-injury loss. The captives have been heralded as the only effective way that insurance can be used to influence physician and institutional behavior. The Illinois study report concluded that the physician-owned captive "may provide an added incentive for more intensive self-policing of the medical profession so that those few doctors who are not sufficiently competent are excluded from practice or from particular areas of practice." As a physician's financial interests will be more visibly on the line, it is assumed that the company will formulate loss-control programs and that the doctors and hospitals will willingly participate in them.

Some hospital-association plans and some hospitals that are self-insuring appear to be making some progress in this area. The program adopted by the Pennsylvania Hospital Association requires stringent safety checks over facilities and equipment, standardization of record-keeping, and reemphasis on surgical-sponge counts as a condition of continued insurance coverage. It is viewed as a model for other hospital plans. Still, even this model plan has not challenged the hegemony or autonomy of the medical staff within the hospital.

The physician mutual companies have direct authority to introduce incentives to reduce malpractice. Because the medical societies dominate the new physician captives, the scope of loss-control efforts will be determined by these groups. Although the captives are legally distinct from the medical societies, the medical society lends seed money to the captive until it can get off the ground, participates in drafting its plan of operation, and actively promotes the company to its members. In New York, the peer-review responsibilities of the captive company have been delegated to the state medical society. The American Medical Association is establishing a national reinsurance company for the state captives. Are individual physicians and the medical societies likely to make more effective use of peer revew in their own malpractice companies? Because most of the captives are just beginning operation, there is not yet much to report. Most of them have established peer-review panels to evaluate the claims history of suspected high-risk practitioners. Many companies have indicated their intention to refuse coverage to some physicians. Companies in high-premium states (New York, California, Illinois) provide premium incentives for specialists who do not provide high-risk treatments. Certainly, the economic pressure of skyrocketing premiums is likely to encourage a higher level of commitment to the company's peer-review activities, and to increase support for more equitable premium-pricing criteria.

There may be other incentives working against some reforms in the setting of premium rates in the physician-controlled companies. For example, it is unlikely that a medical society would support a rating system tied to a physician's surgical load, participation in a program of surgical consultation, or willingness to work in an underserved area. Indeed, premium rates may create incentives that exacerbate problems rather than solve them. For example, both the New York and Northern California captives gave doctors practicing for the first year a 50 percent premium discount, to encourage young doctors to practice in these states. Considering the relative over-abundance of physicians in these areas, this policy is difficult to understand in relation to risks of malpractice liability. Similarly, when the New York company began operations, it required a $1,750 loan from each doctor, regardless of specialty. Although this may be a sensible way to capitalize, it does not make sense if the objective is to relate premiums to risks generated.

Do the captive companies represent a long-term solution to the crisis of malpractice premiums and availability? There is little reason to believe that the number of incidents of malpractice has decreased. Further, patients' awareness that legal remedies do exist has been greatly increased by the publicity surrounding the malpractice crisis. As we have seen, the tort-law reforms enacted to date are not likely to have more than a minimal effect on malpractice recoveries. Hence, it seems reasonable to suppose that malpractice premiums must continue to escalate. Eli Bernzweig, former executive director of the HEW Malpractice Commission, predicted in early 1977 that annual premium increases will be at least 20 percent in the coming years. The ISO projects a 23.6 percent annual trend factor, which would translate into a rate increase of at least that amount.

Many observers suggest that the captive companies are setting their rates too low, or that they may be undercapitalized, or both. A principal fear is that the companies rely on a base of insureds that is too small, and that there is a consequent danger of undercapitalization. *Best's Review* reports:

It is foreseeable that the undercapitalization of these entities and their lack of underwriting and management experience will precipitate a new medical malpractice crisis. . . .

Risk Management warns that the industry must scrutinize the rate filings of the captives, or the "industry will be faced with picking up the pieces while the doctors will have enjoyed several additional years of coverage at bargain rates." Eli Bernzweig also predicts that state insolvency guarantee funds (which pay policy-holder obligations in case of company insolvency) will be needed when some of the captives incur one or two large losses.

It is not possible to know the accuracy of these dire forecasts at this time. We do know that most of the captives are setting rates below those of any remaining competing commercial carriers or the state JUA, though that does not necessarily indicate that the rates will prove inadequate. The Medical Liability Mutual Insurance Company of North Carolina is an exception to this general rule; its policy is to set rates at the same level as its competition. State statutory requirements for minimum insurance-company capital vary widely, seem to have little to do with the relative risks of different lines of insurance, and are often presumed to be inadequate. As a result, some state commissioners require more than the minimum-capital requirements before granting a license to operate.

Further dangers arise from the fact that some of the captive companies are establishing domiciles in Bermuda and Grand Cayman Island to escape state regulatory authority, including minimum-capital requirements, and to avoid U.S. taxation. *Business Insurance* confirms that "Bermuda has a stable government sympathetic to the interests of the 'exempt' captive companies." At least fifteen hospital captives have already been drawn by Bermuda's $120,000 minimum-capital requirement. Not to be outdone, Grand Cayman has no capital requirement at all. Though regulators on both islands claim that in practice they require more than their minimums for malpractice insurers, the California and Oregon commissioners have questioned the financial viability of these offshore operations. As an example, we do know that the fourteen Harvard-affiliated hospitals have formed their own insurance company on Grand Cayman with paid-in capitalization of only $253,000. The Physicians Reimbursement Fund Ltd., also of Grand Cayman, insures seventy San Francisco physicians with no capitalization whatsoever. Finally, several of the physician companies on Grand Cayman are attempting to operate by spreading the risk of malpractice among only twenty or thirty doctors. Because solicitation for more customers in the United States would subject them to the risk of state regulation, these small companies will be unable to expand.

If insurance companies are willing and able to increase premiums to meet higher claim rates, some suggest that more and more doctors will practice without insurance. The American Medical Association reports that one in eight doctors is now "going bare," but its survey is nearly meaningless because it includes retired doctors and doctors whose work does not require insurance coverage. Though some physicians are attempting to go this route, for a number of reasons it is not likely that this will become a significant trend. First, a few cases of proven medical negligence against physicians unable to pay a judgment will encourage more states to pass laws requiring malpractice insurance coverage. Wisconsin has already done so. Second, hospitals, out of their own fear or at the insistence of their insurance companies, increasingly require staff physicians to carry their own malpractice insurance. A federal district court in Louisiana has upheld the right of a hospital to require physicians to carry insurance as a condition of employment. Finally, physicians may be reluctant to practice with or refer patients to a doctor who is not insured.

Presumably, the great majority of doctors and hospitals will continue to purchase malpractice insurance, because of concern for their patients, economic insecurity, or external compulsion. The captive companies, like the commercial companies before them, can survive only so long as premium rates are kept at levels acceptable to their customers. Cosmetic changes in the structure and control of the insurance mechanism are not likely to control insurance rates in the long run. Eventually, physicians and health-providers must address the underlying causes that give rise to malpractice and the high cost of malpractice liability.

11

Conclusions

In the enormous quantity of research and literature generated by the malpractice crisis there is not a shred of hard evidence suggesting that the injuries of malpractice claimants are anything but real, or that the injuries of successful claimants result from anything other than avoidable medical negligence. Despite this, the primary thrust of malpractice reform in the 1970's has been to reduce insurance costs, by making it more difficult for the victims of malpractice to obtain legal redress for their injuries. The most explicit of the newly enacted laws are those that limit the amount the patient can receive after proving that the doctor's actions were unreasonable. Other laws are intended simply to make it more difficult for patients to establish negligence. Among these are redefinitions of informed consent and *res ipsa loquitur*, reductions in the time limits for bringing suit, and guarantees that the findings of peer processes will remain confidential.

Many of these reforms, such as the modifications of legal requirements for proving negligence, and the laws granting doctors immunity against nonexistent risks of suit, were premised on woefully inadequate data and misconceptions of legal doctrines held by medical professionals and legislators alike. These changes have little impact on the costs of malpractice insurance. Although laws that limit the amount of compensation the patient may receive might affect insurance costs, the impact of such laws on the most seriously injured patients would be devastating. Thus far, most courts have refused to approve the crude approach of forcing injured patients to bear the costs of injuries caused by physician negligence.

A second thrust of malpractice "reform" in the 1970's has been predicated on the assumption that the malpractice crisis was caused by aberrational excesses of a few members of the medical profession, the legal profession, and the insurance industry, and not by the basic nature of these three institutions. In relation to doctors, a few states have enacted reforms to discover and control more effectively the "bad apples." In relation to lawyers, a larger number of states has enacted laws to limit the compensation of lawyers who work for patients on a contingent-fee basis, though, as we have seen, the limits mandated by law are not significantly different from the fees which lawyers commonly charge. Therefore, these laws will have little effect in changing the situation in which lawyers take a larger portion of the malpractice-insurance dollar than injured patients do. In relation to insurance, only a few states have required insurance companies to submit more comprehensive information to support their requests for rate increases. In other states with severe availability problems, the industry has been forced to provide coverage, though only by shifting the risk of loss away from insurance carriers and back to health-care providers and, in some cases, to the public. There have been no efforts to challenge the anticompetitive and monopolistic insurance practices that precipitated the crisis, or to question the legitimacy of the industry's underlying assumptions about risk and profitability.

Reforms designed to control the aberrational excesses of doctors, lawyers, and insurance companies are not necessarily bad; indeed, many of these efforts are important and good, and much more could be done along these lines. But the basic problem with an approach that responds to the malpractice crisis by controlling the exceptional few is that the real causes of the crisis are more deeply rooted.

At the heart of the malpractice problem is the fact that many patients receive care from doctors and hospitals that is below any reasonable standard. The overriding public priority, aside from exigencies created by a crisis situation, must be to reduce the human and economic loss caused by medical malpractice: those losses which result in legal claims, and the still greater number of injuries for which redress is never sought. Malpractice will never be eliminated, but its incidence can be sharply reduced. Such a reduction would ultimately be reflected in lower premiums for providers and diminished unnecessary costs to the entire society.

The malpractice debate has focused little attention on the causes of medical malpractice which are rooted in the core operation assumptions of our health-care delivery system. We have seen that the fee-for-service system and the major health-insurance plans encourage overspecialization, unnecessary hospitalization, and excess surgery. Particularly at the federal level, these problems are recognized as legitimately demanding concern in their own right; but the connections between these economic dislocations and medical malpractice are rarely drawn. Economic and professional incentives produce gross maldistribution of physicians. Therefore, in some situations patients receive an abundance of highly skilled, highly technical, and often high-risk specialty care, and in other more common situations no care is available.

This situation has several consequences which bear on the problem of medical malpractice. First, overspecialization, as much as any other factor, is responsible for the deterioration of the traditional doctor-patient relationship. Many observers attribute the increase in malpractice suits to the loss of this personal and trusting relationship, but fail to perceive either the factors that ended the former relationship or the possibility of corrective action. Second, every estimate indicates that maldistribution, combined with loose certification requirements and insurance and fee incentives, produces too many doctors in particular areas who are ready, willing, but only sometimes able to perform surgical and other high-risk procedures. Finally, there is the obvious irrationality of a system whose normal course is to defer ordinary care until medical needs reach a critical state that often demands complex, difficult, and risky treatment.

The plain answer to these problems is that more rational controls must be exercised over who can practice medicine, where they can practice, what specialty procedures they can perform, and how they will be paid. The incentives provided by the existing market are destructive ones. It is not reasonable to assume that professional self-regulation will run counter to these market incentives. Laws that attempt to regulate the excesses of fee-for-service medicine without addressing the root causes of the problem are likely to produce bureaucracy and regulatory red tape that are both ineffective and oppressive.

The notion that doctors and hospitals should be paid on a fee-for-service basis is not written in stone or ordained by some natural law. We, as a society, have chosen this method of paying for medical services, and we could choose otherwise. Doctors could be salaried. Salaries could be adjusted to encourage provision of services which are needed, as well as to reward skill and hard work. Hospitals could operate on budgets. Budgets could be set by a public social process in which needs for ordinary and acute care were weighed and balanced and responsibility for the most technically complex services was assigned to those institutions best able to meet that responsibility. It would be difficult for an individual state to insist that doctors be paid on a salaried basis, since doctors could leave the state; but states could require that hospitals operate on budgets, and a national health-insurance program could mandate that doctors be salaried and that hospitals perform defined responsibilities with defined budgets. Because of the dominant influence of the medical, hospital, and insurance industries in the federal legislative process, none of the current proposals for national health insurance seriously challenges fee-for-service medicine.

Federal and state governments can and should provide appropriate financial incentives to medical schools and hospitals so that the number of residency positions offered in particular specialties would align with actual medical need. The federal Health Professions Education Act has adopted this policy as a goal, though it is questionable whether the regulatory stick and the financial incentives that have been offered will actually produce a significantly greater proportion of primary-care physicians. Stronger measures may well be necessary.

Another basic cause of medical malpractice is the absence of traditions of criticism and self-criticism within and toward the practice of medicine. Physicians are effectively insulated from the judgments of their colleagues and other health-care workers, and from the doubts of their patients. Private office-based physicians, making their daily rounds in the hospital, have little reason or inclination to observe other doctors critically, or to take serious interest in externally mandated review processes. The hierarchical organization within the medical profession prevents junior physicians and students, who are often in a position to observe medical incompetence, from offering criticism or even information that might avoid medical injury.

Similarly, a larger hierarchy within the hospitals, which separates physicians from other health professionals and from nonprofessionals, makes it difficult if not impossible for nurses and other health-care workers to question a physician's judgment. The power disparities generated by education, income, race, and sex place very real limitations on the likelihood that nonphysician workers will be able to offer criticisms or report what they know is wrong, particularly when there are no established means of eliciting such criticisms or encouraging such reports, as is normally the case. Further, these workers risk losing their jobs should they challenge a doctor's actions.

Patients are at once victims and part of the problem. The 2.38 million people who were subjected to unnecessary operations in 1974 are not simply statistics. These are people who, at least theoretically, have the right to refuse surgery. Often patients do not take responsibility for themselves. Since 1975, New York Blue Cross has offered to pay for second consultations to determine the necessity of elective surgery. Although the studies show that one elective operation in five is unnecessary, very few of the patients undergoing elective surgery in New York in 1976 took advantage of the opportunity to obtain a second medical opinion. Why? Often the patient's perception of the doctor's professional authority, the assumption that the doctor knows and does right, is sufficient to dissuade a patient from seeking another view. In other instances, doctors actually threaten and intimidate patients. We have counseled patients who have been told that if they consult with another doctor and thereby demonstrate their "distrust" of the doctor treating them, he will no longer be willing to care for them.

Patterns of relationship develop over time. Patients seeking treatment for minor problems often do not insist on information about their condition or the treatment prescribed. If they do ask, they are frequently rebuffed by the doctor and do not press the point because they know the condition is not serious. When serious problems do arise, the patient lacks a history of insisting upon being given information and choices. Little in the doctor's experience or training prepares or encourages him to say to patients, "I think you need an operation for the following reasons, but since it is not an emergency and any operation is a serious business, why don't you see another doctor for another judgment?" Little in the patient's experience prepares him to think that this is his or her right or responsibility. The patient wants to trust his doctor, and finds it easiest to establish and experience that trust by abdicating decision-making responsibility to the physician.

The law can be structured to encourage attitudes of criticism and self-criticism within and toward medical practice. For example, it is the law that determines patients' rights to information about their medical treatment, yet during the 1970s, no state enacted laws to give patients the right of access to medical records, and some states restricted patients' rights to informed consent. Profiles of the performance of doctors and hospitals, such as those that the PSRO is mandated to develop, could and should be made available to patients seeking to determine the quality of care they will receive.

· Alternative forms of medical review within hospitals can also be mandated by law. However, the effectiveness of new review forms is likely to depend as much on changes in consciousness, relating to the way in which doctors perceive themselves and how society envisions the professional, as on the particularities of any new review structure. Still, at the very minimum, it seems possible to remove some of the more overt forms of self-interest at work in the traditional review. Physicians from outside the economic and social web of the hospital's medical staff could be brought into the process: these would be doctors whose main interest, both personal and financial, would be the hospital's performance in providing quality care. Nurses should be included in the review process: they, as well as other health-care workers, could also be encouraged to file reports with hospital committees, if the institution guarantees job security to whistle blowers.

Reform in relation to the legal profession has focused on the excesses of a few plaintiffs' attorneys. But, as we have seen, there are basic problems in relation to standard lawyer fees and access to the legal system that have not been addressed. The basic cause of the situation in which lawyers take more of the malpractice premium dollar than patients do is not that patients' lawyers make too much, or even that malpractice lawyers make too much relative to other lawyers, but rather that lawyers generally receive compensation that is very high relative to other people in the society; hence the costs of legal services are very high relative to the compensation of patients. Significant restrictions on the compensation of malpractice lawyers are necessary to increase the patients' share of the malpractice insurance dollar, yet those same restrictions will increase the amount of damage a malpractice victim must suffer before a lawyer will take the case. In other words, such restrictions will make it more difficult for people with less serious injuries, or even very seriously injured people whose lives are not "worth" much in economic terms, to sue. The injustice is readily apparent. In the absence of a general reduction in the disparities in the amounts that people earn for the work that they do, and particularly the amount that lawyers earn, it seems that no equitable remedy exists for this problem. This conclusion, however, does not foreclose a solution to the other end of the problem: access to the legal system for those already denied representation because their damages are insufficient. Free or publicly subsidized legal services are now available to only the poorest in the society, and only for a very limited range of problems.

The contribution of the legal profession to the medical malpractice crisis is not limited to the fact that legal costs consume such a large portion of the malpractice premium dollar. Many people have noted with dismay the increased legalization of life in contemporary America. Of course, lawyers are only partially responsible for this phenomenon, and in the context of medical malpractice it is not surprising that, as human relationships between doctors and patients atrophy, both doctors and patients, to the extent they are able, insist upon rigid and technical mechanisms for resolving disputes.

Legal education, like medical education, is directed to producing an elite group of people—lawyers—trained to deal with the most complex disputes in the context of the courts. When lawyers talk with their clients, they often fail to help people learn to press their own grievances. Lawyers, like doctors, encourage dependency and submissiveness. Neither the bar nor the medical profession has provided leadership in creating patient-advocacy programs that could provide an alternate means of resolving many disagreements between patients and doctors. Such programs can increase patient satisfaction and end the exclusive reliance on medical malpractice as the outlet for the sense of outrage which people often feel about the treatment they have received as patients.

Doctors and some lawyers have instead proposed that medical malpractice disputes be "delegalized" by adopting no-fault insurance or by channeling disputes into arbitration. These proposals are attractive until they are examined in detail. It then becomes clear that difficult problems are not solved by putting them into new procedural forms. The process remains highly adversarial, lawyers continue to collect fees, there is no certainty, amicability, or ease in settling the disputes. Reducing the costs of legal services in malpractice disputes involves more fundamental changes in the relationships among patients, doctors, and health-care institutions so that the instances in which lawyers are needed can be lessened.

Finally, although the malpractice "crisis" was precipitated by the actions of the insurance industry, the only legislative response in the insurance area has been to fashion immediate solutions to availability problems, rather than to address the underlying regulatory void which the crisis made apparent. Regulatory reform is absolutely essential, not merely as a response to the demonstrated excesses of a few malpractice carriers, but because the entire insurance industry has taken extreme advantage of the abysmal regulatory job done in the majority of states. The industry has learned to present its financial posture to its best possible advantage, as determined by the particular necessities of the individual state's regulatory processes, so it is predictable that state regulation has been entirely inadequate. Some, if not all, insurance regulation must be transferred to the federal level. The market's regulators must have the ability to view the industry in the national context in which it operates. Regulators must also begin to analyze those areas which have been fertile for abuse: carriers' reserving practices, investment policies, and asset transfers within holding-company chains.

Regulatory reform by itself does not address the critical questions posed by the industry's growing reluctance to do that which it was established to do: to insure risk. The industry's recent actions with respect to a number of insurance lines, malpractice among them, suggests that it is primarily interested in insuring lines of guaranteed and predictable profits. Life insurance, where average life expectancy is predictable, is perhaps the best example of the type of nonrisk coverage that the industry likes and seeks to peg its future on. The malpractice insurance companies still in the market prefer to insure only good risks, and then only through the claims-made policy which further reduces risks.

Although it is not likely that the industry can be forced to underwrite an entire line of insurance from which it would rather withdraw, the worst possible approach is to allow the industry to skim the best risks and dump the remaining bad risks on the public. Unfortunately, that is the general thrust of the many state JUA plans which oblige state taxpayers or holders of other types of insurance policies to make up for losses not covered by malpractice premium charges. As a matter of principle and economics, if the public is to be burdened with the subsidization of bad risks, it should also have the benefit of insuring the good risks.

Publicly controlled insurance also makes a great deal of sense from another vantage point. The private malpractice-insurance carriers have never had the ability or inclination to engage in serious risk-control activities; and, as we have seen, the JUA's have absolutely no incentive to do so. Similarly, it is unlikely that provider-owned companies, despite the clear financial incentive, will effectively use pricing incentives and innovative risk-control methods that would challenge any of the critical organizational patterns of medical care which create opportunity for malpractice. It is those patterns that must ultimately be changed, on the entire variety of fronts that have been explored here.

Appendix: Excerpts from *Gonzales* v. *Nork* *

The Opinion of Judge B. Abbott Goldberg, Superior Court of the State of California, County of Sacramento No. 228566, November 19, 1973

For 22 weeks with a cast of 84 witnesses presented by four and sometimes six lawyers, this court was a *Grand Guignol* of medical horrors. But the drama played out here was not a fantasy contrived to satisfy a casual fancy for morbid amusement; it was real, permanent and tragic. Here have come "the poor, and the maimed, and the halt" to testify against their once "beloved physician" for the wrongs that he committed against them with evil purpose. The problem is an old one. . . . I cite Plato:

> "No physician, insofar as he is a physician, considers his own good in what he prescribes, but the good of his patient; for the true physician is also a ruler having the human body as a subject, and is not a mere money-maker."

Although the problem is old, what is unusual in this case, but unfortunately not unique, is the extent to which one doctor abused the confidence reposed in him by inflicting his incompetence on the unsuspecting and defenseless public. The defendant, Dr. Nork, for nine years made a practice of performing unnecessary surgery, and performing it badly, simply to line his pockets.

The case began simply enough. The plaintiff, Albert Gonzales, was living happily in West Sacramento with his wife and two small children, working as a grocery clerk in Willie's market full time and as a tree trimmer and floor polisher part time. He has been characterized as an "over-achiever,"

---

* Dr. Nork appealed arguing that he should have been allowed to revoke his waiver of a jury trial. The court of appeals accepted his arguments. *Gonzales* v. *Nork,* 131 Cal. Rptr. 717 (1976). In 1978 the California Supreme Court reversed, holding that Nork had waived his right to a jury.

and there is no question but that at age 25 he was sober, industrious, athletic, devoted to his family and popular among his fellows. In October 1967 his car was rear-ended by Ira Storey, an employee of the F. B. Hart Co. After the accident he had some pain in the neck and back, and following two or three days of light work he consulted Dr. Porter in the absence of his family physician, Dr. Liddil. Dr. Porter sent him to an orthopedist, but the orthopedist's nurse said he would have to wait for an hour and a half. So Gonzales, being in pain, made the apparently innocuous, but actually critical, if not fatal, decision to go to his mother-in-law's home in the neighborhood to relax. His mother-in-law, Mrs. Leonard, suggested that he see Dr. Nork, because Dr. Nork had operated successfully on her daughter. Gonzales accepted the suggestion, called Dr. Nork's office, was told to come in, and went. Thus, the die was cast.

On November 1, 1967, the date of Gonzales' first visit, John George Nork, M.D., had been practicing in Sacramento for some six years. . . .

Dr. Nork was graduated from Columbia Medical School in New York City in 1953, interned for one year at the University of Wisconsin at Madison, and then had a residency in general surgery at the Milwaukee County Hospital for part of one year. . . . During his residency he served at a hospital where laminectomies were done only by neurosurgeons, at a hospital where they were done by orthopedic surgeons because the hospital had no neurosurgeons, and at a hospital where they were done by both types of specialists. During his residency he began assisting at laminectomies, but he has no idea how many he did as a resident. At the completion of his residency he was obligated to serve four more years, and he served two of those four years at Travis Air Force Base as an orthopedist. After some sort of difficulty with the chief surgeon at Travis, Dr. Nork was allowed to resign from the Air Force, and he came to Sacramento. While at Travis he had done some laminectomies with Dr. Hal Holland, who was then chief of neurosurgery at Travis and who had also had a problem with the chief surgeon. . . . Dr. Holland had come to Sacramento and suggested to Dr. Nork that he come here, too.

In Sacramento Dr. Nork was first employed on a salaried basis by, and later entered into a profit-sharing arrangement with, Dr. Wallerius. Dr. Wallerius was then the oldest practicing orthopedist in Sacramento and enjoyed a good reputation. Dr. O. W. Jones, a severe critic, considered Dr. Wallerius "O.K." Dr. Wallerius did not approve of orthopedists doing laminectomies and did not want them done in his office. Nevertheless, Dr. Nork felt capable of doing them and did not heed Dr. Wallerius' advice. Instead he did a number of laminectomies with poor results, which he has now admitted were unnecessary and improperly performed, and he admits his incompetence to do them.

Despite his poor results, at the time Gonzales consulted him, Dr. Nork had a fine reputation. He was a member of the staff of the Mercy Hospital and other hospitals, active in Mercy Hospital affairs, and esteemed by his fellow physicians and by the nurses. [The court goes on to list a number of Dr. Nork's patients who were on the staff of Mercy Hospital and who had heard nothing but praise of Dr. Nork's medical expertise.]

Unfortunately, Dr. Nork's good reputation did not reflect the facts of his professional life. In November 1967, when Gonzales first consulted him, Dr. Nork says he was a secret drug user. He now admits that from 1963 through the fall of 1970 he was taking excessive amounts of Preludin, an amphetamine-like compound. He prescribed these for himself to relieve depression due to the fact that his work had been curtailed by a period of illness (possibly viral encephalitis) in 1962, and he felt he was not producing. He settled on Preludin after a period of experimentation, because his usage of this drug would not be noticeable to others. He developed some tolerance for Preludin and increased his dosages. These larger dosages made him feel extremely active, and he used Equanol, a tranquilizer, to counteract them. In street language, he was on "uppers" and "downers." He knew that such self-prescription was in violation of the ethics of his profession, but he continued to use these drugs in excessive amounts. In addition to admitting the use of these and another drug, Donatol, Dr. Nork now admits that the drugs rendered him incompetent, and that they caused him to treat his patients improperly. His usage was controlled and sophisticated and escaped detection by presumably skilled observers. . . . During argument, counsel for Mercy Hospital presented a list of 17 witnesses who were in a position to observe aberrant behavior or discover the drug use. None were aware of anything. Dr. Nork was able to conceal his use of drugs even from his wife. This amazing list lends color to the hospital's contention that the admission of drug use is a recent contrivance, and to the plaintiff's contention that the drugs did not prevent Dr. Nork from forming an intent to defraud. These points are discussed hereafter.

In 1965, 1966 and 1967, Dr. Nork had failed the examinations given by the American Board of Orthopedic Surgeons, and he never became a "Board Certified" specialist. He stated that the examinations tested clinical judgment and refused to analogize them to a driving test, *i.e.,* a test to determine no more than minimal acceptable proficiency. So his repeated failures did not cause him to question his own competency. [A discussion about Dr. Nork's "need to operate for personal gain" is omitted.]

Doctor Nork's History of Bad Surgeries, All Admittedly Negligent, or Unnecessary, or Both

Dr. Nork's formal and testimonial admissions that he treated the plaintiff improperly and his testimonial admissions that he treated other patients improperly are corroborated by the appalling list of patients on whom he performed surgery that was either unnecessary, or bungled, or both. Evidence was adduced as to 38 patients and, since several underwent multiple surgeries, something in excess of 50 operations. . . . I have concentrated largely on the 13 other cases antedating Dr. Nork's surgery on Gonzales.

These 13 cases have a dual relevance. Dr. Nork denies that he defrauded Gonzales, and Mercy Hospital denies that it knew or should have known that Gonzales was liable to be a victim of malpractice by Dr. Nork. . . .

[The court tells of its reliance on the testimony of two expert witnesses testifying for the plaintiff. The main reason the court gives so much weight to the testimony of Drs. Jones and Bernstein is their "independence of attitude and forthrightness of manner." The court finds their honesty in discussing malpractice in marked contrast to most other doctors in the same situation.]

[A technical discussion of the operation involved in most of Dr. Nork's acts is omitted. Essentially, a laminectomy is a very delicate operation on the spine designed to correct a "ruptured disc." If the surgeon is not skilled and careful, a condition known as arachnoiditis is often the result. The effect of arachnoiditis is a "gumming up" of the nerves.]

I accept the testimony of Dr. Jones in this trial that arachnoiditis is the end stage of postoperative trauma; it is the result of poor technique; it is not an inherent risk of the operation if the operation is properly performed. But as will appear hereafter, many of Dr. Nork's patients suffer from this painful and disabling condition. Dr. Jones has collected cases of arachnoiditis, but has not yet found another surgeon who has a number even close to Dr. Nork. [He testified] that there "never was such a series in medical history."

Arachnoiditis is permanent; it is essentially inoperable except under a recently developed microscopic technique, and even this is only 50% successful. It tends to get worse rather than better with time, apparently because activity causes tugging on the traumatized nerve roots.

Arthur J. Freer, laminectomy, August 21, 1962

This is the first such surgery known to have been done by Dr. Nork with the assistance of only a general practitioner, Dr. Go. The operation was bloody, but Dr. Nork recorded in his notes only a minimal loss of blood. The patient was in the recovery room for 5–6 hours, about five times longer than normal, and his condition was critical. The patient developed arachnoiditis after the surgery, which caused bowel and bladder incontinence. Dr. Wallerius took over the care of this patient and saw him until September 14th, the date of his discharge from Mercy General. The hospitalization was about twice as long as for the normal case of this sort.

Dr. Nork was sued by Freer, the first malpractice suit against him. Freer's attorney, Mr. Freidberg, engaged Dr. Nork's friend, Dr. Holland, as a consultant, and Holland told him there was no case, and the suit was dismissed. . . .

Despite Dr. Holland's report, Dr. Nork now admits that his surgery on Mr. Freer was performed below the standard of care, and agrees with Drs. Jones and Bernstein that Mr. Freer should not have developed arachnoiditis. He says, however, that in 1962 he thought that the surgery was properly performed, and nothing about the case then made him think his technique was deficient.

[The court proceeds to examine Dr. Holland's behavior in both the Freer lawsuit and in *Gonzales v. Nork*. Holland gave varying opinions on whether Nork had committed malpractice on Freer, explaining the differences in opinion by the fact that he had not originally studied Freer's medical records. The court goes on to point out that Holland had not told Mr. Freidberg about his friendship with Dr. Nork when Freidberg was investigating for the Freer suit. Additionally, Dr. Holland failed to disclose to hospital authorities the symptoms for which he was treating Dr. Nork professionally—dizziness and "unsteadiness of the legs." In short, a picture of a doctor doing his very best to protect his peer from a justified malpractice suit is painted by the court.]

Keith Wilson, laminectomy, October 6, 1964

Dr. Nork's notes, which he denies falsifying, report that he diagnosed a herniated disc after a relatively complete physical examination during which the patient would have had to have his clothes off. The patient and his wife, who accompanied him to the doctor, was present throughout the discussion, and would have had to help him disrobe, both stoutly deny that Dr. Nork examined Mr. Wilson. Instead they agree that Dr. Nork diagnosed a ruptured disc by the way the patient grunted with pain, and that not only was the patient not required to undress, but Dr. Nork performed no physical examination in his office. . . . Mrs. Wilson recalled that Dr. Holland said there might be some tingling or numbness after the surgery. Neither Holland nor Nork said anything about any other risks. . . .

The laminectomy was done by Drs. Nork and Holland as co-surgeons, Nork doing the left side and Holland the right. After the surgery Mr. Wilson had motor weakness in his left leg. Before the surgery the weakness had been on the right. Then he developed pain radiating down the groin and left leg. He had been hospitalized six times since the surgery. On June 25, 1966, he was discharged by the Veterans' Administration in San Francisco whose discharge summary states: "The discharging diagnosis is that of most likely postoperative arachnoiditis."

Dr. Bernstein reviewed Mr. Wilson's case. It is one of those supporting his conclusion that Dr. Nork cannot perform laminectomies properly. Dr. Jones was questioned about the procedure of having two co-surgeons, one on one side and one on the other. He did not understand it and had never heard of it before. . . .

In the case of Mr. Wilson, as in the case of Mr. Freer, Dr. Holland appears again to have attempted to disguise the disagreeable truth. He hospitalized Mr. Wilson as recently as May 7, 1972, and discharged him six days later with the diagnosis: "(1) neuropathy of left lower extremity, cause undetermined; probably diabetic; superimposed upon chronic low back syndrome." Nork Ex. AE, p. 89. The fact that Mr. Wilson had diabetes was discovered during this hospitalization, and Dr. Holland called in Dr. Kalinske, an internist, as a consultant. Dr. Kalinske stated in his report that there was "an outside possibility that there might be some connection between the diabetes and the neuropathy.". . . Similarly he sweetened the Veterans' Administration diagnosis of "probable post-operative arachnoiditis" into "post-operative 'low back syndrome.' ". . .

Mrs. Jo Austin Branson, laminectomy, November 12, 1964; spinal fusion, December 4, 1964 [The court notes Mrs. Branson was the medical secretary at Mercy Hospital. She was originally referred to Dr. Nork for severe back pain, treated by him and ostensibly cured. One and a half years later she was involved in an automobile accident and injured her back. Her X-rays, according to the radiologist, showed "no recent bony injury." Dr. Nork then performed a myelogram on her back despite the risks of such a procedure. The court elsewhere explained a myelogram as being a test to determine where a ruptured disc is in the spine of someone *already diagnosed* to have such a condition. The radiologist, reporting on Mrs. Branson's myelogram, found "no X-ray evidence of herniated (disc). . . ." Nonetheless, Dr. Nork performed a laminectomy three days later. The result of the operation was a fractured disc.]

The fractures were not seen on the October x-rays; they were not seen on the myelogram three days before the surgery; they were not seen on the lateral x-rays performed during surgery, but they are clearly visible in the photographs taken during the surgery. . . .

[The court examines the various theories of how the broken back occurred and rejects Dr. Holland's version as that of an interested, biased party.]

Reading it as it stands, it is obvious that no fractures were noted until after Dr. Nork began to work. . . .

To Dr. Bernstein it was obvious that things had happened during the operation, which were not written down. He explained how the fractures might occur by surgery done below the standard of care and concluded that they did occur during surgery. To come to the opposite conclusion would require not only reliance on the testimony of highly-interested witnesses but also disregard of the plain tenor of all the documentary evidence. . . .

[The court next documents discrepancies between Dr. Nork's "roseate" reports of Mrs. Branson's recovery and other reports of her worsened condition. The conclusion reached is that "Dr. Nork's entries are arrant falsifications."]

[Dr. Nork's decision to re-operate is reported by the court in the context of Dr. Nork's continued falsifications of records. A spinal fusion was performed by Drs. Nork and Holland during which a different disc than the one originally injured was removed.] Dr. Bernstein found that there was "no diagnostic basis" for this removal and that the operative report of December 4 "does not make sense.". . . After a harrowing month in the hospital, she was discharged on December 31, 1964, with a note by Dr. Nork, "Complication: none.". . .

[The court describes how Mrs. Branson was misled by Dr. Nork into believing Nork responsible for saving her life. She actually testified in his behalf at a malpractice trial *(Hendrick v. Nork).* Her condition following the surgery by Dr. Nork was "serious and disabled". . . "obviously impaired." Dr. Nork now admits his surgery caused her condition.]

After the fusion in December, Mrs. Branson was seen in the hospital by Dr. Fong for a medical condition, by Dr. Hickey, a neurosurgeon, in the temporary absence of Dr. Holland, by Dr. Gammel, another neurosurgeon, and by an orthopedist whose name she cannot recall. In 1969 she was seen by a neurologist, Dr. Sheehy. No doctor ever suggested to her that there was anything wrong with her surgery.

Dr. Holland referred Mrs. Branson to counsel, Mr. Adrian Palmquist, for her automobile accident. He had, himself, consulted Mr. Palmquist. Mr. Palmquist tried unsuccessfully to get the doctors to reduce their bills. He generously waived his own fees. Mr. Palmquist did not, however, suggest to her that she might have been a victim of medical malpractice. His lack of suspicion, coupled with the similar lack of suspicion of Mr. Brown in the case of Mr. Miyahara, *infra.*, and of Mr. Friedman in the case of the plaintiff, Gonzales, is striking evidence of how powerless at the hands of physicians are even experienced lawyers with, to use Dr. Bernstein's expression, "a high index of suspicion."

The patient is even more powerless than a lawyer. Throughout the trial numerous patients have testified how impressed they were with Dr. Nork's competence and interest. As Dr. Jones, hardly an emotional man, said, doctors like Nork have "charisma" and many patients develop a fondness for such doctors that is "unbeatable and unexplainable." This is well illustrated by Mrs. Branson. Even now, when the whole sorry story of how she was maltreated, deceived and victimized has been exposed, she wept on the stand and said that she did not want to know if Dr. Nork had done anything wrong to her back. . . .

Mrs. Betty Jean Jones, laminectomy, April 14, 1965 This patient was operated on by Dr. Nork five times, three laminectomies and two fusions. . . .

Mrs. Jones denies that he advised her of the risks and hazards of the operation, and Dr. Nork now admits that this first laminectomy was unnecessary, that it was not properly performed, and his own incompetence to perform it. Since the four subsequent surgeries were done only in vain efforts to correct the first, it follows that they, too, were unnecessary. . . .

Mrs. Jones did not do well after the second laminectomy, and Dr. Nork referred her to Dr. Gammel, a neurosurgeon, while still in the hospital, because the hospital rules required a consultation under the circumstances. . . .

Mrs. Jones was subjected to a third laminectomy by Dr. Nork on September 18, 1967, although this was contrary to Dr. Gammel's advice. She asked for another consultation with a neurosurgeon, but Dr. Nork said this was unnecessary. She did not improve and later had two spinal fusions by Dr. Nork. . . . [Neither of these later operations helped her, and she was eventually told she would just "have to learn to live with her pain."]

Shirley Diane Hart, Pantalar Arthrodesis, April 5, 1965 [the court describes Dr. Nork's use of a risky medical procedure to repair an injury to Miss Hart's ankle which eventually resulted in the amputation of her leg below the knee.]

The importance of the case of Miss Hart in the present context is that it shows Dr. Nork's readiness to embark on a reckless course of conduct. He now admits that the operations he performed were improper, were done below the standard of care and were responsible for the amputation. Furthermore, the case is another in the pattern of Dr. Nork's discouragement of consultation with other doctors. Miss Hart testified that while hospitalized with a postsurgical infection she once suggested a consultant be called, and Dr. Nork refused to do so. . . . She decided to stay with Dr. Nork, "Because I was afraid to change doctors. I was sick in the hospital and needed somebody to take care of me. And I really wasn't in any condition to go looking around for another doctor. Besides I thought he wouldn't do anything wrong. I trusted him."

Thus threatened with abandonment by the physician on whom she had heretofore relied and trusted, Miss Hart dropped the subject. . . .

[The court accepts the testimony of Gonzales's expert witnesses that:]

Dr. Nork's operations on Miss Hart were "absolutely senseless." Not only
should Dr. Nork have known this, but it should have been obvious to the
assistant surgeon, Dr. Stanford, that basic surgical principles were being
violated.

[Omitted is a brief discussion of a man whose surgery was "unnecessary
but lucky."]

[Also omitted is a discussion of a man whose surgery was unnecessary,
"below the standard of care," and resulted in permanent injury. In this case
both the myelograms and the surgery were improperly performed.]

Miss Fumiye Nishioka, laminectomy, November 15, 1965

[This patient was a nurse who was referred to Dr. Nork for back pain.
Dr. Nork performed a myelogram.] Although the radiologist found the myelogram entirely normal, Dr. Nork found disc disease between the 4th and 5th
lumbar vertebrae. Miss Nishioka asked for Dr. Maass as a consultant, because
he had treated her brothers and sisters. Dr. Maass also found that the myelogram was normal and recommended that she not be treated for an interverte-
bral disc. She was thoroughly confused by the discrepancy between Drs. Nork
and Maass and requested a third opinion. She was then seen by Dr. Gammel,
who found the myelogram equivocal. . . .

Dr. Nork, however, told Miss Nishioka that Dr. Gammel said that surgery
should be done. . . .

[When after the surgery Miss Nishioka experienced the same symptoms
as before, she sought the advice of several other physicians, none of whom
mentioned the possibility of unnecessary surgery.]

Dr. Bernstein was shown the records [of Miss Nishioka] and testified that
it was improper to fail to inform her of the consultant's reports and even
worse to falsify them. In his language, it was "medically and morally wrong."
Miss Nishioka's case is the worst "cover-up" that Dr. Bernstein had ever seen
or heard of. . . .

[Another "unnecessary but lucky" case is omitted.]

*Mrs. Dorothy Gebhardt, 2 laminectomies, September 2, 1966, and May
2* Mrs. Gebhardt came to Dr. Nork with minimal symptoms. He now admits
that she should have been treated conservatively. Not only was the surgery
on her unnecessary, she should not even have had a myelogram. Nevertheless,
Dr. Nork performed a laminectomy on her. During the course of the operation
he removed some material, which he could not identify. All the material removed was sent to the Mercy Hospital pathologist, Dr. Friedlander, who reported finding among the material "a mass of white fibrotic material . . . 12
mm. in diameter" as a separate specimen. It consisted of "bundles of myeli-
nated nerve fibers. . . ."

Mrs. Gebhardt was another patient whom Dr. Nork terrorized into surgery.
He told her that unless the surgery were performed she would be crippled

or paralyzed within six months to a year. She was not eager for the surgery and wanted another way out, but Dr. Nork said that considering her myelogram, the hospital would not release her without surgery. So she consented. . . .

Dr. Nork now admits that he should have advised her that he had pulled the nerve fibers from her back. He admits that he misrepresented her condition by failing to list the removal as a complication in his hospital notes. He concedes that she had arachnoiditis, which he had previously stated was basically inoperable and that he did the work of a neurosurgeon by operating on her dura and injecting saline solution into it, a procedure that he had seen only once before and for which he had no training. . . .

She was in such agony in October of 1969 that she was rehospitalized. But Dr. Nork never came to see her. Instead she was seen by Dr. Bard, who has been treating her since. Neither he nor Dr. Nork ever mentioned arachnoiditis to her. She was not aware that she was a victim of malpractice until she met Mr. Cooper, an investigator for Mr. Freidberg. . . .

It was or should have been obvious to the pathologist where the nerve roots had come from. Dr. Bernstein was sure that the pathologist must have been astonished when he found them and that he should have been aware of the malpractice, for his report shows that he knew that the operation was a laminectomy, not a neurectomy. But the pathologist, Dr. Friedlander, not only was not astonished, he did not even consider finding these fibers "remarkable.". . .

Drs. Bernstein and Jones also agreed that finding the nerve fibers should have been included in the "Diagnosis" in the pathologist's report. As Dr. Jones explained, nerve tissues are not supposed to be found in a disc; they are, in effect, "foreign bodies" in a laminectomy. In Dr. Bernstein's opinion the failure to mention the nerve fibers in the "Diagnosis" was a device to make them less obvious, and he "suspects" that the pathologist was aiding the surgeon. Dr. Friedlander now wishes that he had listed them in the "Diagnosis," but only because of what has happened to Dr. Nork. The Nork experience has brought to the attention of Dr. Friedlander and other doctors the fact that one cannot assume that a colleague is honest.

At Mercy Hospital the Medical Audit and Tissue Committee is required to review: "all tissue with discrepancies between preoperative and postoperative diagnoses." Dr. Jones considered finding the nerve fibers a discrepancy. But even if the nerve fibers were a "discrepancy" within the meaning of the Mercy rule, all four doctors equivocated on whether they should have been reported to the Audit and Tissue Committee. . . . The Committee had told him [the pathologist] to report the removal of normal appendices, gall bladders and uteruses, and to report procedures showing "a pattern of irregularities." Of course, one case did not show a pattern, and "anyone is entitled to one mistake or questionable judgment." If there had been a second case, they would have taken action. Since the only record of the first case is in the memory of the pathologists, it is hard to see how one would know whether the case was the first or second, and it is impossible to see how cases of questionable conduct not manifested by pathological specimens would be discovered at all. [This was the introduction of what later in the case came to be called the "First Bite Rule."]

The "First Bite Rule" got its name from my recollection of the old proverb: "Every dog is entitled to one bite." This "is not and never has been the law" for dogs. W. Prosser, Torts §76 at 501–02 (4th ed. 1971). . . . If it is not a good rule for dogs, it is not a good rule for doctors.

Mrs. Roberta (Lindstaedt) Hendrick, laminectomy, November 17, 1966 [The court notes that this patient was the records clerk at Mercy Hospital. Following a sudden onset of back pain, she was operated on by Dr. Nork.] He offered her no course of alternative conservative treatment, but terrorized her into surgery by telling her that if she did not have surgery, she would be paralyzed. . . .

[During the operation, Dr. Nork's assistant surgeon, Dr. Stanford, left with Dr. Nork's permission. Testimony agrees that an assistant is necessary in a laminectomy. Dr. Nork apparently had a surgical nurse assist him—"an unheard of" procedure.]

Dr. Nork now admits that the surgery on Mrs. Hendrick was unnecessary, negligently performed, and that he was not competent to do it. He admits that even the myelogram should not have been performed. Nevertheless, both he and the absconder, Dr. Stanford, had the effrontery to dun Mrs. Hendrick for their fees, and Dr. Nork literally added insult to injury by doing so publicly and loudly in the presence of her co-workers during an interval when she was attempting to return to her employment. . . .

To this day Mrs. Hendrick has leg, bowel, and bladder problems. Her left leg has atrophied, and she limps. She is unable to work. But she never suspected that she was a victim of malpractice until her son, an insurance adjuster, read a newspaper account of a suit against Dr. Nork and recommended that she consult Mr. Freidberg. She sued and recovered a substantial verdict in the fall of 1972. . . .

The premature departure of Dr. Stanford was corroborated by Dr. Stanford himself and by the nurse, Mrs. Rowe. Dr. Stanford said he was "bothered" by this but felt he could leave since he had the permission of Dr. Nork. He claimed not to know that if he left, a nurse would have to hold the retractor. Mrs. Rowe, however, was emphatic that he left even before the "specimen" had been removed from the patient, and she functioned as assistant surgeon for about 1½ hours.

It is conceivable that an assistant may properly leave in an emergency. . . . But Dr. Stanford left to repair an anal fistula, an operation so minor in comparison to a laminectomy, that Mrs. Rowe, when told this was the reason for his departure, first laughed with astonishment and then said: "Who was the patient? I wish I knew. It must have been the president."

Mrs. Rowe promptly reported to her supervisor, Mrs. Stephens, that she was being required to "scrub" as an assistant. All the doctors questioned agreed that her conduct was proper. Mrs. Stephens, who is now retired, had no recollection of the incident. Apparently no record was made of it. Dr. Martin explained the absence of a record on the ground that it may not have been considered "unusual" and was not a "recurring phenomenon."

This is another example of the "First Bite Rule." It shows how the doctor may have more than one "First Bite." Dr. Nork had already had a "First Bite" at the pathologist. Then he had a second "First Bite" within the Surgical Department. Neither was aware of what the other knew, because neither reported to any central point. Even if there may be reasons for not disciplining a doctor for his first misconduct, it is obvious that a record must be made of that misconduct.

[Most of a discussion about a patient undergoing two unnecessary laminectomies is omitted. An interesting aspect of the case is that the patient was originally referred to Dr. Nork by a lawyer for whom Nork often testified as an expert witness.]

One significance of Mr. Miyahara's case is the information it provides on the difficulty of realizing that a patient has been the victim of malpractice. When Mr. Brown saw Mr. Miyahara after the first laminectomy, he was "surprised and in a way astonished" by the fact that he was wearing a leg brace for a foot drop. But Mr. Brown could not say that he was "suspicious" of Dr. Nork but only that this made him "wonder." "Suspicion is too strong a term." Mr. Brown's law firm continued to use Dr. Nork as a witness as late as 1970, and Mr. Brown never suspected that there had been malpractice by Dr. Nork in Mr. Miyahara's case. . . .

[Another "unnecessary but lucky" case is omitted.]

Doctor Nork's Systematic Scheme of Fraud

Dr. Nork made a practice of operating not only on the basis of inadequate preoperative findings, but also on the basis of false findings. Drs. Jones and Bernstein testified from a recapitulation of 26 laminectomies Dr. Nork performed between 1966 and 1970. They found that Dr. Nork's preoperative findings were statistically inconceivable in a sample of this size. . . .

Another practice followed by Dr. Nork was to operate on patients without giving them a period of conservative treatment within the hospital. . . .

The case of Jerome Keating is most affecting. In 1967 and 1968 he had back problems and received some relief from the administrations of a chiropractor. . . . Nevertheless, Dr. Nork persuaded him that surgery was necessary by saying: "You don't want to go through life taking medicine." Dr. Nork performed a myelogram and told Keating he not only had one disc, but two, and "I might as well take them both out." The surgery was done, and after a gruelling postoperative course, Mr. Keating is still afflicted with bowel difficulties and cannot tell when he has to void; he has urinary incontinence; he is impotent; when he sits down he cannot tell when his buttocks meet the chair. . . .

Another deficiency of Dr. Nork was his faulty myelographic technique. . . . [Omitted is the technical discussion of the myelogram referred to earlier.

In essence, a myelogram is an X-ray of the spine after the injection of radio-opaque fluid into the back. The point of injection is critical and, as mentioned before, a myelogram is not done until "the need for surgery has been determined from clinical symptoms." The court finds Nork's technique clearly substandard.]

One of Dr. Nork's least endearing habits was that of inducing patients to undergo surgery. Some he actually terrorized; others he merely gulled. [An extended list of the instances in which Nork terrorized his patients is omitted.]

That Dr. Nork was pursuing a plan of purposeful fraud appears from the way he handled patients' requests for consultants and the way he treated consultants' reports when he had them. To recapitulate briefly: In the case of Mrs. B. J. Jones he ignored Dr. Gammel's advice and discouraged Mrs. Jones from obtaining another consultation; he threatened to abandon Shirley Hart if she insisted on a consultant; he falsified Dr. Neblett's consultation report in his summarization in Mr. Heppner's record; he lied to Miss Nishioka about Dr. Gammel's recommendation and Dr. Treanor's electromyogram; and although he referred Mrs. Gebhardt to Dr. Hickey before her 1968 surgery, he never took any steps to see that this consultation occurred and operated without it. . . .

[The court's discussion of Dr. Nork's "practice of falsifying progress reports" is deleted.]

The Adversities of Albert Gonzales Caused
or Aggravated by Dr. Nork

Dr. Nork's treatment of the plaintiff was in accordance with the pattern of professional misconduct, which has been developed above at such length. He performed a perfunctory examination of Gonzales, made no substantial effort to treat the patient conservatively, discouraged consultation, hurried him into unnecessary surgery, which he bungled, and achieved a bad result, which he concealed. Gonzales' case differs from the others in that one of the consequences of the unnecessary and bad surgery was to upset his ability to cope with life to such a degree that it impaired his amenability to treatment for cancer. In a nutshell: Dr. Nork not only harmed Gonzales' back, but he also ruined his personality. And he is liable for the bodily harm resulting from the emotional disturbance caused by his misconduct. Restatement (Second) of Torts §456, Comment f (1965).

The plaintiff first saw Dr. Nork on November 1, 1967, in his office. Dr. Nork now admits he should have been aware even then of his own incompetence from the sorry history related above. His own witness, Dr. Hanzel, agrees. Nevertheless, he undertook to treat Mr. Gonzales, examined him, and hospitalized him forthwith with the diagnosis "Acute slipped spondylolisthesis (traumatic) L5-S1 & acute disc herniation L4–5." Dr. Nork placed the plaintiff in traction and reported that he was intermittently better and worse. . . .

After Gonzales had been in traction about a week, he no longer had his original severe pain and thought the traction was helping. But Dr. Nork denied it was helping and said a myelogram and surgery were needed.

Gonzales, was "scared to death by surgery." At the insistence of his wife, he asked Dr. Nork to call in Dr. Howard Black as a consultant. Dr. Nork said that he would do so, although he did not need a consultant because he had done this surgery many times, and it had always been successful. This misrepresentation itself makes Dr. Nork liable for both fraud, Restatement (Second) of Torts §299A, Comment *d* at 74 (1965), and breach of fiduciary duty.

Dr. Nork did contact Dr. Black. On November 10 he noted: "Has been scheduled to be seen by Dr. Black with whom I discussed the patient's situation. He will see the patient today." Dr. Black, however, did not visit Gonzales, and Dr. Nork told him that Dr. Black "was too way up to come," meaning that he was "too high class" to bother with Gonzales. Naturally, Gonzales was insulted by this answer. Actually, Dr. Black overlooked Dr. Nork's request and on November 27 wrote a contrite note of explanation and apology [saying that it] "was simply a case of oversight on my part." But Dr. Nork, following his pattern of discouraging consultation, made no effort to ascertain why Dr. Black had not kept the appointment for November 10 or to accommodate Gonzales by suggesting another consultant, although he knew it was his duty "within reason" to get a consultant.

Rather than seeking consultation, Dr. Nork ordered a myelogram, which was performed on November 13. The radiologist, Dr. Johannessen, reported his impression [that the results were] . . . "within normal limits of appearance." Dr. Nork admits that at this point the proper treatment for Gonzales was to proceed conservatively. . . .

Dr. Nork also knew that a fusion should not have been performed unless a patient in Gonzales' condition had severe symptoms for a prolonged period of time. Dr. Bernstein testified that the proper treatment for a young man undergoing his first episode of back pain was traction in the hospital to enforce rest and rest at home for three to six weeks or, considering Gonzales' anxiety and tension and involvement in his auto accident litigation, perhaps up to three months. Dr. Nork agreed substantially, except that he added the possibility of putting the patient in a cast for an interval. Both Drs. Bernstein and Nork stated that had Gonzales been given conservative care, he would probably have become asymptomatic, and in Dr. Nork's opinion he would probably be back at work now. . . .

The point here is not that Dr. Nork's surgery was unnecessary, because he has admitted not only that it was unnecessary but incompetently performed. The point is the fact that the surgery was unnecessary was obvious. Indeed, Dr. Bernstein concluded that Gonzales did not even have the herniated disc Dr. Nork purported to find. . . .

The surgery was performed on November 17 by Dr. Nork with Dr. Stanford assisting. . . . The patient was under anesthetic for 4 hours and 25 minutes, and received 5 units, 2500 cc. of blood. Dr. Nork conceded that this amount of blood was "grossly excessive." It was needed because he had to withdraw the bone graft for the fusion, repack the site, and start over. He believes that he performed the surgery negligently.

Before surgery the anesthetist had noted that Gonzales was a "nervous young man," and after surgery he was worse. He complained of back pain immediately on his return to his room, and 45 minutes later the nurse noted he complained of "severe back pain" and was "very apprehensive about moving and turning." He continued through most of his hospitalization to have various complaints of pain in the back, legs and right thigh, chills, nausea, headache, and said he did not "feel right." Dr. Nork agreed that Gonzales' complaints after surgery were justified.

Dr. Nork discharged Mr. Gonzales from the hospital on November 30 with the note: "Has done extremely well and has no complaints. Is ambulatory and doing very well. Now ready for discharge." Like other of Dr. Nork's notes, this appears to be fictitious. In fact, Gonzales could not walk with ease; the nurse noted that the afternoon before his discharge he "ambulated in hall with help for 10 min." Mrs. Gonzales stated he still had to be helped to the bathroom, and he complained of "terrible" pain in the back and right leg and felt "paralyzed.". . .

From the day he came home, Mr. Gonzales was unhappy and like an invalid. He was pale and thin. . . . He spent most of his time lying in bed or on the sofa complaining of pain in his back constantly and weeping. Whereas before he had been an affectionate father, now he could not bear to have his children near him, because he was afraid they would bump him and hurt his back. . . .

By January 1968 he was complaining of headaches. Although on January 15 Dr. Nork noted "Doing extremely well," he also noted that the patient was "very apprehensive," and on January 29 he noted "severe headaches without apparent cause—sometimes nausea and vomiting.". . .

[Following a referral by Dr. Nork to an ear, nose and throat specialist, Gonzales was told his headaches were "not of sinus origin." Apparently feeling that he could not be helped, Gonzales took an overdose of pills and was hospitalized under Dr. Nork's care. Gonzales was referred at this time to Dr. Sebastian, a psychiatrist friend of Dr. Nork.

Although Mr. Gonzales saw Dr. Sebastian for several months, "Mr. Gonzales never developed toward Dr. Sebastian any attitude resembling the almost filial affection he had for Dr. Nork." During his treatment with Dr. Sebastian, Gonzales had two more "suicidal episodes" which Dr. Sebastian classified as either a "suicidal gesture" or an actual "attempt."]

Gonzales' depression is perfectly understandable. He was in constant pain; he could not work although he tried; he could increase his activities only marginally and with great effort; he was upset by his financial difficulties; and felt degraded by the facts that the family had to go on Welfare and Mrs. Gonzales had to go to work. He complained repeatedly to Dr. Sebastian that he had been relegated to the role of baby-sitter. . . .

Dr. Sebastian felt that Gonzales' constant complaints of back pain were due to his injuries in the auto accident, and that the pain was preventing his usual adaptation to life. He believed this "strained his [Gonzales'] defense mechanisms," and that this, in turn, intensified the pain. He described Gonzales as a man with a physical orientation, who would have had no need for psychiatric help had he been able to work. With his disability, the plaintiff showed evidence of a personality change at best of moderate to severe degree and sometimes severe. This evaluation accords well with that of Dr. Solomon, a psychiatrist who examined Gonzales in May and June 1973, and has since treated him, who described him as "upwardly mobile," and that of Dr. Greene, another psychiatrist who testified on the basis of the hypothetical question. . . .

Two points that Dr. Solomon made are particularly important. One is that the mistreatment suffered at the hands of Dr. Nork has made Gonzales unable to trust other doctors. This is reflected in the difficulties Dr. Caggiano has since had in treating Gonzales for cancer, which will be described hereafter. The other is the fact that Gonzales became an alcoholic. This was the result of his reliance on intoxication to avoid both his painful emotions and his use of alcohol as an anodyne to allay his physical discomfort. . . .

Dr. Sebastian's description of Mr. Gonzales as a physically oriented man is fully substantiated. Before his accident he worked regularly at two jobs, grocery clerk and evening janitorial work, and intermittently at a third as a tree trimmer. He was athletic. Indeed, Mrs. Gonzales was concerned that she never saw him because he was so frequently involved in work or sports. Immediately after the accident in October 1967 he tried to work for a few days. And as early as January 1968 he tried to return to Willie's Market, but he had so much pain that all he could do was some dusting. He tried to work in his yard, but could not. After this succession of frustrated efforts he developed the headaches and vomiting, for which Dr. Nork referred him to [the ear, nose and throat doctor].

There has been no material change in his pain since 1969. His inability to work at the market is due almost entirely to his back pain. He has been seen or treated for his pain intermittently since his surgery. In June 1969 and September 1970, Dr. Nork advised Gonzales' insurer that he was still temporarily disabled. But by November 12, 1970, Dr. Nork had come to the conclusion that the disability, which he said had existed since November 1, 1967, was both total and permanent. On February 10, 1972, Dr. Canaan, to whom Gonzales was referred by Dr. Nork when he left Sacramento, found the patient still totally disabled from his laminectomy but indicated it might be temporary and "possibly" Gonzales would be able to resume some sort of work by April of 1972. Dr. Caggiano has prescribed Darvon, a compound for the relief of pain, rather regularly, and Mr. Gonzales reported to Drs. Bernstein and Hanzell that he was using it. He continues to use about fifty capsules per month. In the face of this evidence, the suggestion of Dr. Nork's counsel that Gonzales' pain has ameliorated is not acceptable.

In June 1971, a little more than a year after the removal of his right testicle for cancer, Gonzales, with the encouragement of Dr. Caggiano, returned to work for about six months. He worked only part-time, because his back, rather than his cancer, still disabled him. He worked again in the Summer of 1972 for sixty-two hours, and in 1973 for eighty-three hours. . . . At that time Gonzales' stomach ulcer was still acute; regardless of his hours of attendance, he could actually work no more than three or four hours a day. . . .

Dr. Nork's counsel tried to raise the inference that these episodes of work show that the plaintiff is a malingerer. But the explanation given by Gonzales and the DaPratos is more convincing. The plaintiff worked to maintain his eligibility for health insurance through the Retail Clerks' Union, and Mr. Da-Prato "threw in" hours that the plaintiff did not work to help him achieve this end. [Mr. DaPrato's acts were admirable and constituted no more than aid to a loyal employee.]

The plaintiff's medical history must be considered because of its bearing on the amount of damages. Mr. Gonzales suffers from three physical conditions, which all contribute to his present disability. In order of occurrence they are gastro-intestinal problems preceding the surgery, the back and leg pains caused by the surgery, and the cancer, which became manifest after the surgery. All three physical conditions are complicated by what Dr. Caggiano called "an emotional overlay," or what Dr. Solomon repeatedly referred to as emotional "vulnerability." The plaintiff suffers from what can be described as psychic fragility; he breaks where less delicately adjusted people might bend and spring back. The emotional and gastro-intestinal problems rendered him more susceptible to injury by the surgery, and the surgery aggravated them and reduced his ability to accept treatment for the cancer. These factors bear on the extent of Dr. Nork's liability. Restatement (Second) of Torts §§458, 461 (1965).

Two years before the surgery by Dr. Nork, Dr. Liddil had the impression that Mr. Gonzales had an irritable colon and probably had colitis. On April 5, 1967, he was admitted to Sutter Hospital with a diagnosis of questionable appendicitis, and later questionable ileitis. . . . None of this past history appears in Dr. Nork's notes although the Mercy history form clearly calls for it.

Since an actor may be held liable for harm based on a peculiar physical condition, which he could not have discovered even by the exercise of reasonable care, Restatement (Second) of Torts §461, comment a, a fortiori, he may be liable where he was under a duty to discover the condition. Dr. Colbert, who first admitted Mr. Gonzales for cancer, was able to elicit this history. It is significant because both colitis and ileitis are in the category of psychosomatic diseases according to a number of defense witnesses, in which emotions cause a physiological reaction. Dr. Nork should, therefore, have been on guard.

There is no doubt Dr. Nork injured the plaintiff's back. Even Dr. Nork's own witness, Dr. Hanzell, concedes: "The patient's lumbo-sacral pain and intermittent right sciatic pain can presumably be considered to be related to the patient's initial injury *and subsequent surgery.*". . . The best that can be said is that the plaintiff's back is not as severely damaged as those of some of Dr. Nork's other patients.

The important point, however, is not what Gonzales has, but that whatever he has is due to Dr. Nork's surgery as both Drs. Hanzell and Bernstein agree. Dr. Hanzell qualified his opinion by stating in his report that it was also due to his prior injury and in his testimony that it might also be due to the cancer treatment. But he could give "no solid opinion" on how much of the condition was due to any of the separate causes. Accepting Dr. Hanzell's testimony for purposes of discussion, we have a case of substantial concurrent causes without a reasonable basis for apportionment among them, and Dr. Nork must, therefore, be held liable for the whole. Restatement (Second) of Torts §433A and comment *i* (1965).

In the Spring of 1970, while still disabled with his back and leg, the plaintiff noticed a lump on his right testicle. He ignored it for three or four months and then saw Dr. Ma. Dr. Ma referred him to Dr. Colbert, a urologist, who admitted him to Sutter Hospital on May 11, 1970. Dr. Colbert performed a radical right orchiectomy (removal of testicle) on May 12 and Dr. Montemayor did an exploratory laparotomy on May 20. The pathologist, Dr. Glassy, diagnosed an embryonal carcinoma or teratocarcinoma of the testicle, and, as a result of the laparotomy, found that it had already metastasized to the perirenal lymph nodes. Drs. Montemayor and Colbert found that the metastatic mass was inoperable: "It was felt that because of the extent of the disease the procedure should be abandoned and he [Gonzales] will be given chemotherapy and radiation therapy later." Dr. Glassy reported that his pathological findings suggested "a poor prognosis."

Dr. Caggiano, a specialist in internal medicine, particularly hematology and oncology, called in by Dr. Montemayor, has treated the plaintiff from May 21, 1970, the time of the diagnosis of cancer, to date. Of Mr. Gonzales Dr. Caggiano says, "He's been a difficult patient to treat." This testimony is either a triumph of understatement or a model of irony. The record shows that the plaintiff has had a dismal history relieved only by the excellence of Dr. Caggiano's treatment. The excellence of the treatment has been substantiated by at least three of Dr. Nork's witnesses. . . . Nevertheless, Dr. Caggiano estimates the plaintiff's chance of surviving another three years at between 10 and 20%. . . .

The plaintiff contends that his cancer was caused by Dr. Nork's surgery, either because of the debility produced by the surgery, or because of his severe depression consequent to the surgery. I shall not go into the mechanisms by which either debility or depression are claimed to result in cancer, because I am satisfied by the testimony of Dr. Nork's witnesses that neither the cause nor progression of cancer can, in the present state of medical knowledge, be attributed to emotional depression, and, assuming that such cause or progression can be attributed to debility, that the plaintiff's degree of debility was sufficient to allow such attribution in this case.

The plaintiff's emotional state due to his surgery cannot, however, be disregarded. . . . [An extended discussion of Gonzales's emotional difficulties is omitted.]

This series of uncontrollable physical and emotional reactions, attributable in a substantial degree to Dr. Nork's surgery, prevented treatment for the cancer. Thus Dr. Nork is liable for the consequences of diminishing the treatment.

The foregoing was complicated by Gonzales' continued use of alcohol, against which Dr. Caggiano cautioned him on numerous occasions. Gastric problems reappeared, not in the relatively vague or inconclusive form that Gonzales suffered before his accident, but in the form of a perforated ulcer, which required surgical repair in February 1971. "Since that time he has not been able to take full courses of chemotherapy because of persistent worsening of epigastric discomfort.". . .

To recapitulate: Gonzales was psychologically vulnerable; the surgery caused physical pain that prevented his usual adjustment to life; being psychologically vulnerable, the alteration in his adjustment caused him to become severely depressed; the depression led, if not to alcoholism, to episodes of aggravated abuse of alcohol; all three, the psychic vulnerability, the depression, and the abuse of alcohol, resulted in an "emotional overlay," which rendered him unable to accept treatment for cancer with the drugs of choice, in the desirable amounts, at the desirable intervals; the interference with and interruption of his treatment has reduced his life expectancy from a 50% chance of surviving ten years, a cure, to about a 10% chance of surviving three years. Thus we have the surgery as a cause which, in natural and continuous sequence, has produced an abbreviation of his life, and without which such abbreviation would not have occurred. Cf. BAJI 3.75. The incompetent surgeon, who operated needlessly and negligently, is, therefore, liable for such abbreviation.

Dr. Nork's Defenses

Dr. Nork waived his defense under Code Civ. Proc. §340.5 and formally admitted his professional negligence in the treatment of Gonzales. He expressly reserved, however, his rights to contest the nature of the harm caused by his negligence, the extent of such harm, and the amount of Gonzales' damages. He resisted the claim for punitive damages on the theory that he had no intent to defraud. He claims he treated his patients improperly because the drugs altered his memory and judgment.

. . . Dr. Nork's counsel during the trial raised the issue of improper collusion between counsel for the plaintiff and the hospital. This was not pleaded as a defense, and it does not appear to be a defense. For lack of a better term, I call it a "quasi-defense.". . .

Thus, in summary there are six defense issues: (1) the release; (2) the statute of limitations; (3) the denial of fraud; (4) causation and extent of damage; (5) amount of damage; and (6) collusion. I have already disposed of the 4th item and given my reasons above. I will dispose of the 5th separately. In this section I shall consider only the first three and the "quasi-defense" of collusion. . . .

The release was executed by Mr. Gonzales on April 28, 1969, in consideration of $55,850.00 to settle his claim against Storey and Hart arising out of the automobile accident in which he first injured his back. It is in the usual form used by defense lawyers. It purports to release not only Storey and Hart but "all other persons, firms or corporations, of and from any and all claims, demands, actions and causes of action, arising out of or which are in any way incident to" the accident of October 24, 1967. And it purports to extend to "any and all claims, demands, actions and causes of action of any and every kind or nature whatever, present or future, known or unknown, contemplated or uncontemplated, arising out of or connected with said accident."

Dr. Nork never heard that he might be covered by the release until this case was being prepared. Nevertheless, through his counsel, he claims that he is a third-party beneficiary of this release—a donee beneficiary, because he gave no consideration for it. There are two reasons why his claim that the release was some sort of a gift to him cannot succeed.

The first reason is that there is no evidence of an intent on the part of Gonzales to release Dr. Nork. . . . The release of "unknown injuries," without more, does not even release the defendants actually named in the release. There must be evidence, independent of the words of the release, that the releaser actually intended to discharge such claims. . . . If such a blanket release does not avail a defendant named in the release, *a fortiori* it does not help a defendant claiming as a donee beneficiary of the release. . . .

The second reason is that at the time I had to rule on this defense a *prima facie* case of fraud had already been presented against Dr. Nork. By no stretch of the imagination can this fraud case be considered a claim "arising out of" or "incident to" the prior auto accident. It is an independent tort of a different nature. It would be an affront to conscience to hold that a patient defrauded by a doctor cannot hold the doctor because of a release given to the original tortfeasor before the patient even knew of the doctor's deception. [Here the court goes through the arithmetic of computing Dr. Nork's liability with due regard to the consideration Gonzales received for his release. Since a plaintiff may not recover twice for the same injury, the court subtracts the amount of damage *not caused* by Dr. Nork (property damage to Gonzales' car and lost wages during the period immediately after the accident) to arrive at a total figure of $51,950 which must be subtracted from the total award of damages to the plaintiff in order to prevent his double recovery.]

This action was filed on November 17, 1972, five years and one day after the surgery. Dr. Nork contends that it is barred by the one-year statute of limitations, Code Civ. Proc. §340(3). . . .

Despite the language of §340(3), "it is well established in [medical] malpractice actions that the statute does not commence to run until the patient discovers his injury, or through the exercise of reasonable diligence should have discovered it." [A discussion of California law is omitted.]

The physician-patient relationship between the plaintiff and Dr. Nork lasted until at least March 29, 1971. The first actual notice that the plaintiff had of Dr. Nork's malpractice was no earlier than February 1972. At that time he was hospitalized for metastasis of his cancer to the orbit or brain, and Mr. Cooper, Mr. Freidberg's investigator, unsuccessfully sought to contact him through his wife. The contact was sought to ascertain whether Mr. Gonzales might be a witness in the Hendrick case, which was then awaiting trial. Some three or four months later Mr. Cooper succeeded in contacting Gonzales. Mr. Gonzales insisted upon meeting with Mr. Freidberg and thereafter allowed Mr. Freidberg to examine his records. Later, although he did not believe what Mr. Freidberg told him about Dr. Nork, he retained him. Thus the likely date of actual notice is June 1972, about five months before the action was filed, and the plaintiff is protected by the rule as stated in *Rawlings v. Harris,* supra. . . .

Even by the exercise of the utmost diligence Gonzales could not have had notice of Dr. Nork's malpractice before he spoke to Mr. Freidberg. . . . [The court lists all the doctors and nurses who failed to inform the plaintiff of the cause of his condition.] Since not one of the doctors who treated him, and who were, presumably, devoted to his best interests, told him his pain was due to bad surgery, either they did not suspect it was, or, if they did, they would not tell him. Thus there was no way he could discover the fact. . . .

This pattern of lack of communication by doctors is a manifestation of the "conspiracy of silence" that has been seen in other aspects. . . .

The medical profession cannot have its cake and eat it. Either it has to disclose the facts to the patients, or it has to live with the judicial applications to the statutes of limitation. . . .

Dr. Nork resists liability for fraud, *i.e.,* for punitive damages, on the ground that his malpractice "was the result of his unfortunate situation of being gradually addicted to mood-elevating drugs interfering with his clinical judgment. . . ." Although I have treated this as a defense, it is actually only an effort to escape liability for punitive damages predicated on the rule that such damages may not be awarded for a merely negligent act committed while intoxicated. . . .

The basis in law for the proposition that intoxication reduces liability for fraud was never made clear. Counsel cited no authority to this effect, and I have found none. . . .

I am, however, satisfied from the evidence that Dr. Nork successfully engaged in a deliberate and purposeful course of conduct intentionally designed to deceive a class of persons, his patients. . . . And I am further satisfied that he had the mental capacity to form and execute the intent to defraud. Restatement of Torts §531, comment *b* (1938). . . .

The only evidence that Dr. Nork's use of drugs in any way affected his ability to distinguish right from wrong or to appreciate the nature and consequences of his acts is that which came from his own mouth. His testimony is uncorroborated; it is contradicted directly and circumstantially by a host of credible witnesses; it is belied by his position in other litigation; and it appears to be a recent contrivance invented for the purposes of this case. . . .

Dr. Nork used Preludin, a trade name for an amphetamine-like substance. It is used principally to effect weight control by reducing the appetite for food. Its use does not impair memory; on the contrary, it causes the user to remember "explosively." A user would certainly be aware of what he was doing, such as falsifying medical records, unless the use were so excessive as to produce a "frank psychosis." Although Dr. Nork's use was excessive, it did not produce a "frank psychosis.". . .

Dr. Nork's assertions that his admitted malpractice on numerous patients was due to the alteration of his judgment and memory by the use of drugs were attacked by the plaintiff and the Hospital as a recent contrivance. The attack was based largely, but not exclusively, on his failure to make such defensive contentions in the Hendrick trial in 1972. . . .

Dr. Nork said that he testified as he did in Hendrick, because he was "threatened, forced and coerced" to do so by his then attorneys, Mr. Gray and Mr. Huber. They had been retained for him by his malpractice insurer, the American Mutual Liability Company. He gave a rather vivid account of a meeting with Mr. Gray at the Brigadoon Lodge in Vacaville at which Mr. Gray "read the riot act" to him, "whipped [him] into shape," and said "you've got to cooperate and do as we say." Dr. Nork knew that his lawyers were telling him to lie, but he felt that he had to cooperate with them in order to have insurance coverage and counsel at the trial. . . . In all of this he was more concerned with protecting himself than he was by compounding his patient's problems. . . .

On the immediate problem of the effect of the use of drugs, the balance of credibility is clearly against Dr. Nork. . . .

Dr. Nork's use of drugs amounted to thousands of pills. His use of Preludin, the amphetamine-like compound, was clearly "excessive." But he made no disclosure of the extent of his use until after he retained his present co-counsel, Mr. Harper, in January of 1973. He told Mr. Harper that he used only three or four Preludin per day. Mr. Harper pointed out that the records showed he had used about three times those amounts, and that such usage might enhance the argument as to their effect. This seems to have been the birth of Dr. Nork's present contention.

Although Dr. Nork denies the drug defense is a device to "wipe the slate clean" with the State Board of Medical Examiners, he does hope that his use of drugs will be considered a reason for disregarding his past history so that he can continue to work. . . .

On reviewing this background it is apparent that the contention that the use of drugs altered Dr. Nork's thinking to the point where he could not entertain a fraudulent intent is unacceptable. I shall find that he used the drugs, but that they did not have the effect he claims. That claim is a recent contrivance, which I shall find to be false. . . .

Throughout the trial Dr. Nork's counsel were, understandably, vexed by the fact that Mercy Hospital was as aggressive in presenting a case against Dr. Nork as was the plaintiff. Their vexation was compounded by the fact that the plaintiff presented only a comparatively casual case against the hospital. Mr. Freidberg testified that his attitude toward the hospital was "neutral." He did, however, present a *prima facie* case against the hospital. And Mercy did not move for a nonsuit, or, after it waived the jury, make a motion for judgment under Code Civ. Proc. §631.8. Dr. Nork's counsel have claimed that the conduct of Mr. Freidberg, for the plaintiff, and Mr. Rust, for Mercy, shows that they have engaged in some improper form of collusion. . . .

There never was a possibility that holding the hospital liable would be of advantage to Dr. Nork. What Dr. Nork was seeking to do was to protect his potential right of contribution against a co-tortfeasor. Since I intend to hold him guilty of deliberate fraud, he is an intentional tortfeasor and has no right of contribution under the statute. Code Civ. Proc. §875(d).

The Amount of Mr. Gonzales' Damages

The plaintiff originally asked for $1,000,000 general damages, plus medical expenses and loss of earnings. His motion to amend the prayer to $2,000,000 general damages was granted on May 30, 1973, but this was omitted from the minutes. The minutes were corrected on October 1, 1973. He also asked for $1,000,000 in punitive damages against Dr. Nork only. His motion to amend this prayer to $2,000,000 was granted on July 23, 1973.

The plaintiff's damages are conveniently considered under two headings: (A) compensatory damages; and (B) punitive damages. The item of compensatory damages can be subdivided into four categories: (1) medical expenses; (2) wages lost to date; (3) wages to be lost in the future; and (4) pain, suffering, and emotional distress. In determining the net item of compensatory damages, allowance will be made for a portion of the amount Gonzales recovered by his settlement with Storey and Hart.

[A discussion of Gonzales' medical expenses is omitted.]

[In treating the issue of wages lost to date, the court rejects Dr. Nork's argument that Gonzales' inability to work dates from his cancer and holds Nork liable for the entire amount requested by the plaintiff, minus the compensation for the release.]

On the question of loss of future wages, Dr. Nork and the plaintiff are at loggerheads. Dr. Nork claims that since the plaintiff has a life expectancy of but two or three years, he can recover future wages for that period only. Gonzales, he says, can recover no more, because he is going to die. This argument is made in the face of the fact that Dr. Nork's surgery is a cause of Gonzales' impending death. Dr. Nork is thus arguing that he can have the benefit of the plaintiff's decreased life expectancy and consequent diminished expectation of future wages, even though his own acts caused these circumstances. In short, Dr. Nork seeks to profit from his own wrong.

For example, he argues that allowing the plaintiff to recover future earnings for anything more than two or three years will amount to a double recovery, because the plaintiff will not be obligated to support himself or his family after his death. I reject this contention because I cannot find any authority that damages are to be computed on the basis of the plaintiff's costs of living. . . .

Dr. Nork also predicates his argument that Gonzales' recovery should be limited to his actual life expectancy on the proposition that such limitation is necessary to protect his heirs under Code Civ. Proc. §377 and his estate under Probate Code §573. He cites no authority for this proposition. . . .

I accept the reasoning in *Coffman v. St. Louis–San Francisco Ry. Co.*, 378 S.W. 2d 583, 594–95 (Mo. 1964), and *Roberts v. United States*, 316 F.2d 489,

497 (3d Cir. 1963). And following the latter, in determining Gonzales' life expectancy I shall not consider "the injury for which redress is sought, as that would permit the defendant to benefit by [his] own wrong.". . .

Gonzales' argument is as extreme as Dr. Nork's. He contends that his loss of future earnings and retirement benefits should cover the period of 39 years from now. This period is the average life expectancy of a white male aged 32. (Mr. Gonzales was born on August 18, 1941.) This period would be proper if Dr. Nork's surgery had caused Gonzales' cancer. But I find that it did not cause the cancer. I accept the testimony of Drs. Caggiano and Whitmore that had the plaintiff been amenable to more treatment, he would now have a better than 50% chance of surviving ten years, and surviving ten years is a cure. Therefore, I shall reduce the plaintiff's claim for future wages and retirement benefits by 50%. . . .

In this case there is evidence that shows that the intensity of the emotional distress Gonzales incurred at the hands of Dr. Nork was extraordinary. I have already noted that Gonzales developed almost filial affection for Dr. Nork. [An extended discussion of the plaintiff's feelings for Dr. Nork and his betrayal of his patient's feelings is deleted.]

There is, of course, no relation between the special damages and the monetary value of pain and suffering. Assuming, as a rule of thumb, that a day of pain is worth a day of work, I considered fixing the general damages at the total of the wages lost to date and to be lost in the future. But here the intensity of Gonzales' suffering caused by his own nature and Dr. Nork's abuse and betrayal of that nature, and the fact that Dr. Nork is partly responsible for Gonzales' having to be a witness to his own dissolution are peculiar elements of pain, suffering and emotional distress that cannot be ignored. I shall, therefore, allow for general damages the amount of the total special damages, $862,397.17 (before credit) plus $50,000 rounded down to $900,000 to avoid a delusive appearance of certainty. This may seem to allow the plaintiff to recover for pain, suffering, and emotional distress after his death, but it is not so intended. It is intended to allow the plaintiff to recover for having to face the awful prospect of his impending death.

Medical expenses	$ 37,271.84
Wages lost to date	75,125.33
Future wage loss	750,000.00
	$ 862,397.17
Pain, suffering and emotional distress	$ 900,000.00
	$1,762,397.17
Less consideration for release in *Gonzales v. Storey* (adjusted)	51,950.00
Total compensatory damages	$1,710,447.17

"The purposes of awarding punitive damages or 'exemplary' damages as they are frequently called, are to punish the person doing the wrongful act and to discourage such person and others from similar conduct in the future." Restatement of Torts §908, Comment *a* at 554 (1939). Dr. Nork argues that since he has already been subjected to a judgment for punitive damages in the Hendrick case, he cannot be subjected to a judgment for punitive damages in this case. This argument of "double jeopardy" is totally unacceptable. In Mrs. Hendrick's case he was punished for what he did to her. Here he is to be punished for what he did to Mr. Gonzales. There are two distinct causes of action, although they arise from the one course of misconduct. A thief is not to be punished less because he steals repeatedly. His prior offenses are a reason for increasing rather than mitigating the penalty. . . .

Consideration has also been given to the deterrent purpose of punitive damages. Civil Code §3294 says they may be awarded "for the sake of example." And the Restatement of Torts says they may be awarded "to discourage . . . others from similar conduct." §908, Comment *a* at 554. The need for deterrence is obvious, because the failure of the medical profession to discipline itself has been recently remarked. R. McCleery, One Life–One Physician 69 (1971); Holman, *Hard Cases Make Bad Law,* 226 Jl. Am. Med. Assoc. 562 (1973). . . . The problem is illustrated by this case. No action has been taken against Dr. Nork by the Board of Medical Examiners, and he is still practicing at the Veterans Administration Hospital in Martinez. The Board has, or should have, knowledge of the malpractice judgments or settlements in Dr. Nork's cases since January 1, 1971. . . . Licensing of persons to practice medicine in itself "furnishes no continuing control with respect to a physician's professional competence and therefore does not assure the public of quality patient care. The protection of the public must come from some other authority. . . ." *Moore v. Board of Trustees of Carson-Tahoe Hosp.,* 495 p. 2d 605, 608 (Nev. 1972).

In this case the other authority is the Court. The beneficial effect of malpractice litigation in improving medical performance has been established by evidence in this case. Consider the following fragment from the testimony of Dr. Nesbit:

> "The legal profession has helped the medical profession a great deal
> by having malpractice litigation, pointed out several flaws in our sys-
> tem that we are working under. . . ."

Based on the foregoing, it would appear reasonable to award punitive damages in an amount twice the actual damages, *i.e.,* $3,420,894.34. This amount is so large that I would reduce it by the amount of the Hendrick award of punitive damages, $300,000, to $3,120,894.34. However, even this amount should not be awarded. The plaintiff has asked for $2,000,000, and that is what I shall allow. . . .

[The court goes on to dismiss Dr. Nork's objection that he is "not a man of means."] Here, of course, we are not concerned with the "amount of damage suffered," as that has already been considered. But we are concerned with the award of a sufficient amount to serve as an example to discourage others. Collectibility of the amount is, nevertheless, still immaterial.

The Liability of Mercy Hospital

Mercy Hospital did not plead the release and statute of limitations. . . . Instead it has raised two defenses: (1) that it cannot be held for the torts of its independent medical staff; and (2) that it not only conformed to the standards of the industry but went somewhat beyond them. (Although Mercy did not plead the release, I intend, nevertheless, to allow it the credit of $51,950 that I shall allow to Dr. Nork. This is to avoid the paradox of holding the less culpable tortfeasor to a greater compensatory liability than the more culpable tortfeasor, the intentional and oppressive wrongdoer, Dr. Nork.)

In coming to the conclusion that Mercy Hospital should be held liable I have considered the following: the fact that Mercy had no actual knowledge of Dr. Nork's propensities until May 1970, why it did not have such knowledge, and how it obtained it; the general duty of hospitals to protect patients from fraudulent surgery by members of their staffs; . . . that this duty could not, in 1967, be discharged merely by compliance with the then prevailing standards of the Joint Commission on Accreditation of Hospitals (hereinafter JCAH); and that Mercy had opportunities to acquire actual knowledge, which it neglected by failure to investigate properly and by violations of its own rules by its agents or employees.

Throughout this part I have relied very heavily on the testimony of Dr. Reed M. Nesbit and Mercy's exhibits, which corroborate and amplify his testimony. Dr. Nesbit, a surgeon of stellar eminence, was Mercy's principal witness. He is one of the nation's outstanding urological surgeons. [Omitted is a discussion of Dr. Nesbit's credentials.] He came here, not because of his concern in the case as such, but to find out how a case of this sort could arise in a properly accredited hospital. His expenses were paid not by Mercy but by JCAH. . . .

The burden of Dr. Nesbit's testimony was that Mercy had complied meticulously with the JCAH standards, but that the standards in effect in 1967 provided no means of detecting a fraudulent physician like Dr. Nork. . . . The burden of this opinion is that compliance with such a standard is not due care in discharging the hospital's obligations to protect a patient from fraud. Thus I accept the testimony of Dr. Nesbit, but I do not accept the conclusion Mercy would have me draw from it. . . .

Mercy Hospital has been accredited by JCAH since the inception of that organization in 1953. . . . Mercy at all times complied strictly with the JCAH standards. . . . It practiced, through its medical staff, the system of "peer review" of the quality of patients' treatment required by JCAH. But the methods of review required by JCAH in 1967, and before, were random, casual, subjective and uncritical. . . . Thus in November 1967, the time of

Mr. Gonzales' surgery, Mercy Hospital did not have actual knowledge that Dr. Nork was using it as the vehicle for the systematic perpetration of fraud and incompetence.

A natural supposition is that a physician of Dr. Nork's ineptitude would have revealed his lack of skill by his techniques in the operating room. But the performance of a laminectomy is such that no one in the operating room can tell whether the surgeon is mishandling the dura or nerve roots. The aperture through which the surgeon must work is so small that only the surgeon himself need know what he is doing.

Mercy Hospital did not become aware of the fact that it had a problem with Dr. Nork until May of 1970, when Mr. Dresel, its administrator, heard a rumor that Dr. Nork's malpractice insurance had been cancelled. Like many hospitals, Mercy . . . has a requirement that staff doctors have malpractice insurance. It inquired and found the rumor was true. Dr. Nork's insurance was cancelled in May 1970 when three lawsuits, Curtis Jackson, De La Torre and Darling, were pending, and a fourth, Tower, had been filed but not served. . . .

Whatever the reason for the cancellation, Mercy acted promptly and put Dr. Nork under a monitoring program, under which he was forbidden to operate without another designated surgeon present. And Dr. Nork did no further back surgery at either Mercy General or Mercy San Juan after June 1970. . . .

Dr. Nork also tried to have the restrictions removed. He approached his friend, Dr. Quillinan, then a member of the State Board of Medical Examiners, who spoke to Mr. Gray on Dr. Nork's behalf. Mr. Gray and his law firm wore three hats: counsel for the Sacramento Society for Medical Improvement; counsel for American Mutual; and counsel for Dr. Nork. American Mutual knew that the Society had reviewed the Nork cases and found them indefensible. . . . So Mr. Gray doffed his Society hat, donned his other two hats, and approached Mr. John Diepenbrock, Mercy's corporate counsel, to have the restrictions removed. He was unsuccessful; Mercy proceeded to conduct an intensive review of Dr. Nork's cases; thereafter it reduced Dr. Nork's surgical privileges; almost simultaneously Dr. Nork resigned from the Mercy staff and left Sacramento. . . .

In considering the duty of a hospital to protect its patients from malpractice by its staff, the term "staff" should be defined, and a legal distinction should be made clear. The terms "medical staff" or "hospital staff" are ambiguous. They may refer to doctors employed by the hospital, *e.g.* a pathologist or anesthetist, or they may refer to doctors who have been granted the privilege of using the hospital's facilities to treat their own patients. The latter definition is the one principally involved in the present case. See Annot., 69 A.L.R. 2d 305, 321–22 (1960).

The difference in the meanings of the word "staff" raises another problem— the legal distinction between vicarious liability of the hospital and what has come to be called its "corporate" liability. If the doctor is an employee of the hospital, the hospital is liable for his acts of malpractice under the doctrine of *respondeat superior.* If the doctor is a member of the staff only in the second sense, *i.e.,* simply allowed to treat his private patients in the hospital, the hospital is not liable under the doctrine of *respondeat superior* for his acts of malpractice. But if the hospital knew or should have known that a patient was liable to be a victim of malpractice by a doctor on its staff, in either of the senses of the term, it is liable on the basis of its corporate liability. *Darling v. Charleston Community Memorial Hospital,* 211 N.E. 2d 253, 14 A.L.R. 3d 860 (Ill. 1965); *Fiorentino v. Wenger,* 227 N.E. 2d 296 (N.Y. 1967).

[Description of *Darling* and *Fiorentino* omitted.]

The rule I distill from these cases is this: the hospital, by virtue of its custody of the patient, owes him a duty of care; this duty includes the obligation to protect him from acts of malpractice by his independently retained physician who is a member of the hospital's staff, if the hospital knows, or has reason to know, or should have known that such acts were likely to occur.

Mercy Hospital claims that it cannot be liable for Dr. Nork's fraud, because it is, in effect, required by Bus. & Prof. C. §2392.5(c) to function through a "medical staff [that] shall be self-governing with respect to the professional work performed in the hospital." This argument is in flat opposition to the views of Mr. Charles W. Jacobs, Assistant Director of JCAH and a lawyer. Mr. Jacobs says:

> "Delegating authority to its medical staff for performance of specific quality maintenance functions does not, of itself, relieve a hospital of its ultimate responsibility. . . ."

Mercy's argument is also contradicted by some fundamental principles. There was a substantial body of old law that hospitals were not vicariously liable even for the torts of physicians whom they employed, because they could not control the professional conduct of such physicians. . . . But the more recent rationalization of the doctrine of *respondeat superior* is that the rule is a device to place the risk of harm on the employing enterprise, which can insure or guard against the harm, even though the tortfeasor may not be controlled by the enterprise. *Hinman v. Westinghouse Elec. Co.,* 2 Cal. 3d 956, 960 (1970). The policy of placing the risk of harm on the enterprise is so pervasive that it has virtually swallowed up the old general rule that there was no liability of the acts of an independent contractor. . . .

The above mixture or obliteration of the distinction between liability for the acts of employees or agents on the one hand, and the acts of independent contractors on the other, cannot be ignored. I suggest that it may be the genesis of a development similar to what has happened in the law of strict liability. . . . [T]he rights of the victim of medical malpractice should not be made to depend on the intricacies of the law of master and servant or principal and agent.

> "The concept of corporate responsibility for the quality of medical care was forcibly [*sic.* forcefully?] advanced in *Darling v. Charleston Community Memorial Hosp.* . . . , wherein the Illinois Supreme

Court held that hospitals and their governing bodies may be held liable for injuries resulting from imprudent or careless supervision of members of their medical staffs. The role of the hospital vis-a-vis the community is changing rapidly. The hospital's role is no longer limited to the furnishing of physical facilities and equipment where a physician treats his private patients and practices his profession in his own individualized manner." *Moore v. Board of Trustees of Carson-Tahoe Hosp.*, 495 P. 2d 605, 608 (Nev. 1972).

Who is better able to guard against the use of a hospital as a means of perpetrating frauds, the operator of the hospital, or the patient in the hospital? To put the question is to answer it.

[The court's discussion of the statutory bases for Mercy's arguments about its liability is omitted.]

The JCAH standards and the Mercy Medical Staff By-Laws illustrate the point made in *Moore v. Board of Trustees of Carson-Tahoe Hosp.*, 495, P. 2d 605, 608 (Nev. 1972), a revocation case, that "All powers of the medical staff flow from the board of trustees, and the staff must be held accountable for its control of quality." If quality is not controlled, the hospital may be subjected to corporate liability. The Nevada Court then cites *Darling v. Charleston Community Memorial Hospital.* . . . These principles were applied in a corporate responsibility case, *Mitchell County Hospital Authority v. Joiner,* 189 S.E. 2d 412 (Ga. 1972). The Georgia Court arrived at them independently and without considering *Darling*. It held that a hospital could be liable in a wrongful death action for its independent negligence in allowing a licensed, but incompetent, physician to practice as a member of its staff. There, as here, the hospital sought to escape liability on the grounds that the function, in that case admission to the staff, had been properly delegated to its medical staff. But the Georgia Court of Appeals held, "This is not defensive, as these members of the staff are agents of the Hospital Authority and it is responsible for any default or negligence on its [the staff's] part. . . ." *Joiner v. Mitchell County Hospital Authority,* 186 S.E. 2d 307, 308 (Ga. App. 1971). The Georgia Supreme Court expressly approved this holding. *Mitchell County Hospital Authority v. Joiner, supra.,* 189 S.E. 2d at 414. *Purcell v. Zimbelman,* 500 P. 2d 335, 341 (Ariz. App. 1972) follows *Joiner*. Thus it appears that the standards and by-laws are means whereby the hospital meets its corporate responsibility; they are not means whereby it insulates itself from liability.

[The court then distinguishes a contrary case.]

To recapitulate briefly: the hospital is required to have a medical staff by the regulations in the California Administrative Code. That staff is required to be "self-governing" or independent by Bus. & Prof. C. §2392.5. The hospital has met these obligations by adopting Medical Staff By-Laws in accordance with the JCAH Standards for Hospital Accreditation. But this does not immunize it from liability, because the medical staff acts for the hospital in the discharge of the hospital's responsibilities to protect its patients.

Mercy contends that because it complied with the Standards for Hospital

Accreditation of the Joint Commission on Accreditation of Hospitals, it cannot be held negligent. . . . I understand Mercy's argument, it is that proof of compliance with the JCAH standards "is evidence of what should be done and may assist in the determination of what constitutes due care, [but] it does not conclusively establish the standard of care."

Even if the question of the hospital's negligence is considered to be one on which expert testimony is required, the hospital is not helped. The evidence given by its own expert, Dr. Nesbit, shows the JCAH standards of clinical review in 1967, the standards which the hospital followed faithfully, were inadequate.

The testimony of Dr. Nesbit shows that the JCAH standards being followed by Mercy at the time of Mr. Gonzales' surgery, Mercy Ex. AR, were deficient in the following respects: (1) They were predicated on the assumption that the doctor was reporting honestly and that the records were truthful and accurate. Such assumptions cannot be made, since the hospital has a duty to protect its patients against fraudulent doctors. (2) The required clinical review was subjective according to the personal standards of the reviewer. The review in court done by Dr. Maass showed that such a subjective review will not disclose known deficiencies. (3) The review was random. Therefore, bad cases were picked up only by chance. (4) The review was infrequent. (5) The review was casual, uncritical and sandwiched in between the doctors' other work. (6) The review did not include a comparison of the doctors' progress records and the nurses' notes. (7) No protocol, profile or record was made of doctors' deficiencies so that there was no common fund of knowledge available to the hospital.

An aggravating factor is that the "peer review" system of clinical audits operates generally in an atmosphere of hostility from the profession. Dr. Nesbit referred to the social or club pressures on the reviewers, economic pressures and fear of reprisal. His testimony is completely corroborated by other evidence in the record. Schlicke, *American Surgery's Noblest Experiment,* 106 Archives of Surgery 379, 381 (1973); Jacobs, *Procedure for Retrospective Patient Care Audit in Hospitals* (1973). . . .

I am deeply sympathetic with Mercy Hospital. It, in a sense, is a prisoner of the prevailing system. But in face of the known and admitted inadequacies of the system, I cannot in conscience come to the conclusion that following it constitutes due care. To hold that Mercy was not negligent would fly in the face of its own evidence, would put an imprimatur of approval on manifest impropriety, and would undercut the efforts to reach "the optimum achievable" standards. The law, both here and elsewhere, recognizes that I need not and should not do so.

In his written argument, Mr. Rust, on behalf of Mercy, says: "Any Court that takes it on itself to say that the system has been a failure means that it has to make a determination that the whole United States' medical system has been a failure because the system admittedly was never designed to catch fraud.". . . This statement is a little overblown, of course. The Court does not have to say and should not say the system is a failure. It has operated admirably to bring us from the days when "hospitals [were] in many cases walk-in garbage cans, which people entered reluctantly as a last resort before death." Schlicke, *American Surgery's Noblest Experiment*, 106 Archives of Surgery 379 (1973). But the system is only a minimum one, and one of its deficiencies is that it has no means of detecting fraud.

As long as Justice Lazansky's proposition, reiterated in *Fiorentino v. Wenger, supra*, 227 N.E. 2d, 299–300, remains law, the hospital "owes to every patient . . . the duty of saving him from . . . false, fraudulent or fictitious medical treatment. . . ." This implies a duty to acquire knowledge of possible fraudulent conduct, because to hold the hospital only in cases of actual knowledge would be to place a premium on ignorance. *Foley v. Clarkson Memorial Hospital, supra.*, 173 N.W. 2d at 884. Since the system admittedly does not provide a means of acquiring any knowledge of fraud, except by accident, the system must be held deficient.

This may amount to holding the whole "health care industry," Schlicke, *supra*. at 379, negligent. And if it does, so be it. Precedent is not wanting for such a holding. As Judge Learned Hand said:

> "[A] whole calling may have lagged in the adoption of new and available devices. It may never set its own tests, however persuasive be its usages. Courts must in the end say what is required; there are precautions so imperative that even their universal disregard will not excuse their omission." *The T. J. Hooper*, 60 Fed. 2d 737, 740 (2d Cir. 1932).

The Restatement is in accord. . . . Restatement (Second) of Torts §295A, Comment *c* (1965).

This case is actually easier than the *T. J. Hooper, supra*. It does not involve the "adoption of new and available devices." It involves simply making better use of available information. It takes no great ingenuity or medical knowledge to compare nurses' notes and doctors' progress records. It is no triumph of intellect to record a doctor's deficiencies. Omission of such precautions cannot be excused, because they are imperative to adequate patient care. The need for an incentive to adopt such precautions is apparent from the evidence. This is shown by Dr. Nesbit's testimony about the opposition to peer review, and is expanded on in Dr. Schlicke's paper heretofore cited. California law permits the application of an incentive. And the care of the public requires it. I, therefore, hold that Mercy Hospital was negligent in failing to have any means for detecting Dr. Nork's frauds. . . .

A cursory review of the thirteen surgeries by Dr. Nork, which antedate the plaintiff's surgery, shows that Mercy should have had actual knowledge of Dr. Nork's deficiencies.

In the case of Arthur Freer in 1962, Mercy had two opportunities to acquire actual knowledge. In Freer's case, Dr. Nork's first laminectomy at Mercy, he reported a complication. According to Dr. James Martin, who was on the Mercy Executive Committee from 1962 to 1969, and on its Surgery Committee in 1961 and 1962, the standard of practice for many years had been to list complications, *i.e.,* any major deviation from anticipated convalescence. . . .

Assuming that Freer's complications were not routinely reviewed by Mercy's surgical department, the failure to review may have been perfectly proper. But this does not excuse Mercy, because it had a specific reason to review Freer's case.

Freer brought an action against Mercy and Dr. Nork, no. 144180, on June 5, 1963. This was the first known malpractice suit against Dr. Nork. . . . Mercy answered on July 5, 1963. Thus it had actual notice of the suit. Such notice required it to make a proper investigation. . . .

I conclude that if Mercy had made a proper review of the Freer case, either routinely, or after it had been sued, Dr. Nork's incompetence to do laminectomies would have been exposed as early as 1963. . . .

[The court's discussion of Mrs. Gebhardt and the pathologist *(supra)* is omitted. See the earlier discussion of the "First Bite" rule.]

The hospital has a duty to protect its patients from malpractice by members of its medical staff when it knows or should have known that malpractice was likely to be committed upon them. Mercy Hospital had no actual knowledge of Dr. Nork's propensity to commit malpractice, but it was negligent in not knowing. It was negligent in not knowing, because it did not have a system for acquiring knowledge; it did not use the knowledge available to it properly; it failed to investigate the Freer case, which would have given it knowledge; and it cannot excuse itself on the ground that its medical staff did not inform it. . . .

I have reached the conclusion that the hospital is liable with great reluctance, because I am sure that the Sisters of Mercy have done everything within their power to run a proper institution. But they, like every hospital governing board, are corporately responsible for the conduct of their medical staff. I do not anticipate that they will suffer financially, because the ultimate responsibility rests on Dr. Nork. "A person . . . who by the improper exercise of a legal power, intentionally creates liability against the other, is liable to the other for the . . . creation of liability." Restatement of Torts §871 (1939). Mercy is a culprit, but it is also a victim.

As for the doctors on the Mercy staff, two thoughts keep going through my mind. The one is from Dr. Jones: "No one told anyone anything." The other is from Edmund Burke:

> "The only thing necessary for the triumph of evil is for good men
> to do nothing."

[A brief epilogue is omitted. The court closed with its order directing Dr. Nork to pay the plaintiff $2,000,000 in punitive damages and $1,710,447.17 in compensatory damages, these sums to be divided between Mercy Hospital and Dr. Nork.]

Notes on the Text

1. An Introduction to Malpractice Law

Page

1 For general background on the law of torts and the two functions it serves, see Prosser, *Law of Torts* (4th ed., 1971), pp. 6–16; Harper & James, *The Law of Torts* (1959), §11.5

One recent economic theorist argues that loss-spreading is not an economic objective of the tort law, and that even if it were, it would be irrelevant since potential victims are as capable of self-insurance as potential injurers. See Posner, *Economic Analysis of the Law* (Little, Brown, 1972), p. 94.

Punishment is also sometimes a purpose of the tort law. This is particularly so when the injurer acts in a deliberate and willful way and the victim is given "punitive" damages above the amount of compensation. Also where the injury that the victim complains of is largely dignitary, as, for example, in libel or slander or some cases of false imprisonment one of the prime objectives of the law is to punish the injurer as well as to encourage good future behavior. See Morris, "Punitive Damages in Tort Cases," *Harv. L. Rev.* 44 (1931): 1173.

2 On the history of the development of tort law, see Wigmore, "Responsibility for Tortious Acts: Its History," *Harv. L. Rev.* 7 (1894): 315, 317; Harper & James, *supra,* §12.3; Prosser, *supra,* p. 28 *et seq.;* Wigmore, *op. cit.,* p. 443.

2 *Brown v. Kendall,* 6 Cush 292 (Mass. 1850), is generally cited as the first cases requiring that tort liability be based on fault. Kendall hit Brown on the head while trying to separate some fighting dogs. Even though Brown was killed as a direct result of Kendall's blow, Chief Judge Shaw denied liability, saying Brown "must come prepared with evidence to show either that the intention was unlawful, or that the defendant was in fault; for if the injury was unavoidable, and the conduct of the defendant was free from blame, he will not be liable." *Id.,* p. 296. See also Winfield, "The History of Negligence

in the Law of Torts," *L.Q. Rev.* 42 (1926): 184; Gregory, "Trespass to Negligence to Absolute Liability," *Va. L. Rev.* 37 (1951): 359; Harper & James, *supra*, p. 752.

3 Holmes, *The Common Law* (1881), pp. 79–96, quoted at p. 95. The person suing in a tort action is the plaintiff. The person being sued is the defendant. Holmes used these terms. We have substituted *victim* and *injurer* throughout this book so that people not trained in the law will not be confused by the identity of the parties.

For a good critique of Holmes, see G. Gilmore, *The Death of Contract* (1974), p. 16.

4 The basic definition of negligence was written by Learned Hand in *Conway v. O'Brian*, 111 F. 2d. 611, 612 (2nd Cir. 1940), *rev'd on other grounds*, 312 U.S. 492 (1941). See also Terry, "Negligence," *Harv. L. Rev.* 29 (1915): 40.

4 A. P. Herbert, *Uncommon Law* (7th ed., 1952), pp. 1–6.

5 The quote is from *Titus v. Bradford B. & K.R. Co.*, 136 Pa. 618, 626, 20 Atl. 517, 518 (1890). There are some early cases in which courts refused to be bound by industry practice in determining the standard of care. See, e.g., Mr. Justice Holmes in *Texas and Pacific Railway Co. v. Behymer*, 189 U.S. 468, 23 S. Ct. 622 (1903).

6 The tugboat case is *The T. J. Hooper*, 60 F. 2d 737 (2nd Cir. 1932).

For a delightful discussion of early English malpractice law, see Goldberg, "Horseshoers, Doctors and Judges and the Law of Medical Competence," *Pac. L. Rev.* 9 (1978): 107.

6 The 1767 malpractice case is *Slater v. Baker and Stapleton*, 95 Eng. Rpts. 860, 862 (King's Bench). A very similar tale is told in *Madame Bovary*, Chapter 11.

7 See Morris, "Custom and Negligence," *Colum. L. Rev.* 42 (1942): 1147, 1163 *et seq.* Harper & James, *The Law of Torts*, §17.3, n. 6, explain that the two aspects to the medical-custom rule are that the patient must produce expert testimony and that conformity to custom usages precludes negligence. Gregory & Kalven, *Cases and Materials on Torts* (Little, Brown, 1969), p. 149, explain, "The rule as to medical custom has two aspects. Not only is compliance 'the unbending test' of due care, but the doctor is presumed to have complied. Hence the plaintiff in a malpractice case cannot get to the jury without *expert* testimony that the doctor fell below the customary standard."

2. The Maldistribution of Malpractice

11 The comparison between New Hampshire and California is based on the rating information of the Insurance Service Organization. The ISO compiles information on the relative cost of constant-level medical malpractice coverage for various rating areas and specialties. The national average index was 100 in 1966. The index for New Hampshire physicians was 18.8 in 1972; for California surgeons, it was 252.2 in that year. *HEW Secretary's Malpractice Commission Report*, 1973, Appendix, pp. 539–40.

11 The figures on malpractice actions against doctors in Maryland are reported in Evans *et al.*, "A Survey of Profession Liability Incidence in Maryland," reported in *HEW Secretary's Malpractice Commission Report*, 1973, Appendix,

p. 626, and W. Pabst, "Comments on a Survey of Professional Liability Incidence in Maryland," reported in *HEW Secretary's Malpractice Commission Report,* 1973, Appendix, p. 634.

12 The *Medical Opinion* survey is reported in B. Scott, "A Survey of Medical Opinion: The Malpractice Crisis Is Worse Than We Thought," *Med. Opinion,* Vol. IV, No. 7 (July 1975), p. 40

12 Data on geographical maldistribution is reported in *A Report on the Health Professions Educational Assistance Act of 1974,* Sen. Comm. on Labor and Pub. Welfare, S.R. No. 93–1133, 93rd Cong. 2d Sess. 55–57 (1974). The figures for this report were obtained from AMA, *Distribution of Physicians in the United States,* Vol. 1 (1972) (physicians), and *Current Population Reports,* Series P-25, No. 508 (Nov. 1973) (population, excluding military personnel). See also National Health Insurance Resource Book, Staff Report, House Comm. on Ways and Means, 93rd Cong. 2d Sess. 118–123 (1974).

12 On urban-rural maldistribution, see P. DeVise, "The Changing Supply of Physicians in California, Illinois, New York, and Ohio, *Working Paper 1.21 Chicago Regional Hospital Study,* April 1974, pp. 4–5, 59; D. Dewey, "Where the Doctors Have Gone," *Ill. Regional Medical Program, Chicago Regional Hospital Study,* 1973, p. 80; and P. DeVise, "Health Planning in Illinois," *Illinois Regional Medical Program,* Vol. 2, No. 3 (Fall 1971), p. 5. The quote from the Chicago study is from Dewey, *supra,* p. 149. On physicians in the Bronx, see Harris, *The Economics of Health Care Finance and Delivery,* 1975, p. 225.

13 On medical-school enrollment, see AMAM, "Medical Education in the United States," *J.A.M.A.* 236 (1976): 2960.

14 On specialty maldistribution, see *A Report on the Health Professions Educational Assistance Act of 1974, supra,* pp. 42, 73.

On excesses in the supply of neurosurgeons, see Dr. Hugh Luckey, Vice President for Medical Affairs, Cornell University, quoted in C. T. Stewart and C. M. Siddayao, "Increasing the Supply of Medical Personnel," American Enterprise Institute for Public Policy Research, Washington, D.C., 1973, p. 35, and Dr. John Bunker, Stanford University Medical Center, Testimony Before the Senate Labor and Public Welfare Comm. Hearings on Health Personnel, reported in *A Report on the Health Professions Educational Assistance Act of 1974, supra* at p. 87.

One study, based on the standards and opinions of physicians, estimates that primary medical care of good quality requires the services of about 133 physicians per 100,000 persons, or one primary-care physician for every 750 people. The United States has about half that number. The *New England Journal of Medicine* reports:

> Obviously with a shortage of this magnitude in the supply of physicians for primary care not all who require such care can receive it. What now occurs is that some people receive no primary care, some receive only part of the needed care, and only some fraction of the population receives all necessary primary care indicated by current clinical standards and judgements.

The *New England Journal* report, Schonfeld *et al.,* "Numbers of Physicians Required for Primary Medical Care," *N.E.J. of Med.* 286 (1972): 545.

The American Academy of Family Practitioners has set a more modest standard of the need for primary-care physicians. They estimate that we need one family physician for every 2,500 people. Even by this standard, in 1972 only three states—Arizona, Iowa, and Maine—had enough family practitioners. Even states which have very large total numbers of doctors have dramatically fewer general practitioners than this modest standard recommends. For example, as of 1972, it was estimated that California needed 1,304 additional general practitioners and New York needed 2,243. See: Testimony of James G. Price, American Academy of Family Practitioners, Before the Senate Comm. on Labor and Public Welfare Hearings on Health Personnel, June 25, 1974, reported in *A Report on the Health Professions Educational Assistance Act of 1974, supra,* pp. 81–2.

14   The National Academy of Science report is Institute of Medicine, *Medicare and Medicaid Reimbursement Study,* March 1976.

15   The basic source of data on residency positions offered and filled and on the distribution of physicians in the United States is the annual report of the AMA entitled "Medical Education in the United States," which is published each year in the December issue of the *Journal of the American Medical Association* and also released as a separate document.

On the continuing problem of specialty maldistributions, see *Cost and Quality of Health Care: Unnecessary Surgery,* Subcomm. on Oversight and Investigations, Comm. on Interstate and Foreign Commerce, U.S. House of Rep., 94th Cong., 2d sess., January 1976; G. D. Zuidema, ed., *Surgery in the United States: A Summary Report for the Study on Surgical Services for the United States* (R. R. Donnelley & Sons, 1975) (this study was sponsored by the American College of Surgeons and the American Surgical Association); J. O'Rourke & S. Wallack, U.S. Dept. of HEW, *A Health Manpower Strategy for the 70's,* June 29, 1973, p. 27; U.S. Dept. of HEW, *Health Resources Statistics,* 1973, Public Health Service Pub. No. 1509; *The National Health Insurance Resource Book,* Staff Report of the House Comm. on Ways and Means, April 11, 1974, pp. 121–22; G. I. Weber, *An Essay on the Distribution of Physicians Amongst Specialties,* U.S. Dept. of HEW, 1973, pp. 12–13; Victor Fuchs, *Who Shall Live* (Basic Books, 1974), p. 68.

On trends in medical education, see E. Levit *et al.,* "Trends in Graduate Medical Education and Specialty Certification," *N.E.J. of Med.* 290 (1974): 545–49.

16   See Statement of Charles C. Edwards, Assistant Secretary for Health, Department of Welfare, Hearings on Health Personnel, June 25, 1974.

16   On doctors' incomes in 1973, see AMA, *Profiles in Medical Practice,* 1974, Table 63, p. 192. The estimate that surgeons earn 20 percent more than other doctors is from W. Houck *et al.,* "Surgeons in the U.S.," *J.A.M.A.* 236 (1976): 1864, 1871. The *Med. Economics* data is reported in the Oct. 18, 1976, issue at p. 154.

The amount of work which individual surgeons do varies enormously. As long ago as 1965, a surgeon observed in a professional journal, "There are a few surgeons who are doing all or more than they humanly can do. Many, though, are working at a pace far below their capacity and this is a tremendous waste of highly skilled talent." One comprehensive study of general surgeons in a suburban community showed that the workload of the typical surgeon was only about one third of what the profession deemed to be a reasonably full schedule. The busiest surgeon in the community was doing four times as much work as the average surgeon. One fourth of the surgeons were doing half of the surgery and their average workload was triple that of their colleagues. In this same community, the average surgeon was "at work" only thirty-four hours a week. "At work" included all the time the surgeon was at the office or hospital, including time for lunch and the conduct of personal affairs. See W. P. Longmire, "Problems in the Training of Surgeons and in the Practice of Surgery," *Amer. Jour. of Surgery* 110 (1965): 16; Hughes *et al.*, "Surgical Work Loads in a Community Practice," *Surgery*, Vol. 71, No. 3 (March 1972), pp. 315–17.

A 1976 study found that surgeons surveyed worked an average of forty-six hours a week. The study concludes that "there are too many physicians in surgical practice in the United States. The low operative work loads per surgeon are the primary evidence." Hauck *et al., supra,* p. 1871.

16 On health insurance coverage, see M. S. Mueller & Paul A. Piro, "Private Health Insurance in 1974: A Review of Coverage, Enrollment, Financial Experience," *Soc. Sec. Bull.* 39 (March 1976): 3,4.

For general information on insurance payments for physician services, see National Academy of Sciences, Institute of Medicine, *Medicare-Medicaid Reimbursement Policies,* 1975. The Attorney General of Ohio has instituted an antitrust action against Blue Shield and the Ohio Medical Society, alleging that they have conspired to fix prices. *Ohio v. Ohio Medical Indemnity,* Civ. No. C–2–75–473 (D. Ohio, filed 1975).

17 For a readable introduction to economic assumptions, see G. Calabresi, *The Costs of Accidents: A Legal and Economic Analysis* (Yale Univ. Press, 1970).

17 For general background on Medicare and Medicaid reimbursement for physician services, see Stevens & Stevens, *Welfare Medicine in America* (Free Press, 1974); S. Law, *Blue Cross: What Went Wrong?* (Yale Univ. Press, 1974); Institute of Medicine, *Medicare-Medicaid Reimbursement Policies,* 1975; Butler, "The Medicaid Program: Current Statutory Requirements and Judicial Interpretations," *Clearinghouse Rev.* 8 (1974): 7,16. For a good description of Congressional action to deal with rising physicians' fees under Medicare, and the effects on old people, see Iglehart, "Health Report: Explosive Rise in Medical Costs Puts Government in Quandary," *Nat'l J. Rep.* 7 (1975): 1319, 1321.

A study of the American Geographers of Washington concludes that there is a direct link between the provision of federal funds under Medicare and Medicaid and the migration of doctors to the east and west coasts. Reported in T. Shabad, "Faulty Distribution of Doctors Linked in Part to Federal Aid," *New York Times,* Nov. 11, 1973, p. 30.

18 On unnecessary surgery, see J. P. Bunker, "Surgical Manpower," *N.E.J. of Med.* 282 (1970): 143; C. E. Lewis, "Variations in the Incidence of Surgery," *N.E.J. of Med.* 281 (1969): 884; L. Williams, *How to Avoid Unnecessary Surgery* (Nash Publishing, 1971), p. 210; E. G. McCarthy & G. W. Widmer, "Effects of Screening by Consultants on Recommended Surgical Procedures," *N.E.J. of Med.* 291 (1974): 1331; *Cost and Quality of Health Care: Unnecessary Surgery,* Subcomm. on Oversight and Investigations, Comm. on Interstate and Foreign Commerce, 94th Cong., 2d Sess., 1976; Blue Cross/Blue Shield of

Page

Greater New York, "Study Finds Need for Elective Surgery is Unconfirmed in One out of Four Cases," Feb. 27, 1978.

19 For various estimates of the number of deaths from unnecessary surgery see *Cost and Quality of Health Care: Unnecessary Surgery, supra.*

19 The information on Medicaid surgery rates is reported in R. Lyons, "Medicaid Surgery Rate Reported to Be Twice U.S. Rate," *New York Times,* Sept. 1, 1977, p. 17.

20 On welfare-department policies requiring repayment of welfare grants from personal-injury settlements, see S. Law, *The Rights of the Poor* (Avon, 1974), p. 44.

20 Data on the distribution of physicians is presented in *Distribution of Physicians in the U.S., 1972,* Vol. 1, Center for Health Services Research and Development, AMA, 1973.

21 Data on specialty rate variations is presented in ISO, "Relative Costs of Constant Level of Medical Malpractice Coverage for Various ISO Rating Areas, 1960–72," reported in *HEW Secretary's Malpractice Commission Report,* 1973, Appendix, p. 539.

21 For classification descriptions, see *The Problems of Insuring Medical Malpractice,* 1975, prepared by All-Industry Medical Malpractice Insurance Committee. The ISO classifications are slightly different, putting anesthesiologists in Group V rather than IV. See *HEW Secretary's Malpractice Commission Report,* 1973, Appendix, p. 533.

Data on specialty rate variations is presented in *HEW Secretary's Malpractice Commission Report,* 1973, Appendix, p. 534. There are geographical exceptions to these rates, notably New York City (1969–72).

For data on specialty maldistribution, see C. Stewart & C. M. Siddayao, "Increasing the Supply of Medical Personnel," American Enterprise Institute for Public Policy Research, Washington, D.C., 1973, pp. 33–5.

22 The ratio of surgeons to population was obtained by comparing surgeon data reported in *Distribution of Physicians in the U.S., 1972,* Vol. I, Center for Health Services Research and Development, Dept. of Survey Research, 1973, Table 9, pp. 67–122, with population data reported in *Reader's Digest 1973 Almanac and Yearbook,* pp. 213–52. Correlation data is obtained by comparisons with ISO rating information reported in *HEW Secretary's Malpractice Commission Report,* 1973, Appendix, p. 540.

The NAIC study is *Medical Malpractice,* 1976, p. 11. The comments on the study were reported in Stuart, "Highly Trained Called Targets of Malpractice Claims," *New York Times,* May 10, 1976, p. 230.

22 The survey of physician relocation is reported in B. Scott, "The Malpractice Crisis Is Worse Than We Thought," *Med. Opinion,* Vol. 4, No. 7 (July 1975), p. 40. The Rand Study is reported in "Coast Doctors Cope with Insurance Crisis," *New York Times,* March 6, 1977, p. 36.

On factors influencing doctors' decisions where to practice, see Fein & Weber, *Financing Medical Education* (Carnegie Commission on Higher Education, 1971); Hadley, *Physicians' Specialty and Location Directions: A Literature Review,* Economic Analysis Branch Discussion Paper No. 10, National Center for Health Services Research and Development 1973, p. 49.

23 On the failure of the federal loan-forgiveness programs, see GAO, Annual Report of the Comptroller General of the U.S., *Congressional Objectives of*

Federal Loans and Scholarships to Health Professions Students Not Being Met, May 24, 1974, p. 100.

The original 1965 loan-forgiveness program provided that up to 50 percent of a student loan could be forgiven at a rate of 10 percent for each year served in an underserved area. Amendments in 1966 allowed 100 percent of student loans to be forgiven at a rate of 15 percent a year. The 1971 amendments allowed all student loans to be forgiven if a person worked for two years in an underserved area. These provisions are described in the GAO report, *supra*, pp. 38–39.

23   The 1974 bill was Sen. Bill No. 3585, and it is discussed in *Report on Health Professions Educational Assistance Act of 1974,* Sen. Comm. on Labor and Public Welfare, S.R. No. 93–1133, 93rd Cong. 2d Sess. pp. 55–57 (1974).

The 1976 legislation is the Health Professions Educational Assistance Act of 1976, P.L. 94–484, enacted Oct. 12, 1976.

24   For a good recent analysis of the federal loan-forgiveness programs and the reasons they have failed, see *The Role of Aid to Medical, Osteopathic and Dental Students in a New Health Manpower Education Policy,* Staff Working Paper, Congressional Budget Office, Aug. 10, 1976.

3. Bad Apples

28   The stories on the Marcus twins are reported in B. Rensberger, "Death of Two Doctors Poses a Fitness Issue," *New York Times,* Aug. 15, 1975, p. 1; B. Rensberger, "N.Y. Hospital Defends Its Actions on Marcus Twins," *New York Times,* Aug. 19, 1975, p. 1; B. Rensberger, "Unfit Doctors Create Worry in Profession," *New York Times,* Jan. 26, 1976, p.1.

29   The editorial on aged doctors is Spiro & Mandell, "Visceral Viewpoints: Leaders and the Swan—Who Should Do Family Practice?" *N.E.J. of Med.* 295 (1976): 90.

The opinion in *Gonzales v. Nork* is included in the Appendix. The colleague's quote was reported in "How Well Does Medicine Police Itself?" *Med. World News,* Vol. 15, No. 11, March 15, 1974, p. 62.

29   The Altchek case is reported in M. Lifflander, *Report to the Medical Practice Task Force,* Comm. on Health and Insurance, New York State Assembly, April 7, 1977.

30   The self-analysis of error was written by R. Gambino, "The Genesis of Medical Error—Three Case Histories," *New York Times,* March 20, 1976, p. 27.

The surgical study is Child, *The Critical Incident Study of Surgical Deaths and Complications, 1973–1975* (10th and final SOSSUS Report in the Study of Surgical Sciences for the United States).

30   The study of anemic children in Starfield & Scheff, "Effectiveness of Pediatric Care: The Relationship Between Process and Outcome," *Pediatrics* 49 (1972): 547.

The studies of gastro-intestinal problems are: Brook, Berg & Schechter, "Effectiveness of Non-Emergency Care via an Emergency Room: A Study of 166 Patients with Gastro-intestinal Symptoms," *Annals of Internal Med.* 78 (1973): 333, 337 (university hospital); and Brook & Stevenson, "Effectiveness of Patient Care in an Emergency Room, *N.E.J. of Med.* 283 (1970): 904–07 (public hospital).

Page

31   The major work by Dr. Derbyshire is *Medical Licensure and Discipline in the United States* (Johns Hopkins Press, 1969).

Dr. Egeberg is quoted in Rensberger, "Unfit Doctors Create Worry in Profession," *New York Times,* January 26, 1976, p. 1, at p. 20.

31   The twelve-million figure is obtained by multiplying the 16,000 who are estimated to be chronically incompetent by 781, the national average physician/patient ratio.

In a recent year-long study, federal judges in New York and Connecticut were asked to evaluate the 2,396 lawyers who had appeared before them. The judges rated 7.1 percent of the lawyers incompetent. The most common problem was lack of preparation. See "U.S. Judges Rate 92.9% of Lawyers Competent," *N.Y.L.J.,* Aug. 31, 1977, p. 1.

The figures on the revocation of medical licenses were obtained from the National Federation of State Medical Boards. Although the board of every state belongs to the federation, some states do not provide the federation with data. Hence, the figures are incomplete and approximate, though this is the best source of information available. Their reports are available, 1612 Summit Ave., Suite 308, Fort Worth, Tex. 76102. Other figures on grounds for disciplining physicians are reported in Dr. Derbyshire's book, *supra,* Table 5, p. 78.

A detailed survey of state licensing laws is Forgotson *et al.,* "Licensure of Physicians," *Wash. U.L.Q.* (1967): 249. Additional data through 1975 were provided by the National Federation of State Medical Boards. Revocation figures exclude cases in which licenses were revoked for nonpayment of fees or failure to obtain citizenship, licenses which were placed on inactive status, and licenses voluntarily surrendered.

32   The 1957 estimate on drug addiction among doctors was made by the U.S. Commissioner of Narcotics. See H. J. Anslinger, "Interview," *Mod. Med.* 25 (1957): 170. The 1969 estimate is reported in S. Garb, "Drug Addiction in Physicians," *Anesthesia & Analgesia* 48 (1969): 129. The 1975 article is R. Green *et al.,* "Drug Addiction Among Physicians: The Virginia Experience," *J.A.M.A.* 236 (1975): 1372. The Moldin quote is reported in Clark, "Physician, Heal Thyself," *Newsweek,* Aug. 8, 1977, p. 74. Other useful articles on the problem of the addict doctor include: Jones, "Narcotic Addiction of Physicians," *N.W. Med. J.* 66 (1967): 559; Putnam & Ellinwood, "Narcotics Addition Among Physicians: A Ten Year Follow-up," *Amer. J. Psychiat.* 122 (1966): 745.

32   Testimony of Frank Moss before the Senate Subcommittee on Long Term Care, reported in Hicks, "Total of Medicare Fraud Put at $300 Million a Year," *New York Times,* July 29, 1976, p. 11.

33   The California cases upholding the suspension of doctors convicted of Medicaid fraud are: *Carey v. Board of Medical Examiners,* 66 Cal. App. 3d 538, 136 Cal. Rptr. 91 (1977), *People v. Brown,* 61 Cal. App. 3d 476 (1976).

33   The New York study is *First Interim Report on Medical Practice Problems in the State of New York,* a Joint Study by the Assembly Standing Committee on Health and the Assembly Standing Committee on Insurance, May 10, 1977, p. 7.

33   The data on disciplinary actions for incompetence were obtained from the National Federation of Medical Boards, *supra.*

34   The data on 1967–75 increases in malpractice payments are taken from Steves, "A Proposal to Improve the Cost to Benefit Relationships in the Medical Professional Liability Insurance System," *Duke L.J.* 6 (1975): 1305, 1315–16.

34   The NAIC data are reported in *Malpractice Claims,* 1976, pp. 66–67.

The information on Dr. Nork is reported in "Argonaut and Malpractice: The Tangled Web," *Med. World News,* Vol. 16, No. 15 (July 14, 1975), pp. 23, 25, quoting from the testimony of Mr. Bruce Woolery in *Argonaut v. Florida Medical Association* (U.S.D.C. M. Dist. Fla.), 75–140 Civ. J.T. 1975. As of 1976, Mr. Gonzales had still not received any money because the case was on appeal. However, in 1974, when judgment was entered, the insurance company, in accordance with general practices, placed money in a special reserve account to pay the judgment.

35   In general, on malpractice premium rating, see Kendall & Haldi, "The Medical Malpractice Insurance Market," in *HEW Secretary's Malpractice Commission Report,* 1973, Appendix, p. 494. For more recent discussion, see *Report of the Special Advisory Panel on Medical Malpractice, State of New York,* 1976, p. 216; Roddis & Stewart, "The Insurance of Medical Losses," *Duke L.J.* 6 (1975): 1281.

To the extent that medical science does not provide reliable means of testing for drug or alcohol addiction where the individual to be tested is given advance notice, the insurance companies could offer lower rates to doctors who agreed to random, unscheduled testing.

35   On the lack of correspondence between continuing medical education and reduction of malpractice, see Bernstein & Greene, *Competence, Relicensure and Continuing Medical Education,* Issue Paper, Georgetown University Health Policy Center, 1976.

36   An excellent discussion of the nature of professionalism can be found in Freidson, *Professional Dominance* (Atherton Press, 1970). See also Carr-Saunders & Wilson, *The Professions* (Oxford Univ. Press, 1933); Everett Hughes, *Men and Their Work* (Free Press, 1958); H. Vollmer & D. Mills, eds., *Professionalization* (Prentice-Hall, 1966).

37   For a recent examination of state medical boards, see Bernstein & Greene, *Competence, Relicensure and Continuing Medical Education,* Issue Paper, Georgetown University Health Policy Center, 1976.

37   The PRSO statute is 42 U.S.C. §§1320c-1320c-19. The constitutionality of the program was upheld in *Association of American Physicians and Surgeons v. Weinberger,* 395 F. Supp. 125 (D. Ill. 1975), *aff'd.* 423 U.S. 975 (1976). For a general description, see A. Gosfield, *P.S.R.O.'s: The Law and the Health Consumer* (Ballinger, 1975).

The PSRO confidentiality statute is 42 U.S.C. §1320c-15 (Supp. 1973). In 1973, HEW authorized the release of sanction reports to state medical boards, HEW, HSA, BOA, PSRO Transmittal No. 16, and in 1976 the authorization was retracted. PSRO Transmittal No. 41. The current HEW regulations are 41 Fed. Reg. 53215, amending 42 C.F.R. §101.1701 and 101.1702 (Dec. 3, 1976). See Miller, "P.S.R.O. Data and Information: Disclosure to State Health Regulatory Agencies," *Boston U. L. Rev.* 57 (1977): 245.

38   The immunity provisions are described and discussed in Note, "Professional Standards Review and the Limitation of Health Services: An Interpretation of the Effect of Statutory Immunity on Medical Malpractice Liability," *Boston*

U.L. Rev. 54 (1974): 931; Note, "Federally Imposed Self-Regulation of Medical Practice: A Critique of the Professional Standards Review Organization," *Geo. Wash. L. Rev.* 42 (1974): 822; Comment, "PRSO: Malpractice Liability and the Impact of the Civil Immunity Clause," *Geo. L.J.* 62 (1974): 1499.

39 *HEW Secretary's Malpractice Commission Report,* 1973, p. 52, found that professional imcompetence was a ground for discipline in only fifteen states, and it recommended amendments in state laws.

In 1975 and 1976, California, Michigan, Minnesota, New York, New Hampshire, Ohio, Oregon, Tennessee, and Washington enacted laws providing, in slightly varying terms, that a physician may be disciplined for gross incompetence, gross ignorance, gross negligence, or gross malpractice in the course of medical practice. Illinois enacted a somewhat more limited law providing that a physician may be disciplined for "gross malpractice resulting in permanent injury or death of a patient." Florida and North Carolina have enacted broader laws. The North Carolina law provides that a physician may be disciplined for

> any departure from, or the failure to conform to, the minimal standards of acceptable and prevailing medical practice, or the ethics of the medical profession, irrespective of whether or not a patient is injured thereby, or the committing of any act contrary to honesty, justice or good morals, whether the same is committed in the course of his practice or otherwise, and whether committed within or without North Carolina. *N.C. Gen. Stat. §90–14 (1975 Supp.).*

40 The Kansas case is *Kansas State Board of the Healing Arts v. Foote,* 436 P. 2d 828, 833–34 (Kan. Sup. Ct. 1968).

40 In 1975–76, the following states enacted laws to provide state medical boards with a broader range of sanctions: Ala. Code tit. 46 §271 1975 Supp.; Alaska Stat. §8.64.325 1976 Supp.; Calif. Bus. & Prof. Code §2372 (West) 1975 Supp.; Conn. Gen. Stat. Ann. §20-13f(b) (West) 1976 Supp.; Del. Code tit. 24 §1730–31 1976 Supp.; 1975 Fla. Sess. Laws §458.1201 3(a); Ga. Code Ann. §84–916 1974 Supp.; Idaho Code tit. 54 §1806 A(10) & (6) 1976 Supp.; Ky. Rev. Stat. §311.595(1) 1976 Supp.; La. Rev. Stat. Ann. §37–1285 (West) 1976 Supp.; Me. Rev. Stat. tit. 32 §3284 1973 Supp.; Md. Ann. Code art. 43 §130(h) 1976 Supp.; Mass. Gen. Law Ann. Ch. 112 §5 (West) 1977 Supp.; Mich. Stat. Ann. §147.021 (West) 1976 Supp.; Mo. Ann. Stat. §334.100 (1) (14)a (Vernon) 1976 Supp.; Mont. Rev. Codes Ann. §66–1038 (1969); Neb. Rev. Stat. §71–155 (1976 Supp.); Nev. Rev. Stat. §630.330 (3) (1973); N.M. Stat. Ann. §67–5–9 (A) (1969); N.Y. Educ. Law §6511 (Consol.) (1975 Supp.); N.C. Gen. Stat. §90–14 (1975 Supp.); Ohio Rev. Code Ann. §4731.22 (1976 Supp.) (Page); Okla. Stat. Ann. tit. 76 §17 (1976 Supp.) Ore. Rev. Stat. §677.205 (2) (1975 Supp.); R.I. Gen. Laws §5–37.1–13 (1976 Supp.); S.C. Code §40–47–200 (1976 Supp.); Tenn. Code Ann. §63–618(a) (1975); Utah Code Ann. §58–12–35 (1) (1976 Supp.); Vt. Stat. Ann. tit. 26 §1361(b) (1975 Supp.); Va. Code §54–316 (1966).

The AMA has prepared model state legislation which would establish a national repository of information about disciplinary actions, to be available to state medical boards and hospitals. See AMA, Report of the Board of Trustees, Preliminary Report of the Ad Hoc Committee on Medical Discipline, A-76, Report V.

42   The comprehensive reporting laws are Fla. Stat. Ann. §458.01 *et seq.* (1975–76 Cum. Pocketpart); and Vt. Stat. Ann. tit. 26 §1362 (1976 Supp.). Probably the state does not have authority to order the reporting of P.S.R.O. data, where federal law prohibits such reporting.

42   The following states require that information be reported to either the state medical board or the state insurance commissioner when a malpractice action is filed: Ark. Stat. Ann. §72–625 1975 Supp.; Ariz. Rev. Stat. §32–1451.02 1976 Supp.; Md. Code Ann. §3–2A02 1976 (claim must be more than $5,000); Ill. Ann. Stat. Ch. 73 §767.19 (Smith-Hurd) 1976 Supp.; Mich. Stat. Ann., §14.542 (11)(c) (1977 Supp.; New York Ins. Law §335 (Consol.) 1975 Supp.; Okla. Stat. Ann. tit. 76 §17 1976 Supp.; Ore. Rev. Stat. §752.120 (1975 Supp.); S.C. Code §38–3–320 (1976 Supp.); Tex. Ins. Code Ann. art. 5.82 (5) (1975) (Vernon); Wyo. Stat. §§33–340.1(a),(b) (1976 Supp.).

The following state laws require that the state medical board be informed when a malpractice claim has been reduced to judgment or settlement: Ala. Code Ann. tit. 46 §297a 1973 Supp.; Ariz. Rev. Stat. §32–1451.02 1976 Supp.; Calif. Bus. & Prof. Code §801, 802 (West) 1976 Supp.; Colo. Rev. Stat. §10–1–124 1976 Supp.; Del. Code tit. 24 §1728(c) 1976 Supp. and tit. 18 §6821 1976 Supp.; Ind. Code Ann. §16–9.5–6–2 (Burns) 1976 Supp.; Kan. Stat. §40–1127 1976 Supp.; Ky. Rev. Stat. §304.40–310 1976 Supp.; La. Rev. Stat. Ann. §40–1299.48 1976 Supp.; Mich. Stat. Ann. §24.12477(6) 1977 Supp.; Mo. Ann. Stat. §383.125 (Vernon) 1976 Supp.; Neb. Rev. Stat. §44–2835(1), (2) (1976 Supp.); N.M. Stat. Ann. §58–33–27 (1976 Supp.).

The following laws require courts to report to the state board when a physician is convicted of a crime: Calif. Bus. & Prof. §803 (West) 1976 Supp.; N.J. Stat. Ann. §45:9–19 (West) (1921); Mich. Stat. Ann. §140542(11c) (2) 1977 Supp.; Wis. Stat. Ann. §448.18(3) (1973) (West).

These laws require courts to report to the state board when a physician is formally declared incompetent: Mich. Stat. Ann. §14.542(12) 1977 Supp.; Minn. Stat. Ann. §147.021 (2) (West) 1976 Supp.; N.M. Stat. Ann. §67–5–25 (1961); Ore. Rev. Stat. §677.225 (1975).

The following laws require that hospitals report disciplinary actions to the state medical board: Calif. Bus. & Prof. Code §805 1976 Supp.; Conn. Gen. Stat. Ann. §20–13(d) 1976 Supp.; Ga. Code Ann. §88–1912 1977 Supp.; Idaho Code tit. 39 §1393 1976 Supp.; Tenn. Code Ann. §53–1330 (1976 Supp). See also N.Y., "Medical Practices Act of 1977," N.Y.S. Session Laws, ch. 773, §11 (1977).

Five states require that the state and local medical societies report their disciplinary actions to the state medical board: Mich. Stat. Ann. §14.542(11a) 1977 Supp.; Nev. Rev. Stat. §630.341 1975 Supp.; Ore. Rev. Stat. §677–415(2) 1975 Supp.; N.Y. "Medical Practices Act of 1977," Session Laws, ch. 773, §11 (1977); Vt. Stat. Ann. tit. 26 §1362 (1975 Supp.).

Florida requires that all medical disciplinary boards report their actions to the state medical board: Fla. Stat. Ann. §458/1201 (West) 1976 Supp. Under Kentucky law, the local boards of health must report evidence of physician incompetence to the state board: Ky. Rev. Stat. §311.605 (1976 Supp).

Delaware requires that a physician must report to the state board any action taken against him by a hospital or medical society. Del. Code tit. 24 §1728(b) 1976 Supp. Arizona, Connecticut, Michigan, and Vermont require the state board to report its decision to all other medical bodies. Ariz. Rev. Stat. §3-1451 1976 Supp.; Conn. Gen. Stat. Ann. §20–13f(c) 1976 Supp.; Mich. Stat. Ann. §14.542 (11c) (3) 1977 Supp.; Vt. Stat. Ann. tit. 26 §1352(3) (1975 Supp.). Florida and Colorado require medical-review committees to report their findings to the state board. Fla. Stat. Ann. §768.43 (4) (West) 1976 Supp.; Colo. Rev. Stat. §43.5–102 1976 Supp. Nevada requires malpractice screening panels to report their findings to the state medical board and county medical society. Nev. Rev. Stat. §41A.090 (2) (1975).

44   The laws imposing a general requirement on physicians to report to the state medical board any evidence of incompetence on the part of other doctors are: Ala. Code Ann. tit 46 §271 (1975 Supp.); Ariz. Rev. Stat. Ch. 13, §32–1451 (1976 Cumm. Supp.); Idaho Code tit. 54 §1818 (1975 Cumm. Supp.); Ohio Rev. Code Ann. §4731.22(c) (2) (1975) (Page); Ore. Rev. Stat. §677.415 (1975 Supp.); Ill. Ann. Stat. Ch. 91 §16b(13) 1976 Supp.; Utah Code Ann. §58–12–23 (1967); Va. Code §54–317.2 (1974).

Laws requiring that doctors report when they have treated another physician for drug addiction, alcoholism, or mental illness include: Alas. Stat. §8.64.336 (1976); Me. Rev. Stat. tit. 32 §3286 (Supp. 1973); Va. Code, §54–317.2 (1974); Del. Code tit. 24 §1728(a) 1976 Supp.

The effectiveness of the Arizona law is discussed in "How Well Does Medicine Police Itself?" *Med. World News*, Vol. 15, No. 11 (March 15, 1974), p. 62.

44   On the common-law privilege to report information to state licensing boards, see Prosser, *The Law of Torts* (4th ed., 1972), p. 792.

The following laws provide doctors with specific immunity from civil suit when they report information about other doctors to the state medical board: Ala. Code tit. 46 §297 (a3) 1973 Supp.; Ariz. Rev. Stat. §32–1451 1976 Supp.; Ark. Stat. Ann. §71–5101 1975 Supp. (immunity for medical-society or medical-committee members); Calif. Civ. Code §43.7, 43.8 (West) 1976 Supp.; Conn. Gen. Stat. Ann. §20–13(h) (West) 1976 Supp.; Colo. Rev. Stat. §12–43.5–113 1976 Supp. (immunity for medical-committee members or any witness before the committee); Del. Code tit. 24 §1728(a) 1976 Supp.; 1975 Fla. Sess. Laws §458.1201; Ga. Code Ann. §88–3202 1975 Supp. (immunity for medical-review committee members); Hawaii Rev. Stat. §36–663–1.7 1975 Supp. (immunity for medical-review committee members); Idaho Code tit. 54 §1818 1976 Supp.; Ind. Code Ann. §25–22.5–6–3 (Burns) 1977 Supp.; Iowa Code Ann. §147.135 (West) 1976 Supp. (immunity for peer-review committee members); Kan. Stat. §65–2898 1976 Supp.; Ky. Rev. Stat. §311.377 1976 Supp.; La. Rev. Stat. Ann. §37–1287 (West) 1976 Supp.; Me. Rev. Stat. tit. 32 §3286 1973 Supp.; Md. Ann. Code art. 43 §130 *et seq.* 1976 Supp.; Mich. Stat. Ann. §14.542 (5) 1977 Supp.; Minn. Stat. Ann. §145.62 (West) 1976 Supp.; Miss. Code Ann. §73–25–67 1976 Supp.; Mo. Ann. Stat. §334.100 (5) (Vernon) 1976 Supp.; Mont. Rev. Codes §66–1052 (1975) (immunity for peer-review committee members); Neb. Rev. Stat. §44–2844 (immunity for medical-review committee); Nev. Rev. Stat. §630.341(2) (1975); N.J. Stat. Ann. §2A:84A–22.9 (1970) (West) (immunity for utilization-review committee members); N.M. Stat. Ann. §67–42–11 (1976 Supp.); N.Y. Pub. Health Law §230 (8) (Consol.) (1975) (immunity for members of committee on professional conduct): N.D. Cent. Code §23–01–02.1 (1969); Ohio Rev. Code Ann. §4731.22(c) (2) (1975 Supp.) (Page); Okla. Stat. Ann.

tit. 76 §16 (1977) (immunity for peer-review committee members); Ore. Rev., Stat. §677.425 (1975 Supp.); Pa. Stat. Ann. tit. 63 §425.3(a) (1974); R.I. Gen. Laws §23–16–25 (1976 Supp.); S.C. Code §40–47–216 (1976) (immunity for medical board); S.D. Compiled Laws Ann. §36–4–25 (1975) (immunity for professional-review committee members); Tenn. Code Ann. §63–623(B) (1975); Tex. Rev. Stat. Ann. art. 4447d(3) (1971); Utah Code Ann. §58–12–43 (1976 Supp.); Vt. Stat. Ann. tit. 26 §1442 (1975) (immunity for peer-review committee members); Va. Code §54.317.2 (1974); W. Va. Code §30–3C–2 (1975); Wash. Rev. Code Ann. §4.24.260 (1976 Supp.); Wyo. Stat. §33–340.13 (a)(ii) (1971 Supp.).

45　The survey of patient knowledge about where to complain is reported in "Complaints Against Doctors," *Consumer Help* 2 (1976): 1, 8. This article also reports the lack of consumer complaints against the Marcus twins, and suggests that complaints about failure to process insurance claims may provide an early warning signal that a physician has problems which may affect practice in more substantial ways.

　　The information on complaints to the medical society about Dr. Nork is reported in "How Well Does Medicine Police Itself?" *Med. World News*, Vol. 15, No. 11 (March 15, 1974), p. 68.

45　The Massachusetts case is *Berman v. Board of Registration in Medicine*, 244 N.E. 2d 553, 355 Mass. 358 (1969).

46　The material on the composition of state medical boards is taken from Derbyshire, *Medical Licensure and Discipline in the United States* (Johns Hopkins Press, 1969), Chapter 3.

47　*HEW Secretary's Malpractice Commission Report*, 1973, pp. 53–5.

　　On California appointments, see J. Nordheimer, "Brown Places 60 on California Regulatory Boards as Lobbyists for People Instead of Special Interests," *New York Times*, Feb. 7, 1977, p. 1.

　　The California board has established local offices to receive complaints from patients and to help resolve grievances in cases that do not necessarily lead to formal disciplinary action against a physician. More fundamentally, the board is considering proposals to require that people seeking a license to practice medicine in California must take examinations in subjects that are of importance to patients but are traditionally ignored in medical education—for example, human sexuality. They are also considering proposals to allow people with medical experience—for example, nurses—to take the licensing exam and become doctors without going to medical school. Interviews and correspondence with Hope Blacker, member of the California Board of Quality Assurance, on file with authors.

47　The staffing situation in New York and New Jersey is discussed in "How Well Does Medicine Police Itself?" *Med. World News*, Vol. 15, No. 11 (March 15, 1974), p. 62. See also N.Y. State Consumer Protection Board, *Rights Without Remedies: A Study of Complaint Handling Mechanisms in Professional Misconduct Cases in New York State*, 1977, p. 23.

48　On California staffing, see J. Nordheimer, "Brown Places 60 on California Regulatory Boards as Lobbyists for People Instead of Special Interests," *New York Times*, Feb. 7, 1977, p. 1.

　　On financing of state medical boards, see correspondence with Hope Blacker, member of the California Board of Quality Assurance, Nov. 15, 1977,

Page

on file with authors; L. J. Sullivan, "Doctor Accountability: The Peer Review Hoax?" *Health Law Project Library Bulletin 337* (November 1977): 1.

49 Due-process requirements are summarized and discussed in "Medical Discipline: Constitutional Considerations—Protection of Physicians' Rights," *J.A.M.A.* 234 (1975): 1062. In 1975, the U.S. Supreme Court held that a doctor was not denied due process when his license was revoked by a board which had also been involved in the process of investigating the charges against him. The Supreme Court held that, while the doctor was entitled to a fair and impartial decision-maker, the fact that investigative and adjudicatory functions were given to the same agency under state law did not in itself deny him a fair decision-maker. *Withrow v. K. Larkin*, 421 U.S. 35, 95 S. Ct. 1456 (1975). For other cases on due-process requirements in the context of professional discipline, see Dorsen, Bender & Neuborne, *Political and Civil Rights in the United States, Vol. 1* (Little, Brown, 4th ed., 1976), pp. 1301–16.

49 On delay in enforcement of board orders, see *HEW Secretary's Malpractice Commission Report*, 1973, pp. 53–54.

Statutes which prohibit staying actions are: Md. Ann. Code art. 43 §130(m) 1976 Supp.; Iowa Code Ann. §148.7 (9) (West) 1976 Supp.; Va. Code §54–320; Kan. Stat. §65–2850 1976 Supp.

The California law is Calif. Code of Civil Procedures §§1094.5(f) and (g) 1976 Supp.

50 The New York law which provides for nine reviews is N.Y. Pub. Health Law, Art. II, Title II-A §230 (Consol.) 1975.

The study of the New York process is N.Y. State Consumer Protection Board, *Rights Without Remedies: A Study of the Complaint Handling Mechanisms in Professional Misconduct Cases in New York State*, 1977, p. 23.

4. The Hospitals: The Doctor's Workshop

51 The information on Dr. Ashkenazy is contained in *Confidential Report* (now public), prepared by the New York State Assembly Medical Practice Task Force, April 1977.

52 The American Hospital Association position was expressed in a memorandum to member institutions, "Update on Malpractice Situation—Report on the May 16 House of Delegates Meeting," June 9, 1975.

53 In 1975, there were 36,157,000 hospital admissions in the United States. AHA, *Hospital Statistics*, 1976, p. 13, Table 1.

The HEW statistics are from two studies in the Appendix to the *Secretary's Malpractice Commission Report*, 1973. They are: Mirabella, Myers, *et al.*, "Medical Malpractice Insurance Claims Files Closed in 1970," p. 1; and Pocincki, Dogger *et al.*, "The Incidence of Latrogenic Injuries," p. 50.

The NAIC study is *Malpractice Claims*, May 1977.

The survey of nurses' attitudes was conducted by the journal *Nursing 77* and reported in the *New York Times*, Jan. 7, 1977, p. 21.

The AHA's consultant's report was in *Hospitals: Journal of the A.H.A.*, Vol. 50, No. 13 (July 1, 1977), p. 17.

54 The distribution of hospital injuries is reported in Mirabella, Myers, *et al.*, "Medical Malpractice Insurance Claims Files Closed in 1970," *HEW Secretary's Malpractice Commission Report*, 1973, Appendix, p. 10. The increase

in claims against hospitals is in another report included in the Appendix, William Pabst, "American Hospital Association Professional Liability Insurance Survey," pp. 610–17. In 1971, 69.1 percent of hospitals had no sole-defendant claims; 83.8 percent had no co-defendant claims. *Id.,* p. 617.

On the history of hospital charitable immunity see Prosser, *The Law of Torts,* pp. 992–996, (West: 1971).

55 The legal characterization of the physician as independent contractor is indicated in *St. Paul Fire and Marine Insurance Co. v. Aetna Casualty and Surety Co.* 394 F. Supp. 1274 (D.C. Penn., 1974). Here the court determined that a radiologist was an independent contractor, although her appointment was considered by the personnel committee, she was provided equipment and working space by the hospital, and she was paid a gross percentage of X-ray bills with a basic annual dollar guarantee. The court focused on the fact that the hospital could not supervise the physician's work and that no fringe benefits were provided and no withholding taxes taken. Prior to *Bing v. Thunig* 2 N.Y. 2d 656 (1957) even a salaried physician was regarded as an independent contractor.

56 The JCAH history is described in Worthington and Silver, "Regulations of the Quality of Care in Hospitals," *Law and Contemporary Problems* (1975) 35.

56 Dr. Porterfield was quoted in Bird, "Substandard Care is Found in the Majority of 105 Hospitals in Federal Spot Check," *New York Times,* March 23, 1975, p. 43.

On state licensing, see Somers & Somers, *Hospital Regulation: The Dilemma of Public Policy* (Princeton Univ. Press, 1969), pp. 107–9. For a statistical report on enforcement activities, see National Center for Health Statistics, State Licensing of Health Facilities, U.S. Dept. of Health, Education and Welfare, 1968.

56 JCAH standards for accreditation were made the upper limit for hospital standards in the 1965 Social Security Act on Health Care for the Aged, Title 42 §1395x(e) (8).

57 The *Darling* case is reported at 211 N.E. 2d 253 (1968). The applicable standards are not reported in the opinion, but were described in "The Darling Case," *J.A.M.A.,* Vol. 206, No. 7, (Nov. 11, 1968), p. 1665.

The cases in which a hospital was held liable under the *Darling* standard were *Purcell v. Zimbleman* 500 P2d 335 (Arizona 1972); *Mitchell County Hospital Authority v. Joiner* 189 S.E. 2d 412 (Georgia 1972); *Guidley v. Johnson* 476 S.W. 2d 475 (Missouri 1972); *Corleto v. Shore Memorial Hospital* 350 A2d 534 (N.J. 1975). There was no breach of the *Darling* duty in *Hull v. North Valley Hospital* 498 P.2d 136 (Montana 1972) and *Ferguson v. Gonjaw* 236 N.W. 2d 543 (Michigan 1975). *Darling* was cited in staff-privilege context in *Moore v. Board of Carson-Tahoe Hospital* 495 P.2d 605 (Nevada 1972), *cert. den.* 409 U.S. 879 (1972); *Khan v. Suburban Community Hospital* 45 Ohio St. 2d 39 (1976), and *Huffaker v. Bailey* 540 P. 2d 1398 (Oregon 1975). In other cases, *Darling* has supported a court's rejection of the locality rule; but the cases did not reach the question of the hospital's duty to review the medical care provided by physicians. See, for example, *Dickinson v. Maillard* 175 N.W. 2d 588 (Iowa 1970) and *Skillkret v. Annapolis Emergency Hospital Association* 349 A.2d 245 (Md. 1975).

Page

58   The state law regarding the self-governing medical staff is Calif. Bus. and
      Prof. Code §2392.5(c) (West) (1965).

59   The survey of hospital boards was Porter, "A Profile of the Hospital Trustee,"
      Trustee 28: (January 1975): 21.

60   The Stanford study is reported in Brody, "Study Finds Danger in Surgery
      Varies Greatly Among Hospitals," *New York Times*, Dec. 15, 1976, p. 1. The
      importance of hospital staffing and organization in explaining differing surgical
      outcomes was also suggested in National Academy of Sciences, *Study of Institu-
      tional Differences in Postoperative Mortality*, Dec. 1974.

      The information on staff privileges in New York City hospitals is contained
      in a summary report prepared by the NYC Health and Hospitals Corporation,
      and is on file with the authors and available on request.

      The study of hospital privileges was in Roemer & Friedman, *Doctors in
      Hospitals* (Johns Hopkins Press, 1971), pp. 206–10. See also Claude Welch,
      "Professional Licensure and Hospital Delineation of Clinical Privileges—Rela-
      tionship to Quality Assurance," in Egdahl & Gertman, eds., *Quality Assurance
      in Health Care* (Aspens Systems Corp., 1976). On methods and approaches
      for defining physician privileges on hospital medical staffs, see Jacobs & Stein-
      wald, "Defining Clinical Privileges for the Hospital Medical Staff," J.C.A.H.,
      1975.

61   The report on differing mortality rates is contained in *Getting Ready for
      National Health Insurance: Unnecessary Surgery*, Hearings Before the Sub-
      comm. on Oversight and Investigation of the House Comm. on Interstate
      and Foreign Commerce, 94th Cong., 1st Sess., 191–92 (1975) (testimony of
      Dr. George Crile).

61   The report on the JCAH's attempt to delineate surgical privileges is in Welch,
      op. cit., p. 196.

62   The estimate of unnecessary surgery was in the Report by the Subcomm.
      on Oversight and Investigations of the House Comm. on Interstate and Foreign
      Commerce, *Cost and Quality of Health Care: Unnecessary Surgery*, pp. 5–
      6, 94th Cong., 2nd sess. (1976). The AMA's criticisms of the subcommittee's
      report are contained in AMA, "A Critique on . . . 'Cost and Quality of Health
      Care: Unnecessary Surgery,' " May 11, 1976. The study conducted by the
      professional surgical associations is *American College of Surgeons and Ameri-
      can Surgical Association, The Critical Incident Study of Surgical Deaths and
      Complications, 1973–75*, 1977. The 1977 hearings were "Quality of Surgical
      Care," Subcomm. on Oversight and Investigations of the House Comm. on
      Interstate and Foreign Commerce, 95th Cong., 1st sess. (1977).

63   The Congressional Budget Office estimate is in Congressional Budget Office,
      Expenditures for Health Care: Federal Programs and Their Effects, August
      1977, p. 23. The estimate includes both physician and hospital billings.

      It is about two thirds as expensive for a hospital to maintain an empty
      bed as it is to have a paying occupant for it. See Paxton, "Whatever Happened
      to the Hospital Bed Shortage?" *Med. Economics*, Feb. 28, 1972, p. 34.

      On hospital resistance to internal utilization review see e.g. D. Bird, "Hospi-
      tals in New York City Balk at Drive on Unneeded Surgery," *N.Y. Times*, p.
      40, col. 1, May 10, 1976.

63   The practice of allowing a doctor to resign without any deficiencies being
      noted in his record is based on a report from Dr. Robert Derbyshire in Rensber-

ger, "Few Doctors Ever Report Colleagues' Incompetence," *New York Times,* Jan. 29, 1976, p. 1.

64 The report on hospital surgical-review committees was based on the testimony of Dr. William Stahl in *Getting Ready for National Health Insurance: Unnecessary Surgery, op. cit.,* p. 91.

64 The study of medical review in hospitals is Marcia Millman, *The Unkindest Cut* (William Morrow, 1977), pp. 99–100.

On JCAH review procedures, see Worthington & Silver, "Regulation of the Quality of Care in Hospitals," *Law & Contemporary Problems* 35 (1975): 305, and Cunningham, *Governing Hospitals* (AHA, Chicago, 1976), p. 83.

65 For a thorough examination of the history and purposes of JCAH audit requirements, see Jacobs, Christoffel & Dixon, *Measuring the Quality of Patient Care: The Rationale of Outcome Audit* (Ballinger, 1976).

65 The audit case history was in Christoffel, Jacobs *et al.,* "Audit Results," *Quality Rev. Bull.,* Vol. 2, No. 4 (April 1976), p. 32.

66 A JCAH audit analysis of one hospital's efforts to review the treatment of disc disease (Dr. Nork's specialty) found that the doctors had chosen treatment criteria so insensitive that they allowed actual deficiencies to go undetected. Lippe, "Disc! Disc!" *Quality Rev. Bull.,* Vol. 2, No. 1–2 (Jan.-Feb. 1976), p. 18.

66 The information on JCAH surveys of New York City Hospitals is based on a summary report prepared by the NYC Health and Hospitals Corporation, and is on file with the authors and available on request.

The Florida Statute is Fla. Stat. Ann. 768.41 (1976).

67 The New York report is *Report of the Special Advisory Panel on Medical Malpractice, State of New York,* 1976, p. 50. The Florida study is reported in Macro Systems, *A Preliminary Assessment of Risk Management in Health Care Settings,* July 1975.

Premium rating of individual hospitals, solely on the basis of their own experience exists in some state-hospital-association group plans and is offered as an option to individual hospitals by most of the major insurance carriers. See Kendall & Haldi, "The Medical Malpractice Insurance Market," *HEW Secretary's Malpractice Commission Report,* 1973, p. 494, for a description of the rating policies of several group plans.

The HEW study is Applied Management Services, *A Study of Hospital Injury Prevention Programs,* Nov. 29, 1976.

68 On physicians' liability for participation in peer review, see Jacobs & Weagly, "The Liability Myth Exposed: Hospital Peer Review Activities Pose No Risk," J.C.A.H. paper 1975. Cases on the hospital's discretion in granting privileges are *Huffaker v. Bailey,* 540 P.2d 1398 (1975) and *Khan v. Suburban Community Hospital,* 45 Ohio St. 2d 39 (1976).

States which have enacted laws granting immunity from defamation liability for members of peer-review committees and protecting against examination of committee reports in malpractice actions are: 1976 Ala. Acts Ch. 693; Ariz. Rev. Stat. §§36–441, 36–445, 36–445.03 (1973 Supp.); Calif. Civil Code §§43.7, 43.8 (West Supp. 1976), Calif. Evid. Code §§1157, 1157.5 (West Supp. 1974); Fla. Stat. Ann. §768.131 (1973); Hawaii Rev. Stat. §§624.25.5, 663–1.7 (1973); Idaho Code §§39–1392 to 1392e (1974); La. Rev. Stat. §44.7 (West) (1975 Supp.); Md. Ann. Code art. 43 §§136c (1975 Supp.), 134 A (1976 Supp.);

Mich. Stat. Ann. §§14.57(21)–(23), 14.1179 (12) (1974); Minn. Stat. Ann. §§145.62 to 145.64 (West) (1974); Mont. Rev. Codes Ann. §§66–1052 (1975), 69–6301 to 69–6304 (1970); Neb. Rev. Stat. §§71–147.01 (1976), 71–2046 to 71–2048 (1971); Nev. Rev. Stat. §§630.341 (2) (1975), 49.265 (1973); N.J. Stat. Ann. §§2A:84A–22.8, 2A:84A–22.9 (1975 Supp.); N.Y. Educ. Law §6527–3 (McKinney Supp. 1976); N.D. Cent. Code §23–01–02.1 (1970); Ohio Rev. Code Ann. §§2305.24 (1975), 2305.25 (1976), 2305.28 (1976); Ore. Rev. Stat. §§677.335 (1967), 421.675 (1973); Pa. Stat. Ann. tit. 63 §425.2 (1975 Supp.); R.I. Gen. Laws §23–16–25 (1976); Tex. Rev. Civ. Stat. art. 4447d (3) (1974); Vt. Stat. Ann. tit. 26 §§1442, 1443 (1975); Wash. Rev. Code Ann. §§4.24.240, 4.24.250, 4.24.260 (1976); Wyo. Stat. §§35–140.1 to 140.4, §§35–528 to 530 (1973).

States which have only statutes granting immunity from defamation liability for members of peer-review committees are: Ark. Stat. Ann. §82–3201 (1975); 1976 Conn. Pub. Acts, No. 56; 1976 Colo. Sess. Laws Ch. 91; Del. Code Ann. tit. 24 §1191 (1974); Ga. Code Ann. §105–114 (1972); Ill. Ann. Stat. Ch. 91 §2c (1973); Ind. Code Ann. §16–10–1–6.5 (1973); Kan. Gen. Stat. Ann. §65–442 (1973); Ky. Rev. Stat. Ch. 311–377 (1972); Me. Rev. Stat. Ann. tit. 32 §3293 (1973); Mass. Gen. Laws Ann. Ch. 231 §85N (1973); Mo. Rev. Stat. Ann. §537.035 (1973); N.M. Stat. Ann. §12–5–16 (1973); N.C. Gen. Stat. §131–169 (1974); S.C. Code Ann. §56–1369.2 (1976 Supp.); S.D. Compiled Laws §§36–4–25, 36–4–26 (1967); Tenn. Code Ann. §63–623 (1974); Utah Code Ann. §58–12–25 (1975).

The public-policy reasoning is stated in *Bredice* v. *Doctors' Hospital,* 50 F.R.D. 249, 251 (1970).

New Hampshire has only a statute protecting against the examination of committee reports in malpractice actions. N.H. Rev. Stat. Ann. §329:29 (1975).

69 Committee reports are inadmissible at trial because they do not qualify under the business-record exception to the hearsay rule. They are not made at the time of, or close in time to, the transaction in question (the patient injury), they are not made by a party to the transaction, and they do not record an act but rather contain opinions and conclusions. Cases denying patients' requests for pretrial discovery are *Matchett* v. *Superior Court for County of Yuba* 40 Cal. App. 3d 623, 115 Cal. Rptr. 317 (1974) and *Oviatt* v. *Archbishop Bergen Mercy Hospital* 191 Neb. 224, 214 N.W. 2d 490 (1974). Cases allowing examination are *Nazareth Literary and Benevolent Institutions* v. *Stephenson* 503 S.W. 2d 117 (Ky. 1973); and *Gureghian* v. *Hackensack Hospital* 262 A.2d 440 (N.J. 1970).

The Arizona statute makes a distinction for purposes of examination in litigation between information considered by review committees and the conclusions reached by the committee. In *Tuscon Medical Center, Inc.* v. *Miseuch,* 113 Ariz. 34, 545 P. 2d 958 (1976), the Arizona Supreme Court distinguished between "purely factual investigative matters" and "materials which are the product of reflective deliberation on policy-making processes."

70 The requirement that there be "utilization review" programs was set out in 42 U.S.C. §1395x(e) (6) (1965); make-up of the utilization-review committees was set out in 42 U.S.C. §1395x(k) (1965).

70 The report on utilization review was in the Report of the Senate Committee on Finance, *Medicare and Medicaid—Problems, Issues, and Alternatives,* Feb. 9, 1970, p. 105.

The 1972 amendment is set out in 42 U.S.C. §1395x(e) (9) and §1395bb (a) (4) (1972).

The federal spot-check is reported in Bird, "Substandard Care is Found in the Majority of Hospitals in Federal Spot Check," *New York Times,* March 23, 1975, p. 43.

71 The preference for in-house PSRO review is stated in the Social Security Act, 42 U.S.C. §1320 C-4(e) (1) (1972). The Bureau of Quality Assurance position is stated in Transmittal #15, Feb. 12, 1975.

The original BQA transmittal on confidentiality provided for limited disclosure of nonprivileged institutional data (medical-care evaluation studies would be privileged) and the disclosure of sanction reports to state licensing authorities. A later BQA transmittal withdrew these disclosure provisions because a "recent examination of the PSRO statute" had convinced the department that these disclosure provisions could be provided for only by regulations. While a literal reading of the statute would dictate this result, nothing in the law envisions that the Secretary would avoid issuing regulations for over four years and administer the program by the more flexible method of transmittal letters. When and if regulations are ever issued, there is little likelihood, based on prior communications from the BQA, that meaningful disclosure will be mandated. See Bureau of Quality Assurance, Transmittal #41, Oct. 6, 1976.

72 The federal report on PSRO's is Health Services Administration, "Draft—P.S.R.O.: An Evaluation of the Professional Standards Review Organization," No. 77–12, October 1977. The reported findings are in Volume 1: Executive Summary.

73 The proposal to focus malpractice liability on the hospital is discussed in Steves, "A Proposal to Improve the Cost to Benefit Relationships in the Medical Professional Liability Insurance System," *Duke L.J.* 6 (1975): 1305. See also "Medical Malpractice: Changing the System," *Consumer Reports,* November 1977, p. 674.

76 The efforts of one organized consumer group to affect the governance and policies of hospitals in New York City is chronicled in Consumer Commission on the Accreditation of Health Services, *Health Perspectives.*

5. Lawyers: How Much Is Too Much?

81 The first quote is from Gerald M. Branower, M.D., letter to *New York Times,* March 22, 1975, p. 30. The condemnation of the contingent fee is by Norman S. Blackman, M.D., President, Kings County Medical Society, letter to *New York Times,* April 7, 1975, p. 30.

82 The information about lawyers is found in Dietz, Baird & Berul, "The Medical Malpractice Legal System," *HEW Secretary's Malpractice Commission Report,* 1973, Appendix, p. 87.

A national random survey of lawyers in private practice showed that 50 percent of all potential malpractice clients were rejected. A selected survey of lawyers who regularly handle malpractice cases showed that they rejected 71 percent of potential malpractice clients. *Id.,* p. 97.

About two thirds of the plaintiffs' lawyers get formal written expert medical opinion before deciding to take a malpractice case. The other third obtains informal medical opinion. *Id.,* p. 99.

Information about hours devoted to unsuccessful cases in *id.*, p. 116.

See also R. Harley and P. Rheingold, "New Survey of Malpractice Litigation," *N.Y.L.J.* April 28, 1976, p. 1.

82 Information about the number of cases in which patients recover and the insurance-company expert's estimates of valid malpractice claims is reported in Rudov, Myers & Mirabella, "Medical Malpractice Insurance Claim Files Closed in 1970," *HEW Secretary's Malpractice Commission Report*, 1973, Appendix, p. 1. HEW commission's conclusion on meritorious claims is *HEW Secretary's Malpractice Commission Report*, 1973, p. 10.

83 For an article arguing that the contingent-fee system does not provide appropriate economic incentives, see M. Schwartz & D. J. B. Mitchell, "An Economic Analysis of the Contingent Fee in Personal Injury Litigation" *Stan. L. Rev.* 22 (1970): 1125. The basic problem with this analysis is that, in the style that seems fashionable in current economic thinking, it makes assumptions that are directly contrary to our experience in the real world. For example, it begins by assuming that (a) both client and lawyer have "perfect knowledge" of whether a case is winnable and the amount that will be recovered; (b) if lawyers' fees go down, the legal profession will become less attractive and the number of lawyers will decrease; and (c) there is a perfect free market of both buyers—i.e., every claimant can afford a lawyer or can borrow the money to hire one. The first assumption is modified in the course of the work. The last two are clung to until the end. These assumptions destroy any utility which the analysis might have in the world we actually inhabit.

83 On the constitutionality of abolishing the contingent-fee system without providing a substitute, see *Person v. Association of the Bar of City of New York* 414 F. Supp. 144 (E.D.N.Y. 1976). This case held that a ban on contingent fees for witnesses violated equal protection because it had the effect of keeping lower-income people out of court and the state had not shown any substantial reason in support of the rule, even though there are practical problems inherent in hiring witnesses on a contingent-fee basis. Since the witness has a direct financial interest in the success of the side for which he testifies, the testimony may be less credible than that of a witness who is assured payment whatever the outcome of the case.

84 On malpractice and the contingent fee in Great Britain, see Addison, "The Malpractice Problem in Great Britain," in *HEW Secretary's Malpractice Commission Report*, 1973, Appendix, p. 54; Dorsey Woodson, "Malpractice Coverage for $58 a Year," *Med. World News*, Vol. 16, No. 8 (April 21, 1975), p. 40.

The HEW Malpractice Commission concluded that the differences between the British and Canadian "social, legal, and health-care systems and ours make discussion of the comparative effect of the contingent legal fee essentially irrelevant." *Report*, p. 32.

A recent leftist critique of the health-care delivery system suggests that the incidence of medical malpractice suits is lower in England because "when the doctor is taken out of the marketplace, . . . the patient is less likely to treat him like any other supplier of a commodity who fails to deliver." Singer, "Blood, Markets, and Medical Care," *Working Papers for a New Society* Vol. 4, No. 2 (1976), pp. 56, 59. While the generalization may be correct, the example does not provide evidence to support it. English patients cannot bring medical malpractice actions because they cannot obtain legal assistance. It is impossible to know whether the English would sue their doctors more if they could.

There is some movement in Britain to allow the use of contingent fees. When the Turkish Airlines DC-10 crashed outside Paris in March 1974, the families of the British people killed could obtain legal representation only by hiring American lawyers on a contingent-fee basis. This case has raised questions in Britain about the fairness of the ban on contingent fees. See Lloyd's List, Aug. 21, 1976, reprinted in N.Y.L.J., Sept 17, 1976, p. 1.

84 Whether an injured patient can find a lawyer to assert a malpractice claim depends in large part on the economic loss to the patient, which in turn depends in large part on race, sex, and economic class of the patient. In 1974, the median income of employed black women was $6,371, and $12,434 for employed white men. U.S. Dept. of Commerce, Bureau of Census, *The Social and Economic Status of the Black Population in the U.S., 1974,* Special Studies P-23, No. 54., p. 28. In 1974, the unemployment rate for black women was 8.4 percent, while the unemployment rate for white men was 3.5 percent. *Id.,* p. 53 In the first quarter of 1975, the unemployment rate was 11.0 for black women and 5.8 for white men.

If the patient is unemployed at the time the injury occurs, there is no economic loss in terms of earning capacity. See, e.g., *Toal v. United States,* 306 F. Supp. 1063 (D. Conn. 1969), *aff'd,* 438 F.2d 222 (2d Cir. 1969).

On the importance of economic loss in lawyers' decisions whether to take a malpractice claim, see Dietz *et al.,* "The Medical Malpractice Legal System," *HEW Secretary's Malpractice Commission Report,* 1973, Appendix, p. 98. The analysis arguing that a likely recovery of $25,000 is necessary to justify a malpractice action is Lieberman, "Examining the Cases for Universal No Fault," *Bus. Week,* April 28, 1975, p. 56. The survey showing that New York lawyers generally insist upon a likely recovery over $40,000 is R. Harley and P. Rheingold, "New Survey of Malpractice Litigation," *N.Y.L.J.* April 28, 1976, p. 1.

A recent article urging malpractice lawyers to ask patients to pay the costs of malpractice claims investigation in advance is N. Shayne, "Economics and the Law," *N.Y.L.J.,* Oct. 12, 1976, p. 1.

85 The law often protects interests which are not simply monetary. For example, in actions for libel and slander, the interest protected is often largely dignitary. Sometimes actions for battery—the slightest touching without expressed or implied consent—are allowed to redress dignitary injury. A relatively new tort, the intentional or negligent inflection of mental distress, protects dignitary interests, and in some states is tied to a requirement that the person injured show some physical manifestation of the injury in order to guard against trivial claims.

The recommendation of legal services for small claims is in *HEW Secretary's Malpractice Commission Report,* 1973, p. 35.

85 Data on the compensation of patients who are successful in malpractice cases are reported in I.S.O., *Report of the All Industry Committee, Special Malpractice Review—1974 Closed Claims Survey,* 1975.

86 Information on countersuits against lawyers is reported in AMA, *State by State Report on the Professional Liability Issue,* Oct. 1976. The following

medical societies have promised financial support to physicians instituting countersuits: Florida, Georgia, Iowa, South Carolina, Utah, Vermont, and Wyoming. In addition, societies in Ohio, Oregon, and Texas will provide expert testimony and society support. Such programs are being considered in Idaho, Kansas, Nebraska, New Mexico, New York, Tennessee, Virginia, and Wisconsin.

Legal developments are discussed in Birnbaum, "Physicians Counterattack: A Lawyer's Liability for Instituting an Unjustified Medical Malpractice Action," *Fordham L. Rev.* 45 (1977): 1003.

87   The data on the characteristics of malpractice lawyers and their fees are taken from Dietz *et al.*, "The Medical Malpractice Legal System," *HEW Secretary's Malpractice Report*, 1973, Appendix, p. 87, quote on p. 113. For a critique of the methodology and scope of this study, see Curran, *How Lawyers Handle Medical Malpractice Cases*, HEW, Public Health Services, NCHSR Research Report, 1976.

88   The first estimate of the distribution of the malpractice premium dollar is based on ISO and other data, and is set fourth in O'Connell, "An Alternative to Abandoning Tort Liability: Elective No-Fault Insurance for Many Kinds of Injuries," *Minn. L. Rev.* 60 (1976): 501, 506–09. The other estimates were offered by malpractice insurers testifying in Congress. See Subcomm. on Executive Reorganization of the Sen. Comm. on Government Operations, 91st Cong., 2nd Sess., *Medical Malpractice: The Patient Versus the Physician* (1969), p. 50. In 1975 the actuary for Employers Insurance of Wausau, N.Y.'s medical malpractice insurer, estimated that patients receive 40 cents of each malpractice dollar, patients' lawyers, 30 cents, and doctors' lawyers and insurance companies, 40 cents. Letter to author from Robert G. Harley, October 13, 1977.

89   N.J. Stat. Ann. §1:21–7(c) (1971) (West). The New York sliding scale is set forth in N.Y. Court Rules §603.7(e) (McKinney 1975). Both the New Jersey and New York schedules were attacked as unconstitutional and were upheld by the courts. See *American Trial Lawyers Association v. New Jersey Supreme Court*, 126 N.J. Super 577, 316 A. 2d 19, *aff'd*, 66 N.J. 258, 330 A. 2d 350 (1974); *Gair v. Peck*, 6 N.Y. 2d 97, 160 N.E. 2d 43, 188 N.Y.S. 2d 491 (1959), *cert. denied*, 361 U.S. 374 (1960).

The Ohio law is reported in Amend. Sub. H.B. 682, §7 (1975) Page's Ohio Legis. Bull. No. 3 at 183.

The California scale is reported in *Medical Injury Compensation Reform Act*, ch. 1, 2d Extra Sess., §24.2 (1975) West's Cal. Legis. Service No. 9, at 3789 (codified at Calif. Bus. & Prof. Code §6146) (1975 Supp.).

Laws mandating a fixed limit on contingent fees include: Idaho Code §39–4213 (1975 Supp.); 1975 Ore. Laws 2319, ch. 796, §27; Tenn. Code Ann. §23–3419 (Supp. 1976).

An Iowa law requires the trial court to determine the reasonableness of contingent-fee arrangements. Iowa Code Ann., §147.

90   The most precise and recent data on relative earnings of different kinds of lawyer are collected on the state level. The data do not isolate medical malpractice lawyers from other personal-injury lawyers.

In Michigan in 1972, plaintiff's-negligence lawyers ranked 11th in income out of 25 classifications, while defendant's-negligence lawyers ranked 13th. Rankings for other groups of lawyers were: (1) public-utility law; (2) admiralty;

(3) labor law; (4) antitrust; (5) condemnation; (6) securities; (7) banking and commercial; (8) corporations; (9) insurance law; (10) administrative law; (11) patents; (12) natural-resources law; (13) municipal law; (14) bankruptcy; (15) workmen's compensation; (16) probate; (17) other; (18) tax; (19) real property; (20) domestic relations; (21) government contracts; (22) criminal law; (23) collections. *The Economics of Law Practice in Michigan—a Survey*, State Bar of Michigan, 1974, p. 25.

Another study in Indiana in 1971 ranks the mean income of lawyers by specialty areas as follows: antitrust; workmen's compensation; labor; corporations; appellate practice; banking; bankruptcy; estate planning; insurance; negligence—plaintiff; negligence—defendant; patent; real estate; probate; criminal law; municipal corporations; administrative law; tax; domestic relations; mineral law; collections; motor carriers. *Economics of Indiana Law Practice*, Indiana State Bar Association, 1971, p. 48. See also *Economic Survey Conducted by the Massachusetts Bar Association, 1973*, Massachusetts Bar Association, 1975.

90   USDL, Bureau of Labor Statistics, *National Survey of Professional, Administrative, Technical and Clerical Pay*, March 1974, p. 46.

92   The provision of the ABA Code of Professional Responsibility is Disciplinary Rule, 2–106(A).

The case involving minimum-fee schedules is *Goldfarb v. Virginia State Bar Association*, 421 U.S. 773 (1975).

92   Gillers, "Money and Lawyers, Lawyers and Money," *The Commentator*, April 14, 1977, p. 3. See also, Frankel, "An Immodest Proposal," *New York Times Magazine*, Dec. 4, 1977, p. 92, in which a federal district-court judge argues that all lawyers should be paid from public funds.

93   In 1976, the average annual salary of production or nonsupervisory workers on nonagricultural payrolls was $9,025.64. U.S.D.L. Bureau of Labor Statistics, *Employment and Earnings*, Vol. 23, No. 3, p. 73. In 1976, the mean salaries of attorneys within the Bureau of Labor Statistics classifications ranged from $15,413 for inexperienced lawyers to $43,747 for attorneys in the most experienced group. USDL, Bureau of Labor Statistics, *Average Salaries of Employees in Selected White Collar Occupations in Private Establishments*, March 1976, p. 7.

93   The figures on the distribution of income in the United States are available from the U.S.D.L. Bureau of Labor Statistics. The distribution of income has remained relatively stable since 1947, when data were first collected. Since 1968, there has been a slight increase in the proportion of income received by the richest fifth.

Wealth is even more seriously maldistributed than income. In 1972, 25.9 percent of all personal wealth in the United States—including real estate, cash, stock, life insurance, trusts, etc.—was owned by 1 percent of the population. Six percent of the population owned 52.4 percent of the personal wealth. J. D. Smith & S. D. Franklin, "The Distribution of Wealth Among Individuals and Families," Internal Revenue Service, *Personal Wealth*, 1976.

94   For a good discussion of the allocation of attorney fees in America and Great Britain, see *Alyeska Pipeline Services Co. v. Wilderness Society*, 421 U.S. 240 (1975).

94   There is little concrete data on whether juries inflate verdicts to help the

patient pay lawyer's contingent fees. One of the few empirical studies suggests that they do not. H. Kalven, "The Jury, the Law, and the Personal Injury Damage Award," *Ohio State L.J.* 19 (1958): 158, 176–77. However, the study is quite old, and its data are inconclusive.

95 On the mechanisms for passing along the costs of malpractice to patients and taxpayers, see: McGill Commission, *Report of the Special Advisory Panel on Medical Malpractice,* State of New York, Jan. 1976, pp. 22–23, and Lewis *et al.,* Dept. of Community Health, Albert Einstein College of Med., *Hospital Malpractice Insurance in New York State,* 1977, pp. 1–4.

6. The Rules of the Malpractice Game

97 Statements that the increase in malpractice premiums is caused by a slackening of legal standards are so common as almost to require no citation. The comments quoted appear in D. H. Mills, "Malpractice Litigation: Are Solutions in Sight?" J.A.M.A. 232 (1975): 369, 372; P. Blume, Speech to the Conference of Insurance Legislators, July 25, 1975, on file with authors.

98 For discussion of general principles in malpractice cases, see W. Prosser, *Law of Torts* (4th ed., 1971), §30 p. 143 *et seq.*

98 The Michigan case was *Naccarato v. Grob,* 12 Mich. App. 130, 162 N.W. 2d 305 (1968) *rev'd* 384 Mich. 248, 180 N.W. 2d 788 (1970).

99 The Massachusetts case is *Brune v. Belinkoff,* 354 Mass. 102, 109, 235 N.E. 2d 793, 797–8.

Other cases abandoning the locality rule include: *Gambill v. Stroud,* 258 Ark. 766, 531 S.W. 2d 945 (1976); *Kronke v. Danielson,* 108 Ariz. 400, 499 P. 2d 156 (1972); *Fernandez v. Baruch,* 96 N.J. Super. 125, 232 A. 2d 661, at 666 (1967), *rev'd on other grounds* 52 N.J. 127, 244 A. 2d 109 (1968); *Doublas v. Bussaberger,* 73 Wash. 2d 476, 438 P. 2d 829, 837–8 (1968). See also *Pederson v. Dumouchel,* 72 Wash. 2d 73, 431 P. 2d 973 (held reversible error to limit the standard of care solely to that of the same or similar community); *Hundley v. Martinez,* 151 W. Va. 977, 158 S.E. 2d 159 (1967) (court allowed a New York Specialist to testify as to standard of care in a suit tried in West Virginia against a physician with the same special training); *Blair v. Eblen,* Ky., 461 S.W. 2d 370 (where the court called for the adoption of a national standard of care) (1970). *Harris v. Cafritz Memorial Hospital,* 364 A2d 135 (D.C. Ct. App. 1976) (a physician must exercise the degree of skill exercised by members of the medical profession); *Caron v. U.S.,* 548 F2d 366 (1st Cir. 1976) (standards for inoculations in Michigan are the same as those throughout the U.S., any state); *Shea v. City of Spokane,* Wash. App, 562 P. 2d 264 (1977) (a physician must exercise the degree of care expected of the average practitioner in the class in which he belongs). See, generally, Waltz, "The Rise and Gradual Fall of the Locality Rule in Medical Malpractice Litigation," *DePaul L. Rev.* 18 (1969): 408, 418; Note, "Locality Rule in Malpractice Suits," *Calif. W. L. Rev.* 5 (1969): 124, 128–31; Note, "Malpractice and Medical Testimony," *Harv. L. Rev.* 77 (1963): 333, 338; Note, "An Evaluation of Changes in the Medical Standard of Care," *Vand. L. Rev.* 23 (1970): 729, 737–38.

99 On the importance of expert testimony in a patient's lawyer's decision to take a case, see *HEW Secretary's Malpractice Commission Report,* 1973, Appendix, p. 130.

100 The Boston University study is reported in M. Gross, *The Doctors* (1966), p.

120. For general information on the difficulty of finding experts, see Kelner, "The Silent Doctors—the Conspiracy of Silence," *U. Richmond L. Rev.* 5 (1970): 119; Belli, "An Ancient Therapy Still Applied: The Silent Medical Treatment," *Vill. L. Rev.* 1 (1956): 250, 254.

On the difficulties which doctors have obtaining experts to help in their defense, see Comm. on Medicine and Law, "The Medical Malpractice Insurance Crisis," *The Record* 30 (1975): 336, 352.

100 The Tennessee statute is Tenn. Code Ann. §23–3414 (Supp. 1975). The Louisiana statute is La. R.S. 9:2794 (1975).

The Arkansas case is *Gambill v. Stroud,* 531 S.W. 2d 945 (Ark. 1976). These cases may indicate a return to the locality rule. A federal court, interpreting Texas law, required a patient in a malpractice action to produce an expert from the Texarkana area. A dissenting judge argued that the locality rule had been abandoned in Texas. *Edwards v. United States,* 519 F. 2d 1137 (5th Cir. 1975). See also *Knight v. Holder,* 324 So. 2d 765 (Miss. 1975) *cert. denied* 425 U.S. 972 (1976), pet. for cert. filed, 44 L.W. 3647, in which a patient's claim was dismissed because he did not produce an expert from within 150 miles of the area in which the treatment occurred.

102 The case of the falling barrel is *Byrne v. Boadle,* Court of Exchequer Chamber, 159 Eng. Rep. 299, 30 (1863). The mock newspaper story was supplied by the authors.

102 Lord Shaw's comment can be found in *Ballard v. North British R. Co.* [1923] Sess. Cas. H.L. 43, 56.

103 On the procedural effect of *res ipsa loquitur,* see W. Prosser, *The Law of Torts* (4th ed., 1971), p. 214 *et seq.*

103 For a general discussion, see Comment, "The Application of Res Ipsa Loquitur in Medical Malpractice Cases," *Nw. U. L. Rev.* 60 (1966): 852; *HEW Secretary's Malpractice Commission Report,* 1973, Appendix, p. 124, and Comment, "Res Ipsa Loquitur in Medical Malpractice Cases in Oregon," *Willamette L.J.* 6 (1972): 253.

103 The case of the hypothermal-blanket injury during surgery is *Fogal v. Genesee Hospital,* 41 App. Div. 2d 468, 344 N.Y.S. 2d 552 (1973).

The case in which the painful shoulder was not X-rayed is *Heins v. Synkonis,* 58 Mich. App. 119, 227 N.W. 2d 247 (1975).

Negligence cannot be inferred when the arm loses feeling after blood is drawn. *Pipers v. Rosenow,* 39 App. Div. 2d 240, 333 N.Y.S. 2d 480 (1972).

The case in which the drug was improperly administered is *Ohligschlager v. Proctor Community Hospital,* 303 N.E. 2d 392, 55 Ill. 2d 411 (1973).

104 The case of the patient paralyzed after radiation treatment is *Zebarth v. Swedish Hospital Medical Center,* 81 Wash. 2d 12, 499 P. 2d 1 (1972).

The 1973 Washington case is *Younger v. Webster,* 9 Wash. App. 87, 510 P. 2d 1182 (1973).

104 The 1944 California case is *Ybarra v. Spangard,* 25 Cal. 2d 486, 494, 154 P. 2d 687, 691.

105 The case applying *res ipsa* to the group of people in charge of the hemorrhaging post-operative patient was *Cline v. Lund,* 107 Cal. Rptr. 629, 31 Cal. App. 3d 755 (Ct. App. 1973).

The case of the fourteen-year-old boy in Louisiana is *McCann v. Baton Rouge General Hospital,* La. 276 So. 2d 259 (1973).

The case of the Ohio hemodialysis patient is *Shields v. King,* 40 Ohio

App. 2d 77, 317 N.E. 2d 922 (Ct. App. 1973), motion to certify record overruled (1974).

The New Jersey case is *Anderson v. Somberg,* 67 N.J. 291, 338 A2d 1, *cert denied* 423 U.S. 929 (1975). Articles discussing this case are "Torts—Medical Malpractice—Procedural Effect of Res Ipsa Loquitor," *Tenn. L. Rev.* 43 (Spring 1976): 502; "Medical Malpractice—Unconscious Patient—Liability for Defective Instruments—Hospitals and Enterprise Liability—Anderson v. Somberg," *Wash. L. Rev.* 51 (1976): 981. For general discussions, see Note, *"Res Ipsa Loquitur:* Its Place in Medical Malpractice Litigation," *U. San. Fran. L. Rev.* 8 (1974): 343; Note, *"Res Ipsa Loquitur* and Multiple Defendants: Time for Betrothal," *Fla. L. Rev.* 26 (1974): 311.

106   The statistics on the use and success of *res ipsa* in malpractice cases are reported in *HEW Secretary's Malpractice Commission Report,* 1973, Appendix, pp. 122–42. A comprehensive analysis of the *res ipsa* cases in the states studied by HEW and reported between 1971, when the HEW data were gathered, and 1975 is on file with the authors and available upon request.

The study of 1974 resolved claims is All-Industry Medical Malpractice Committee, *1974 Closed Claim Survey,* Dec. 1975. See also American Bar Association Fund for Public Education, *Legal Topics Relating to Medical Malpractice,* Jan., 1977, p. 63.

The NAIC study is *Malpractice Claims,* April 1976. The *res ipsa* claim category was eliminated from the final report; hence the use of the earlier report's data.

106   The *Medical World News* comments is in an article by Rhein, "Malpractice: Grim Outlook for '76," Jan. 12, 1976, p. 71 at p. 77. The conclusion of the Governor's Special Advisory Committee is in *Report of the Special Panel on Medical Malpractice,* State of New York, 1976, p. 35.

106   The Alaska statute is Ala. Stat. §9.55.550 1976 Supp.

107   The Washington law is Wash. Rev. Code §4.24.290 (Supp. 1975).

The Tennessee law is Tenn. Code Ann. §23–3414(c) (Supp. 1976). Nevada's law is Nev. Rev. Stat. §41A.100 (1975).

A good example of a scholarly article providing a somewhat misleading view of the effect of these new statutes is Comment, "An Analysis of State Legislature Responses to the Medical Malpractice Crisis," *Duke L.J.* 6 (1975): 1417, 1426.

107   On legislative attempts to alter Pi, see Issac Asimov, *Adding a Dimension* (Avon, 1977), pp. 49–50.

108   A collection of pre-1960 consent-to-medical-treatment cases can be found in Prosser, *The Law of Torts* (4th ed., 1971), pp. 101–08.

108   The 1914 New York case is *Schloendorff v. Society of New York Hospital,* 211 N.Y. 125, 129–30, 105 N.E. 92, 93, *overruled Bing v. Thunig,* 2 N.Y. 2d 656, 143 N.E. 2d 3 (1957) on the subject of hospital immunity. For further discussion on hospital immunity, see Chapter 4 *supra.*

The Prosser statement is from *The Law of Torts* (4th ed., 1971), p. 165.

109   On the lack of any discernible medical custom about information, see *Canterbury v. Spence,* 464 F. 2d 772, 783 (D.C. Cir.) *cert. denied,* 409 U.S. 1064 (1972).

109   On the information practices of physicians at Yale-New Haven Hospital, see Duff & Hollinshead, *Sickness and Society* (Harper & Row, 1968) pp. 124, 308–14.

Page

110 On doctors' lack of firsthand knowledge about the effect of information on patients, see Oken, "What to Tell Cancer Patients," *J.A.M.A.* 175 (1961): 1120. On the doctors' fear of death, see Arling, "Intimations of Mortality," *Annals of Internal Med.* 69 (1968): 137, 139.

110 On information being good for patients, see I. Janis, *Psychological Stress* (Wiley, 1958), pp. 358, 368.

The policy of opening hospital records is discussed in "How to Reduce Patients' Anxiety: Show Them Their Hospital Records," *Med. World News* 16 (1975): 48.

The angiogram study is reported in Alfidi, "Informed Consent—a Study of Patient Reaction," *J.A.M.A.* 216 (1971): 1325.

111 Good general discussions include Note, "Restructuring Informed Consent," *Yale L.J.* 79 (1970): 1533, and Comment, "Informed Consent—a Proposed Standard for Medical Disclosure," *N.Y.U.L. Rev.* 48 (1973): 548.

Canterbury v. Spence, 464 F. 2d 772, 780–81 (D.C. Cir.) *cert. denied*, 409 U.S. 1064 (1972).

111 Cases since 1970 which have required the patient to produce expert testimony to support a claim that not enough information was provided to allow an informed consent include: *Miriam v. Mascheck, Inc. v. Masner*, 264 So. 2d 859 (Fla. 1972), dicta affirming *Ditlow v. Kaplan*, 181 So. 2d 226 (Fla. App. 1965); *Green v. Hussey*, 127 Ill. App. 2d 174, 262 N.E. 2d 161 (1970); *Ohligschlager v. Proctor* 283 N.E. 2d 86 (Ill. 1972), *rev'd on other grounds*, 55 Ill. 2d 411, 303 N.E. 2d 393 (1973); *Tatro v. Laeken*, 212 Kan. 606, 512 P. 2d 529 (1973); *Charley v. Cameron*, 215 Kan. 750, 528 P. 2d 1205 (1974); *Marchlewicz v. Stanton*, 50 Mich. App. 344, 213 N.W. 2d 317 (1973); *Ross v. Sher*, 483 S.W. 2d 297 (Tex. App. 1972); *Karp v. Cooley* 493 F. 2d 408 (5th Cir.), *cert. denied*, 419 U.S. 845 (1974); *Zebartz v. Swedish Hospital Center*, 81 Wash. 2d 12, 499 P. 2d 1 (1972); *Collins v. Stoh*, 503 P. 2d 36 (1972); *Butler v. Berkeley*, 25 N.C. App. 325, 213 S.E. 2d 517 (1975); *Llera v. Wisner*, 557 P. 2d 805 (Mont. 1976); *Casey v. Penn*, 360 N.E. 2d 93 (App. Ct. Ill. 1977). See also *Perin v. Hayne*, 210 N.W. 2d 609 (Iowa 1973), in which the patient's claim was rejected because she did not prove that if she had been informed, she would have rejected treatment. In *Downer v. Veilleux*, 322 A. 2d 82 (Maine 1974), the court declined to decide whether consent standards should be based on medical practice or the patient's need for information, but dismissed the patient's claim because she did not produce experts to show that there were alternative treatments she could have sought if she had been informed of the risks.

Courts adopting an informed-consent standard based on the informational needs of a reasonable patient include: *Fogal v. Genesee Hospital*, 41 App. Div. 2d 468, 344 N.Y.S. 2d 552 (1973); *Cobbs v. Grant*, 104 Calif. Rptr. 105, 8 Calif. 3d 229, 502 P. 2d 1 (1972); *Congrove v. Holmes*, 37 Ohio Misc. 95, 308 N.E. 2d 765 (Ct. of Common Pleas, Ross County 1973); *Cooper v. Roberts*, 220 Pa. Super. 260, 286 A. 2d 647 (1971); *Miller v. Kennedy*, 11 Wash. App. 272, 522 P. 2d 852 (1974), *aff'd* 85 Wash. 2d 151, 530 P. 2d 334 (1975); *Wilkinson v. Vesey*, 110 R.I. 606, 295 A. 2d 676 (1972); *Getchell v. Mansfield*, 260 Ore. 174, 489 P. 2d 953 (1971); *Trogun v. Fruchtman*, 58 Wis. 2d 569, 207 N.W. 2d 297 (1973). *Jeffries v. McCague*, Pa. Super., 363 A. 2d 1167 (1976). The status of the law in Louisiana is unclear. In *Goodwin v. Aetna Casualty and Surety Co.*, 294 So. 2d 618 (La. App), *aff'd*, 299 So. 2d 788 (La. App.

1974), the patient complained because she had not been informed that a fractured jaw was a possible consequence of extraction of wisdom teeth. Her claim was dismissed because she failed to show that she would not have had the teeth removed if she had had this information, but the court seems to indicate that expert testimony is not needed to show the need for the information. Tennessee adopted an informed-consent standard based upon the reasonable patient's need for information in *Ray v. Scheibert*, 484 S.W. 2d 63 (Tenn. 1972). But in *Longmire v. Hoey*, 512 S.W. 2d 307 (Tenn. 1974), the court dismissed the claim of a patient complaining that she had not been informed of a 1 percent risk of a fistula associated with a hysterectomy. The court said that the risk was not sufficiently serious to require disclosure, though it indicated that a 1 percent risk of death, paralysis, or blindness should be disclosed.

112 The HEW data on appeals raising a consent issue are reported in *HEW Secretary's Malpractice Commission Report*, 1973, Appendix, p. 147. A comprehensive analysis of the cases decided in the states studied by HEW between 1971, when the HEW data were gathered, and 1975 is on file with the authors and available upon request.

The NAIC study is *Malpractice Claims*, May 1977, p. 93.

113 The New York statute can be found N.Y. Public Health Law, §2805–3 (1–4) (1975) and C.P.L.R. §4401 A (1975).

113 On the lack of practical effect of informed consent laws see, Association of the Bar of the City of New York is Committee on Medicine and Law, "The Medical Malpractice Insurance Crisis," *The Record* 30 (1975): 336, 349.

114 See Idaho Code, §39–4304 (Supp. 1975); Iowa Code Ann. §147.137 (1975); La. Rev. Stat. Ann. §40.1229.40(a) (1975); Ohio Rev. Code Ann. §2317.54 (1976); Utah Code Ann. §78–14–5(2) (e) (Supp. 1976); Wash. Rev. Code Ann. §7.70.060 (1976); Nev. Rev. Stat. §41A.110 (1975); Ga. Code Ann. §88–2906 (1971). The decision interpreting the statute is *Young v. Yarn*, 136 Ga. App. 737, 222 S.E. 2d 113 (1975).

114 For the origin of the distinction between positive and negative defensive medicine, and also a systematic study showing that it is not so common as physicians believe, see "The Malpractice Threat: A Study of Defensive Medicine," *Duke L.J.* 5 (1971): 939–993.

115 The AMA study of physician beliefs about defensive medicine is reported in *1970 Professional Liability Survey* (AMA, 1970). See also L. Altman, "Poll Indicates 3 in 4 Doctors Order Extra Tests to Protect Against Suits," *New York*, March 28, 1977, p. 19. Analyses of defensive medicine often focus on excess laboratory tests. The total number of lab tests performed in U.S. hospitals has increased from about 2.9 billion in 1971 to an estimated 5.0 billion in 1975. Over the last six years, the number of lab tests has risen by more than 8 percent annually. The Congressional Budget Office, commenting on this increase, states: "Federal reimbursement policies have contributed to the rapid diffusion and expansion of laboratory tests and procedures, and federal research and development expenditures have spurred advances in technology." Congressional Budget Office, *Expenditures for Health Care: Federal Programs and Their Effects*, Aug. 1977, p. 24.

Another systematic study of defensive medicine is Hershey, "The Defensive Practice of Medicine, Myth or Reality," *Milbank Memorial Quarterly*

20 (1972): 69. See also Bernzweig, "Defensive Medicine," in *HEW Secretary's Malpractice Commission Report,* 1973, Appendix, p. 38.

115 See "Child Head X-Rays: Value Doubted After a Study of 570 Cases," *Med. Tribune* 11 (Oct. 26, 1970): 1. See also Rourke, "Are All Those X-Rays and Tests Really Necessary?" *Modern Hospital* 118 (1972): 106.

116 On the lack of legal courses in medical schools, see Hirsh, "Educational Opportunities in Forensic Medicine in Medical and Law Schools," *J. of Legal Med.* 2 (March 1974): 41.

116 For the lack of reported cases against Good Samaritans, see *HEW Secretary's Malpractice Commission Report,* 1973, p. 15. See also Kelner, "The Silent Doctors—the Conspiracy of Silence," *U. Richmond L. Rev.* 5 (1964): 119.

117 On the development of state Good Samaritan laws, see Comment, "Good Samaritans and Liability for Medical Malpractice," *Colum. L. Rev.* 64 (1964): 130.

On doctors' unwillingness to render aid even with Good Samaritan protection, see AMA, 1963 Report of the Law Department, cited in *HEW Secretary's Malpractice Commission Report,* 1973, p. 16.

States which expanded the Good Samaritan laws in 1975 include Alabama, California, Connecticut, Idaho, Kansas, Louisiana, Maine, Michigan, Mississippi, Montana, Nebraska, Nevada, New Hampshire, South Dakota, Washington, and Wyoming. See NAIC, *Malpractice Claims,* 1976, p. 81.

118 The Washington case is *Helling v. Carey,* 83 Wash. 2d 514, 519 P. 2d 981 (1974).

Useful articles discussing the case include: Comment, "Comparative Approaches to Liability for Medical Maloccurrences," *Yale L.J.* 84 (1975): 1141; Note, "Physicians and Surgeons—Standard of Care—Medical Specialist May Be Found Negligent as a Matter of Law Despite Compliance with the Customary Practice of the Specialty," *Vand. L. Rev.* 28 (1975): 441; Note, "Medical Malpractice: The Standard of Care," *Gonzaga L. Rev.* 10 (1974): 220; Note, *"Helling v. Carey:* Medical Malpractice Standard of Care Determined by Court," *Willamette L.J.* 11 (1974): 152.

7. Techniques of Dispute-Resolution

120 Various estimates of the allocation of the medical malpractice dollar are discussed *supra,* p. 88. There are also various estimates of the time it takes to settle malpractice disputes. These data are discussed *infra,* pp. 123 and 188.

121 For general background on the purpose and operation of statutes of limitations, see Note, "Developments in the Law—Statutes of Limitations," *Harv. L. Rev.* 63 (1950): 1177. For more specific discussion of statutes of limitations in the context of medical malpractice, see S. Sacks, "Statutes of Limitations and Undiscovered Malpractice," *Cleve. Mar. L. Rev.* 16 (1967): 65; Comment, "Discovery Rule: Accrual of Cause of Action for Medical Malpractice," *Wash. & Lee L. Rev.* 25 (1968): 78; Kroll, "The Etiology, Pulse and Prognosis of Medical Malpractice," *Suffdk. L. Rev.* 8 (1974): 598, 612–14; Comment, "An Analysis of State Legislative Responses to the Medical Malpractice Crisis," *Duke L.J.* 6 (1975): 1417, 1429–36; Association of the Bar of the City of New York, "The Medical Malpractice Insurance Crisis," *The Record* 30 (1975): 336, 347–8.

Page

122   The following statutes enacted in 1975 and 1976 restrict the time for bringing suit in medical malpractice cases: Ala. H.B. 300, §28 (1975); Ariz. Rev. Stat. §12–564 (1976); Calif. Civ. Pro. Code §340.5 (West) (1975); Del. Code tit. 18 §6856 (1976); Fla. Stat. Ann. §95.11 (4) (1975); Ill. Ann. Stat. ch. 83, §22.1 (1975); Ind. Ann. Stat. §§16–9.5–3–1, –2 (Burns Supp. 1975); Iowa Code Ann. §614.1 (9) (1975); Kan. Stat. §60–513 (7) (1976); La. Rev. Stat. Ann. §9:5628 (West) (1975); Md. Cts. & Jud. Pro. Code Ann. §5–109 (Supp. 1975); Mass. Ann. Laws ch. 231, §60 D (1975); Mich. Comp. Laws Ann. §600.5838 (1975); Miss. Code Ann. §15–1–36 (1976); Mo. Ann. Stat. §516.105 (1976) (Vernon); Neb. Rev. Stat. §44–2838 (1976); Nev. Rev. Stat. §11.400 (1975); N.M. Stat. Ann. §58–33–13 (1976); N.Y. Civ. Prac. Law §§203 (f), 208, 214 (6), 214–a (McKinney Supp. 1975); N.D. Cent. Code §28–01–18 (3) (Supp. 1975); Amend. Sub. H.B. 682, §1, (1975); Ohio Rev. Code Ann. §2305.11 (1975); Okla. Stat. Ann. tit. 76 §18 (1976); Pa. Stat. Ann. tit. 40 §1301.605 (1976); S.D. Compiled Laws Ann. §15–2–15.1 (Supp. 1975); Tenn. Code Ann. §23–3415 (a) (Supp. 1975). The new Tennessee statute actually liberalizes that state's limitations period for medical malpractice claims. Compare *Clinaid v. Pennington,* 438 S.W. 2d 748 (Tenn. App. 1968) (reaffirming strict application of act or omission rule), with Tenn. Code Ann. §23–3415 (a) (Supp. 1975). Utah Code Ann. §78–14–4 (1976); Wash. Rev. Code Ann. §4.16.350 (1976); Wyo. Stat. §1–18.1 (1976).

123   The NAIC data are reported in *Malpractice Claims,* 1976, Tables 1a, 2a, p. 17. It examines claims closed from July 1975 through June 1976 and shows the following with respect to time from when the incident occurs and is reported to the insurance company until final payment is made or the case closed.

	Minors		All Claims	
	% of incidents reported	% of claims paid	% of incidents reported	% of claims paid
1 yr.	60.2%	53.1%	62.2%	56.8%
2 yr.	80.4%	76.6%	84.2%	82.5%
3 yr.	88.8%	86.7%	93.7%	93.2%
4 yr.	92.3%	91.2%	96.9%	96.7%

The HEW data are reported in Mirabella *et al.,* "Medical Malpractice Insurance Claim Files Closed in 1970," of the *HEW Secretary's Malpractice Commission Report,* 1973, Appendix, p. 9.

123   The following studies support the conclusion that restrictions on the time for filing suit are not likely to have a significant impact on malpractice premiums. *Report of the Special Advisory Panel on Medical Malpractice (McGill Commission),* State of New York, Jan. 1976, pp. 36–37. American Bar Association Fund for Public Education, *Legal Topics Relating to Medical Malpractice,* Jan. 1977, pp. 62–63.

124   The statute of limitations for children in New York is set forth in N.Y. C.P.L.R. Law §208 (Consol.) (1975). Other states with special provisions for minors: Ala. Code tit. 7 §176 (10) (1975); Ariz. Rev. Stat. §12–564 (1976); Calif. Civ.

Pro. Code §340.5 (West) (1975); Del. Code tit. 18 §6856 (1976); Ill. Ann. Stat. ch. 83 §22.1 (Smith-Hurd) (1975); Ind. Code Ann. §16–9.5–3–1 (Burns) (1975); Kan. Stat. §60–515 (1976); Md. (Cts. & Jud. Proc.) Code Ann. §5–109 (1975); Mich. Stat. Ann. §27A.5838 (1975); Miss. Code Ann. §15–1–36 (1976); Mo. Ann. Stat. §516.105 (Vernon) (1976); Nev. Rev. Stat. §11.400(4) (1971); N.J. Stat. Ann. §2A:14–2.1 (West) (1964); N.C. Gen. Stat. §1–17(b) (1975); Tex. Ins. Code Ann. art. 5.82(4) (1975) (Vernon); Wyo. Stat. §1–18.1(a) (ii) (1976).

The portion of payments made in cases involving minors is reported in NAIC, *Malpractice Claims Survey,* No. 3, 1976, p. 7.

124 The Bar Association of the City of New York found that sometimes providers of health-care services are made defendants in a malpractice action solely to obtain the patient's records. It recommended that "the legislature enact a statute which mandates the access to medical records on the part of a patient or his authorized representative at the patient's expense within thirty days of demand; failure to comply should result in imposition of reasonable attorney's fees and costs incurred as a result of noncompliance." "The Medical Malpractice Insurance Crisis," *The Record* 30 (1975): 336, 351. See also California Select Commission on Medical Malpractice, Preliminary Report, 1974, p. 11.

The HEW Secretary's Malpractice Commission found that "the unavailability of medical records without resort to litigation creates needless expense and increases the incidence of unnecessary malpractice litigation." *Report,* p. 75. It recommended that the states "enact legislation enabling patients to obtain access to the information contained in their medical records through their legal representatives, public or private, without having to file suit." *Report.* p. 77.

For other disucssion of the policy considerations with respect to patient access to medical records, and legal rights to such records, see Kaiser, "The Patients' Rights of Access to Their Own Medical Records: The Need for New Law," *Buff. L. Rev.* 24 (1975): 317; Shenkin & Warner, "Giving the Patient His Medical Record," *N.E.J. of Med.* 289 (1973): 688.

124 On the need for early notice to providers of intent to file suit, see *HEW Secretary's Malpractice Commission Report,* p. 37.

The California Law is Calif. Civ. Pro. Code, §364 (1975) (West). The Utah law is Utah Code Ann. §78–14–8 (1976).

125 On the difficulty in obtaining experts to evaluate and testify as to medical malpractice claims, see *HEW Secretary's Malpractice Commission Report,* 1973, p. 36; Calif. Assembly Select Comm. on Medical Malpractice, Preliminary Report, 1974, p. 27.

For a description of earlier voluntary medical malpractice screening panels, "Documentary Supplement, Medical-Legal Screening Panels as an Alternative Approach to Medical Malpractice Claims," *Wm. & Mary L. Rev.* 13 (1972): 695.

125 The following statutes have implemented screening plans in one form or another. Alaska Stat. §9.55.536 (1976); Ariz. Rev. Stat. §12–567 (1976); Ark. Stat. Ann. 34–2602 (Supp. 1975); Calif. Code Civil Pro. (1975); P.A. 17–249 Conn. Legis. Serv. 1977; Del. Code tit. 18 §6803 *et seq.* (1976); Fla. Stat. Ann. 768.44 (1975); Idaho Code tit. 6 §1001 (1976); Ill. Ann. Stat. ch. 110 58.2–.10 (1976); Ind. Code Ann. 16–9.5–9 (West) (1975); Kan. Stat. §65–4901

(1976); La. Rev. Stat. Ann. 40:1299.47 (1975); Mass. Gen. Laws Ann. ch. 231 §60B (West) (1975); Md. (Cts. & Jud. Pro.) Code Ann. §3–2A01 *et seq.* (1976); Mo. Ann. Stat. §538.015 *et seq.* (Vernon) (1976); Neb. Rev. Stat. §44–2840 (1) (1976); Nev. Rev. Stat. 41A.020 (1975); N.H. Rev. Stat. Ann. §519–A:1 (1971); N.M. Stat. Ann. §58–33–14 (A) (1976); N.Y. Judiciary Law 148–a (McKinney Supp. 1975); Ohio Rev. Code Ann. 2711.21 (c) (1975); R.I. Gen. Laws §10–19–1 (1976); Tenn. Code Ann. 23–3403 (1976); Wis. Stat. Ann. 655.021–.21 (1975) (West).

126   The states where the decision of the Pretrial Screening Panel is admissible as evidence in later judicial proceedings are: P.A. 77–249 Conn. Leg. Serv. 1977; Del. Code tit. 18 §6812 (1976, Supp.); Fla. Stat. Ann. §768.47 (West) (1975); Ind. Code Ann. §16–9.5–9–9 (West) (1975); La. Rev. Stat. Ann. §40:1299.47 (1975); Mass. Gen. Laws Ann. ch. 231 §60B (West) (1975); Neb. Rev. Stat. §44–2844 (3) (1976); N.H. Rev. Stat. §519 A:3 (1971); R.I. Gen. Laws §10–19–8 (1976); Wis. Stat. Ann. §655.19 (1) (1975).

The states where the decision of the pretrial screening panel is not admissible as evidence are: Ark. Stat. Ann. §34–2609 (1975); Idaho Code tit. 6 §1001 (1976); Ill. Ann. Stat. ch. 110 §58.8 (Smith-Hurd) (1975); Kan. Stat. §65–4904 (c) (1976 Supp.); Mo. Ann. Stat. §538.050 (Vernon) (1976); N.M. Stat. Ann. §58–33–20(D) (1976).

In New York the panel decision is admissible only if the verdict of the panel members is unanimous (N.Y. Jud. Law §148–a (4), (8) (Consol.) (1974).

126   For an article arguing that nonadmission of panel findings is unfair to physicians, see Comment, "An Analysis of State Legislative Responses to the Medical Malpractice Crisis," *Duke L.J.* 6 (1975): 1417, 1461.

The ABA comment is from ABA Fund for Public Education, *Legal Topics Relating to Medical Malpractice,* 1977, p. 58.

126   Cases holding that it is unconstitutional to allow introduction of the findings of screening panels include: *Wright v. Central DuPage Hospital Association,* 347 N.E. 2d 736 (Ill. Sup. Ct. 1976); *Arnold v. Tennessee ex. rel. Blanton* (Nashville Chancery Court, Part Two, Dec. 1975); *Simon v. St. Elizabeth Medical Center,* 355 N.E. 2d 903 (Ohio Court of Common Pleas). Cases holding that panel findings may be admitted in evidence include: *Carter v. Sparkman,* 335 So. 2d 802 (Fla. Sup. Ct. 1976), *cert. denied,* 429 U.S. 1041 (1977), *Comiskey v. Arlen,* 55 App. Div. 2d 304, 390 N.Y. Supp. 122 (Second Dept., 1976); *Prendergast v. Nelson,* 199 Neb. 97, 256 N.W.2d 657 (1977). See also "Note: Medical Malpractice Mediation Panels: A Constitutional Analysis," *Ford L. Rev.* 36 (1977): 322.

127   The Massachusetts law is Mass. Gen. Laws Ann. Ch. 231, §60B (1975). The Arizona law is Ariz. Rev. Stats. §12–567 (1976).

The Massachusetts data is reported in W. H. McLaughlin, "A Look at the Massachusetts Malpractice Tribunal System," *Am. J. of Law and Medicine* 3 (1977): 197. The author argues that the bond required should be increased from $2,000 to $5,000.

The ABA recommendation is reported in ABA, Fund for Public Education, *Legal Topics Relating to Medical Malpractice* (1977), p. 60.

Information about the voluntary screening programs is reported in Documentary Supplement, "Medical-Legal Screening Panels as an Alternative Approach to Medical Malpractice Claims," *Wm. & Mary L. Rev.* 13 (1972): 695.

In 1971, an experimental screening program was instituted in Manhattan and the Bronx. It required that every malpractice case be referred to a special panel consisting of a doctor specializing in the area of the dispute, a lawyer with trial experience, and a judge. The panel conducted hearings which were informal and confidential, and no panel finding was admissible in a subsequent judicial action. The hearings generally took between sixty and ninety minutes. The doctor examined the medical records; the lawyer studied the legal papers; the judge looked at the entire case file. The panels proceeded in different ways to discuss the case with the lawyers and encourage settlement. About 25 percent of the cases heard by these panels were settled without further legal proceedings. Even where settlement was not possible, those participating in the experiment found that there was a substantial benefit because the issues were narrowed, positions clarified, and a more realistic view of the case was achieved by both sides. One major problem encountered was that the attorneys often came to the panel hearing unprepared. (Also many attorneys, particularly those representing the City of New York, lacked authority to settle the case.) The New York program is described in Comment, "The Medical Malpractice Mediation Panel in the First Judicial Department of New York: An Alternative to Litigation," *Hofstra L. Rev.* 2 (1974): 261.

A 1977 study of screening panels in four states—New York, New Mexico, New Jersey, and Pennsylvania—concludes that "panels must be mandatory for all medical malpractice actions if they are to be effective in producing dispositions. . . . The panelists should be expert, the physicians and attorneys experienced, the chairpersons disposition-oriented with knowledge of medical malpractice law and strong negotiating skills. . . . [I]f the mechanism for settling out of court is forceful and demonstrably impartial, the panels will be able to dispose of cases fairly and will save all participants time, money, and energy." *Medical Malpractice Panels in Four States,* a study prepared by the Institute of Judicial Administration, Inc., for the American Bar Association, Commission on Medical Professional Liability, 1977, pp. 60–61.

128 For medical-journal articles advocating arbitration as an alternative to malpractice litigation, see Averback, "A Plaintiff's Attorney Says: Malpractice Cases Don't Belong in the Courts," *Hosp. Physician* 56 (Jan. 1969); Coulson, "The Malpractice Mess: Is Arbitration the Answer?" *Med. Times* 99 (Oct. 1971): 131; Ludlam & Hassard, "Arbitration," *Cal. Med.* 114 (May 1971): 102; Bergen, "Arbitration of Medical Liability," *J.A.M.A.* 211 (1970): 175.

For general discussion of the legal doctrine applicable to the arbitration of medical disputes, see Henderson, "Contractual Problems in the Enforcement of Agreements to Arbitrate Medical Malpractice," *Va. L. Rev.* 58 (1972): 947; Baird, Munsterman & Stevens, "Alternatives to Litigation, I: Technical Analysis," in *HEW Secretary's Malpractice Commission Report,* 1973, Appendix, p. 214; Note, "Arbitration of Malpractice Claims," *Ariz. Med.* 28 (1971): 391.

The following states passed laws specifically allowing malpractice claims, already in existence, to be submitted to arbitration: Code of Ala. Title 7 §176.14 (1975); N. Dak. Century Code, Ch. 32–29.1, §01–110 (1977); 12 Vermont Stat. Ann. Ch. 215, §512(4) (1976). The following state laws specifically allow agreements to arbitrate future malpractice disputes: Alaska Code Ch. 102, §09.55. 535–6 (1976); Calif. Code of Civ. Proc. Ch. 1, §1295 (1975), Ch. 1185, §1295

(f) (1976); Ill. Rev. Stats. Ch. 10 §101 (1976); La. Rev. Stat. §9:4230–4236 (1975); Mich. Comp. Laws Ch. 50 A §600.5033, 600.5040–5065 (1975), Comp. Laws Ch. 30 A §500.3051 (1975); Ohio Rev. Code Ann. §§2711.01, .22–.24 (1975); S. Dak. Comp. Laws Ann. §21–25A–58–41–38 (1976); Code of Va. §8–911–922 (1976). In addition, Puerto Rico has passed a law requiring that malpractice claims be submitted to binding arbitration. Ins. Code of Puerto Rico, §41.000–41.140 (1976).

128   The data of the American Arbitration Association are reported in I. Ladimer *et al., Medical Malpractice Arbitration: Laws, Programs, Cases* (AAA, 1977), pp. 38–40.

129   The evaluation of the California experience is Heintz, "An Analysis of the Southern California Arbitration Project: Jan. 1966 through June 1975," HEW, Public Health Service, National Center for Health Services Research, Nov. 1975 (hereinafter cited as Heintz).

130   The composition of the California panels and the characterization of the "consumer" member is from Heintz, *supra,* p. 30.

    The composition of panels under the state laws enacted 1975–77 is discussed in Ladimer, *supra,* pp. 16–19.

131   The Heintz study of the Southern California Arbitration Project found that attorneys for both doctors and patients were deeply disturbed by the absence of rules of evidence for the arbitration proceedings. Hearsay evidence was allowed, and there was no right to cross-examination. Officials of the Arbitration Association and hospital and medical associations believed that the attorneys' objections were unfounded, since the arbitrators were sufficiently sophisticated to discount hearsay evidence and information which was supplied without opportunity for cross-examination. Neither side offered any concrete data in support of its position. Because of limited experience with medical malpractice arbitration, and the difficulty in evaluating what constitutes a "fair" decision-making process, it is difficult to know whether the lawyers for the parties are correct in suggesting that these procedural protections are an essential aspect of a fair process, or whether the professional associations are correct in maintaining that it does not matter.

    For a discussion of rules of evidence and rights of appeal under the California plan, see Heintz, *supra,* pp. 31–33.

131   Data on the time from incident to settlement are presented in Heintz, *supra,* pp. 22–23.

132   Under the California project, parties are charged $300, $150 of which must be paid when the claim is filed. Costs may be adjusted or reapportioned by the arbitrators at the close of the proceedings. Heintz, *supra,* p. 3. Under the New York plan, the maximum cost to the patient is $500, of which $200 is a "nonrefundable initial administrative filing fee." American Arbitration Association, *An Arbitration Program for Patient, Physician and Hospital,* Draft 5/17/76, p. 5.

    The information on defense costs in California is reported in Heintz, *supra,* pp. 20–21.

132   The information on amounts paid to patients under the California experiment is reported in Heintz, *supra,* pp. 17–19.

133   For discussion of common-law attitudes toward arbitration, see 6A Corbin, Contracts §1433 (1962), also Henderson, *supra,* pp. 948–54.

133 The Puerto Rico law requiring arbitration of malpractice disputes is Ins. Code of Puerto Rico, §§41.000–41.140 (effective July 1, 1976). The Michigan law is Mich. Compiled Laws, §§500.3051–500.3062 (1975), and South Dakota's is S. Dak. Compiled Laws, §58–51–58 (1976).

For a discussion of constitutionality of laws forcing parties to arbitrate, see Note, "An Analysis of State Legislative Responses to the Medical Malpractice Crisis," *Duke L.J.* 6 (1975): 1417, 1463–67.

134 The California law, Calif. Code Civ. Pro. §1295 (1975), seems to go furthest in validating arbitration agreements. It provides that agreements may be made with any health-care provider. They are revocable within thirty days of being signed. The law provides that agreements which comply with the statute are not "a contract of adhesion, nor unconscionable nor otherwise improper."

The Alaska law, Alaska Stat. §9.55.535 (1976), provides that the patient may revoke the arbitration agreement within thirty days of its execution. However, the health-care provider may not revoke at any time.

The Alabama law, Ala. Code tit. 7 §176 (14) (1975 Supp.), the Louisiana law, La. Rev. Stat. Ann. §9:4235 (1) (1976), and the Ohio law, Ohio Rev. Code Ann., §2711.22 (1975) (Page), provide that agreements which comply with statutory forms are "valid, irrevocable, and enforceable, save upon such grounds as exist at law or in equity for the revocation of any contract." Michigan goes somewhat further and provides that agreements meeting statutory standards shall be presumed valid. Mich. Comp. Laws Ann. §600.5041.

The Michigan law also provides that the agreement is revocable by the patient within sixty days of being signed, and expires of its own force after one year. The Illinois law, Ill. Ann. Stat. ch. 10 §208 (Smith-Hurd) (1976), and the Ohio law, Ohio Rev. Code Ann. §2711.23 (1975) (Page), provide that the agreement may be revoked within sixty days after "the patient's discharge from the hospital for any claim arising out of hospitalization, or within sixty days after the termination of the physician-patient relationship for the physical condition involved for any claim against a physician."

The South Dakota law, S.D. Compiled Laws Ann. §21–25B–1 (1976), and the Vermont law, Vt. Stat. Ann. tit. 12 §7002 (1975), provide that the agreement to arbitrate may be terminated on written notice to all parties before a claim is filed. Once the claim is filed, in Vermont it can be withdrawn from arbitration only upon the written consent of all the parties. In South Dakota, the claimant is bound by the claim once it is filed, and cannot terminate after that point.

134 Information about the New York arbitration program is based on various drafts of the agreement to arbitrate sponsored by the New York Medical Society, New York Hospital Association, and the American Arbitration Association. These documents have been considered and criticized in unpublished reports by the Committee on Law and Medicine of the Association of the Bar of the City of New York. S. Law is a member of that committee, and its unpublished reports are available upon request. Published material about the New York plan include articles in support of the plan by Richard E. Lerner, Associate Counsel of the AAA, published in the *New York Law Journal* on Feb. 19, Sept. 17, Oct. 8, and Dec. 1, 1975, all on page 1. A criticism of the New York plan is P. Rheingold, "Malpractice Arbitration Plan—an Analysis," *N.Y.L.J.*, Dec. 12, 1975, p. 1.

The Texas statute requiring advice of counsel prior to an agreement to arbitrate is Tex. Rev. Civ. Stat. Ann., art. 224 (1965).

135 The United States Supreme Court has recognized the difficulty in obtaining a valid consent to arbitrate where one party is substantially weaker and less informed. The court has said, "We note that categories of contracts otherwise within the Arbitration Act but in which one of the parties characteristically has little bargaining power are expressly excluded from the reach of the Act." *Prima Paint Corp. v. Flood & Conklin Mfg. Co.*, 388 U.S. 395, 403, n. 9 (1967). Although the federal statute expressly excludes only contracts of employment of seamen, railroad employees, or any other class of workers engaged in foreign or interstate commerce, the Supreme Court dicta seem to indicate a broader reading.

135 The bar group's findings are in Association of the Bar of the City of New York, Committee on Law and Medicine, *Report on Medical Malpractice Arbitration Plan*, Feb. 4, 1976, p. 8.

135 Dr. Ralph Emerson, past president of the New York Medical Society, acknowledged that information about whether a patient had signed an arbitration agreement would affect the total doctor-patient relationship. Public meeting, Association of the Bar of the City of New York, April 12, 1977. See also Association of the Bar of the City of New York, *Report on Medical Malpractice Arbitration Plan*, Feb. 4, 1976, p. 3.

136 On the revocability of arbitration agreements in the New York and California plans, see Heintz, *An Analysis of the Southern California Arbitration Project: January 1966 through June 1975*, HEW, Public Health Service, National Center for Health Services Research, Nov. 1975, p. 2; and American Arbitration Association, *An Arbitration Program for Patient, Physician and Hospital*, Draft 5/17/76, p. 2.

137 The California case upholding the agreement to arbitrate is *Madden v. Kaiser Foundation Hospitals*, 17 Calif. 2d 699, 131 Calif. Rptr. 882, 552 P. 2d 1178 (Calif. Sup. Ct. 1976). The case invalidating the agreement to arbitrate is *Wheeler v. St. Joseph Hospital*, 63 Calif. App. 2d 357, 133 Calif. Rptr. 775 (Calif. Ct. of App., 4th Div. 1976).

138 The New York case is *Linden v. Baron, N.Y.L.J.*, July 21, 1977, p. 21 (Sup. Ct. Part 1).

139 Laws limiting the amount which an injured patient may receive are: Idaho Code, Section 39–4204 (Supp. 1975); N. Dak. Cent. Code, Section 26–40–11 (1975); Ind. Ann. Stat., Section 16–9, 5–2–2(b) (1975); La. Rev. Stat. Ann., Section 40:1299.42 (B) (2) (1975); Ill. Rev. Stat., ch. 70, Section 101 (1975); Neb. Rev. Stat., Section 44–2825 (1976); New Mexico Stat. Ann. §58–33–6 (1976); Virginia Code, Section 8–654.8 (1977).

140 Cases upholding the abolition of the action for alienation of affections are *Rotwein v. Gersten*, 160 Fla. 736, 36 So. 2d 419, (1948), *Hanfgarn v. Mark*, 274 N.Y. 22, 8 N.E.2d 47 (1937).

141 The notion that a reasonable substitute must be provided if common-law rights are abolished originates in the Supreme Court opinion in *New York Central R.R. Co. v. White*, 243 U.S. 188, 201 (1917), in which the court said: "Nor is it necessary, for the purposes of the present case, to say that a State might, without violence to the constitutional guarantee of 'due process of

law' suddenly set aside all common law rules respecting liability as between employer and employee, without providing a reasonably just substitute. . . ."

An automobile no-fault case in which the court required that an adequate substitute be provided for common-law rights is *Lasky v. State Farm Ins. Co.*, 296 So. 2d 9 (Fla. Sup. Ct. 1974). In other cases, courts have examined the adequacy of the substitute provided without requiring that an adequate substitute is necessary. See *Montgomery v. Daniels*, 38 N.Y. 2d 41, 340 N.E. 2d 444, 378 N.Y.S. 2d 1 (1975).

In addition to the state laws limiting the amount which may be paid to seriously injured victims of medical malpractice, Congress has enacted a law which places a limitation of $560,000,000 on the maximum amount of liability for damages resulting from a nuclear accident involving an atomic power plant. The Price-Anderson Act, 42 U.S.C. §2210(e) (1957). The law was held unconstitutional in *Carolina Environmental Study Group v. United States*, 431 F. Supp. 203 (1977). This case is discussed *infra*.

For commentary arguing that no substitute remedy is required, see Comment, "An Analysis of State Legislative Responses to the Medical Malpractice Crisis," *Duke L. Rev.* 6 (1975): 1417, 1420–22; Redish, "Legislative Response to the Medical Malpractice Crisis: Constitutional Implications," *Texas L. Rev.* 55 (1977): 759.

141 The Illinois case is *Wright v. Central Du Page Hospital Association*, 347 N.E. 2d 736 (Ill. Sup. Ct. 1976). The court cited several factors in support of its finding that the $500,000 limit was unconstitutional. First, it noted that the legislature did not provide seriously injured patients with any benefit in exchange for the rights abolished. But it also stated that "we do not hold or even imply that under no circumstances may the General Assembly abolish a common law cause of action without a concommitant *quid pro quo*." *Id.*, p. 743.

Second, it rejected the doctor's argument that the law provides a "societal *quid pro quo*," in the form of lower insurance premiums and low medical-care costs for all patients. This alleged social benefit is of no particular value to the seriously injured. Third, it noted that in some cases the victim "might be unable to recover even all the medical expenses he might incur, in which event he would recover nothing for any other loss suffered." *Id.*, p. 742. See "Note: Medical Malpractice Statute Declared Unconstitutional," Wisc. L. Rev. (1977): 203.

142 A good discussion of recent Supreme Court cases on equal protection is Gunther, "The Supreme Court, 1971 Term—Foreword: In Search of Evolving Doctrine on a Changing Court: A Model for a Newer Equal Protection," *Harv. L. Rev.* 86 (1972): 1. See also Dorsen *et al., Political and Civil Rights in the United States*, (Little Brown, 1978) for a comprehensive examination of equal-protection law.

142 The Ohio decisions indicating disapproval of the limits set by that state's malpractice statute are: *Graley v. Satayatham*, 74 Ohio Op. 2d 316, 343 N.E. 2d 832 (Ohio Comm. Pl. 1976) and *Simon v. St. Elizabeth Medical Center*, 30 Ohio Op. 2d 164, 355 N.E. 2d 903 (Ohio Comm. Pl. 1976).

142 For commentary arguing that caps on malpractice recoveries should be upheld under relaxed equal-protection standards, see Redish, "Legislative Response

to the Medical Malpractice Crisis: Constitutional Implications," Texas L. Rev. 55 (1977): 55. The middle-level equal-protection standard quoted is from *Royster Guano v. Virginia*, 253 U.S. 412, 415 (1920).

143 The Idaho Supreme Court decision is *Jones v. State Board of Medicine*, 555 P. 2d 399 (1976).

143 A United States District Court in *Carolina Environmental Study Group v. United States*, 431 F. Supp. 203 (D N. Car. 1977), found that the constitutional guarantee of equal protection was violated by a federal statute limiting the total potential liability of a nuclear-power company. The court found that the law "irrationally places the risk of a major nuclear accident upon people who happen to live in the areas which may be touched by radioactive debris. [It] irrationally and unreasonably places a greater burden upon people damaged by nuclear accident than upon people damaged by other types of accidents. . . . [It] unreasonably and irrationally relieves the owners of power plants of financial responsibility for nuclear accidents. . . . [And] the limitation is unnecessary to serve any legitimate public purpose." 431 F. Supp. at 225. The court relies upon Idaho and Illinois decisions invalidating limitations upon recovery for medical malpractice.

In another related area, in recent years several state courts have considered the constitutionality of state laws providing that a nonpaying guest in an automobile may recover for injuries caused by the host driver only when the guest proves that the driver was grossly negligent.

The United States Supreme Court upheld such a law in 1929, *Silver v. Silver*, 280 U.S. 117, and such laws have existed in most states for many years. In 1973 the California Supreme Court struck down that state's guest statute as a violation of the constitutional guarantee of equal protection. See *Brown v. Merlo*, 8 Calif. 2d 855, 506 P. 2d 212, 106 Calif. Rptr. 388. Since that time six other state courts have held guest statutes unconstitutional and eleven state courts have upheld the statutes. See C. Gregory *et al., Cases and Materials on Torts*, 3rd ed. (Little, Brown, 1977), p. 426. See also Note, "Judicial Activism in Tort Reform," *U.C.L.A. Rev.* 21 (1974): 1566; Notes, "Legislative Purpose, Rationality, and Equal Protection," *Yale L. J.* 82 (1972): 123.

144 The NAIC study is *Malpractice Claims Survey*, No. 3, 1976, Table 27, p. 63.

144 The criticism of the Idaho decision is from Redish, *supra*, at p. 67. See also Prendergast v. Nelson, 199 Neb. 97, 256, N.E. 2d 657 (1977) in which three of the seven judges on the Nebraska Supreme Court ruled that a $500,000 ceiling on malpractice judgments is constitutional. Three judges thought the limit was not constitutionally valid. The seventh judge thought the issue was not properly before the court.

145 An appeal of the case invalidating the federal limitation on liability for atomic accidents has been filed in the United States Supreme Court, *Carolina Environmental Study Group v. United States*, 46 U.S.L.W. 3222 (1977). It is possible that this case will be decided in a way that provides guidance on the issue of the constitutionality of limitations on damages in medical malpractice actions. However, most state constitutions also contain a guarantee of equal protection of the laws, and state-court judges interpreting state constitutional provisions are not bound to follow the rulings of the United States Supreme Court.

146 For medical criticism of recovery for pain and suffering, see Holder, "Damages

for Pain and Suffering," *J.A.M.A.* 222 (1972): 1473; Holder, "Recent Decisions on Pain and Suffering," *J.A.M.A.* 227 (1974): 1204.

Laws limiting recovery for pain and suffering include Calif. Civil Code, §3333.2(b) (1975), Ohio Rev. Code, §2307.43 (1975).

146 The Idaho and North Dakota laws provide that recoveries against hospitals and doctors shall be limited to "compensatory damages not previously paid or satisfied by any other person or from any other source." Idaho Code, §39–4204 (1975). N. Dak. Cent. Code, §26–40–11 (1975).

For general discussion of the collateral source rule, see Note, "Unreason in the Law of Damages: The Collateral Source Rule," *Harv. L. Rev.* 77 (1964): 741; Schwartz, "The Collateral-Source Rule, *Boston U.L. Rev.* 41 (1961): 348.

147 Statutes limiting malpractice recovery for injuries compensated through collateral sources include: Tenn. Code §23–3418 (Supp. 1975) (malpractice recoveries reduced by all amounts received from collateral sources "except the assets of the claimants or of the members of the claimants' immediate family and insurance purchased in whole or in part, privately and individually"); Iowa Code, §147.134 (1975 Supp.) (malpractice recoveries reduced by all amounts received from collateral sources except "the assets of the claimant or of the members of the claimant's immediate family"); Calif. Civ. Code, §3333.1 (1975 Supp.) (malpractice recoveries reduced by any amounts paid to obtain the insurance coverage); Ala. Stat. §9.55.548(b) (1976 Supp.) (malpractice recoveries reduced by all amounts received by claimant from collateral sources, "whether private group or governmental, and whether contributory or noncontributory"); Ariz. Rev. Stat. §12–565 (1976) (defendant may introduce evidence of any compensation claimant is receiving from a collateral source); Del. Code tit. 18 §6862 (1976) (evidence may be introduced on any public collateral source of compensation, but not life insurance or private collateral sources of compensation); Fla. Stat. Ann. §768.50 (West) (1976) (malpractice recoveries reduced by the total amounts paid or to be paid from all collateral sources available to the claimant, including Social Security and health, accident, disability, or income insurance, but not life insurance); Ill. Ann. Stat. ch. 110 §68.4 (Smith-Hurd) (1976) (malpractice recoveries may be reduced by no more than 50 percent by deducting benefits received from collateral sources); Pa. Stat. Ann. tit. 40 §1301.602 (1975) (malpractice recoveries reduced by no more than 50 percent by deducting benefits received from collateral sources); Pa. Stat. Ann. tit. 40 §1301.602 (1975) (malpractice recoveries reduced by any public collateral source of compensation or benefits); R.I. Gen. Laws §9–19–34 (1976) (evidence may be introduced of any amount, public or private, payable as a benefit to the claimant as a result of the personal injury, and the jury will be instructed to reduce the award to the claimant by that amount); Wash. Rev. Code Ann. §7.70.080 (1976) (malpractice recoveries reduced by any amount the patient has already been compensated for, except from the assets of the patient, or his immediate family, or insurance purchased with such assets, including insurance provided by an employer for an employee).

148 The Ohio decision on collateral sources is *Graley v. Satayatham*, 343 N.E. 2d 832 (Ohio Comm. Pleas 1976).

The ABA study is Fund for Public Education, *Legal Topics Relating to Medical Malpractice*, 1977, pp. 64–65.

8. The No-Fault Alternative

149 Perhaps the leading proponent of no-fault insurance for medical injuries is Professor Jeffrey O'Connell. See his book *Ending Insult to Injury: No-Fault Insurance* for *Products and Services* (Univ. of Ill. Press, 1975). See also O'Connell, "No-Fault Insurance for Injuries Arising from Medical Treatment: A Proposal for Elective Coverage," *Emory L.J.* 24 (1975): 21; O'Connell, "An Alternative to Abandoning Tort Liability: Elective No-Fault Insurance for Many Kinds of Injuries, *Minn. L. Rev.* 60 (1976): 501; O'Connell, "Expanding No-Fault Beyond Auto Insurance: Some Proposals," *Va. L. Rev.* 59 (1973): 749.

For a free-market economic analysis of the no-fault idea, and a concrete proposal for implementing it, see Havighurst & Tancredi, "Medical Adversity Insurance—a No-Fault Approach to Medical Malpractice and Quality Assurance, *Milbank Memorial Fund Q.* 51(1973):125; Havighurst, "Medical Adversity Insurance—Has Its Time Come?" *Duke L.J.* 6 (1975): 1233.

The American Public Health Association supports a no-fault system for ensuring compensation of patients injured by medical treatment. See APHA, "Policy on Malpractice," *A.J.P.A.* 67 (1977): 96. While the HEW Secretary's Malpractice Commission opposed wholesale adoption of a no-fault compensation system for medical injuries, it did recommend further study and demonstration projects to test the idea. *Report,* pp. 100–02. Dr. Charles A. Hoffman, commission member and president of the American Medical Association, dissented and argued that a no-fault system should be adopted. *Report,* pp. 127–29. New York's McGill Commission recommends creation of "a system of compensation for adverse medical outcomes resulting from medical treatment, whether or not caused by negligence." State of New York Special Advisory Panel on Medical Malpractice, Report 4, 1976, p. 57.

150 The quoted definition of compensable events is adapted from Ross & Rosenthal, "Non-Fault Based Medical Injury Compensation, *HEW Secretary's Malpractice Commission Report,* 1973, Appendix, p. 460. The definition is advocated by O'Connell in the *Emory* article, *supra* at p. 32.

A similar definition is used in the Kennedy-Inouye no-fault bill, S. 215, 94th Cong., 1st Sess. (1975). This bill would provide "compensation for loss from any injury suffered as a result of health care services provided by an insured. . . ." *Id.,* §1711(a). The bill further specifies that "an injury 'results' from the provision of health care services when it is more probably associated in whole or in part with the provision of such services than with the condition for which such services were provided." *Id.,* §1721(8).

On the difficulty in determining whether an injury or illness "arises out of employment," see *The Report of the National Commission on State Workmen's Compensation Laws,* 1972. The commission states that disputes as to workers' compensation coverage include such questions as "Is the employer insured? Does the law apply to the particular event, worker, or impairment? Did the impairment arise out of and in the course of employment? Is the disability related causally to the injury or exposure? . . . How real or serious is the impairment or disability? How long will the disability endure? How much earning power has been lost and how much should be replaced? Who, in the event of death, are legitimate dependents?" *Id.,* p. 106. Although the data was limited, the commission found that a substantial portion of workers' compensation claims are contested, and that attorneys' fees constitute a significant portion of the costs of workers' compensation. *Id.*, pp. 107, 109.

151 The detailed no-fault proposal is described in Havighurst & Tancredi, "Medical Adversity Insurance—a No-Fault Approach to Medical Malpractice and Quality Assurance," *Milbank Memorial Fund Q.* 51 (1973): 125; Havighurst, "Medical Adversity Insurance—Has Its Time Come?" *Duke L.J.* 6 (1975): 1233.

152 The statistics on the number of contested workers' compensation cases were provided to the authors by the NYS Workmen's Compensation Board. Attorney involvement is indicated in NYS Workmen's Compensation Board, *Compensated Cases Closed 1974.* The figure of 18,000 cases in which attorneys were involved is almost certainly an underestimate, because it refers only to compensated cases.

153 Inadequacies in state workers' compensation payments are described in *The Report of the National Commission on State Workmen's Compensation Laws*, 1972, pp. 18–19. This broad-based commission concluded, without dissent, that "the evidence compels us to conclude that State workmen's compensation laws are in general neither adequate nor equitable." *Id.*, p. 25.

154 O'Connell relies on general arguments made in support of enterprise liability with respect to the manufacture of products to support the internalization of the costs of injuries resulting from medical treatment. See *Minn. L. Rev.* 60 (1976): 551–56, *supra*, p. 222.

Havighurst also advocates the goal of internalizing the costs of adverse outcomes, but suggests that costs should be internalized to specific procedures, rather than to the general enterprise of the practice of medicine. *Duke L.J.* 6 1237–52, *supra*, notes p. 220.

156 The notion that there should be different principles of liability depending on whether risks are generated and encountered on a reciprocal or a nonreciprocal basis is discussed at length in Fletcher, "Fairness and Utility in the Law of Torts," *Harv. L. Rev.* 85 (1972): 537.

156 On the conditions leading to the enactment of the Occupational Health and Safety Act of 1970, see United States Senate Committee on Labor and Public Welfare, *Report on the Occupational Health and Safety Act of 1970*, 91st Cong., 2nd sess. (1970).

On the lack of correlation between workers'-compensation premiums and the level of workplace accidents, see *Report of the National Commission on State Workmen's Compensation Laws*, 1972, pp. 87–98.

9. Malpractice Insurance: The Blood-Money Industry

161 The 1975 NAIC profitability report is *Property and Liability Insurance 1975 Profitability Results*, Oct. 19, 1976. The unreleased document is on file with the authors. The 1976 report is *NAIC Report on Profitability by Line and by State*, Aug. 12, 1977. The caveats concerning the 1975 data are included in the *Proceedings of the 1977 NAIC Annual Meeting*, June 1977.

162 The premium-increase surveys were reported in Arthur Owens, "How Much Have Malpractice Premiums Gone Up?" *Med. Economics*, Dec. 27, 1976, p. 102. Average loss figures are in NAIC, *Malpractice Claims*, May 1977.

164 Deficiencies in ISO data were noted in Kendall & Haldi, "The Medical Mal-

practice Insurance Market," in Report of the Secretary's Commission on Medical Malpractice, D.H.E.W., 1973, Appendix, p. 533.

The New York decision is NYS Insurance Department, *In the Matter of the MMIA and ISO,* Nov. 7, 1975, p. 29.

On Argonaut's withdrawal from New York see "Argonaut and Malpractice: A Tangled Web," *Medical World News,* July 14, 1975; and from New Jersey see N.J. Department of Insurance, "State Owned and Operated Non-Profit Medical Malpractice Insurance Company," June 12, 1975.

165 Estimates of the number of insurance companies writing malpractice insurance vary widely. The number noted here is based on a report of the Insurance Information Institute, Press Release, June 30, 1975.

The HEW report is in Kendall & Haldi, "The Medical Malpractice Insurance Market," in Report of the Secretary's Commission on Medical Malpractice, D.H.E.W., 1973, Appendix, p. 551.

The Connecticut insurance situation is reported in Peter Kihss, "Doctors Premiums Less in Jersey and Connecticut," *New York Times,* June 4, 1975, p. 22.

The advantages to physicians of the group plans are noted in Philip Harsham, "Malpractice Insurance Outlook Brightens," *Med. Economics,* Aug. 2, 1971, pp. 214–26.

166 For purposes of this discussion, a monopoly position is assumed either by a medical-society-sponsored plan or by one company holding at least 60 percent of the individual market in the few states without sponsored plans. The market distribution is reported in Steves & McWhorter, "Notes on the Malpractice Insurance Market," *C.P.C.U. Annals,* Dec. 1975, p. 225.

The North Carolina experience is indicated in the statement of John Ingram, Insurance Commissioner of North Carolina, Dec. 19, 1974.

167 The HEW report indicates that the premium value for physicians' and surgeons' professional-liability insurance does not exceed 2.5 percent of the total property-liability insurance market. Report of the Secretary's Commission on Medical Malpractice, D.H.E.W., 1973, p. 41.

Insurance-industry losses are reported in "Insurance Group Says Underwriting Losses for 1975 Set Record," *Wall Street Journal,* April 7, 1976, p. 7.

The cycle theory is discussed in Herman, "The Risk Business: Insurers Hit Hard by Losses in Stocks," *Wall Street Journal,* Jan. 20, 1975, p. 1.

The former commissioners' analysis is in Roddis & Stewart, "The Insurance of Medical Losses," *Duke L.J.* 6 (1975): 1281, 1288.

168 The California report is California Joint Legislative Audit Committee, Office of the Auditor General, *Doctors' Malpractice Insurance,* Report 265.2, Dec. 1975.

Investment losses of insurance companies are reported under the heading of each particular company in A. M. Best Co., *Best's Insurance Reports (Property-Casualty),* 1976. See index, pp. xiii–xxvii, for listings of individual companies.

168 St. Paul's losses were reported in Herman, "The Risk Business: Damage Insurers Hit by Large Losses in Stocks," *Wall Street Journal,* Jan. 20, 1975, p. 1; Argonaut's losses were reported in "Teledyne Sees Threat to Insurance Unit from Suits," *Wall Street Journal,* April 4, 1975, p. 34.

Page

169   The *Wall Street Journal* report was "Heard on the Street," Oct. 16, 1974, p. 39.

The insurance-industry executive was Lester Senger of the Aetna Life and Casualty Co.; Hearing on the Examination of the Continuing Medical Malpractice Insurance Crisis, 1975, Before the Subcommittee on Health of the Senate Committee on Labor and Public Welfare, 94th Cong., 1st Sess. (1975), p. 235 (statement of Lester Senger).

169   Evidence of increasing frequency and severity of malpractice claims is fragmentary and imprecise. See *Report of the Special Advisory Panel on Medical Malpractice, State of New York,* 1976, p. 246; Steves, "Medical Malpractice in Perspective," *C.P.C.U. Annals,* Dec. 1975, pp. 213–14; St. Paul Insurance Co., *The Problems of Insuring Medical Malpractice,* 1975, p. 3.

On the California insolvencies, see California Joint Legislative Audit Committee, Office of the Auditor General, *Doctors' Malpractice Insurance,* Report 265.2, Dec. 1975, p. 22. Between 1964 and 1974, 129 property-liability insurance-company insolvencies were reported nationwide. NAIC, *Strengthening the Surveillance System* (McKinsey, 1974), p. 3–1.

170   On the dividend payments of the individual companies, see A. M. Best Co., *Best's Insurance Reports (Property-Casualty),* 1976.

171   The Wisconsin report is in Czerwinski, "Wisconsin's Medical Malpractice Crisis," in Warren & Merritt, eds., *A Legislator's Guide to the Medical Malpractice Issue* (Georgetown Health Policy Center, National Conference of State Legislatures, 1975), p. 51. The Idaho report is in the same document, p. 35. The Massachusetts report is from an interview with Edward Brennan, Executive Director, Massachusetts Special Committee on Medical Malpractice, Jan. 17, 1977.

172–175 On Argonaut's history and the Teledyne takeover see *Best's Insurance Reports (Property-Liability),* 1975, p. 142–144. *Best's* also provides data on the company's miscellaneous liability policy commitments. On the company's market participation and withdrawals see A.M.A., *State By State Report on the Professional Liability Issue,* Oct. 1975; and "Argonaut and Malpractice: A Tangled Web," *Medical World News,* July 14, 1975. The latter article also reports the Teledyne tax credit policy, and the company's activities in the Florida and Pennsylvania markets. The New York withdrawal is reported in "When a Malpractice Carrier Says Goodbye," *Medical World News,* Feb. 24, 1975; and Lindsey, Robert, "For Argonaut, Profits Proved Illusory," *N.Y. Times,* June 8, 1975, p. 49. Argonaut's losses are reported in the Lindsey article; see also "Teledyne Sees Threat to Insurance Unit From Suits," *Wall St. Journal,* April 4, 1975, p. 34.

The dividend payment is reported in "Argonaut and Malpractice: A Tangled Web," *supra.* The California Commissioner's review is California Department of Insurance, *Report of Financial Examination—Argonaut Insurance Company,* Dec. 31, 1974.

See also "Malpractice Insurance for Doctors Reviewed by Public Health Unit," *Wall St. Journal,* Dec. 30, 1974, p. 10; "Henry Singleton's Singular Conglomerate," *Forbes,* May 1, 1976, p. 38; Sasweet, "Teledyne Takes Drastic Steps in an Effort to Salvage Its Argonaut Insurance Unit," *Wall St. Journal,* Jan. 30, 1975, p. 26.

The report on the transfer in the St. Paul companies was in "Heard on the Street," *Wall Street Journal,* Oct. 16, 1974, p. 39; the Aetna transfer was reported in Herman, "The Risk Business: Damage Insurers Hit by Losses in Stocks," *Wall Street Journal,* Jan. 20, 1975, p. 1.

Argonaut's activities in the hospital-insurance market were reported in Phillips, "Malpractice Coverage: The Long and the Short of It," *Hospitals,* April 16, 1975.

The New Jersey analysis is based on the information reported by Argonaut in its Annual Statement, 1974.

The Florida case was *Argonaut v. Florida Medical Association* (U.S.D.C. M. Dis. Fl.) 75–140 Civ-J-T. 1975.

175 The other company whose investment income was insufficient to overcome underwriting loss was the Federal Insurance Co. (Chubb). See A. M. Best Co., *Best's Insurance Reports (Property-Casualty),* 1976, pp. 400–02.

176 The Singleton quote is in "Henry Singleton's Singular Conglomerate," *Forbes,* May 1, 1976, p. 38.

Argonaut's expansion into overseas markets is reported in A. M. Best Co., *Best's Insurance Reports (Property-Casualty),* 1975, pp. 142–44; the report on the general expansion of U.S. companies into the foreign market is "U.S. Insurance Companies Grow Abroad," *Wall Street Journal,* Jan. 28, 1974, p. 6.

176 The AMA report is the *State by State Report on the Professional Liability Issue,* Oct. 1976. No doubt many insurance companies doing only a small amount of malpractice business have withdrawn from the field. In Pennsylvania, for example, forty carriers offered hospital malpractice insurance in 1975; in 1976, only fifteen remained active. See Lewis & Clyman, *Hospital Malpractice in New York State* (Albert Einstein College of Medicine, 1977), p. 51. The hospital premium increases for New York State are also indicated in this report. Insurance premium increases are reported in A.M.A., "State by State Report on the Professional Liability Issue," Oct. 1976. The New York hospital rates are reported in Report of the Special Advisory Panel on Medical Malpractice, State of New York, 1976.

177 That most physicians were more interested in the availability of insurance than in its price was noted in interviews with Edward Brennan, executive director of the Massachusetts Malpractice Study Commission, and James Sheeran, New Jersey Commissioner of Insurance. The same point was made by Calvin Lodge of Indiana—see Council of State Governments, *Medical Malpractice: The States are Responding,* 1975, p. 2.

177 Herbert Denenberg's comments are included in an interview, "A Noted Doctor Baiter Dissects the Malpractice Crisis," *Med. Economics,* June 14, 1976, p. 39.

178 On the theory and practice of malpractice insurance rate-making see Roddis and Stewart, "The Insurance of Medical Losses," *Duke L.J.,* 6 (1975) 1281.

179 Woolery's testimony is reported in "Argonaut and Malpractice: A Tangled Web," *Med. World News,* July 14, 1975, p. 23.

179 The particular way in which the insurance companies combine local and national experience was illustrated with some degree of precision in Massachusetts, where the Commissioner actually sets the rates rather than merely approving or denying them. The JUA's advisory rate filing for a December 1976 hearing used Massachusetts data for coverage of up to $25,000 per claim

and $75,000 total. While these coverage limits were standard many years ago, almost all physicians now buy coverage of at least $100,000 per claim and $300,000 total. Higher-risk specialists purchase coverage of $1 million to $3 million. In the Massachusetts hearing, national data, including the distorting experience of states with severe malpractice problems, were used as an experience base to determine coverage for all claims above the $25,000–$75,000 limits. The country-wide experience was also used to determine development and trend factors. There is every reason to suspect that this policy was and is used for rate filings in other states. The testimony in the Massachusetts hearing indicated that a similar process is used in Pennsylvania. See Commonwealth of Massachusetts, Department of Banking and Insurance, Division of Insurance, *Hearing to Establish . . . Premium Charges,* Dec. 7, 1976. It is also used in Washington state—see Health Policy Analysis Program, *The Malpractice Issue in Washington,* 1976, p. 4—and in Kansas—see *Report of the Special Committee to the 1976 Kansas Legislature,* 1976, p. 1158.

The claims survey was NAIC, *Malpractice Claims,* May 1977.

180 That ISO data do not include Medical Protective experience is reported in the "Advisory Filing of the Massachusetts Medical Society," for the Dec. 1976 Massachusetts hearing noted above.

180 The difficulties of the "long tail" are expounded in St. Paul Insurance Co., *Preserving the Medical Malpractice Insurance Market: Problems and Remedies,* 1975. See also *HEW Secretary's Malpractice Commission Report,* 1973, p. 42.

181 The malpractice crisis has led many state insurance departments to begin collecting data on the reserves established for individual claims. The New York report is Committee on Medicine and Law, "Medical Malpractice Insurance Crisis," *The Record,* Vol. 30, No. 516 (May/June 1975), p. 341.

The HEW report's comments on reserves were in Kendall & Haldi, "The Medical Malpractice Insurance Market," in *HEW Secretary's Malpractice Commission Report,* 1973, Appendix, p. 531.

182 The North Carolina analysis is reported in North Carolina Department of Insurance, *In the Matter of Physicians and Surgeons Professional Liability Filing of the St. Paul Fire and Marine Co.: Temporary Order of the Commissioner,* Dec. 19, 1974. The New Jersey experience is reported in Donald F. Smith & Associates, *Hospital Insurance Company Study for the New Jersey Hospital Association,* Jan. 8, 1975. The Washington report is in Health Policy Analysis Program, *The Malpractice Issue in Washington,* 1976, p. 28.

182 The NAIC report is *Malpractice Claims,* May 1977. The averages weighted by the value of the claims are fifteen months from incident to report, and thirty-six months from incident to disposition.

183 The Employers disclosure was made in a letter from Mr. Imse of Employers of Wausau to the New York State Insurance Department, March 26, 1975. MMIA's rate increase was denied in NYS Insurance Department, *In the Matter of MMIA and ISO,* Nov. 7, 1975, p. 26. ISO's policy toward carrier settlement processes is also reported in this decision, p. 25. One available source of information might also be seen to support the conclusion that Employers' policy was shared by other parts of the industry. *Medical Economics* reports that large jury awards in California peaked at 50 in 1972 and fell to 24 by 1975. It attributes this decrease to the crisis rebounding in favor of physicians:

juries had become more sympathetic to the physician's plight. However, an equally plausible conclusion is that the companies had settled many large claims in the earlier years, so that they simply never came to trial. See "A Change of Heart in Malpractice Juries," *Med. Economics,* June 14, 1976, pp. 240–41.

183   The impact of rising awards on rates, through application of the trend factor, is indicated in the various advisory filing of the Massachusetts Medical Society for the 1976 Massachusetts malpractice-rate hearings. The quote is an ISO statement in Massachusetts Department of Insurance, *JUA v. Commissioner,* Reservation and Report, 1975, Vol. 2, p. 325.

183   Claim reports and settlement periods are reported in NAIC, *Malpractice Claims,* May 1977.

184   The industry's position with respect to investment income was made in a paper, *The Problem of Insuring Medical Malpractice,* in Hearings Before the Senate Committee on Labor and Public Welfare, Subcommittee on Health, Examination of Continuing Medical Malpractice Crisis, Dec. 3, 1975, p. 210. The California report was made by the Booz, Allen Consulting Actuaries and included in California Joint Legislative Audit Committee, Office of the Auditor General, *Doctors' Malpractice Insurance,* 1975. The North Carolina Insurance Commissioner's statement was made on Dec. 19, 1974.

    The Federal Insurance Administrator's statement was contained in a letter to Senator Kennedy in Hearings on the Examination of the Continuing Medical Malpractice Insurance Crisis, 1975, Before the Subcommittee on Health of the Senate Committee on Labor and Public Welfare, 94th Cong., 1st Sess. (1975) (Statement of Robert J. Hunter), p. 423.

185   The disparity between the payout period for development and for investment purposes was noted in the brief of the Massachusetts Medical Society, submitted for the Dec. 1976 hearing, p. 32.

    The comment regarding the various jurisdictions' handling of investment income was made in *Report of the Special Advisory Panel on Medical Malpractice, State of New York,* 1976, p. 218. For a discussion of prior approval and competition, see State of New York Insurance Department, *Cartels vs. Competition,* 1975, pp. 71–83.

186   The New York Insurance Department's review of MMIA's rate request was in NYS Insurance Department, *In the Matter of MMIA and ISO,* Nov. 7, 1975. The New York statute is N.Y.S. Insurance Law §175 (2) (1975).

    The Massachusetts insurance law requiring consideration of investment income potential is Mass. Gen. Laws Ann. ch. 175A §5(a) (1) (1970) (West).

187   On St. Paul's claims-made policy see St. Paul's *Communique,* Winter 1975. See also N.Y.S. Insurance Department, *Opinion and Decision in the Matter of Claims Made Form,* May 7, 1976.

188   For an example of the sophisticated analysis done by malpractice insurance consumers see "Advisory Filing of the Massachusetts Medical Society," 1976.

    Conglomerate composition and holding company relationships are indicated under the heading of the various companies in *Best's Insurance Reports (Property-Liability),* 1975.

189   The federal insurance cases were *Paul v. Virginia* 75 U.S. 357 (1869) (8 Wall) and *United States v. Southeastern Underwriters Association* 322 U.S. 533, 653 (1944). In *St. Paul Fire and Marine Insurance v. Barry,* 555 F. 2d 3 (1977) a

group of Rhode Island doctors sued four malpractice insurance companies that refused to continue providing malpractice insurance coverage on an occurrence basis. The Federal District Court ruled for the insurance companies because they were exempt from the federal antitrust laws, but the first Circuit Court of Appeals reversed. The appellate court held that under the McCarran-Ferguson Act insurers remain subject to the antitrust laws if they engage in acts of or agree to boycott, coercion, or intimidation. The court held that the carriers' activities in this case could constitute a boycott, meaning a concerted refusal to deal with a disfavored purchaser. The case is now on appeal before the U.S. Supreme Court.

On the influence of the insurance lobby at the state level, see "Industry Lobbies Are Powerful at the State Level," *Wall Street Journal,* June 6, 1974, p. 1.

190 Dean Spencer L. Kimball's comment on state insurance laws was in "Unfinished Business in Insurance Regulation," *Wis. L. Rev.* 4 (1969): 1019. General analysis of the American insurance law's focus is in State of New York Department of Insurance, *Cartels vs. Competition,* 1975. It quotes the New York Superintendent's testimony before the Joint Legislative Committee on Insurance Rates and Regulation on Feb. 20, 1969: "Prior approval does not, and was not designed to keep rates down. Doing away with prior approval will not, therefore, make rates go up—unless rates have been artificially suppressed beforehand, which is not the case in this state." NYS Insurance Department, *Cartels vs. Competition,* 1975, p. 87, note 43.

The state's financial examinations are conducted under the primary responsibility of the department in which the company is domiciled. The country has been divided by NAIC into zones, and personnel from other zones may participate in the examination.

The New York Superintendent's comment was made in NYS Insurance Department, *Regulation of the Financial Conditions of Insurance Companies,* 1974, p. 46.

191 The subsidiary insurers' underwriting capacity was reduced by $1 billion. *Best's Review (Property-Liability)* Vol. 70, No. 6 (Oct. 1969), p. 5.

191 The survey of state capability to regulate insurance holding companies was NAIC, *Strengthening the Surveillance System,* (McKinsey, 1974), pp. 1–5. The NAIC Subcommittee's report was *Report of the Insurance Holding Company Task Force,* 1976.

192 That stricter state regulation leads to the migration of insurance companies is reported in Note, "The Insurance Holding Company Phenomenon and the Search for Regulatory Control," *Va. L. Rev.* 56 (1969): 636, 655.

The recommendation of the federal task force was reported in "Federal Law for Insurance and Dairy Coops," *New York Times,* Jan. 17, 1977, p. 14.

192 The federal malpractice-insurance proposals were introduced in the first session of the 94th Congress (1975). The House bill number was H. R. 6100; the Senate's S. 188, and S. 482, 94th Cong. 1st Sess. (1975). Administrator Hunter's prediction was in Hearing on the Examination of the Continuing Medical Malpractice Insurance Crisis, 1975, Before the Subcommittee on Health of the Senate Committee on Labor and Public Welfare, 94th Cong., 1st Sess. (1975) (letter to Senator Kennedy from Robert J. Hunter, Jr.), p. 428.

194   Opposition to the federal proposals is reported in "A Malpractice Solution Almost No One Wants," *Med. World News,* May 5, 1975, p. 23.

The variables by which insurance premiums might be gauged are suggested in Steves, "A Proposal to Improve the Cost to Benefit Ratios in the Medical Malpractice Insurance System," *Duke L.J.* 6 (1975): 1305. They are considered in the context of the Steves' proposal to focus all malpractice liability on the hospital, which was discussed on page 74. To some extent, they might still be attempted in premium determination for individual physicians.

The private companies' reluctance to insure high-risk physicians is reported in Andrew Markovits, "Why Should I Pay for Other Doctors' Malpractice?" *Med. Economics,* May 17, 1976, pp. 88–94.

10. Insuring Insurance: When the Private Market Fails

195   A summary of state legislative activity in forming insurance pooling devices is in Grossman, "Analysis of State Legislative Activity," in Warren & Merritt, eds., *A Legislator's Guide to Medical Malpractice,* Georgetown Health Policy Center and The National Conference of State Legislatures, Washington, D.C., 1976, p. 3.

States which enacted insurance legislation include: Alabama Code 7 §176 (13) (1975 Supp.); Arizona Rev. Stat. §20–1702 (1976); Arkansas Stat. Ann. §§66–5301, 66–5317 (1975); California Insurance Code §§11890, 11915 (1975); Colorado Rev. Stat. §§10–4–901, 10–4–911 (1976 Supp.); Delaware Code Ann. 18 §§6830, 6841 (1976); Florida Stat. §768.53 (1976 Supp.); Georgia Code §56–512.1 (1975); Hawaii Rev. Stat. §435C–1–11 (1975 Supp.); Idaho Code §§41–4101, 41–4116 (1976); Illinois Ann. Stat. 73 §1065.201 *et seq.* (1975); Iowa Code Ann. §§519A.1, 519A.13 (1975); Kansas Stat. Ann §40–3401 *et seq.* (1976); Kentucky Rev. Stat. §§304.40–010, 330 (1976); Maine Rev. Stat. Ann. 20 §2401, 2414 (1975); Maryland Ann. Code. Art. 48A §557, 564 (1975); Massachusetts Laws Ann. 175A §5A (1975); Michigan C.L.A. 500 §§2500, 2517 (1975); Minnesota Stat. Ann. §62F (1976); Miss. C. Ann. §83–36–1 *et seq.* (1976); Missouri §383.150 *et seq.* (1976); Nebraska Rev. Stat. §§44–3001, 44–3019 (1976); Nevada Rev. Stat. 57 §§686B.180 *et seq.* (1975); New Hampshire R.S.A. §404–c (1975); N.J.S.A. §17.30D–1 *et seq.* (1975); N.M.S.A. §58–34 (1–14) (1976); N.Y. Stat. 18 §§681–695 (1975); N.C. Stat. §58–173.34 *et seq.* (1975); Ohio Code Ann. §3929.71–.85 (1975); Oklahoma Stat. Ann. 76 §22 (1976); Penn. Stat. §§1301.801, 1301.805 (1975); R.I. Rev. Stat. 42 §14.1 (1) (1976); S.C. Code §38–3–310 (1975); Tennessee Code Ann. §§56–4301, 56–4315 (1975); Texas Ins. Code Art. 21.49–3 (1975); Utah Code §78–14–9 (1976); Virginia Code §38–1–21 (1976); Wisconsin Stat. Ann. §619.01–.04; §655.23 (1975).

196   The states which have operating JUA's are Arkansas, Florida, Kansas, Louisiana, Maine, Massachusetts, Michigan, New Hampshire, New York, Ohio, Pennsylvania, Rhode Island, South Carolina, Tennessee, Texas, Virginia, and Wisconsin.

197   St. Paul's activities in a JUA servicing capacity were reported by William Torgerson, phone conversation with authors, Mar. 7, 1977,.

The states in which JUA's are or would be the exclusive source of malpractice insurance are Alabama, Hawaii, Idaho, Illinois, Maine, and Tennessee.

197   The states which have authorized stabilization reserve funds are Alabama, Colorado, Delaware, Idaho, Illinois, Iowa, Kentucky, Maine, Maryland, Minne-

sota, Mississippi, Nebraska, New Jersey, New York, Ohio, Pennsylvania, and Tennessee.

The states with patient compensation funds are Indiana, Kansas, Kentucky, Louisiana, Nebraska, and Wisconsin. Reinsurance mechanisms were authorized in New Jersey, North Carolina, and Oklahoma.

197   Two states, Georgia and Maryland, have JUA-enabling legislation in which the provisions for company recoupment of assessed losses could conceivably prove inadequate. Neither state has actually established a JUA.

198   The case holding the North Carolina plan unconstitutional was *Hartford Accident and Indemnity Co. v. Ingram,* Decision of Justice I. Beverly Lake, July 14, 1976.

198   The states allowing a surcharge on premiums in other insurance lines are Alabama, Delaware, Kentucky, Maine, Minnesota, Mississippi, New Hampshire, Ohio, Rhode Island, and Tennessee. The states allowing deductions in premium taxes are Alabama, Arizona, Colorado, Delaware, Idaho, Illinois, Minnesota, Mississippi, Nevada, Rhode Island, Tennessee, and Texas.

199   The medical-society and insurance-industry positions were reported in Tarky Lombardi, "New York's Medical Malpractice Insurance Crisis," in Warren & Merritt, eds., *id.,* p. 45. The American Life Insurance Association's activities were reported in George Lenz, "Malpractice Storm Passes, Clouds Linger," *Nat'l Underwriter (Life-Health),* Vol. 79, No. 21, (May 24, 1975), p. 1.

199   On the problems of products-liability insurance see "The Overload on the Nation's Insurance System," *Bus. Week,* Sept. 6, 1976. Frederick Watkins, president of Aetna Insurance Co., was quoted in this article: "The medical malpractice insurance crisis could turn out to be a firecracker compared to an explosion in products liability litigation, which could rip our industry apart and wreak havoc with the whole economy." See also "Product Liability—the Search for Solutions," *Nation's Business,* June 1977, p. 24; Brummond, *A Comparison of Products Liability and Medical Malpractice,* NAIC Paper, Nov. 29, 1976.

200   The Illinois report is State of Illinois, *Report and Recommendation of the Medical Injuries Reparation Commission,* June 1976, p. 39.

200   The MMIA official was Edwin Reeg; his statement was made in a phone conversation with the authors, Feb. 21, 1977.

The New York study is State of New York, *Report of the Special Advisory Panel on Medical Malpractice,* Jan. 1976, p. 124.

The New York Superintendent's evaluation was NYS, *An Evaluation of the Operation of the Medical Malpractice Insurance Association,* Feb. 15, 1976, p. 8.

The executive director was William Klein of Long Island College Hospital. Letter to authors, Jan. 17, 1977.

201   The report on the Massachusetts JUA was Massachusetts Rating Bureau, *Derivation of Increased Limits Factor,* 1976.

The St. Paul official was William Torgerson. Phone conversation with authors, March 7, 1977.

201   On the formation of the New York captive, see Howard Eisenberg, "Malpractice Insurance: These Doctors Fooled the Experts," *Med. Economics,* June 14, 1976, pp. 91–100.

The Pennsylvania Medical Society President was quoted in Grant Hubbard,

Page

" 'Bedpan Mutuals': Will They Survive?" *Best's Review, (Property-Liability)* Vol. 77, No. 5 (Sept. 1976), p. 14.

202 The captive's adoption of a restrictive policy toward claim settlement is similar to a rather unique policy provision that many doctors once had with their private insurer: that the carrier could not settle without the consent of the insured. The expense in fighting claims that doctors refused to settle has led many companies to drop this policy provision in recent years. See *HEW Secretary's Malpractice Commission Report*, 1973, Appendix, p. 508.

202 The Illinois report is State of Illinois, *Report and Recommendation of the Medical Injuries Reparation Commission*, June 1976, p. 39.

On the Pennsylvania Hospital Association plan, see Meyer, "Medical Malpractice Insurance Crisis May End Up Improving Hospital Care," *Wall Street Journal*, Dec. 27, 1976. See also, the HEW study, Applied Management Services, *A Study of Hospital Injury Prevention Programs*, Nov. 29, 1976.

203 Eli Bernzweig was quoted in "Why the Medical Malpractice Crisis Has to Get Worse to Get Better," *Med. Economics*, Jan. 24, 1977, p. 37. The ISO projection is reported in a Harvard report, *Malpractice Crisis—A New Approach for Harvard Institutions*, Feb. 1976.

204 The *Best's Review* report was Grant Hubbard, " 'Bedpan Mutuals': Will They Survive?" *(Property-Liability)*, Vol. 77, No. 5, p. 14.

The *Risk Management* report was Grant Miller, "The Medical Malpractice Insurance Dilemma." Vol. 23, No. 2 (Feb. 1976), pp. 29–42.

204 On the adequacy of required capitalization, see Mayerson, "Ensuring the Solvency of Property and Liability Insurance Companies," in Kimball & Denenberg, eds., *Insurance, Government, and Social Policy* (Univ. of Pennsylvania), p. 159. A report of the State of New York Insurance Department entitled *Regulation of Financial Condition of Insurance Companies*, 1974, p. 63, says, "The focus upon minimal capital and surplus requirements expressed in absolute dollars, bears only an accidental relationship to a prescription for financial soundness." See also *Strengthening the Surveillance System*, Report to NAIC, (McKinsey and Co., April 1974).

Colorado is a state with no absolute minimum-capital requirements. The Commissioner is, however, requiring $1 million in capital and surplus for the malpractice captive. See Margaret LeRoux, "Colorado Gives O.K. to 13 New Captives," *Bus. Insurance*, Feb. 21, 1977, p. 7.

The *Business Insurance* report is Margaret LeRoux, "Bermuda an Adolescent Planning to Make Waves," March 7, 1977, p. 11. Other reports on the offshore captives are Margaret LeRoux, "Malpractice Captive Has Problems Only in California," *Bus. Insurance*, Sept. 6, 1976, p. 22; Philip Harsham, "Offshore Malpractice Insurance: Is It the Answer for You?" *Med. Economics*, Feb. 7, 1977; David Gumpert, "Doctors and Hospitals Start Insurance Concerns in Caribbean to Beat Malpractice Premium Rates," *Wall Street Journal*, July 6, 1977, p. 30.

The initial capital for the Harvard hospital company is stated in a Harvard report, *Malpractice Crisis—a New Approach for Harvard Institutions*, Feb. 1976.

205 The AMA survey is reported in "More Physicians are Disregarding Insurance," *Bus. Insurance*, Oct. 4, 1976, p. 40. The Wisconsin statute is Wis. S.A. 655.23 (1975).

205 The Louisiana case is *Pollock v. Methodist Hospital* 392 F. Supp. 393 (E.D. La. 1975).

11. Conclusions

209 For a summary of the provisions of the eighteen national-health-insurance bills introduced in the 94th Congress, see: Saul Waldman, *National Health Insurance Proposals: Provisions of Bill Introduced into the 94th Congress as of 1976* (USD-HEW, Office of Research & Statistics, Pub. No. SSA 76–11920, Supt. of Documents).

210 In 1976 only 2,000 New York Blue Cross subscribers took advantage of the opportunity to obtain a second opinion prior to surgery, even though six million subscribers were entitled to that benefit. Telephone interview, Malcolm McKay, Executive Vice President, New York Blue Cross–Blue Shield, Sept. 13, 1977. As we have noted, national figures show that there are 9,583 operations per 100,000 people each year. While some of these operations are done on an emergency basis, nonetheless 2,000 is a very small number of people electing the second-opinion option. (In one third of the cases in which second opinions were sought, the second doctor recommended against surgery.) Fifty-five of the first one hundred people seeking second opinions asked that their first physician not be informed that they had sought a second opinion. Telephone interview, John Byrnes, December 8, 1977.

213 See *St. Paul Fire and Marine Ins. Co. v. Ins. Comm'n,* 339 A.2d 291 (Md. Ct. of Appeals 1975), exploring the power of the insurance commissioner under Maryland law to force an insurance company to continue writing malpractice insurance.

Index

accreditation of hospitals, 51, 52, 54, 56, 57, 58, 64–65, 75
adhesion, contract of, 138–39
admitting privileges, hospitals and, 60–61, 63, 75
Aetna (insurance company), 165, 166, 173, 176, 177, 188
Altcheck, Dr. Edward, 29
American Arbitration Association (AAA), 128, 135
American Bar Association, 126
American College of Physicians, 56
American College of Surgeons, 30, 56, 62
American Hospital Association, 52, 53, 54, 56, 59
American Insurance Association, 85, 199
American Medical Association (AMA), 15, 16, 19, 20, 30, 40, 52, 56, 62, 63, 86, 115, 117, 162, 176, 202, 205
American Mutual Liability Company, 34, 179
American Public Health Association, 46
American Surgical Association, 30, 62
arbitration, 128–39
 adhesion, contracts of, 138–39
 appeal, right to, conflicts in, 131
 consent to, 132–36
 costs, 131–32
 court cases and, differences between, 128
 court scrutinizing of, 136–38
 forms of agreement to, 129
 revoking agreement to, 135–36
 rules for conduct, conflicts in, 130–31

Argonaut (insurance company), 164, 166, 167, 168, 170, 171–77, 179, 181, 183, 186, 188, 191
Ashkenazy, Dr. Moses, 51, 52

"borrowed servant," doctrine of, and malpractice suits, 55
Bernzweig, Eli, 203, 204
Best's Review, 191, 204
Blue Cross, 70, 75, 153
Blue Shield, 16, 18
boards, state medical, 37–39, 43, 44, 45, 46, 48, 49
 complaints to, 45–46
 financing of, 48
 hospitals and, legal structure of, 54–65, 76–77
 legal powers of, 39–41, 42, 45
 staffing and leadership problems of, 46–48
 suspension of physicians by, 49–50
bond requirements, adverse screening panel findings and, 127
Bunker, Dr. John, 18
Bureau of Quality Assurance (B.Q.A.), 71, 72
Business Insurance, 204

California Hospital Association, 129
California Medical Association, 129
"caps," *see* recovery amounts
"captive" insurance companies (physician-hospital owned), 201–202, 204–205
 medical societies and, 202
 peer review of, 202–203

"captive" insurance companies *(cont'd)*
   rates, problem in setting of, 204
   undercapitalization of, 204, 205
Cardozo, Benjamin, 108
Chubb (insurance company), 166, 170, 177
claims-made system, insurance system and, 187–88
CNA (insurance company), 166, 176
Code of Professional Responsibility, 92
collateral sources, limitations on damage recovery and, 146–47
   premiums and, 147–48
Committee on Interns and Residents, 46
Congressional Budget Office, 63
Conrad, Joseph, 43
consent
   to arbitration, 132–36
   to treatment, 108–109
   see also informed consent
constitutional limits, recovery amounts and, 139–44
   and due process, 141
   and equal protection, 141
   and "special" legislation, 141
Continental (insurance company), 171
contingent-fee system, 81, 82–86
   abolition of, 84
   doctor's role in malpractice action, 82
   limitations on, 89
   payments to patients, 82–83
   remedies to harassed doctor, 86
   strengths of, 83–84
   weaknesses of, 84–85
   see also earnings of lawyers
continuous-treatment rule, statutes of limitation and, 122
contracts of adhesion, arbitration and, 138–39
costs, legal, payment of, 94–96
   arbitration and, 131–32
   disparity in source of funds of patients' and doctors' lawyers, 94–95
countersuits, by harassed doctors, contingent-fee system and, 86
customs, professional, disclosure and, 109–111

Darling v. Charleston Community Hospital (1968), 57–58, 60
death, disclosure of, patients' vs. doctors' attitudes, 109–10
defensive medicine, informed consent and, 114–16
Denenberg (insurance commissioner of Pennsylvania), 176, 177, 178

Derbyshire, Dr. Robert, 31, 46, 47
disclosure of information, settlement of claims and, 124–25
discovery rule, statutes of limitation and, 122
dispute resolution, techniques of, 120–48
   arbitration, 128–39
   encouraging settlement, 124–28
   recovery amounts, limits on, 139–48
   time limitations, statutes of, 121–24
distribution of medical care, problems of
   financial aspects, 24–25
   geographical, 12–13
   health services, maldistribution of malpractice rates and, 19–27
   legislation and, 23–24, 25
   malpractice and, 208
   specialization in medical practice, maldistribution by, 13–16
doctors, *see* physicians
drug abuse, physicians and, 32, 35, 40, 44

earnings of lawyers, 86–94
   compensation, patient's lawyer–doctor's lawyer, 88–89
   contingent-fee percentages for patient's lawyer, 87
   excessiveness of, criteria for judging, 87–88
   hourly fees for doctor's lawyer, 87
   limits to contingent fees, 89
   of other lawyers, compared to, 90
   limits on percent of recovery, 89
   premium dollar, patient-doctor ratio, 88
   regulation of, 90–94
Edwards, Dr. Charles C., 16
Egeberg, Dr. Roger O., 31
Employers Insurance of Wausau, 166, 183
expert testimony
   basis for claims and, 124–28
   consent and, 108, 109
   disclosure standards and, 111
   locality rule and, 98, 99, 100
   reasonable due care and, 101
   res ipsa loquitur and, 103–104

family practice, physicians and, 14–15, 24
fault system, 1–8
   compensation of victim, 1–3
   deterrence of injury, 1–2
   Industrial Revolution and, 2–3
   laissez-faire philosophy and, 2–3
   liability, malpractice suits and, 22, 27
   medical malpractice and, 6–8
   see also no-fault insurance

federal action on hospital responsibility, 56–57, 62, 70–72
Federal Insurance Administration, 193
"file and use" statutes, 185
Florida Medical Association, 172, 174, 175
Forbes, 176
fraud
  exposure of, discovery rule and, 122
  forms of, physician's, 108

Goldberg, Judge B. Abbott, 58, 59
Gonzales, Albert, 34, 42
Good Samaritan laws, 44, 116–17

Hand, Learned, 5, 6
Hartford (insurance company), 166, 170, 176, 177
Hastings, Congressman James, 192
HEW Malpractice Commission, 11, 47, 49, 53, 67, 70, 71, 82, 85, 86, 87, 88, 89, 97, 98, 112, 123, 164, 165, 169, 181, 203
health-insurance programs, public, 17–18
Health Policy Analysis Program (University of Washington), 182
Health Professions Education Act, 209
Herbert, A. P., 4
Hill-Burton Hospital Survey and Construction Act (1946), 56
Holmes, Oliver Wendell, 3
hospitals, 51–77
  accreditation of, 51, 52, 54, 56, 57, 58, 64–65, 75
  admitting privileges and, 60–61, 63, 75
  board members, composition of, 59–60, 76–77
  as dangerous places, 53–54
  economic interests of, 63, 75–77
  injuries in, malpractice suits and, 53–54, 55, 57–58, 61, 74
  insurance companies, ownership by, 201, 202, 204–205
  legal structure of, 54–65
  liability for malpractice and, 55–56, 57–58, 59, 67, 73, 74
  malpractice crisis, Joint Commission on Accreditation of Hospitals and, 65–69
  monitoring of, 70–72, 73, 74
  power over physicians, admitting privileges and, 60–61, 63, 75
  reform of, suggestions for, 72–77
  res ipsa loquitur, application to, 104–105
  risk-control programs and, 67–68

hospitals *(cont'd)*
  "utilization review" programs and, 70
  see also insurance system; legal system; medical system
Hunter, J. Robert, 185, 193

INA (insurance company), 166, 176
inadvertence, as cause of malpractice, 3
income, physicians' *(see also* earnings of lawyers), 16–17
incurred but not reported claims (IBNR's), 121
Industrial Revolution, 2, 3, 6
"inevitable necessity," 2
informed consent, 108–19
  death disclosure and, 109–10
  defensive medicine and, 114–16
  development of obligation for, 109
  education of physicians about laws and, 116
  reasonable-patient standard, 111–12
  and risk information, customs of, 109
  vs. simple consent, types of cases, 108
  terminally ill cancer patients and, 109–10
  written consent, forms, 113
injuries
  deterrence of, 1–2
  in hospitals, malpractice suits and, 53–54, 61, 74
Insurance Service Office (ISO), 21, 164, 179, 180, 183, 184, 203
insurance system, 161–214
  Argonaut Insurance Company, as example of crisis in malpractice premiums, 171–77, 179, 181, 183, 186, 188, 191
  claims-made system, 187–88
  cost of malpractice insurance, 162–63, 178–88
  crisis in, malpractice premiums and, 149, 161–62, 164–67, 168, 170, 171, 177–78, 193, 203–204, 213
  data on premiums and losses of insurance companies, 163–64, 173, 177–78, 182–85, 194
  group plans and, 165–66
  income of physicians and, 16–17
  investment, losses and gains and, 163–64, 167–70, 184, 185, 186
  in market economy, deficiencies of, 188–205
  as monopoly, 165, 166–67, 186, 207
  no-fault compensation, effects on, 150–51, 152–53

insurance system (*cont'd*)
"occurrence" basis, malpractice policies and, 169
physician-hospital-owned insurance companies ("captives"), 201–202, 204–205
premium rates for malpractice, 34–36, 163–64, 165, 168, 173, 177–88, 189, 190
profitability of, 161–62, 164, 167–68, 170, 176
public control of, 214
publicly sponsored programs and, 195–205
regulation of, problems in, 188–94, 213
reserve levels, malpractice premium rates and, 180–83
risks, types of, companies' policies concerning, 213–14
setting of malpractice rates, 178–88, 189, 190
underwriting malpractice insurance, 167–69, 195, 197–98
uninsured physicians and, 205
see also legal system; medical system; premiums
"internalization" of costs, no-fault programs and, 155, 156
Internal Revenue Service (IRS), 181
interns and internship, 14
investments, insurance, *see* insurance system

Joint Commission on Accreditation of Hospitals (JCAH), 52, 54, 56, 57, 58, 59, 60, 61, 62, 64, 69, 70, 71, 73, 74, 75, 76
Joint Underwriting Associations (JUA's), 195, 196–97, 198, 199, 200, 204, 213, 214
performance of, 200–201
as public subsidy, 198–99
reactions to, by insurance companies, 199–201
Journal of the American Medical Association, 32

Kaiser Foundation Health Plan, 129
Kansas State Board of Healing Arts, 39
Kennedy, Senator Edward, 193
Kimball, Spencer, 190

laissez-faire, as philosophical basis of fault system, 2
Lewis, Dr. C. E., 18

legal system, 81–157
arbitration, 128–39
contingent-fee system, 82–86
earnings of lawyers, excessive, 86–94
ethics and, professional, 43–44
expert testimony, locality rule and, 98
fault system and, origins of, 1–8
hospitals, legal structure of, 54–65
informed consent, 108–19
no-fault program proposals and, 149–57
payment of legal costs, 94–96
professional competence, presumption of, 6–7
reasonable due care, standards to judge, 101–102
recovery amounts, limits on, 139–48
res ipsa loquitur, 102–107
settlement, encouraging, 124–28
standards of physician behavior, legislation and, 97
state medical boards, legal powers of, 39–41
statutes of limitations, 121–24
see also insurance system; medical system
liability, malpractice, education of physicians about, 116
license, revoking physician's, 32
Lloyd's of London, 166
locality rule, 98–99, 100, 101
Lombardi, Senator (New York State), 199
losses, insurance, data on, 163–64, 168, 173, 177–78, 182–85, 194

McCarran-Ferguson Act, 189
McCarthy, Dr. Eugene, 62
McGill Commission (New York), 185
McKinsey and Co., 191
market economy, insurance and, 188–205
Medicaid, 17, 18, 19, 33, 37, 54, 70, 71, 75
Medical Liability Mutual Insurance Company (North Carolina), 204
Medical Malpractice Insurance Association (MMIA), 200
Medical Opinion, 12
Medical Protective Company, 166, 170, 176, 180
medical services, *see* health services
medical system, 11–77
ethics and, professional, 43–44
federal action on hospital responsibility, 70–72
"free-market" theory of, myth about, 17–19

medical system (*cont'd*)
health services, maldistribution of, malpractice rates and, 19–27
hospitals and, 51–65, 67–68, 70–73
Joint Commission on Accreditation of hospitals, malpractice crisis and, 65–67
market for medical services, 16–19
medical-care evaluation studies (MCE's), 71
overspecialization, 208
peer review of physicians, 63–64, 68–70, 156
physicians, obtaining information about, 41–46
premiums, malpractice insurance, substandard physicians and, 34–36
self-regulation by medical profession, 36–39
specialization in medical practice, maldistribution by, 13–16
state medical boards and, 39–41, 46–48, 54–65
surgery, "surplus," 18–19, 61–62, 63
see also boards, state medical; insurance system; legal system; physicians
Medical World News, 106
Medicare, 17, 32, 37, 54, 56, 70, 71, 75
Menninger Foundation, 32
minors, statutes of limitations and claims by, 122, 123–24
Modlin, Dr. Herbert C., 32
monopolies, insurance system and, 166–67, 186, 207
Morris, Clarence, 7

National Academy of Science, 14
National Association of Independent Insurers, 97, 199
National Association of Insurance Commissioners (NAIC), 22, 34, 53, 106, 112, 123, 144, 161, 162, 163, 164, 170, 179, 182, 184, 191
National Commission on State Workmen's Compensation Laws, 153
National Federation of State Medical Boards, 31
National Medical Association, 46
negligence, 3–6, 7, 8
definition of, 4
"reasonable person," concept of, 4–5, 8, 111–12
Nelson, Senator Gaylord, 192
Nesbit, Dr. Reed, 58
New England Journal of Medicine, 29
New Jersey Hospital Association, 182

New Mexico State Board of Medical Examiners, 31
New York City Bar Association's Malpractice Report, 181
New York Insurance Department, 164
New York's Joint Underwriting Authority (JUA), 183, 184, 185, 186
New York State Board of Regents, 29
New York State Malpractice Report, 67
New York State Medical Practice Task Force, 52
New York State Medical Society, 166, 174
no-fault insurance program proposals, 149–57
compensable event, defining, 150–52
compensation, determining amount to injured party, 153–54
conclusions about, 157
cost of, 152–55, 156, 157
disputes about, 151–52
deterrence of incompetency, problem of, 155–56
financing of, 154
Nork, Dr. John, 29, 34, 42, 45, 51, 58, 61, 151
court case against, 51, 52, 58, 59, 60, 63, 65, 69, 73, 179

Occupational Safety and Health Act, 156
"occurrence" basis, malpractice insurance policies and, 169
"open rating," malpractice insurance and, 185
overspecialization, as problem in distribution of health services, 208

pain and suffering, limitations on damages and, 145–46
patient's compensation, funds for, 197
peer review
physician's response to, 63–64, 68–70
weaknesses of, 64–65
Pennsylvania Hospital Association, 202
Pennsylvania Medical Society, 201
physicians
competence, presumption of, 6–7
"conspiracy of silence" among, 43–44
defamation liability and, 68
disclosure of death risk and, 110
drug abuse among, 35, 40, 44
education about malpractice liability and, 116
ethics of, law and, 43–44
family practice and, 14–15, 24
harassed by lawyers, remedies to, 86
incomes of, 16–17

physicians (cont'd)
  information about, obtaining, 41–46
  insurance companies, ownership by,
    201–202, 205
  interns, 14
  law and, fear and misinformation about,
    116, 117–18
  license, revoking of, 32
  peer review, response to, 63–64, 68–70
  residents, 14
  res ipsa loquitur application to, 103–104
  substandard, malpractice premiums
    and, 34–36
  suspension of, 49–50
  training of, malpractice rates and, 14–
    15, 22
  see also expert testimony; insurance sys-
    tem; legal system; medical system
Physicians Reimbursement Fund Ltd., 205
Porterfield, Dr. John, 56
premiums, malpractice insurance, 19–27,
    34–36, 147–48, 163–64, 165, 168, 173,
    177–78; 189, 190
  recovery amounts and, effects on, 144–
    45
  see also insurance system
Presidential Task Force on Antitrust Im-
    munities, 192
prima facie negligence, see res ipsa
    loquitur
products-liability insurance, malpractice
    insurance and, 199
Professional Standards Review Organiza-
    tions (PSRO's), 37, 41, 52, 71, 72, 193,
    211
profits, malpractice insurance and, 161–62,
    164, 167–68, 170, 176
Prosser, Dean William, 109
punitive damages, limitations on recovery
    of, 146

Quality Review Bulletin, 66
Quality Review Center of Joint Commis-
    sion on Accreditation of Hospitals, 65

rates, malpractice insurance, see insurance
    system; premiums
"reasonable person," standard, 4–5, 8
  informed consent and, 111–12
recklessness, as cause of malpractice, 3
records, patients' examination of, 110
recovery amounts, limits on, 139–48
  absolute limits ("caps"), constitutional as-
    pects of, 139–41, 144–45
  collateral sources, 146–47
  common-law remedies and, 140–41

recovery amounts (cont'd)
  equal protection, 141–44
  kinds of damages, 145–48
  noneconomic loss, 146
  "pain and suffering," 145–46
  premiums, effect on, 144–45
  premiums, malpractice and, 147–48
  primary and secondary sources of pay-
    ment, 147
  punitive damages, 146
  see also contingent-fee system
reinsurance plans, 197–98, 199
reserve levels, malpractice insurance and,
    180–83
resident physicians and residency, 14
res ipsa loquitur, 102–107, 206
  abolition attempts, 106–107
  as controversial issue, 106–107
  hospital application of, 104–105
  institutions, application to, 104–105
  multiple defendants, application to,
    105–106
  physicians, application to, 103–104
  see also negligence
respondeat superior, 55
risk-control programs, hospitals and, 67–68
Risk Management, 204
risks, insurance companies' attitudes to-
    ward, 213–14
Roddis, Richard, 167, 168

St. Paul (insurance company), 166, 168,
    170, 171, 173, 176, 177, 182, 186, 187,
    188, 197, 201
screening panels, basis for malpractice
    claims and, 124–28
self-regulation, professional, 36–39
  social control and, 36–38
settlement, encouraging, 124–28
  information disclosure, 124–25
  penalty fees, adverse screening panel
    findings and, 127
  screening panel laws and, 125–28
Shelby Mutual (insurance company), 166,
    171
Singleton, Henry, 176
Slater, Phillip, passim
"socialized medicine," 199
Southern California Arbitration Project,
    129, 130
specialization in medical practice
  maldistribution of health services by, 13–
    16, 208
  public health insurance programs and,
    17–18

specialization in medical practice (*cont'd*)
  training of physicians and, 14–15
stabilization reserve fund, 197, 198
State Board of Professional Medical Conduct (New York), 29
State Consumer Protection Board (New York), 47
state medical boards, *see* boards, state medical
statutes of limitations, 121–24
  discovery rule, 122
  fraud exposure time, 122
  legal age and, 122, 123–24
  legislation restricting, recent, 122–23
Stewart, Richard, 167, 168
substandard medical practice, chronic, 28–34
Suffolk County Medical Society, 29
surgery, abuse and overuse of ("surplus"), 18–19, 61–62, 63

Teledyne, Inc., 171, 173, 174, 175, 176, 186, 188, 191
torts, law of, 1, 3, 4
  reform regarding, 203
Travelers (insurance company), 166, 176, 188

"unavoidable accident," 2
underwriting, malpractice insurance and, 167–69
  Joint Underwriting Associations, 195–97, 198
  patient-compensation funds, 197
  reinsurance plans, 197–98
  stabilization reserve funds, 197, 198
  see also insurance system
Unfair Insurance Trade Practices Act, 186
U.S. Department of Labor, Bureau of Labor Statistics, 90
U.S. House of Representatives Interstate and Foreign Commerce Committee, 19
U.S. House of Representatives Subcommittee on Oversight and Investigation, 19
U.S. Justice Department, 32
U.S. Senate Finance Committee, 70
U.S. Supreme Court, 49, 92, 145, 189
"utilization review" programs, 70

Wall Street Journal, 169, 173, 175, 176, 189
Waxman, Congressman, 97
Williams, Dr. Lawrence, 18
Woolery, Bruce, 172, 173, 179

X-rays, defensive medicine and, 115–16

About the Authors

Sylvia Law grew up in Minnesota, South Dakota, and Montana. She received her B.A. degree from Antioch College, and her J.D. from the New York University Law School. As a Reginald Heber Smith Community Lawyer at the Columbia University Center on Social Welfare Policy and Law, Ms. Law was involved in test-case litigation asserting the rights of the poor, and worked with the National Welfare Rights Organization.

In 1970–3 she worked with the Health Law Project at the University of Pennsylvania, where she represented consumers of health services on a variety of issues, and wrote *Blue Cross: What Went Wrong?*, a book cited by the *New York Times* as one of the Outstanding Books of 1973. In 1971 she became an adjunct professor of law at New York University, and in 1973 joined the faculty, where she is an associate professor teaching health law, women's rights, torts, and insurance law, and is Associate Director of the Arthur Garfield Hays Civil Liberties Program. She is also the author of *Rights of the Poor* (1973) and co-editor of *Political and Civil Rights in the United States*, Vol. II. She lives in New York with her husband and baby son.

Steven Polan was born and raised in the Albany, New York, area, graduated from Tufts University, and received his J.D. from the New York University Law School. His interest in the health field developed when he worked as a legislative aide to Congressman Bob Eckhardt (Democrat, Texas). During his years in law school, he worked as a legislative assistant to the New York City Council Committee on Health, investigating abuses in the health-care delivery system; he has also worked as a Hays Fellow at the Children's Rights Project of the New York Civil Liberties Union. He now works as a lawyer and health specialist with Carol Bellamy, President of the New York City Council, and lives in New York City.